SOCIETAL DEVELOPMENT

Five Approaches with Conclusions from Comparative Analysis

SZYMON CHODAK

In the past societal development was praised as the source of Western prosperity and the basis of democracy. By the seventies, it had been damned as having caused the destruction of the natural environment, the exhaustion of resources, the decline of community life, and the alienation of man. In either case, being able to predict and so affect the growth of societies became a matter of vital import especially in connection with the needs of the Third World.

But do societies develop in a positive predeterminable pattern? Is it possible for the social scientist to predict societal development in the same manner and with the same exactitude that the biologist anticipates growth patterns in living organisms? Unlike the physical sciences, where cause and effect often relate directly, the social sciences deal with one highly unpredictable factor—assemblages of unique people evaluating situations individually in an attempt to exploit these situations for their own ends.

Economists and political scientists maintain nowadays that it is possible to study respectively economic and political aspects of societal development. Sociologists often shun the concept and consider the substance of societal development as part of the theory of social change. Taking an interdisciplinary overview, Professor Chodak asserts that societal develop-

$12.50

Societal
Development

Five Approaches with Conclusions
from Comparative Analysis

Szymon Chodak

New York
OXFORD UNIVERSITY PRESS
1973

To Nina

Copyright © 1973 by Oxford University Press, Inc.
Library of Congress Catalogue Card Number: 73-82663
Printed in the United States of America

Preface

Issues in the social sciences raised hundreds or even thousands of years ago are still pondered. Philosophers, social and political theorists, and social scientists return to these same questions, to pose them anew from the perspective of their own time, to propose answers only to discover that these answers pose new questions, requiring review of the issues. Old writings are reinterpreted in the light of new discoveries and contemporary understanding. Concepts are redefined and given new meanings. And, after a time the questions will be posed again, and the answers reviewed and reformulated. The social sciences grew not only as a result of new discoveries, the examination of new phenomena, the application of new more strict methods, and the borrowing of ideas from other disciplines, but even more as a result of constant reinterpretation of existing ideas and concepts.

This book takes up one such constantly reviewed and reinterpreted topic: societal development. More strictly, it is about diverse aspects of development processes occurring in societies. It is a search for new answers and explanations, undertaken with the understanding that final answers and explanations cannot be found. It is an attempt to present some new aspects of the problem. The method I have used is comparative analysis, both of theories on the subject and of diverse societal and political orders. Weight is given to the presentation of conclusions from work which I have carried out earlier, however, and from the work of other writers.

It seems to be pertinent to state here the principles which were adopted in the writing of this volume. Although it is possible to discern a body of beliefs and propositions generally regarded as facts of life and acknowledged by all or most social scientists as truths about social living, most theories (including my own) are merely the opinions of experts. The more the opinions of the experts on a subject agree, the greater the probability that they approximate a real state of affairs. Two or more contradictory opinions can be valid simultaneously and, in spite of their contradictions, can be combined in making judgments. This is especially true of theories expressing diverse perspectives. Experts in science tell us that in their fields, "The early developmental stages of most sciences have been characterized by continual competition between a number of distinct views of nature, each partially derived from, and all roughly compatible with, the dictates of scientific observation and method."[1] In the later stages of development of a discipline, when it becomes "mature," scientists learn to accommodate themselves to the many-sidedness of phenomena and to the validity of diverse, seemingly contradictory, interpretations. An element of arbitrariness, scientists assert, is always involved in any interpretation and theory.

Could it be different in the social sciences? The societal phenomena of our concern run a wide gamut. Any one theory has to focus on only some aspects. Thus research, exploration, and theories reflect an arbitrary selection and exposition of the aspects considered at the time to be especially important, or for one or another reason considered determinant or appropriate. Besides, societal phenomena are portrayed differently not only because selection is based on different aspects in researchers' experience and knowledge, but also because of the different perspectives from which they are viewed. Even historical facts and data do not look the same when viewed from diverse perspectives. Complementary approaches allow the same topic to be viewed from many sides.

Many societal phenomena have a dichotomic and contradictory nature. Processes of development may be so described. They are generated most often in conflict, when individuals or parties strive to improve their position vis-à-vis other parties, to attain personal or group goals which indirectly produce the consequences regarded from a historical and societal perspective as development. Societal development, or the developments that occur in social interactions and change the character of social living, are a continuing of the past and an ongoing introduction of cumulative changes engendering new qualities, structures, and relations. Viewed as a process of change in the societal structure, development is simultaneously a process of differentiation of new societal roles and specializations, which produces more options and choices for mobility, and a process of imposing interdependencies that subordinates people within diverse frameworks of growing systemness. It bears simultaneously desirable and undesirable, predictable and unpredictable results.

Science explores phenomena related in strict causality in which the organization of similar conditions leads to similar results, and a combination of similar sets of factors produces with a high degree of probability similar consequences. However, the phenomena and processes analyzed in the social sciences include at least one highly unpredictable factor: assemblages of unique people evaluating situations individually in an attempt to exploit them for their own benefit. The social sciences inevitably have to deal with cases in which "similar initial conditions may lead to dissimilar end-states. Thus two cultures developing in very similar ecological environments may end up with very different sociocultural systems."[2] Thus societies are at the same time unique assemblages of unique people and uniform systems that exhibit similar properties.

In short, I am attempting to view the processes of development in society from a multidimensional synthesizing perspective. I do not claim that this is a royal road to the truth. It is only a voice in the ongoing discussion of the subject.

As I complete this book I wish to express my deepest gratitude to my colleagues, especially of the Department of Political Science at Berkeley (University of California) for their unstinting support and most generous willingness to spend time reading all or parts of this manuscript, for discussions with them helped to make the publication of this study possible. In the community of this Department full of innovative ideas, in its atmosphere of constant intellectual exchanges of opinions and provocative insistent demands of students for explanations of social and political processes, in the atmosphere of sympathetic attitudes with which I was surrounded, I found most suitable conditions for the formulation of this work.

I owe my greatest debt to Professor David E. Apter (now at Yale University). His work on modernization and the discussions that I had with him in Africa and in the United States were an inspiration for my own thoughts. I would like to express my appreciation also to Professor Carl G. Rosberg for his encouragement and aid, including help in obtaining a small grant for typing and editing the manuscript. I also thank Professors Warren F. Ilchman, Leroy E. Graymer, Rufus Davis, and Aaron Wildavsky for reading and commenting on separate chapters; Professor Benjamin Nelson for comments on Chapter IV. Professor Ernst B. Haas read the entire manuscript and gave valuable constructive criticism on parts of it. I benefited also from the help of the Institute of International Studies which he headed, especially in editing and typing the text. In the final stage of my work I had the opportunity to discuss some of the chapters and ideas contained in this book with Professor Neil J. Smelser.

I profited greatly from these discussions. I was lucky to have my office close to that of Professor Philip Siegelman. Discussions with him, whether or not on subjects analyzed in this book, had a stimulating impact on my work. And I am grateful to Professor Maria Hirszowicz (now at the University of Reading in England) for long discussions on the project of this book during my short visit in Oxford. I am also thankful to Bojana Ristich, Betsy Scheiner and Patricia Spoerl for their skill and patience in editing and typing the manuscript.

Szymon Chodak

Montreal, Canada
Berkeley, California
May 1973

Contents

Societal Development

*Once upon a time there was a very long
snake. A very, very, very long one.
One day, when it was hanging from the
trees and bushes, it saw its own tail,
which appeared to it as very ugly.
The snake wanted to kill it, and so it
chased it among the bushes. The faster
it ran, the faster the tail escaped.
Finally it died from exhaustion.
Which one died, the tail or the snake?*

An African story

Introduction

From the moment he became self-conscious, man has been fascinated by the phenomenon of development and growth around him. Seeds put in the ground miraculously changed into plants bearing flowers and fruits. Insects developed from eggs into larvae, and eventually into adults. Man himself grew from a fetus into a baby, and then into a full-grown, self-conscious individual. Even the societal environment in which he lived showed tendencies toward change, admirably fitting the scheme that seemed everywhere to exist behind development and growth. His family grew as a result of the proliferation of its membership. It changed into an extended family, became a part of a unilineal kinship group, and subsequently a tribe and nation. What kind of power was behind this overwhelming general process and order of growth and development? Was it possible to grasp that great secret of nature? Was it possible to control it? Was it possible to generate development, especially in the direction and at the pace of man's own will?

In the middle of the nineteenth century, great achievements and discoveries in biology and related sciences seemed to bring man to the threshold of knowledge where the secret of life and growth of organisms could be explained if not controlled. Philosophers and social thinkers began to see in these discoveries a key to questions they had raised about the character of society. The world appeared to be organized in a clear order. Men were a part of the nature, and the society in which they lived seemed to be simply a natural extension of their surroundings. Even ideas, theories, philosophies, morality, norms, and laws produced by men looked like still another manifestation of nature's unfolding capacity for development, a continuation of the same order of things. A vivid and comprehensive picture emerged, pregnant with formidable explanations and solutions for the many problems and immense scarcities facing people. The task, too, looked simple. Once it seemed clear that everything was part of a great general process of evolution flowing into the future, general laws could be formulated. The general trend could be characterized. Specific laws of developmental processes, of parts and elements of that general trend could be formulated. The ends of these processes could be anticipated. Then man could become master of the flow of events and the societal economic and political consequences. The writers concerned with development at that time described the world as evolving toward prosperity, abundance, rationality, supreme justice, and even total happiness. A science was needed which would utilize the discoveries of other sciences, especially of biology, not only to derive explanations of the chain of events and transformations of the past but also to obtain a perspective from which to envision the future. It was hoped that this science would use its combined knowledge of the past, present, and future to relieve mankind from constant uncertainty, and help him avoid costly deflections from the straightforward march toward the untroubled future.

Sociology germinated in the atmosphere of such beliefs and hopes, and early sociologists attempted to produce theories fulfilling such expectations. Comte, Spencer, Marx, and other forefathers of the discipline were concerned with problems of societal development as they attempted to procure solutions to alleviate all of mankind's predicaments and tensions. They combined their understanding of the past with an explanation of the problems of the present, in order to create a projection for the future. They wanted to be simultaneously historians of the past, great priests of new "scientific" religions, engineers of human destiny and societal transformation, helmsmen of progress, and scientists. They tried to gauge reality by means of scientific evaluation and positivistic assessment, measuring the facts as strictly as possible without any prejudices, especially of an ideological kind. And this was the pitfall that they unconsciously dug for themselves. If societal evolution can be traced at all, it must be regarded as a process in which each step is unique. It is a historical process, and only in a metaphoric sense does it resemble the development and growth of biological organisms. Societies are not simply organisms made up of cells or corpuscles. As early as the beginning of the seventeenth century Thomas Hobbes warned in *Leviathan* against misuse of the organismic metaphor. He pointed out that human societies are inherently arenas of conflict and competition. Since men always seek eminence, for them the common good and the private good cannot be identical. Nor are human societies swarms like wasps and bees. Men are continually in competition for dignity and higher positions in society. They transform their organization consciously and come to agreements and consensus in pursuit of common benefits. At the end of the nineteenth and beginning of the twentieth century new arguments against theories of evolutionary development appeared. It was evident that in spite of their highly imaginative conjectures, illuminating interpretations and explanations of the past, the veracity of evolutionist theories of societal development could not be fully sustained. In particular, the visions of the future promoted by evolutionists were nebulous and speculative. The concepts of inevitability, progress, and dialectic which evolutionists seized as key explanations and denotations of propulsive forces behind chains of events and social action were criticized and dismissed as incompatible with reality, or at least as expressing ideas which could not be tested. Thorough explorations of history proved that the stages discerned by the evolutionists were no more than arbitrary abstract constructions, hardly adequate for a serious explanation of the course of societal development. In addition, they were based on an analysis of European history almost exclusively. Evolutionary explanations of societal development were as-sessed then as Europo-centric, naïve, and schematic. The critics con-cluded that the "development" and "growth" of societies were nothing more than shining metaphors and comfortable euphemisms invented by early sociologists to hide the paucity of their understanding of the proc-ess of social transformation. Strictly speaking, not even the most venomous critics, vituperative and fervent adversaries, persistent and strict analysts were able to invalidate fully the beliefs and theories promulgated by the evolutionist. Nevertheless, the criticism was serious enough to raise suffi-cient doubts about the validity of many concepts of the early evolutionists and to demonstrate that such theories do not have a sound scholarly foundation and cannot be proved in a sustained way. In the meantime disciplines other than biology, for example, psychology, physics, and mathematics, gained eminence, and social scientists turned to them for patterns to illuminate social phenomena.

Vindications of theories of evolutionary societal development and growth still appeared from time to time in the pages of sociological and anthropological publications. Some defended the idea of the evolutionary development of societies, pointing to the growth of science and knowl-edge, and to men as becoming more rational and even more moral; evi-dence of evolutionary development, they claimed. Others like Leslie White reformulated the evolutionist approach to bring it up to date. Social scientists on the whole, however, and sociologists especially, shunned the concept of development or growth and avoided studying it as a societal process. Many appeared to be trying to blot out the idea completely and to treat it as a misunderstanding that took place in the childhood of the discipline. Sociologists were, to be sure, still concerned with problems of development, even though they discussed them under the headings of changing structure, solidarity, and functions. They turned to the theory of social change which was putting forth in less controversial though less far-flung conclusions. The only social science discipline that retained the concept and interest in aspects of the theory of development was economics. True, economists were primarily interested not in the social order but in the growth of wealth, yet it was evident that such a growth reflected the growing generation of market-type interdependencies in society and thus an irreversible trend toward greater societal complexity.

Interest in a developmental theory of society became greatly revitalized in the 1950's and beginning of the 1960's in connection with the emergence of new nations in Asia and Africa. The concern was with economic development and nation-building primarily, but it was clear that the two issues were interdependent and that all solutions and courses of events in new nations would depend on how these two basic questions were answered. This time a comprehensive theory of development was needed for immediate practical use, and more urgently than in the middle of the nineteenth century. It was hoped that theories of development would provide ways of overcoming the economic underdevelopment of new nations, of unifying them and generating their own new identity in the most efficient and productive way in the shortest time. The quest for a new theory of development began. Evolutionary explanations were still rejected, but they could not have provided the answers anyway. This time the new tide of interest in problems of societal development coincided with the emergence and remarkable spread of system theories.

System theories and systemic thinking stem from conscious application of a holistic approach, or generally from a tendency to view structures not simply as congeries of individuals or elements or constituents or units but as organized wholes. Though derived from an analysis of many organized wholes in reality, general system theory tends to abstract the logic of systems and to produce models, "analytical systems," schemes of the logical distribution of constituents of a whole in a dimensional domain. From the point of view of a general system theory, it does not matter whether the constituents of a system are human beings, symbols, elements of mechanisms, or abstractions. What matters is not so much the qualities of the constituents but how they are related in the general order of the system, their "positional value," and the logic and general arrangement of the system as a whole.[1] In the application of system thinking to theories of societies as represented in the writing of Talcott

Parsons, Edward Shils, and other functionalists, basically a similar attitude has been adopted. The system is characterized as composed of four subsystems fulfilling four basic functional prerequisites in mutual exchanges, generating the equilibrium necessary for the existence and continuation of the system. The theory is not interested in the identity of the actors or their inherent qualities. If they are considered it is only in the capacity of roles of constituents of the system. It is a theory of society in general. It attempts to describe and characterize the logic of a social structure regardless of whether it is a tribal society in Africa, a modern industrial nation like the United States or the Soviet Union, or any other social structure in the past, at present, or in the future. It is erected as an abstract model of an organism which is by itself a metaphor and a derivation from societal structures. It is a scheme—not a portrait—of societies, a scheme which according to the functionalists' interpretation of general interactions will occur in any society. As a scheme the functionalist paradigm has to abstract some logical interconnections which are important from the particular point of view adopted by that theory. It has to disregard situational and other peculiarities of real societies. All this could even be regarded as correct so long as it is a scheme, or one of a number of possible interpretations, so long as it is a theory designed to depict one selected aspect of the general order of social structure, one especially important aspect from a definite point of view, yet only one among many possibilities. That was not the case, however. Parsons presented his theory as the sole interpretation, superseding any other interpretation, and explaining as no other interpretation could the voluminous complexity of social, political, and even economic reality. Neither it nor any other theory could fulfill these claims and tasks, and eventually it provoked an avalanche of attacks and criticisms.

The list of societal phenomena and factors accounting for variance which are excluded from functionalist theory, and especially from its leading exposition in the writing of Talcott Parsons is, indeed, extensive. I cannot afford to engage in an enumeration of these phenomena here, nor to discuss other shortcomings of functionalism here. I am sure, however that the reader is familiar with this list from other sources. Although on the following pages I shall have to refer to general systems theory and to the functionalist approach to societal systems, neither the systems theory in itself nor the merits and demerits of functionalism is the subject of interest.

To be sure a part of the discussion in this book will revolve around the concepts of system and growing systemness. These concepts have to be used, despite the idiosyncracies they have developed, because they were used as key concepts in functionalist theory. People, institutions, industries, organizations, and entire societies are in the process of becoming more interdependent. Social relations as well as organizational interactions are becoming increasingly standardized, patterned, recurrent, and therefore, systemic. It is not accidental that modern theory in many fields revolves around the concept of "system." In speaking about systems and growing systemness, I do not wish to imply anything akin to a Parsonian paradigm. Societal systems are characterized here not as structures in equilibrium, homeostasis, or as tendencies toward such states of interactions. In the understanding promoted here, systems, whether economic, political, or societal, evolve in organizations of interdependencies. Moreover, let me stress that systems are quite commonly organized around structures of conflict. As a matter of fact they inherently generate conflict which eventually becomes the source of societal development. Introduction of systems and increase of systemness in societal interaction are rarely a goal per se. Such introductions are instrumental, however, in the generation and acceleration of economic, organizational, political, and other processes of development.

In his theory of pattern variables Talcott Parsons addresses himself to problems of societal development only indirectly. Other members of the functionalist school and writers who were influenced by the functionalist approach transformed in one way or another the scheme of pattern variables into a design which allowed for the contrasting of characteristics of what was later called "traditional underdeveloped" (in a more polite version, "developing") and "developed" modern industrial societies.

Herein I propose to view societal development as growing systemness. I believe that this is not an entirely new idea, since it is contained in numerous classical writings, especially those in the field of sociology, such as the works of Marx, Toennies, Durkheim, Weber, and recently Smelser. I shall attempt to extricate, expose, and reformulate this argument, thereby making it relevant in terms of both system and developmental theories, and to demonstrate that its diverse aspects can be examined by means of such paradigms as those provided by exchange, organizational, or economic interaction theories. In my understanding, when development refers to societies, it implies an entwining of numerous and variant threads of separate processes of development and of separate structures, entities, groups, units, and agencies. These are constituents of the general development, but they simultaneously take their form from their own constitutive threads. Separate threads and processes of development, though related and affecting each other, are not necessarily congruent and hence do not necessarily change at the same pace. On the whole, the process of development as discussed here can be characterized as a continuity occasionally interrupted or stalemated, yet nonetheless irreversibly directed toward greater complexity. Thus it is a process which generates wider and larger systems and densification of intrasystemic interdependencies. It is a process which engenders systems of higher levels while engulfing systems of smaller capacity. Toennies described it as an emergence of *Gesellschaft* which absorbs the variety of *Gemeinschaft*. Durkheim characterized it as a growing organic solidarity superseding mechanical solidarities in a more complex division of labor. Today these processes are even more complex and, what is especially important, they are now becoming engulfed by even wider processes regulated and coordinated by the modern state through networks of bureaucracies. Thus societal development generates eventually the need for etatization.

I shall attempt to abstain from considering societal development as either desirable or undesirable. It advances as a result of increased striving for greater outputs and efficiency in production, economic management, and political control. Patterns of activity and of life generally become standardized in achievement of these ends. Human relations become depersonalized. Various forms of alienation are generated which adversely affect the autonomy of individuals. One may add pollution, destruction of the ecological environment, and other plagues besetting us today as the additional costs of societal development.

The subtitle of this book is "Conclusions from Comparative Analysis." This is to expose and stress the main goal and method applied in the book. All elements of the perspective on societal development which I wish to introduce are derived from a comparative analysis of existing concepts and paradigms on societal development in diverse geographical areas and sociopolitical orders. I am comparing theories and societies in an attempt to discern variables of what I think is a new framework for a multidimensional theory of societal development. It must be emphasized that I am aiming for a frame rather than for a comprehensive theory itself. It also needs to be pointed out that the interest here is more in those aspects of different theories and approaches on the subject which could be regarded as complementary, rather than in indicating and listing contradictions. Indeed, many approaches often considered as incompatible are herein regarded simply as views on the same subject from a different perspective. Besides, in this book I am less interested in finding out and exposing the erroneous in other writing and more interested in attempting to utilize the contributions made from very diverse perspectives and, further, in utilizing them as constitutive parts in the construction of the variables of a still more novel approach.

Comparing theories of development in circulation in the current literature, I have been able to distinguish at least five approaches. These are (1) evolutionary theories; (2) theories of development that stress the process of growing interdependencies; (3) theories interested in motivations of action objectively producing the effect of development; (4) theories concerned with specific aspects of the process of societal development, e.g. economic and political development; (5) theories concerned with specific modes of action sparking organized development—in other terms, theories of modernization.

The five approaches on societal development can be portrayed in a sketchy way as follows:

1. Within what may be called a historiosophic approach, which was more widespread in the past, the concept of development was applied to denote a process of continuous evolution within the socioculture of mankind in general; this process was usually described in sequential stages. In a sense, this was an organismic approach, strongly utilizing biological models of growth and evolution. The theories of Morgan, Marx, Comte, Spencer, Hobhouse, Kidd, and Ward represented this understanding in the past. L. A. White's, J. Steward's, and M. Sahlin's theories on the evolution of culture are contemporary versions of such an approach.

2. Macrosociological theories on industrialization, which as a rule avoid applying the term "development," have to be regarded as another discernible approach. This is because such macrosociological theories are focused on what others will regard as resulting from development. A great number of sociological theories may be included here: Cooley's writings on primary groups; Durkheim's on mechanic and organic solidarity; Toennies's on *Gemeinschaft* and *Gesellschaft;* the functionalist characteristic of contrasting pattern variables of traditional and modern societies; the writings of Bendix and Smelser on that topic, and so forth. All these theories are focused on the birth of contemporary modernity, which tend to view it as resulting from change rather than *expressis verbis* of development. Yet such changes are said to be cumulative, irreversible, and unidirectional, and all such theories imply this. What results from the changes described in such theories is not so much a higher stage but a more complex social structure, containing more structural differentiation and functional specialization, albeit in greater societal interdependence and cohesion. Thus, it could be said that such theories assume that development is a growing societal systemness. Rather than tracing these changes in everlasting processes of development throughout the whole history of Man, such theories concentrate on discussing the turn to the present as a result of industrialization. The basic analytical tool employed here is the contrast and confrontation of opposing values, vari-

ables, qualities, structures of the past and of the present, of the old and traditional, and of the new and modern.

3. Theories concerned primarily with exploration of the mechanism that causes development also have to be singled out. Instead of asking "What is development?" or "What happens in its course?" writers of that inclination ask why it happened, and what especially caused the breakthrough from traditional into modern societies. Thus such theories start with the question "What are the causes of industrialization?" The specific point of interest is why people become involved in economic development and other activities that produce affluence. Such theories tacitly assume that societies develop as a result of the work of exceptional and occasional factors. Where such factors are present, development happens; where they are absent, stagnation prevails. Should it be possible to single out these factors, either analytically or empirically, then not only will an explanation be found for why industrialization happened in Europe, but it will also be clear why it did not happen in other parts of the world. Thus a remedy for new nations will be found. This distinctive factor which causes economic development is then usually sought in the sphere of value orientations. Hence such theories strongly rely on psychological explanations. Max Weber, in his study of the Protestant ethic and capitalism, first introduced this approach. Everett Hagen's theory on status withdrawal and David McClelland's theory on achievement motivation are examples of new versions of such an approach to development in modern literature.

4. Most publications on development are on specific types or spheres of development—on economic and political development especially. In other words, they are about the development of an entity, of one of the multitude of overlapping systems or subsystems of interaction in a socioculture. They explore the growing interrelatedness and its institutionalization, which results in greater economic output, the substitution of a market economy for semimarket and subsistence economic relations, and the like, the increase in political participation, growing efficiency in decision-making, the acquisition by the state of more regulative and co-ordinative functions, increase of political institutionalization and other processes or methods of economic, political, or other developments respectively. This approach does not promote the idea that development is a spontaneous evolution. Instead, it implies that development is made by developers. It consists of calculation and planning and of organized, goal-oriented actions which implement such plans; it consists of prescribing solutions, and in applying remedies to problems. In short, theories belonging to this approach are concerned with explanations of how to

organize resources for specific kinds of development in the sphere of economy, nation-building, politics, education, and so forth.

5. Finally, as a separate approach, I wish to consider those theories that are primarily concerned with development in new nations. Some such theories, as Ponsioen pointed out, reserve the concept of development exclusively for these nations. They assume that since such nations are "developing," development applies to them. According to such a view, other nations, especially the industrialized nations, are outside the sphere of development: they change, increase their economic output, transform their political and social organization and their economy, but they do not develop. Some writers call this expansion in contrast to development. From this point of view, development consists of altering the spontaneously ongoing societal life processes in nations which had not achieved higher standards of living, in order to amplify the growth of their economic output, raise their standards of living, increase their political participation, spread education, and the like. These are theories on how to make new nations modern. In the American literature on the subject, they are actually called theories of modernization. Yet some writers also apply the concept of modernization to the European past—hence modernization is viewed as a specific form of development which consists of bridging the gap between the level of development of a given society or some sphere of its life, and a more perfect and modern form achieved in other societies. Thus such theories are concerned with problems of the continuity of traditional cultures, and with ways of transferring innovations and achievements from other nations and cultures. The works of Levy, Bendix, Apter, and Eisenstadt are exemplary cases of such theories.

In all of the five approaches, development and politics are seen as closely related, and hence are to be found in all theories of development. From one point of view, development results from policies, especially from specific political decision; policies are designed and carried out· with a desire to increase and achieve development. From another point of view, politics is only one of the factors in the ongoing process of development. Throughout our discussion of the diverse approaches to development the role of politics is constantly under consideration.

Combining the elements of system theory in the interpretation outlined above, and what I felt could be derived from the variant approaches of the process of development of societies, I am proposing to view development of societies from the perspective of a number of "variables": (1) conflict within consensus as a source of developmental activities; (2) differentiation within expanding interdependence as a process of growing systemness and as the content of societal development; (3) insecurity within a framework of societal security as one of the most important

sources of motivation in developmental activities (manifest in diverse
societies having diverse value systems in terms of attitudes and organized
action which differ considerably though often leading to similar results
and achievements); (4) change within continuity as a characteristic and
content of the process of development; (5) economic and political development as modes of constituent processes, and in some instances goals
of the general developmental process.

All these variables, as is evident in the terminology selected to characterize them, are depicted in a dualistic consistency. Combined together they allow us to view not only the five approaches outlined here
in complementarity, but can also be regarded as a springboard for a new
perspective, the basic elements of which I shall attempt to promote in the
following pages.

Though characterized recently as a mere metaphor whose reality can
hardly be proven, "societal development" belongs to those great and
important concepts around which large sections of social science theories,
and often great endeavors of social praxis, have been organized. Great
hopes have been connected with this idea. Abandoned and rejected in
the past, the idea of societal development and theories pertaining to it
were reintroduced ten or fifteen years ago. It has been viewed as the
source and vehicle of industrialization, affluence, prosperity, democracy,
increasing education, and freedom. It is still the subject of desires and
hopes especially in the Third World nations. Societal development has
also become, however, the subject of despair and lamentations. Nowadays attention tends to be more often focused on its negative consequences: on the destruction of the environment, pollution, uneven
distribution of wealth, alienation of people and social institutions, depersonalization of individuals, destruction of communal life, transformation
of people into elements and cogs of the all-engulfing industrial complexes,
increasing sterility of democracy, and above all generation of gigantic
systems which the individual is often unable to oppose or control. Although we are unhappy about current developments, we are unable to
think of any solution other than that of better development. Thus problems of societal development remain of great importance.

The First Approach:
Evolutionary Theories

During a conference on the concept of development held at the University of Minnesota in December 1955,* most of the participants argued against it in the social sciences because of its biological connotation, claiming that the term has been commonly associated with organization of living structures and life processes. Referring to K. Popper and R. H. Tawney, one of the participants, Norman J. De Witt, pointed out that the "application of the classical concept of growth and development to social institutions leads us via Hegel to Marx, suggesting that we might amend Aristotle to read: 'Having passed through many stages it [society] found its natural form (with the help of the Party) and there it stopped.'"[1] Organic concepts—and in De Witt's opinion development is an organic concept—imply an orderly process, containing implicit teleological assumptions of an organized body with parts, that is, of a finite sum or whole. Such concepts are based not so much on empirical research as on visual imagination. Hence he advises either to refrain from using the concept "development" and other such organic concepts in the social sciences, or to transfer them with the utmost caution, with a full awareness of the limitations they carry when applied to a field where empirical research is common.

The historian Herbert Heaton argued in a similar manner. Historians, he said, have "plenty of examples to warn . . . of the dangers inherent in

* It is worthy of note that sociologists, economists, and political scientists were absent from the writers represented in the volume containing papers presented at this conference.

ambitious, comprehensive concepts capable of projection into the future."[2] Yet all warnings are futile. Social scientists commonly succumb to the temptation of using such concepts. Recently, he tells us, the *nouveaux riches* newcomers into the social sciences, the economists, have become especially notorious for such dangerous and reckless speculations. His library is full of books containing the word "development" even in the title. What is asked in such books is not only "What happened?", but why it happened, and occasionally even what will happen. Heaton is outraged by this. With brilliant irony, he expresses his indignation:

> Meanwhile my near neighbours, the economists, true to their traditional cultural lag in learning the facts of life, have recently appropriated "economic development" as their latest hobby, and are producing a five-foot shelf of books on the nature and cause of economic development in the past or on the methods—including bulldozers and IBM machines—that are needed for the development of "underdeveloped" areas in the very near future—which means before the Communists beat us to the punch.[3]

Looking back on what has happened since, one may say that economists in the meantime have completed at least five (if not more) of the five-foot shelves of books on development, and many political scientists, anthropologists, and some sociologists have joined them in that effort. Some do so using the term "development" in the open, while others prefer to write about it using other terms. Critics argue that we are still in the dark, and that "we do not know enough about the past and the present to formulate any concept of development that permits a broad, sweeping forecast." Or they say, "Expressions of this type plainly involve the notion of more than the merely logical possibility of the realization of alternatives other than those which were in fact realized, namely of differences between situations in which individuals can be reasonably regarded as being responsible for their acts, and those in which they can not."[4] Other objections may be raised, and they are indeed raised. Yet the interest in problems related generally to development—and more specifically, the problems of economic, political, and what is considered societal development—have recently become widespread. In spite of all warnings, this interest is growing. It is furthermore true that new approaches and interpretations of the concept appeared on the wave of revived concern with the topic, which decisively changed its meaning.

The recent growing interest in problems of development, social change and modernization was stimulated especially by the emergence of new nations and their search for solutions to their mounting problems. After the achievement of independence, leaders of new nations, scholars, and even the masses of people in new countries had to pose the question: "What next? How to accomplish nation-building?" How could they increase the economic output so as to raise the standard of living? How could they solve the many problems protracted and accumulated in the past? The experts answered: through development—economic, political, and similar development. Through development of the state, administration, agriculture, industries, education, culture, communications. Through planned, effectively accelerated changes in pursuit of the implementation of goals ideologically defined. All those things that are considered achievements in Western Europe, the United States, the Soviet Union, and in other parts of the world were said to be products of development, and especially of economic development. So it was assumed that if the new nations wanted to achieve the same, they would have to develop, or modernize.

What does development mean? Dale B. Harris* tells us the following: "Discussions of development commonly include as essential the ideas of (1) organism conceived as living systems; (2) time; and (3) movement over time toward complexity or organization; (4) 'hierarchization,' and (5) an end-state of organization which is maintained with some stability and self-regulation."[5] Well, this is not the only or even not the most common way of understanding the concept of development in modern literature. Yet this is certainly a good example of an evolutionary, organismic interpretation of the idea. Other definitions promoting the evolutionary, organismic approach may tell us that development is one or a combination of the following:

1. A spontaneous process of gradual evolution toward higher stages of organization;

2. A process of the exteriorization of a potentiality, and of the realization of an embryonic capacity in a unilinear process of maturization;

3. A process of continuous structural-functional transformation, proceeding as a result of a greater specialization and structural differentiation in a simultaneous augmentation of the degree of cohesion and intricate interdependence of the whole;**

4. A self-generating, complex, ongoing process of change, containing, at any specific time, factors necessitating and inevitably producing

---

* The writer continues: "These last ideas inevitably bring up the troublesome issue of 'purpose,' so easy to dispose of in simple mechanic systems, but so difficult to avoid in one guise or another in discussions of biological systems" Dale B. Harris (ed.), *The Concept of Development*, p. 3.

** As will be seen in the next section, such an interpretation of the concept of development may also promulgate other than a simply evolutionary, organismic understanding of the idea.

subsequently new, even more complex self-revealing structures and inter-actions.*

Taken separately, the above four definitions demonstrate what may be called four diverse leanings—in the first, toward a pure evolutionary under-standing of the concept; in the second, toward a genetic understanding; in the third, toward a structural-functional understanding; and finally in the fourth, a stress on the element of inevitability, toward determinism.

These differences may be important. However, as was already men-tioned, modern literature on the subject promotes still other understand-ings of the concept. Development nowadays is being prescribed as a remedy for the problems of new nations. Development as a policy, devel-opment as a planned, effectively accelerated activity in the implementa-tion of goals which are defined in advance, is indeed different from the development that is a result of spontaneous evolution, or the exterioriza-tion of an implicit, inherent potentiality; it is different from the develop-ment resulting from an interplay of factors not under the control of man, even though one of them may be the common striving toward the im-provement of living conditions. Those who speak of development as discovered in a chain of perpetuation of history, those who prescribe de-velopment, those who struggle to implement the vision of a leader or a party or government, or do the job as designed by a planning committee, those who purposely undertake development as an activity to emulate the desired achievements of other nations—all these certainly do not mean the same thing. Thus Ponsioen asserts:

> Developing, as used for countries today, is rather a euphemism, des-ignated not a spontaneous process of growth, but a process of induced change, induced by consciously framed policies of indigenous as well as of assisting agencies. They aim at introducing new institutions, new social forces into the existing field of social forces. It reorientates

* Regarding the general definition of development, Herbert Heaton (B. Harris, p. 205) states: "Much that has been said about it by Professors Nagel and DeWitt fits the his-torian's general understanding of the term. So also does Sidney Hook's definition or de-scription as penned for the Committee on Historiography over a decade ago: 'Develop-ment is any change which has a continuous direction and which culminates in a phase that is qualitatively new. [Hence the term] should be used to characterize any series of events in thought, action, or institutional arrangements which exhibit a directional cumulative change that either terminates in an event marked off by recognized quali-tative novelty or which exhibits in its course a perceptible pattern of growth.' If that is how a philosopher sees it, it looks very much like the picture painted by Professor Lane, . . . the Johns Hopkins historian, who describes development as those changes which involve passage through successive stages or states, each of which was made possible by that preceding and was prerequisite to that which followed. Further, the movement is one way. As Lane puts it, 'There is no assumption that we will go back from planet to gaseous nebula, from man to ape, from democracy to absolute monarchy, or from one form of class struggle to an earlier form and start over.' "

those existing forces and tries to motivate them in a new way. It frames new instruments to produce that particular brand of social change, called development.

Strangely enough, the word developing is not applied to Western countries. One is inclined to say that their economies are developing in the proper sense of the word. But they are said to have their economies expanding, or growing. Its reservation to the low income countries suggests that development as happening in developing countries is something different and particular.[6]

This does not seem to be entirely correct. True, the prevailing trend is toward new connotations of the concept of development. Some writers tend to differentiate specific kinds of development, that is, economic, political, and so forth and thus concentrate their interests on definite aspects of sociocultural activities. Sometimes development is related to an interest in new nations; at other times, to general theories. Some use the concept to denote the consequences of industrialization. Still others, as asserted by Ponsioen, reserve the notion exclusively to describe the activities undertaken in new nations in their attempts to generate higher standards of living, greater economic outputs, the building of new nations and new structures of government and administration. Some still continue to view development or to speak of it as a spontaneous evolution.

I must start this review of different approaches to societal development with a discussion of what may be called the evolutionist approach. Not only many of the theories which belong herein are commonly regarded as developmental theories, but because these are the theories that have especially triggered most of the stormy criticism against the concept of development in social sciences. A large gamut of theories belong here. I wish to discuss only some of them—the ones that seem to be most representative and controversial: The ideas of Marxism, the theories of Comte, Spencer, and Ward on the development of societies, and L. A. White's more recent writings on the evolution of culture.

1. Marxism on the Process of Societal Development

The idea of societal development and growth is inherent in the whole cultural tradition of Western philosophy.[7] Ancient Greek philosophies were saturated with it. It reappeared in the core of classical Christian philosophical thinking during the Middle Ages. Modern philosophies were organized around it. In the nineteenth century philosophers and social thinkers proclaimed it to be not only a perspective of thinking or a retrospective approach on what had happened but also a goal of societal existence, the purpose of incessant striving. The fascination with it brought about the appearance of the first sociological theories, and it may be said that sociology—in the beginning, at least—was basically a theory of societal development.

The nineteenth-century theories on development in an evolutionary process of societal transformation—going on throughout the history of mankind and promoting historiosophic implications—were especially inspired by two sources: first, the inspiration generated by the glamorous achievements of nineteenth-century biology, and the Hegelian theories of the dialectical development of the Idea, and its subsequent incarnation in the family, the civil society, and the state. The Hegelian inspiration is especially evident in the writings of Marx and Engels on that concept— more in the works of Marx, strictly speaking. Although it is believed that both of the writers on classical Marxism were the coauthors of one theory, and although Engels did in fact endorse the totality of Marx's ideas as his own understanding of the problems, a careful examination of the writings of these theoreticians shows that the Marxism of Marx and the Marxism of Engels were congruent, yet remarkably distinctive.

Of course, as in other cases, when Marx wrote on development in a historical perspective he rejected the philosophical idealism and the sociopolitical implications derived from it by Hegel, while he retained the spirit, phraseology, and indeed the argument of dialectics. Engels's writings on that topic, on the other hand, are strongly influenced by the ideas of L. H. Morgan. To be sure, Engels expanded Morgan's paradigm. He transformed it into his own model, and focused it on the emergence of social classes, class struggle, state coercion to defend the interests of the privileged, exploited classes, and especially the occurrence of private property, which is described as the source of all evil in the history of mankind. He built into Morgan's analysis the mechanism of dialectic, inevitably and automatically converting one form of property, one form of societal structure into another, higher, inevitably ensuing form. Thus he introduced a concept of societal development as an evolution, progressing in convulsions of contradiction and conflict between productive forces and productive relations—in class struggle subsequently generating higher stages of societal development and more complex forms of societal organization. Engels paralleled this with a theory of dialectical development of nature, with the intention of buttressing his vision of societal theory with generalizations of the common features of the processes of development and evolution, both of the inorganic and organic nature and of the society.*

---

* Engels outlined those views especially in *The Origin of the Family, Private Property and the State; The Part Played by Labour in the Transition from Ape to Man,* and *The Dialectic of Nature.*

Marxist theory combines Hegelian dialectic, Morgan's ideas on the evolution of cultures and societies, and a belief in an inevitably ongoing societal progress which leads to the construction of better societies as envisaged by utopian socialism. It views man as originally a product of the humanizing effect of labor, and labor itself as starting with the making of tools. It assumes that man has a natural propensity for improving the conditions of living. Aiming at self-satisfaction and the improvement of his own well-being, man invented, discovered, and organized cooperation and organization, thus producing culture and society in his immediate surroundings, within the wider environment of nature. In acting for his own benefit man is unable, or at least was unable until then, to account for and anticipate what kinds of latent consequences his actions would bear. Thus, development ensues in a sense constantly, as a by-product of all daily activities of all people. In an abstract manner, it is divisible into several threads of interdependent processes. First, Marx distinguishes a steady, ongoing process of perfecting the tools of production, of discoveries and inventions. Constant improvement and sophistication of the means of production and skills in their use require constant reshuffling in organization and structures of societal interaction respectively. Thus the whole economic structure becomes transformed. The belief is that this occurs systematically throughout the history of man, in the chain of sequential stages which constitute the dialectic evolution of a spiral growth of complexity and the perfection of societal structure. A number of stages are distinguished, each containing a diverse economic structure which reflects the level of perfection achieved in the means of production, the level and type of economy, the structure of property in society, and the class relations determined by those factors. The economic structure determines the features of the suprastructure of the social and political relations and institutions (especially those of the state) and the features of beliefs and behavior. Yet some feedback effect from the changing suprastructure on the economic structure is assumed, too. Therefore, parallel with the thread of the development of the means of production, there is a thread of development of the economic structure and of the suprastructure, which are mutually interdependent but which are principally determined by the changes in the sphere of economics.

It is further assumed that each of the stages of development that ensues in the historical process not only constitutes a separate socioeconomic structure, but can also be singled out by its own peculiar set of contradictions. Of these class struggle is the most discernible and determines any of the other kinds of possible societal conflicts and contradictions. Any societal conflict is thus interpreted as a reflection of class struggle. The model of the structure of class struggle at diverse stages of the process of development is said to be the same. As a rule, the established suprastructure of the state, law, dominant ideology, or prescribed norms of behavior is conservative—rather stiff and constant throughout the stage, in subservience to the interests of the ruling class. So,

> At a certain stage of their development, the material forces of production in society come in conflict with the existing relations of production, or what is but a legal expression for the same thing—with the property relations within which they have been at work before. From forms of development of the forces of production these relations turn into their fetters. Then begins an epoch of social revolution. With the change of the economic foundation the entire immense superstructure is more or less rapidly transformed.[8]

As the result of a revolution, development becomes uplifted to the next, higher stage, where the mechanism of contradictions and class struggle which manifests the growing conflict between productive forces and productive relations appears anew. Marx and Engels asserted that this has been going on throughout the history of mankind, and that it will continue until development reaches the stage of a socialist and communist society. Capitalism was said to be the last stage and the last structure based on the existence of private property and class struggle. Through revolution it inevitably leads to socialism, to a classless, stateless society where a new, perfect order will be established on the basis of a supreme rationality derived from the application of science to all important decisions. Thus conditions for the continuous perfection of the means of production will be established. Production relieved of the impeding fetters of private property will become most effective, producing an abundance of products which will satisfy all the needs of all the members of the society. The order of the society will rest on a system of superior norms of social justice. Men freed from constant scarcities or the necessity to struggle for existence will be able to concentrate on self-perfection and create masterpieces of art, thought, and the like. Thus the era will ensue when the free development of each man will secure the free development of all men, and vice-versa.

The tenets of the Marxist theory of development may be concisely stated as follows:

1. In general development is described (rather than defined) as a unilinear, ongoing process of growth in a sequential transformation, which leads spirally from lower to higher stages of the matter, substance, and organization. Its essence also consists of resolving the contradictions through revolutionary changes which produce new and higher forms of organization of the matter and societal structure, that is, accruing in a transformation of quantity into new quality.

2. When applied to the history of humanity, or when employed in the capacity of a generic notion which encompasses the content of all the processes which lift up societal organization into higher stages, development is said to consist in an evolutionary drive toward a perfection of the mode of production progressing in actions resolving contradictions, especially the contradictions of class struggle (as it was asserted above), and the self-perfection of man himself. It is also characterized as a process of evolution interrupted by a revolution which elevates the social structure and its evolution into a higher stage.

3. Development implies an ongoing expansion of production, hence continuous economic growth—in other words, a growing economic output which results from an increasing application of functional rationality and scientific knowledge and leads to what Karl Mannheim later called the "substantive rationality" of social justice.

4. It is understood that development could be stimulated, speeded up or, conversely, held up or impeded by the state and the socioeconomic and political structures, especially by the form of ownership of the means of production and the class struggle generated by it. However, it is also assumed that such an arrest may only be temporary. The static, conservative sociopolitical structure is unable to withhold and divert the pressing, persistent inevitability of the revolutionary breakthrough for a long period of time. Eventually, the inevitability materializes in the birth of the new socioeconomic and political structure.

5. Marxist theory asserts that development is goal-oriented. On the one hand, it rejects the teleologism implied by organismic theories; on the other hand, however, it proclaims that development consists of the implementation of an historical inevitability, and acquires its highest form not in the institutionalization of the state, as in Hegelian philosophy, but conversely, in the stateless society. As has been said, all contradictions and conflicts which have torn apart past societies are supposed to disappear at that stage. Marxist theory mentions nothing about the possibility of the emergence of new conflicts at that point.* Thus it can be said that development leads to an equilibrium based on rational decision-making and social justice. At that point development will reach the equifinality.

6. It must be stressed, however, that Marxism does not view development as simply growth crowned by a happy end. As was pointed out, it flows from struggle and destruction of the outdated, obsolete forms of societal interaction and institutions which embody them; it generates new structures, but—and this is also very important—it generates negative

* In modern Marxist literature one may find the view that contradictions are common in any society, yet it is assumed that in postcapitalist (or what are called socialist) societies they are essentially different and supposedly nonantagonistic.

phenomena, such as uprootedness and alienation. Both Marx and Engels discussed various forms of alienation and attributed them mainly to capitalism. Thus they distinguished the alienation of men in industrial production, the alienation of the product of work from the producers, and the alienation of the state from society. Alienation, from this point of view, spreads and grows as a latent, yet inevitable product of a striving for greater functional rationality. Capitalism, Marx and Engels asserted, is obsolete because it does not contain enough room for still greater acceleration of functional rationality; it impairs the progress of the perfection of the means of production. It is obsolete because of its immanent class system, which vitiates social justice. It is obsolete because it generates the various kinds of alienation which result from increased functional rationality. These were the negative aspects of development in general, and of industrialization and capitalism in particular. Yet, although they describe the past and the present as a chain of struggles and contradictions, Marx and Engels believed that what was inevitable in the past would not be inevitable in the future.

7. The concept of political development as separated and not related to economics does not fit into the Marxist perspective. On the contrary, politics in general, or one or another type of political structuralization, or the type of state are all but reflections of economic interests. Even nationalism, as indeed any political struggle, is regarded as a peculiar form of class struggle. From this point of view, political parties, regardless of their program, are institutions that promote class struggle; palace rebellions are conflicts within the ruling classes; religious movements are manifestations of the undercurrent conflicts of economic interests, and so forth. Political power is sought for economic privileges or in the economic interests of social classes. Marxist theory in general is assuming that authority at any stage of development serves the establishment and the interests of the economically dominant class. The revolutionary party, on the contrary, is said to serve the economic interest of the coerced and exploited class or classes. It may sound paradoxical, but in fact Marx and Engels were philosophers, economists, historians, and ideologists, but not so much political theorists. In any case, they did not demonstrate a great interest in the problems of political representation, democracy, or the structure of decision-making, and so forth. These questions had to be dealt with by Lenin and other communist leaders and theoreticians.

8. It must be mentioned that Lenin and other Marxist theoreticians introduced a number of changes and revisions into classic Marxism in order to make it operational. Some of them concerned the Marxist understanding of development. The following of these amendments at least have to be listed here: Socioeconomic stages in the process of develop-

ment, such as that of the capitalist society may be entirely bypassed. Socialism could be achieved as the result of planned development, even if a society had not passed through capitalism. Marx and Engels applied the concept of development to the whole of humanity; their successors applied it to individual countries and hence proclaimed that socialism may appear in one country or a number of countries while other countries remain feudal and capitalist, and thereby underdeveloped in comparison to the socialist ones. Politics, political institutions, and especially the state could be used for uplifting economic and generally societal development; hence political transformation and institutionalization of the "dictatorship of the proletariat" would spearhead economic development. This led to the conclusion that the state had to be maintained even in postcapitalist societies.

Marxism as a body of thought basically promotes the ideas of an evolutionary, partly organismic approach to the development of societies; it also contains the seeds of a different approach, which is now more common. Proclaiming the discovery of a process of societal development in the chain of history by attributing the meaning of growth to differing facts and structures, Marxist theory envisages development in the future which will consist of planned, organized actions in the pursuit of definite targets, in the acceleration of what is now regarded as economic growth; in consciously shaped development.

The attraction, strength, and weakness of the Marxist theory in general, and of its understanding of development in particular, follow primarily from its ideological implications. Marxism is accepted or rejected more often because of these implications than because of its scholarly, heuristic values. The Marxist theory of development was designed not so much for the exploration of the process of transformation in human societies, but as an ideological weapon to prove the inevitability of the cessation of capitalism. Marx wanted it to be not so much a concept and scholarly theory explaining social change as much as an instrument to rally the masses for revolution. It is a great vision that cannot and does not have to be proved. One may believe in it or not. Of course, it is inspiring, and in one way or another its elucidative ideas inspired many of the theories in the social sciences. It cannot be made into an empirical, testable theory. Its greatness is in the ambiguity of its weakness.

2. Comte and Spencer

Marx and Engels were not the only writers of their time who have related the past, the present and the future of humanity in a historical and evolutionary process of development. Other writers, philosophers, and later, sociologists of the nineteenth century, while explaining the process and its causes differently, all expressed beliefs in the evolutionary and sometimes in the revolutionary development of humanity. Similarly, they wrote that the world was changing in accordance with some rules which would be discovered or had already been discovered by them; that it was progressing toward a better future, which would be seen right after the next turn of history; and it is possible to change the ugly present into a bright future even at the present moment, if the laws of development were to be properly understood, and if this understanding were to be exploited in a rational reordering of society. That was an era of great scientific discoveries and inventions which stimulated the industrial revolution. Science seemed to possess unlimited capacities, and to be able to produce solutions and remedies for any problems, including social and political ones. So the question was how to use it to make the social and political organization of societies rational and effective, and how to use it to rearrange society on the basis of true and full social justice. Fascination with the achievements of science and technology was immense, and many social scientists believed that societies and countries could at least be ruled scientifically, if not by social scientists. The French Revolution was over, but other revolutions erupted from time to time. Parliaments and political parties were established. Growing numbers of people in Western Europe were enfranchised and obtained the rights of citizens. Democratic institutions were in the making. Apart from a few skeptics and pessimists, like Tocqueville and Burckhardt, who cast doubts as to whether humanity had not actually started to move on the line of decay, many writers on societal development and change seemed to believe that man was finally reaching the threshold of an era when all problems would be solved once and for all—an era when scarcity would be replaced by affluence, when people—not rulers, governments or authorities—would directly rule the societies; when man, exonerated from all constraints, relieved from enslaving powers, duties, and scarcities, would be able to devote his talents to art, to thinking, and to other creative activities. It was thought that science and technology, both of which manifested and realized the growing potentiality of the human mind, would provide the means and concepts for such transitions. Development, as understood at that time, inevitably progressed through history in the implementation of the inner, intrinsic law of history and in the self-realization of the human mind, and was envisaged as the vehicle that would carry humanity to the promised destination.

Auguste Comte, known as the founder of sociology, must be listed as the most distinguished theorist who ardently believed in the idea of the development of humanity, and in the possibility of directing it by means of science, especially by means of the positivistic philosophy he delineated. To Comte the development of humanity was but a natural continuation of the development of nature. He stated that development consists of intellectual and moral self-perfection of man and in his increased humanization. Generating new, more abstract, general notions and concepts, man multiplies his ability to understand the essence and relatedness of his own involvement, and of the constitution of his surroundings. Having perfected himself, man engenders more perfect, complex and higher philosophies, approaches to life, economies, and structures of institutions and cultures. Hence, in the course of development, rationality increasingly prevails over emotionalism, altruism over egoism, and knowledge over ignorance. Comte distinguished three basic stages in the development of humanity, each subdivided into several periods: the theological, metaphysical, and the positivist. Each of these is not a different era in the history of humanity, but a stage in the progressing capacity of the human mind and the growing complexity and interdependence of the world directed by man. The positivist stage was supposed to be then in the making, and Comte outlined proposals on how to organize it.

What, then, are the factors of development in Comte's opinion? As has been said, Comte assumed that development consists of man's own intellectual perfection, and of its exteriorization in abstract categories and in societal interactions. Its increasing capacity, in his view, reveals itself in response to the changing challenges of man's surroundings, and in response to questions posed continuously by man in the course of reevaluating his own attitudes and actions. It is affected by a number of other factors, too, such as increasing division of labor, competition, the length of human life, and, to an extent, by climate and by race. However, Comte did not attribute great importance to those secondary factors.

Parallels may be established between his theory of development and that of Hegel and Marx. Like Hegel and Marx, Comte attempted to construct a philosophical system based upon a specific interpretation of history. All three writers presented their understanding of history as the logic of eternity. All three saw it as a process of dialectical development, progressing basically in three sequential stages. To Hegel it was the realization of the Absolute in thesis, antithesis, and synthesis and in the family, civil society, and the state; to Marx it was the transformation of the form of property from a communal ownership of the means of production to private ownership and back again to a higher stage of communal ownership—that of a common societal ownership, resulting in the institutionalization of culture and socioeconomic interactions. Comte assumes a dialectical transformation of philosophies and institutions produced by them. Each of the writers represented a different philosophical approach, but all three claimed that their own theory represented the climax of philosophy and theoretical thought in general. Comte proclaimed his theory as a new secular religion, and though Hegel and Marx did not, both wanted their theories to be treated as full truth bordering on religious belief. In a manner similar to Marx's, Comte designed his theory not only as an interpretation of the past, but as a guide to action for the masses in reconstructing the present evil society. Like Marx, too, he was a zealous missionary of his program, a philosopher, scientist, ideologist, and prophet. Comte was not as militant as Marx, and he rejected violent revolutions and class struggle; yet he also believed in the necessity of a transitional dictatorship. In Comte's words: "The dictatorship which our transitional policy requires as long as the spiritual interregnum lasts must arise in the first instance from their ranks [of the people]."[9] In his opinion, ". . . the proletariat is not, properly speaking, a class at all, but constitutes the body of society. From it proceed the various special classes, which we may regard as organs necessary to the body.[10] Like Marx, Comte viewed politics either as originated by authorities, or as the emanation of the power of "The People." At maximum, they regarded it as an adverse factor for development in some situations, in others as action aimed at the destruction of the existing established order, never as a creative generator of change, development, and progress. Revolutions, they believed, are progressive phenomena and open the avenues for development; politics was the job of the rulers. Both wanted social scientists to deal with social engineering and to become the constructors of the ideal society of the future. Both, too, envisaged the scientists as the future authority, replacing the corrupt and ignorant politicians.

Herbert Spencer is interesting because his theory contains many ideas which were later expanded and in a sense formulated anew by Parsons and other functionalists. Briefly, let us say that Spencer viewed society as an organism comparable to a biological organism. He was probably more persistent in applying that analogy than any of the other writers of the organismic school in the social sciences; hence he is known as the organismist. Although Spencer admits that social and biological organisms differ in certain respects, he at the same time assumes that common features and similarities between them are more profound, more numerous and more important.* He asserts that societies grow like biological organisms. This is a process of multiplication of the composite units of the structure, augmenting the body, producing specialized organs

---

* Among the differences between individual and social organisms that Spencer distinguished, the following seem to be regarded as the most important: in societal organisms consciousness is diffused, while in individuals it is concentrated in one organ; societies do not have a physical appearance and they are constituted as continuous wholes, while individual organisms have such appearances.

and systems within it. The structure becomes more complex and contains specialized agencies, yet its cells, units, organs, and so forth, are not self-sufficient. Hence the life of the whole determines the life of each unit. Further, he assumes that both the individual and the social organisms of a lower stage or form of existence perform functions of life without differentiating and without articulating specialized organs and systems. These, however, do appear in more complex, higher organisms. Comparing Spencer's ideas with T. Parsons's theory on subsystems, it is interesting to note that generally Spencer distinguishes three types of higher systems: (a) the sustaining system, defined as "the parts carrying on alimentation in a living body and the parts carrying on productive industries in the body politics . . . ;"[11] (b) the distributing system, composed of "channels for transferring materials from the sustaining parts to the expending parts";[12]—corresponding to the circulatory system in the body and the exchange system in society; (3) the regulating system, consisting of an internal coordinating apparatus of a political aggregate which fulfills the functions of offense and defense. In Spencer's opinion, organs of a living organism correspond to institutions in societies. He especially differentiates family, ceremonial, political, religious, professional, and economic institutions.

Spencer identifies development with evolution. He explains that it consists in general of the integration of matter and the concomitant dissipation of motion. Promulgating a monist approach, he sought to formulate a universal definition, good enough to explain all forms of development, whether it was for biological organisms, species, or societies. In a set of rather confusing and often controversial contentions, Spencer characterizes the processes which lead to new types of social structures as unilinear, spontaneous and continuous growth. He calls it superorganic evolution. There is also said to be a continuous process of transformation of the incoherent homogeneity of the superorganic matter into a coherent heterogeneity of it; at the same time, there is a process to sift out specialized agencies, institutions and systems which perform specialized functions that maintain the organism intact, and a process of aggregation that unites separate units and individuals into higher, wider, more cohesive, and consolidated orders. At the same time, Spencer asserts that this is a process of transformation of the predominantly military systems of society into predominantly industrial systems, where individuals become less controlled by the system. He assumes that the latter trend consists in a natural, ongoing transformation of strongly centralized, hierarchical orders which function under a strict subordination to central authorities into orders of voluntary, cooperating, free individuals who aim at their own profits and benefits.

Spencer believed that any evolution or growth (including that of societies) is spontaneous and natural, and that it cannot be altered, diverted or speeded up, except perhaps by destruction of the organism. Although he was hesitant to conclude that societies, like organisms, die after a period of growth—as would follow from the close and strict analogy with biology that he applied in his studies—he contended that the integration of matter and the dissipation of motion, which constituted the superorganic growth, eventually reach a stage of equilibrium where society could be maintained in perpetuity. Conservative tones were already present in Comte's approach to development, yet Spencer's concept contains even more of a persistent conservative interpretation.

3. L. F. Ward on the Process of Societal Development

Recently, approximately one hundred years after L. F. Ward's appearance in public as an editor, paleontologist, philosopher, and sociologist, one may note a remarkable rekindling of interest in his publications. "In different eyes at different times he was a great scientist and a dull plodder, a great sociologist and a second-rate social thinker; a great philosopher and cosmic crack-pot."[13] S. Chugerman called him the American Aristotle.[14] J. Gerver tells us that "Ward's work is shot through with a passionate concern for social reform and the promotion of a liberal ideology. His insight and perception reveal him as the epitome of the concerned human being who uses his learning in order to comprehend and help the world about him."[15] R. Hofstadter, another writer who published a critical essay on Ward's work, asserted: "He was one of the ablest and most prescient thinkers in the history of the American mind, indeed in the history of international sociology. But it was his curious fate to be most pertinent as a thinker where he was most negative."[16]

Most of Ward's extensive writings are on evolution and, in a sense, on the concept of development. He proclaimed himself to be a monist, yet many who assessed his contribution felt that since he viewed development as an intertwining of two processes, which will be discussed further, we should regard him as a dualist—at least when he discussed the development of societies. He was preoccupied with the criticism of Comte and especially attacked Spencer, whose ideas he persistently rejected. This makes the reading of his books difficult, and at times rather tedious for one is not interested in those now remote discussions and ideas. Ward, too, like Comte and Spencer, views the evolution of societal structures as a continuation of the previous evolutions of nature.

On the whole, Ward distinguished three stages in the continuous evolution of matter: the primary aggregation of cosmogeny, the second-

ary aggregation of biogeny and anthropogeny, and the tertiary aggregation of sociogeny.[17] It is because of some of the ideas he elaborated in
connection with the description of what he called sociogeny that it is
important to at least briefly remind the reader of Ward's work here.

In Ward's opinion, one has to distinguish two distinctive composite
chains of action within the historical process of the transformation of societal structures, institutions, functions, and the like: the chain of genesis
and that of telesis. Accordingly, in his book, he has two separate parts
that deal with the ideas related to both of these aspects of societal development.[18] Thus Ward assumes that the genesis of social structures and
functions is a confluence of results of the positive and negative actions
of a number of social forces operating in "their natural freedom." These
are subject only to general evolutionary laws. Simultaneously, however,
societal structures, functions, institutions, and cultures are also the results of purposeful molding and conscious actions in pursuit of the fulfillment of man-made plans and targets. This he calls telesis, which is significant for our discussion. He explains it as follows:

> If, then, we take a comprehensive view of all the phenomena of so-
> ciety, we will see that they fall under two radically distinct classes,
> and we shall have the purely spontaneous or natural phenomena of
> society, on the one hand, produced by the dynamic agent, and the
> phenomena that result from intention or design, on the other hand,
> which are the products of the directive agent in the sense that but for
> the directive agent they would not have taken place. . . . Telic phe-
> nomena may also be called artificial, as distinguished from natural in
> the sense of genetic. For all art is telic. The distinction is sometimes
> said to be that between growth and manufacture, for growth is the
> type of the genetic process in organic nature, while manufacture is
> the final stage in art and results in wholly artificial products.[19]

Promoting the idea of telesis,* Ward introduced a new dimension
(and, one may say, a new level of analysis) into the evolutionary historiosophic approach to development. It is the dimension and the level of
psychic factors, "strictly co-extensive with the domain of mind." In doing
so, Ward ascertains that telic phenomena are made in an effort directed
at the implementation of man's vision, as distinguished from genetic
phenomena which are made in spontaneous, uncontrolled motions or
movements of inorganic and organic matter, and which are emanated
by desires residing in the higher forms of animate organisms. In a separate book, *The Psychic Factors of Civilization* (and on many occasions
in other books), Ward stressed the great importance he attached to that

---

* In his earlier work, *Dynamic Sociology*, Ward used the terms "genetic" and "teleological" phenomena.

distinction. Yet he was not a voluntarist, and he searched for laws and rules to be implemented in the process of evolution and development.

It seems that a number of other implications may be drawn from Ward's understanding of the concept of development. He is clearly not a utopian. Thus he expects neither the genesis nor the telesis to lead to either an equilibrium or to any form of an absolutely perfect society. He assumes, rather, that in the future, as in the past, the ongoing process of evolution and growth will continue under the increasing impact of telesis over its institutionalization and structuralization. He believes in progress, and in what must be stressed as the conscious perfection of the structures, functions, and ways of man's actions. This, Ward claims, will increasingly become an affair of the state, more coordinated and manipulated, and less of a spontaneous interplay in a laissez-faire of uncoordinated agencies, acting on their own account. Ward holds the state in great esteem. Its creation is the most important step taken by man in the direction of controlling the chaotic, self-oriented social forces. "Those who attack the state either do not know, or else they temporarily forget, that it is a product of evolution. It would be quite as rational to attack the solar system or the vertebrate type of structure."[20] In contrast to Spencer, Ward assumes that politics in general and political decision-making aimed at directing and stimulating development in particular will become increasingly important in the societies of the future. This, he assumes, is also true for education. In Ward's opinion, the character of politics, its targets, the organization of the state, and the ways it is operated greatly depend on how well its inhabitants are educated. Thus he says that the effectiveness of telesis, as well as its preponderance over genesis, increases with the dissemination and rising standards of education.

It may be said that Ward's approach implies a development made, induced, and stimulated by educated developers who manipulate the society by means furnished by the state. This stress on the decisiveness of telesis in the evolution and development of social structures makes Ward's theory most distinctive from the other theories on the subject discussed earlier.

4. Modern Evolutionism on Societal Development

As was said earlier, it is now uncommon to explore development in general, or even the various aspects of it within the evolutionary theories that encompass the history of humanity.* An interest in the evolutionary

* Apart from Marxists, who are a special case for obvious reasons, and apart from those who promulgate the idea of the cyclical development of civilizations, the writings of Spengler, Toynbee, and others seem to demonstrate a view of the contemporary world in decay rather than in development.

interpretation of the processes and problems of development was always strong in anthropology. The diffusionists, functionalists, and structuralists dominating that field were unable in their turn to eradicate the earlier strong influences of the evolutionists. Luminaries of that discipline, even while opposing evolutionism, have shown a considerable respect for it. Anthropology also seems to be the only field where evolutionism still survives as an active separate school. The book *Evolution and Culture*[21] can be regarded as an indication of it. Published by a group of self-declared evolutionists, it sounds in many parts as a manifesto of revolutionaries who proclaim the following:

> But antievolutionism has run its course, and once more the theory of evolution is on the march. Again it may be significant to note that this is taking place in a world which is once more undergoing rapid and profound change. The so-called backward nations in Africa and Asia are rebelling against the white man and colonialism. The social organization of the whole world is faced with this real possibility. The status quo is fostered precariously by a nation that has assumed "world leadership."
>
> The return to evolutionism was, of course, inevitable if progress was to continue in science and if science was to embrace cultural anthropology.[22]

L. A. White's writing seems to be the most representative and elaborate of the evolutionist approaches in anthropology today.[23] White views history as an evolution of culture, and in culture he includes the material objects made by man, plus beliefs, attitudes, organizations, and institutions. He assumes also that culture is an organized, integrated system transmissible by nonbiological means.

> We may view a cultural system as a series of three horizontal strata: the technological layer on the bottom, the philosophical on the top, the sociological stratum in between. These positions express their respective roles in the culture process. The technological system is basic and primary. Social systems are functions of technologies; and philosophies express technological forces and reflect social systems. The technological factor is therefore the determinant of a cultural system as a whole. It determines the form of social systems, and technology and society together determine the content and orientation of philosophy. This is not to say, of course, that social systems do not condition the operation of technologies, or that social and technological systems are not affected by philosophies. They do and are. But to condition is one thing; to determine, quite another.[24]

Up to this point, White's paradigm resembles the Marxist view on development. The Second Law of Thermodynamics is then applied as the next tenet of the argument. Culture, says White, is a system of harnessing and controlling energy for the service of man who is confronting the natural process of entropy. White does not refer here to Ward's model of a genesis supplemented by a telesis, but his ideas still resemble Ward's. Thus White asserts that while in the process of nature matter becomes less organized and energy more uniformly diffused, in the process of the evolution of culture, matter becomes more highly organized and energy more concentrated.[25]

White distinguishes three basic factors of cultural situations: (1) the amount of energy harnessed per capita per year; (2) the efficiency or the technological means with which energy is harnessed and put to work; and (3) the magnitude of human need-serving goods and services produced.[26] It is assumed that with discoveries of new sources of energy, and with new inventions for its generation and utilization for the benefit of society, the process of evolution of culture subsequently becomes stepped up. More goods and services become available, and in due course a transformation of the societal and political structure ensues, bringing about correspondingly new philosophical ideas and approaches. In this historical process of the evolution of culture, White distinguishes a number of stages which reflect basic changes in man's growing ability to harness energy for a greater prosperity. At first man could utilize only the energy of his own organism. Though this one stage lasted much longer than all the combined subsequent stages of man's history, it did not produce a great advancement in the culture. As a result of the agricultural revolution, man learned how to cultivate cereals and other plants and to domesticate animals. With this knowledge the second stage in the evolution of culture ensued. During this stage the great ancient civilizations appeared. Then, through the discoveries of fuel resources and as a result of what White calls the fuel revolution, man entered a new stage in the evolution of culture. "But before the question of how far cultural development could advance on a Fuel-Agricultural-Animal-Husbandry-Human Energy basis could become anything like a matter of immediate concern, a tremendously significant technological event took place: the energy resources of atomic nuclei were harnessed."[27]

One more point must be added in this outline of White's paradigm: the pace of advancement of culture within each of the distinguished stages is said to be dependent upon the improvements and efficiency of use of the means with which energy is harnessed. Again as in Marxist theory, White assumes that the sociopolitical structure at each stage tends after a time of positive evolution to become conservative. As it petrifies, it acts as a damper on further increases in technological progress. Yet this is eventually overcome, and a new era ensues. "As culture evolves the rate of growth is accelerated."[28]

It was said earlier that the two models—Marx's model of historical development and White's model of societal evolution—correspond remarkably. However, White's theory is not a new version of Marxism, nor is it even a more modern version of the Marxist theory of development. Many problems and ideas essential to the Marxist scheme are not considered by White, and he in turn raises important questions and problems never discussed in Marxism. Thus, although the two theories correspond, they also differ considerably. As a matter of fact, when he presents his approach on societal evolution, White does not refer to Marx at all. Rather, L. H. Morgan and E. B. Tylor could be considered as his spiritual predecessors. So he is not a Marxist and can barely be considered an ideologist. His is a theory of the evolution of culture—of culturology, as he calls it—and is not particularly a theory of the development of societal structures. When discussing societal structures, he does so only to consider them as an element of culture. The changing variable of White's paradigm is the acceleration with which energy is harnessed; it is not the growth and perfection of the means of production which require the transformation of productive and other societal relations. True, the two variables may be equated, but it must be pointed out that White is not a dialectician; his is not a theory of dialectical transformation of the forms of property, of class struggle, or the dictatorship of the proletariat, and so forth. What is especially discernible in a comparison of the two approaches is the lack in White's paradigm of an element or spring of transformation, such as Hegelian logic, which is so pertinent to the Marxist theory of development.

White discusses both societal problems and vices, and he is passionate about them, but he does not prescribe any solutions. What he expects is the following: "In short, the State as the integrative and regulative mechanism of civil society, is destined to acquire ever greater power and to wield more and more control. Social evolution is moving inexorably toward higher levels of integration, toward greater concentrations of political power and control."[29] In this White takes a stand more similar to that expressed by Ward than to that of Marxist theory, rejecting the state as an institution of class domination.

5. The Argument on the Merits and Demerits of the Evolutionary Approach

Approaches that promote the historiosophic and evolutionary interpretations of the concept of development are imminently europo-centrically biased. Although such theories occasionally refer to other cultures and civilizations—especially when they discuss earlier stages of what is being considered as the development or evolution of humanity or of a culture —they are focused basically on the history of Europe, perhaps with some extensions that include the recent history of the United States. It is not difficult to see that the universal rules and laws of history as proclaimed, established, or anticipated within the evolutionary theories of societies are above all, if not at all in fact, the interpretations of European history. Their universalization is proclaimed and justified on the assumption that culture and humanity are constituted not of separate organisms but are a single whole. If culture and humanity evolve or develop, they advance as a whole, unilinearly including all civilizations. The development in one part of the organism spearheads a general transformation. In this way evolution and development are viewed as a process which combines both the succession from the past and the generation of innovations, new institutions and structures, as well as the diffusion, exchange, and spread of knowledge, practices, and cultural patterns from culture to culture.

Critics question these assumptions, pointing out that up until very recently cultures and civilizations were developing not in total isolation, but at least separately and polilinearly. They assert that the courses of change, transformation, and evolution of the cultures of different societies differed more than they corresponded. They doubt whether there is sufficient ground, if any, to either talk of a unified culture of humanity or to impose schemes of parallelism on their histories. Questions are raised as to why the presumed laws and rules of historical inevitability and the transformation of sequential stages did not manifest themselves in the same extent (if at all) in parts of the world other than Europe, and what the grounds are for assuming that Europe's history is a rule rather than an exception.

Indeed, evolutionary theories of development do not explain why, for instance, industrialization originated first in Western Europe and not in other parts of the world, in spite of the known fact that in at least the fifteenth and sixteenth centuries some of those other parts of the world were potentially as ripe for technological and intellectual advancements as was Europe itself.

It is often contended that evolutionary theories which promulgate ideas of societal and historical development are speculative, especially the earlier theories, which include Marxism. Indeed, there is some merit in that assertion. Although such theories usually include unquestionable facts and data, they are primarily based on conjectures, by means of which they link those facts and data in a presumptive, causative, orderly, logical sequential process of growth. To critics this is teleologism.[30]

Some historians are especially indignant that evolutionary theories which promulgate development assume that historical events happen in the exteriorization of an underlying current of societal forces and laws which flow in a definite direction, and that such theories reject the notion that history is made up of acts of free will. They are dismayed by the outlook that individuals—even kings, army commanders, and generals, or other great personalities or, in other cases, masses, classes, and groups "who made history"—were but the vehicles of inevitable processes. Thus Isaiah Berlin writes:

> The process may be thought of as being in time and space or beyond them; as being cyclical or spiral or rectilinear, or as occurring in the form of a peculiar zigzag movement, sometimes called dialectical; as continuous and uniform, or irregular, broken by sudden leaps to "new levels"; as due to the changing forms of one single "force," or of conflicting elements locked (as in some ancient myth) in an eternal Pyrrhic struggle; as the history of one deity or "force" or "principle," or of several; as being destined to end well or badly; as holding out to human beings the prospect of eternal beatitude, or eternal damnation, or both in turn, or neither. But whatever version of the story is accepted—and it is never a scientific, that is empirically testable theory, stated in quantitative terms, still less a description of what our eyes see and our ears hear. . . .[31]

Elsewhere Berlin adds: "We are plainly dealing not with an empirical theory but with a metaphysical attitude which takes for granted that to explain a thing, to describe it as it 'truly' is, even to define it more than verbally, that is, superficially, is to discover its purpose."[32] Indeed, evolutionary theories on historical development cannot be tested either experimentally or empirically. So those who disapprove of the conjectures in "scientific" thinking and those who dislike speculations or think that social science, as all other sciences, must include nothing but empirically testable statements and quantitatively measurable data are right to reject the concept of development based on the idea of evolution and all the implications connected with them. This is in fact the prevailing attitude in the social sciences today.

On the other hand, however, there are still those social theorists who insist that "Modern civilizations stand higher than previous civilizations in the same sense that they have a far deeper knowledge of the physical world and of life and mind than previous civilizations, a fuller and more articulated conception of their aims and of the nature of the conditions which are needed to achieve them."[33] Morris Ginsberg, for instance, believes that this is what has to be taken into account in societal development. In his opinion, "what remained when the fog of battle . . . [over the concepts of development, evolution, and progress] had cleared" was at least a number of self-evident facts of the advancing growth of knowledge and of the continuous moral progress of humanity.

Greater, more developed knowledge, Ginsberg writes, gives more power to the man over the forces of nature. "Moral progress consists in the clarification of ideals, in obtaining a firmer grasp of the conditions of their realization and in the widening of human sympathies through an extension of the power of imaginative identification."[34] People, he says, become increasingly more sensitive, concerned more about social justice and man's suffering; law becomes rationalized in the "general movement towards rationalization of morality." This, Ginsberg assumes, is a corollary to the institutional and interactional changes brought about by the implicit logic of societal transformation, although it is in a continuous interplay with psychological factors that consist of a multitude of acts of individual wills.

One cannot be satisfied with Ginsberg's stock-taking of "what remained when the fog of battle had cleared." No doubt, one can speak of an ongoing cumulative process of growing knowledge which advances in the course of history,[35] and a scientific development which results from piecemeal discoveries and inventions, in derivative abstractions and paradigms, in concise formulas, and in general theories.

Culture is transmitted from generation to generation. It grows out of new individual and collective experiences, spontaneous and purposeful institutionalization and structuralization.

In his search for answers to questions posed by the inquisitive human mind, for solutions to societal and political problems and conflicts and in his attempts to increase all aspects of security, obtain more freedom and satisfaction from life, man has produced and is constantly reorganizing and producing new religions, sciences, arts, philosophies, institutions, and organizations. Over time, man—and, strictly speaking, some men in some places—learned how to harness more energy, and how to utilize that energy for improving at least the material quality of life. Increasing numbers of people are benefiting from these inventions and achievements, and from the growing scope of knowledge.

On the whole, the productive output of the totality of people is steadily growing, although the growth is uneven in different parts of the world and in different times. One can view these processes as development, and such development and growth is evidently progressing at an accelerated pace. Yet, with the accumulation of more data, with the growth of knowledge and greater understanding of various economic, social, political, psychological and other factors and processes, social scientists seem to be increasingly reluctant to accept theories of societal development as satisfactory explanations. Indeed, the prevailing view now is that if technology determines the character of the structure of the social and political order of societies, it does it in a very complex, indirect way.

New technologies increase man's choices. They open and widen the options for new courses of action rather than univocally and unidirectionally defining what systems will emerge. How technologies are utilized, and for what purposes, depends on the conscious and unconscious will of human beings, although the object of the act of will and what decisions are to be taken depend on the given situation in which man finds himself, and this includes the factor of technology, which is developed to a certain level in a given society.

Comparing modern industrial societies alone, we see a variety of political orders, based on completely different principles, diverse social structures, and different legal systems and property relations, which very often profess alternative value orientations; yet all of them use the same type of technology and harness energy (as White would say) in a similar way. Like technological means might serve to reach diverse ideological, political, economic, etc., ends and might be instrumental in building or maintaining social and political orders of different kinds. These are trivialities, yet they must be mentioned here. Industries, like all other means of technology, require specific skills and professions and produce sets of respective roles to operate them—hense the structures of industrial organization. Industrialization entails specific social processes and consequences. It is also true that many of these are similar in any industrial society, whether it is regarded as capitalist, socialist, communist, First, Second, or Third World, democratic, authoritarian, or totalitarian.

When speaking about the past, one must note, for instance, that similar social and political societal macrostructures existed both in medieval Europe and in some parts of Africa at the same time, in spite of the fact that in the latter societies the plough, the wheel, the use of traction, and the art of writing were unknown. Preindustrial societies were nondemocratic and hierarchical; they contained structures of strongly differentiated castes, estates, and guilds. Was that an historical inevitability or an historical accident? Could agricultural societies not exist as republics of free peasants? Why?

Does technological advancement and increasing scientific knowledge unavoidably or even usually entail the growth of rationality and a progress in morality, as is often implied in the theories on societal development and evolution? Such assertions sound grand. Yet both concepts, rationality and mortality, do have many contradictory meanings and interpretations, and indeed, there are no objective indices, criteria or measurements to rely upon in tackling such contentions. Hence, the ambiguity of such pronouncements requires more questions: Rationality and morality in what sense? one has to ask first. If it is rationality in the sense of an organization of the means in a calculable manner for the attainment of specific goals, or if it is rationality in the sense of finding better appropriateness, greater instrumentality, and more functionality in using more perfect means and efficient actions in one's self-interest, then the answer seems to be: yes. If by rationality we mean an understanding of the interconnections among factors, aspects, events in time and space, and of motives of people; if, in short, we are speaking about functional rationality,* then, of course, we must agree that more knowledge, especially more scientific knowledge, brings about more rational behavior and action. Armed with knowledge, science and technology, man can calculate better, achieve more with less effort, and expand the range of the targets of his daring. If, however, this contention is about so-called substantive rationality; if the assumption is that with the growth of scientific knowledge, increasing numbers of people creatively choose meaningful goals on their own insight; if by greater rationality we mean higher average capacity for independent judgment or rationality of goals, then we must say that such rationality cannot be achieved. Those who believe in it believe in a utopia. People as a rule do not share views on substantive rationality. They usually claim that their rationality is more substantive than that of others. Goals depend on capabilities, experience, predilections, opinions. These cannot be shared by all, and even should they be shared to some extent, as is usually the case, this does not eliminate conflict and competition. Neither does sharing values, ideologies, or beliefs eliminate conflict, disagreements, dissent, and so forth. If greater rationality is supposed to mean growing harmony, and a fuller fusion of the individuals with the supreme whole, then one should not expect it to come from greater development or from growing scientific knowledge. Indeed, a greater autonomy of the individuals, and an increased functional rationality result in independent thinking and lead to more competition and conflict on an increasing number of issues, although it does not necessarily have to lead to violence and war as a resolution of conflict.

True autonomous, creative thought cannot accept any restrictions imposed by any supremacy, even the supremacy of a phantom substantive rationality. Besides, men always were and still are led by emotions, at-

---

* In Mannheim's terms (*Ideology and Utopia*, p. 58), "Increasing industrialization, to be sure, implies functional rationality, i.e., the organization of the activity of the members of society with reference to objective ends. It does not to the same extent promote 'substantive rationality,' i.e., the capacity to act intelligently in a given situation on the basis of one's own insight into the interrelations of events."

tachments, altruisms, irrational antagonisms, and other irrational feelings. To be rational and irrational simultaneously is to be human. As a master of functional rationality, man imposed his control over nature and differentiated himself from the world of animals. As a creative, independently thinking, instantly irrational being, man is distinctive from machines and robots. As a *homo politicus* man must inevitably be substantively irrational.

The task of assessing even in the most general terms what are here called development, evolution, or the progress of morality seems to be even more difficult and elusive. True, beliefs in equality—strictly speaking, beliefs that men ought to have equal rights—have become widespread and are more common now than they were in earlier centuries. The same applies to the respect for human dignity. In a sense, it may generally be contended that throughout the world the degree of respect for human dignity has increased. There has been an expansion in the general concern with the fate and suffering of other people. I must remark, however, that this hapnened more as a result of the build-up of various networks of communications and travel lines throughout the world which facilitated the spread of news, than as a result of any basic improvement in men themselves. In fact, these great norms and values are often used as excuses to punish other people, for cruelties, wars, and the like. Since we live in times of Nazi and Soviet concentration camps, two world wars, wars in Vietnam and in Biafra, in times when only the threat of total destruction by nuclear weapons deters people from starting a new world war, in times when the majority of people live under the rule of various despotic rulers and dictators—how, then, can we speak of steady improvement and growth in morality? The contents of any daily newspaper prove that the grounds for a eulogy on account of a growing rationality and morality are very shaky indeed. Standards of morality are changing, of course, but there seems to be no foundation for viewing those changes as progress or development.

Criticism on the evolutionary approach to development could certainly be expanded further. Yet, although I share many of the views of the critics, I still believe that if the idea of evolutionary development is cleared from excessive pretensions and from biological connotations, that idea (or, rather, that of societal development) retains some amount of validity and hence should be sustained for definite analytical purposes. Assuming that societal development are processes which differ entirely from those that constitute biological evolution, one can at least speak of a self-evident technological and scientific development, related to the increased harnessing of energy. Then, observing the trend of changes in societal history, one can also speak of a self-evident growing systemness in social living, and at least three aspects of it can be distinguished immediately: *

1. It is manifest in the simultaneous multiplication, expansion, and extension, intermediation, depersonalization, and specialization of the scope of interactions which constitute the structures of societies and of the linkages which bond and connect their members.

2. It transpires in the differentiation of greater numbers of inter-dependent specialized systems or subsystems, in correspondence with a greater specialization and role-differentiation within the societal structure.

3. The entire world becomes increasingly transformed into one great system, encompassing all societies and all people; action in one part of it affects other parts.

To view the growing systemness as a process of development is, in fact, to hold an entirely different approach from that contained in evolutionary theories with historiosophic implications. Many sociological theories have appeared on the topic of changing or growing systemness, most often without referring to development or to a growing systemness by name at all. I wish to concentrate on this in the next chapter.

* N. J. Smelser in *Essays in Sociological Explanation* (Englewood Cliffs, N.J.: Prentice-Hall, 1968) described this process most concisely and exhaustively. He refers to it (p. 127) as ". . . ideal-type structural changes, which have ramifications throughout society: (1) Structural differentiation, or the establishment of more specialized and more autonomous social units. (2) Integration which changes its character as the old social order is made obsolete by the process of differentiation. The state, the law, political groupings, and other associations are particularly salient in this integration. (3) Social disturbances—mass hysteria, outbursts of violence, religious and political movements, etc.—which reflect the uneven advances of differentiation and integration respectively."

ii

The Second Approach: Development—the Growing Societal Systemness

1. A Metaphor on Metaphors?

As long ago as 500 years before the birth of Christ the Greek philosopher Zeno of Elea contended that change (and especially motion) entails logically contradictory consequences, and it is, therefore, unthinkable and impossible. For instance, he claimed that to say a flying arrow is moving would mean that the arrow is and is not at a given moment at a definite point in the air. Time is composed of moments, he argued, and the arrow at each moment rests at a different point in space. Hence, space could be divided into portions which could be correlated with portions of time. Motion, therefore, is a euphemism without any correspondence to reality.*

Not long ago scientists were pondering the problem of light. It seemed to be a wave and a beam of particles simultaneously. Eventually, wave mechanics answered the question and solved the apparent contradiction by introducing a new approach to the whole question. Light, it is now asserted, is a self-consistent entity which differs from both waves and particles. In a sense, the controversy over the concepts of development, growth, and the evolution of societies is similar to these issues, and to similar discussions which constantly reappear in man's search to understand his surroundings and his own being.

There are many critics who argue that paradigms which promote the idea of societal development, evolution, and growth are to be rejected because of their contradictory nature and metaphoric character; because such concepts are euphemisms for something that cannot be depicted, em-

* Zeno formulated his objections against the concepts of motion, change, and the like in four related arguments, known as the aporia (ἀπορία): the flying arrow, the stadium, Achilles, and the tortoise.

pirically tested, or examined; and because they are but figurative analogies which contain little if any heuristic value. In other words, they argue not so much that processes which are called societal development, evolution or growth are totally nonexistent, but that we cannot be certain whether such phenomena actually happen, that we are unable to explain how they happen, or that metaphors and analogies are neither the proper and empirical tools of analysis, nor good theoretical concepts. Indeed, they say that development and growth in regard to societies are metaphors and euphemisms, and metaphors and analogies are misleading, confusing, and dangerous. Here we have an attitude of agnosticism directed against speculation.

Can we do without metaphors and speculations in general, and without the metaphor of development and growth in particular? Robert Nisbet, who insistently warns against the abuses, misuses, or irrelevance of the metaphor also tells us that "The usefulness of the metaphor of growth is determined by the *cognitive distance* of the object to which the metaphor is applied. The larger, the more general, abstract, and distant in experience the object of our interest, the greater the utility of the metaphor. Conversely, the smaller, more concrete, finite, and empirical our object, the less the metaphor's utility."[1] This could be treated as the advice: Better do without such concepts as development and growth when you are interested strictly in what is observable, in the behavior of concrete human beings, in a specific period of time under specific circumstances. It is also an acknowledgement that we cannot do without such concepts as development and growth—and without metaphors in general and under specific circumstances. We cannot do without such concepts—and without metaphors in general—when we are aiming at broad historical generalizations which comprise a large span of time and include various peoples in comparative analysis.

However, in general theories on societies, in broad sociological- and economic-perspective analyses on people, cultures, societies, and humanity, at least some understanding of development and growth—if not the concepts themselves—is unavoidable. Such concepts are also useful. Throughout his argument Nisbet demonstrates in a most illuminating way how enduring the concepts of social change, development, and growth were in ancient Greek philosophy, in Christian philosophy, in modern thought, and even in current functionalist sociological theory. Yet he persists in warning us that metaphors are dangerous, especially if integral relevance is attributed to them.

Though Nisbet is right that metaphors may be dangerous, the language of the social sciences cannot be extricated from them. Even the word "dangerous" is a metaphor. We have to be precise and strict in describing social phenomena and processes. True, concepts have to be strictly defined and purged of all equivocalities. However, many definitions now used contain metaphors or words of metaphoric origin. Striving for precision and for accurate expression is undoubtedly a virtue. Yet a notion (especially in the social sciences) is often like a pencil: when sharpened too much it disappears. Concepts made too precise and too rigid become meaningless. Besides, the concepts of development, growth, and evolution as currently used in the social sciences are not exactly metaphors. They are often metaphors of metaphors of metaphors. The use of metaphors permits detachment from the original meaning. When the concept is lifted to a higher level, with its greater frequency of use, and when it is applied to many and varying realities, a new meaning is created. What originally obviously functioned as a metaphor or an analogy seems subsequently and gradually to change into a sort of homonym. The properties of the metaphor do not wither totally, yet it gradually becomes a very distant metaphor. The new meaning is not entirely divorced from the old generic one, but it is remarkably distinctive and does not entirely coincide with the older one.

Development, growth, and evolution are notions used in many other connotations apart from those implied in biology and the social sciences.* It is worth noting that when used outside of biology, development or growth does not necessarily carry the meaning of appearing in cycles, or being an ascending process which, after reaching the apogee, will necessarily move on the line of decline and decay eventually to die. When one speaks of a growing awareness, a growing population, a growing crime rate, the development of projects, development of a child's mental capacity, and the like, one does not assume the same meaning as growth or development implies in regard to biological entities. Societal development and growth are metaphors, concepts which imply some likeness to the processes of the natural biological growth of organisms or the development and emergence of new species, but surely not total identity with them or their courses.

If metaphors are deficient, but we still have to apply them, what can be done? Perhaps neologisms could be substituted for them? Maybe the extent of the metaphor or the analogy, or the euphemism has to be removed from the concept which has acquired new meanings. Perhaps concepts such as development and growth could be purged of their original meaning and established anew in a strictly defined context when applied

---

* In today's newspaper, I read the following: "President Nixon's elite national goal research staff said yesterday the nation can continue to grow in the 1970's and beyond, without destroying itself but must learn to balance progress with the problems it brings" (*San Francisco Chronicle*, July 19, 1970).

to these strongly differing subjects? Should social explorations be abandoned or diverted because of semantic difficulties?

2. The Use of Contrast in the Exploration of Development and Growth

In deference to the nineteenth-century theorists (especially sociologists) who, in advancing the idea of societal development and growth, spent much of their efforts in interpreting metaphors of development and evolution, the twentieth-century sociologists interested in the subject have taken a predominantly evasive, middle-of-the-road stand. Some of them describe, discuss, analyze, and indeed theorize on what may be called societal growth or development without ever calling it that. Others have substituted the metaphor of growth, development, and evolution with another euphemism—that of social change. Social change implies neither any direction in change, nor a continuity or a necessity of occurrence. Instead, it is thought to be a more adequate description for what we are able to state for sure about the state of social reality. Although it is purged from conjectures, it is at the same time less imaginative. It simply assumes that because relations in society are not constant, they may be classified into different types and compared, and so forth.

Sometimes the following question has been asked: What is the relationship between development and social change? While some students dismiss the question as utterly irrelevant, others argue that development is a form, or a case of social change; or, vice-versa, they argue that social change transpires from the process of development. Some distinguish short-range social changes from long-range ones or from changes of societies as a whole.[2] The long-range change is seen as the latent consequences of the short-range changes.

Most important, however, is the fact that instead of discussing the development of humanity or the culture of mankind in all societies and in all areas, interests generally become focused on one decisive period in the West: the period of industrialization and its consequences. Instead of exposing the cumulative effects of continuity, instead of building conjectural bridges between the past, present, and future of all societies at all times, social scientists nowadays confront, compare, and contrast pre-industrial and industrial periods, "developed" and "underdeveloped" or ("developing"), traditional and modern societies. Numerous books have been published on the theoretical bases and characteristics of the two basic types of societies and structures which are contrasted. As a rule, the researchers apply dichotomies which expose the contrasting features of such societies and the systems within them by means of descriptions, scheme, pattern variables, models, and the like. These are not theories strictly on societal growth and development. They discuss industrialization, urbanization, increasing communication, greater mobility, changing cultural patterns, transformation of the pattern variables on which the social structure is based, or simply the changing character of societal structures. Yet, taken together, these theories explain various aspects of one great process of transformation or movement in societal structure, and in human relations, interactions, and interdependencies. They tell us that industrialization, increased productivity, intensified urbanization, the spread of education, increased social mobility, changing social division of labor, greater specialization, changing cultural attitudes, and the like, transpire in an ongoing process of greater mutual interdependence of the individuals and the units, and of the agencies and the subsystems of society; eventually, a greater interrelatedness emerges between the various societies of the world. In short, such theories tell us of a growing societal interdependence and systemness.

For example, Charles H. Cooley described one aspect of what we now call the growing systemness of the socioculture. He told us how the primary groups which exist for their own sake—"characterized by intimate face-to-face associations and co-operation . . . fundamental for forming the social nature of the individual"[3]—become increasingly entangled in the network of larger groups which are constituted on the basis of impersonal relations lacking in any intimacy, and which pursue limited specific objectives. Cooley asserted that when primary groups are absorbed in this larger network of structures (later called "secondary" relations) they lose their strength and persistence, they fall apart easily, or even disappear, leaving the individuals without any significant intimate membership. Sociologists since then have found this breakdown of primary groups to be a major source of many of the ills that confront modern societies.

Ferdinand Toennies discussed another aspect of the growing systemness in his theory of the growing ascendancy of *Gesellschaft* over *Gemeinschaft*—that is, the artificial social construction over the natural social structures which consist of "lasting and genuine forms of living together."[4] *Gemeinschaft*, he assumes, is based on the will and spirit of unity. An individual acts within it on behalf of the other members and on behalf of the whole unit without expecting rewards, because he is a part of it. According to Toennies, *Gemeinschaft* institutionalizes itself in the family (closeness and blood relations), in the neighborhood (physical proximity), and in intellectual proximities. With the spread of trade, education, urbanization, differentiation, and proliferation of the institutions of the state and administration, and especially as a result of industrialization, the bourgeois society comes into being. With it comes the *ens fictivum*, artificial *Gesellschaft*—a limitless totality of a system of conventional rules. The society becomes established, ineluctably engulfing, inexorably permeating and corroding the *Gemeinschaft* unity of genuine togetherness. The *Gesellschaft,* Toennies tells us, is an aggregate, "a multitude of natural and artificial individuals, the wills and spheres of whom are in many relations with one another, and remain nevertheless independent of one another and devoid of mutual familiar relationships."[5] It is an expanding and growing system.

> It is something in the process of becoming, something which should be conceived here as personality of the greater will of the general reason, and at the same time (as we know) it is fictitious and nominal. It is like an emanation, as if it had emerged from the heads of the persons in whom it rests, who join hands eagerly to exchange across all distances, limits, and scruples, and establish this speculative Utopia as the only country, the only city, in which all fortune seekers and all merchant adventurers have a really common interest. As the fiction of money is represented by metal or paper, it is represented by the entire globe, or by a circumscribed territory.[6]

What a vivid and felicitous picture of the unfolding process of the growing societal systemness!

While Charles H. Cooley lamented the wonderful bygone past, and with it the dissolution of the primary groups and Toennies contrasted the idyllic *Gemeinschaft* with the repugnant, mercantile, conflict-ridden *Gesellschaft* to expose the ills of unfolding capitalism, Emile Durkheim admired the growing societal interdependence and systemness engendered in those processes. In this, and in approaching the future with hope, Durkheim followed Comte and Spencer. In a sense, he, too, promoted the vision of organic growth, and he might even be considered a forerunner of functionalism. Yet Durkheim was not seduced into following the pernicious and deceptive concept of development either by the glamorous attraction of its promising analogy with biological ideas, or by the magical prospects of the Hegelian or other dialectics. He was not even drawn by the tradition of Western—and within it, French—philosophical and social thought. He regarded himself as a "social fact" finder. Thus Durkheim writes:

> Why does the individual, while becoming more autonomous, depend more upon society? How can he be at once more individual and more solidary? Certainly, these two movements, contradictory as they appear, develop in parallel fashion. This is the problem we are raising. It appeared to us that what resolves this apparent antinomy is transformation of social solidarity due to the steady growing development of the division of labor.[7]

Durkheim tells us that there is no mystery in the fact that growing societal differentiation entails an accrual of cohesiveness and interdependence. It is a cumulative effect of the growing division of labor. In its course (and also to a lesser extent as a result of population growth and augmentation of the societal structure), the agglomeration or agglutination of the similar small homogeneous societal cells or units, which are comprised of and linked by a mechanical solidarity and are generated by cultural affinity and functional similitude, becomes leveled into a new, inherently heterogeneous structure which is linked in an organic solidarity.* It stems from the growing mutual interdependence of the units and the individuals, each with the other, each with the whole, and the whole working on each one.**

Critics may say that Durkheim was not right—that greater interdependence does not necessarily imply greater cohesiveness and certainly not greater organismic wholeness. They are perhaps right. At this point, however, I do not wish to engage in a critical evaluation of classic theories on development. I wish to discuss these theories because I am interested in the *different ways of portraying the process of growing systemness in societal structures.*

In the rich heritage of Weberian writing one cannot discern a theory that is *expressis verbis* on development or on societal growth. However, Max Weber's works recurrently express the theme of an incessantly ongoing transformation of one "system order" into another, the latter revealing features not only distinctive but as a rule of an opposite nature to those from which it grew, and the idea that new "systems of orders"*** are constantly generated and put above the older ones in a cumulative process of endemic changes.

First, I must point out that Weber reinterpreted Toennies's paradigm, adequately substituting its two principal categories with new ones: for Weber, *Vergesellschaftung*, through the complex process of change, engulfs the earlier established structures of *Vergemeinschaftung*. He basically employs the same dichotomy as Toennies did but views it as processes. The transformation presented by his colleague in static terms becomes thus characterized more dynamically.[8] Both *Vergemeinschaftung*

---

* The concepts of organic and mechanical solidarity appear also in Toennies's work. However, Toennies contends that organic solidarity appears in *Gemeinschaft,* thus preceding the structures based on mechanic solidarity, which are those of the *Gesellschaft.*

** As we know, Durkheim assumed that the mechanical solidarity of traditional societies finds its expression in a body of repressive laws, while the higher type of organic solidarity—that of the modern societies—is based upon and is represented by restitutive law.

*** "System of order" is a Weberian expression.

and *Vergesellschaftung* are regarded simultaneously as ideal types, systems of social action, and processes of cumulative transformative growth. Thus the system is presented as identical to a process of transformation which results from changes in growth. Weber constantly applied the same idea and method. They are reflected in his theory of the subsequent irreversible transformation of a system of traditional authorities (in its course of resolving the inherent structural conflicts of the gerontocratic patriarchal and patrimonial orders into feudalism) to a system of rational-legal authority with bureaucratic administration. The idea of growing systemness could be derived from the theory of the routinization of charisma and its subsequent transformation in the antiauthoritarian direction. The same undercurrent idea is evident in Weber's arresting account of the transformation of the elite—*Honoratioren* political parties—into modern mass parties in an ensuing process of growing membership, performance of new functions, and especially as a consequence of the continuous transformation of the differentiation of a professional party apparatus, internal stratification, and so forth.

Intrinsic conflicts of system orders require new methods of action, new institutions, and new structures of authority. Thus Weber tells us that systems of orders are subsequently substituted for by newer ones. Throughout the ages and for long periods of time systems of orders were oriented toward tradition. The rulers and others in authority in traditional systems are also tradition-oriented. They maintain traditions, and the legitimacy of their rule is based upon traditions. Yet they also have to use the traditions instrumentally in order to achieve their current goals. In Weber's opinion such rules may have been used functionally, but not truly rationally, because orientation toward traditions excludes the rational approach.

Weber argued that capitalism distinctly differs from any other orders primarily because it is based and oriented toward an ascending rationality.* I will return to this point in a later chapter. Let me only mention here that rationalization in the Weberian sense entails (a) a systematization and depersonalization of societal interactions on the basis of market-type relations and by means of a bureaucratic-legal system-ordering; (b) the institution of a supreme norm-orientation toward efficiency over other

* Broadly speaking, one can distinguish four types of actions in the Weberian theory of action: (1) *Zweckrational,* when rationality consists of weighing out and selecting the means of securing maximum attainment with minimum cost—in short, rationality in regard to goals; (2) *Wertrational,* when rationality consists of maintaining or striving for the attainment of certain values at any cost; (3) Actions motivated and oriented toward traditions, and (4) Actions generated by affective or emotional motivations. (These may be regarded as ideal types of actions rather than as a classification.)

values and norms; (c) in connection with (b) an inclination toward progressing specialization; (d) a critical attitude toward traditions which are valued only because they were valued in the past; and (e) a decline in particularistic attachments combined with an increasing preference for universalistic standards.* In short, Weber sharply contrasted the societal growth in those different types of societies. He viewed the postindustrial growth of system orders as dependent on the acceleration of rationality, which by itself contained an imminent self-perpetuating and recurrent contradiction between goal attainment and value maintenance, plus a danger of becoming redundant if it was not kept under control and checked.

While Toennies contrasted *Gemeinschaft* with *Gesellschaft*; Durkheim, mechanic and organic solidarity; and Weber, traditional and rational-legal authority, other sociologists exposed other contrasting features of the preindustrial and industrial (or traditional and modern) societies. Sir Henry Maine focused his attention on what he called differences between societies which are based on status and those which are based on contract; Robert Redfield confronted the folk and urban culture societies; Howard Becker introduced the distinction between sacred and secular. Some sociologists attempted to combine the contrasting features as put forth by their colleagues and incorporate them under two headings —for example, communal and associational societies.[9] F. X. Sutton, who was especially concerned with the structure of political representation, proposed the use of such a classification for differentiating agricultural political systems from industrial-political systems.[10]

The concepts introduced by such theories as those listed above turned out to be very useful and fruitful for sociological explorations. However, the method of contrasting which is employed in such theories is not without deficiencies. It exposes the process of development, societal growth or social change by means of polarizing two types of societies.

Hence from one point of view, such theories are schemes of classification or typologies, but from another, they are theories of social change, development, and growth. Yet at the same time, they are and are not both of the two. As regular, proper classifications, they should obey the rule of extrapolation; they should provide criteria for a strict and full delineation and separation of two entities that possess clearly opposite features. As theories of social change or development, they should contain the characteristics of the processes of generation and birth, and they should have

---

* Some of Weber's arguments imply that at least to some extent he also included secularization among the various facets of accelerated rationality, claiming that Protestantism was in a sense the fountainhead for a variety of trends which promoted the spirit of secularization.

the quality of constantly becoming overwhelmingly new and current; they should describe the accrual of the new and explain its course; they should simultaneously describe the appearance of new qualities and features and the qualities and features of decline, and the withering away of old properties; they should depict from what societies emerge and into what they are transformed. They should, therefore, contain data on a relative intensity of features and properties which are shared by both of the realities under consideration. In actual fact, the contrast exposed in such theories is relative, since they demonstrate differences and differing qualities by degrees; yet the magnitude of those differences eventually becomes so great that extrapolations become justified.

Criticism is waged against such theories because either they are not introducing criteria for a clear-cut delineation and clean polarization, or they contain comparative static instead of a characteristic of a continuity.

Another criticism could also be raised. In the theories that we are now discussing, two characterizations are used: the black and the rosy. In extrapolation, in contrast, the two types of societies, system orders, or the two units, however they are labeled, are presented against each other as negative and positive cases. Cooley and Toennies described the societies of the past as rather pleasant and nice—they fit basic human needs, they were good for the people, and so forth. They described societies in the making and those of the future as somewhat artificial, because they were imposed on people, because they were structures of rather dubious quality and had prospectively gloomy futures. On the contrary, in Durkheim's opinion—and to an extent, in Weber's opinion also—it was the past that looked dark, gloomy, mechanistic; it was the past that had no regard for rationality, while the future of the societies in the making seemed to look radiant, promising, orderly, organic, and hopeful, and seemed to be related to an ascending rationality.

Talcott Parsons proposes a scheme to separate strictly the connotations under consideration and keep them in dichotomous opposition; this scheme would thus fulfill the requirements of fine classification and typology, while at the same time it would use for extrapolation categories with a more neutral character.[11] I am referring to the paradigm on dilemmas of orientation or on pattern variables. Actually, this is neither a theory of development or growth, nor a device for classifying societies of different types. Parsons and Shils regard pattern variables as categories for the description of value orientations of the personality and of cultural and social systems.[12] They introduce them as devices for alternative modes of action, preferences, predispositions, normative expectations, or characteristics of alternative behavior. Altogether five pairs of such dilemmas of orientation are suggested:

Diffuseness	versus	Specificity
Ascription	versus	Achievement
Particularism	versus	Universalism
Collective Orientation	versus	Self-Orientation
Affectivity	versus	Affective Neutrality

Bert F. Hoselitz[13] and other writers of the functionalist school after him have remodeled the paradigm so as to adopt the above categories into a theory on the sociological aspects of economic growth.* Contrasting categories of the above dilemmas of action were utilized to portray two types of societies, which were thought to have a totally opposite nature. Thus the pattern variables were applied to differentiate the "underdeveloped" (traditional) societies and the "advanced" (modern) societies. Actually, three of the five pattern variables were predominantly used to characterize the two types of societies.

It was assumed that societal roles in traditional societies are ascribed, that they are functionally diffuse and geared toward narrow particularistic preferences and standards. In turn, the society as a whole, and the units and individuals belonging to it in particular, exhibit an orientation toward traditionalism in a culture which incites preferential attitudes for ascription, diffuse roles, and particularistic attachments. Conversely, the advanced, modern societies are said to differ alternatively. Here, roles are more strictly delineated and defined; indeed, they are differentiated in accordance with functional specialization. They tend toward specificity and are acquired through a competitive striving for achievement, in an orientation toward universal standards and norms.

Parsonian pattern variables were designed as a device for contrasting alternative choices of action. As I mentioned earlier, then they were applied as a device for contrasting traditional and modern societies, and as a framework for developmental studies. And I must add that regardless of whether one considers them satisfactory or unsatisfactory for the explanation of the phenomena of societal development and growth, modernization and the like, they have served that cause well. The Parsonian paradigm has inspired many area studies and the appearance of many new theories which may or may not support its original contentions. In my opinion, the paradigm serves not only to contrast traditional and modern

---

* He writes: ". . . we may characterize societies at different levels of economic development by describing them in terms of contrasting pairs of pattern variables as these were defined by Talcott Parsons. Economic development may then be considered as being associated with a transformation of social behavior from a form which in its economically relevant aspects is oriented toward ascription, particularism and functional diffuseness to a form of social behavior oriented towards achievement, universalism and functional specificity" (p. 60).

societies, but it also seems to be instrumental in promoting the idea of societal development.

Pattern variables are concepts which can be compared to the flow of a river. No one doubts that the upper part of a river is placed before its lower part, or that the river flows irreversibly and invariably from its source toward its outlet. The same holds for pattern variables. They characterize the direction and the content of the process of irreversible societal transformation which, in fact, takes place in any society.

I must point out that the contrast exposed by a confrontation of pattern variables is in a sense relative. Traditional societies are basically ascriptive, particularistic, and composed of diffuse roles which are acquired on the basis of ascription. Yet within the dominant ascriptive system of role allocation, rewards are given for some achievement, be it for the achievement of maintaining the traditional patterns, for guarding the principles of ascription, for demonstrating other required standards and patterns of behavior, or for innovations which seemingly do not disrupt the establishment. True, it is rather uncommon in such societies to strive for achievement for the sole sake of achievement or acquisition. Yet even this general rule can be disputed, as in the case of the ancient Greek cultural patterns. Some orientation toward achievement, and some competition and conflict in connection with it are immanently present in any society, and this includes traditional societies as well.

Although traditional societies are often described as agglutinations of diffuse roles, they may contain estates and castes, and, of course, some professionalization and specialization, and certainly a social division of labor. They are oriented toward traditionalism; thus the pace for the introduction of innovations is rather slow here, but it is present nevertheless. On the other hand, modern societies, which are oriented toward universalism and achievement and structured in sets of highly specialized roles, as a rule retain in some degree or in certain spheres of social interactions the mechanism of ascription—for example, the form of respect for legal recognition of inheritance and in the form of role acquisition by means of it. In modern societies, people are uprooted and are not particularistically oriented. Yet even in the most modern society local attachments are often still evident. Thus, in my opinion, therefore, the paradigm of pattern variables sounds more correct when formulated in the following way: traditional societies are *predominantly* ascriptive and particularistic with diffuse roles, and modern societies are *predominantly* achievement-oriented, structured of highly specialized roles, and directed toward rather universal attachments. And, of course, in diverse modern societies the subject and the mechanism of achievement differs. Then it may be asserted that from a perspective of longer periods of time, any society seems to tend toward an irreversible transformation from ascription/ diffuseness/particularism toward achievement/specificity/universalism. Traditional societies differ from modern ones in regard to the prevalence of pattern behaviors and orientations. Cases of reverse trends of transformation from modern to traditional societies are unknown.

The irreversible societal transition leading through a process of accretion toward increased complexity and greater interdependence in an advancing differentiation has to be regarded as growing systemness. Although the paradigm of pattern variables can be utilized to construct a theory on growing systemness, societal transition, or development, it does not constitute such a theory by itself. Pattern variables are pillars on which the bridge of a theory of development and growing systemness can be placed. The recent writings of Neil J. Smelser are an excellent example of how this can be done in the most concise yet exhaustive way.[14] Smelser tells us the following:

> For purposes of analyzing the relationships between economic growth and the social structure, it is possible to isolate the effects of several interrelated technical, economic, and ecological processes that frequently accompany development. These may be listed as follows: (1) In the realm of technology, the change *from* simple and traditional techniques *toward* the application of scientific knowledge. (2) In agriculture, the evolution *from* subsistence farming *toward* commercial production of agricultural goods. This means specialization in cash crops, purchase of nonagricultural products in the market, and often agricultural wage-labor. (3) In industry, the transition *from* the use of human and animal power *toward* industrialization proper, or "men aggregated at power-driven machines, working for monetary return with the products of the manufacturing process entering into a market based on a network of exchange relations."[15] (4) In ecological arrangements, the movement *from* the farm and village *toward* urban centers. These several processes often, but not necessarily, occur simultaneously.[16]

Smelser then discusses the various aspects of structural differentiation which consist of ". . . evolution from a multifunctional role structure to several more specialized structures."[17] He arrives at the conclusion that "Development proceeds as a contrapuntal interplay between differentiation (which is divisive of established society) and integration (which unites differentiated structures on a new basis). Paradoxically, however, the course of integration itself produces more *differentiated* structures. . . ."[18] Smelser analyzes the integrative processes in economy, family, community, and political structure; and he then discusses the discontinuities in differentiation and integration.

3. Features of the Growing Societal Systemness

The idea that development is a growing societal systemness seems to be very appealing. Accepting Smelser's formulation as a concise description of one of the essential features of the process, I would now like to trace other phenomena or aspects of that complex trend. Broadly speaking, development could be described as an irreversible, ongoing process of: (1) the multiplication of the channels and volumes of societal exchanges; (2) the differentiation of new, specialized roles, institutionalized organizations, and autonomous systems and their increasing interdependence; (3) the proliferation of systems and systemic interconnections within systems; and (4) generation of worldwide systemic structures. The process is especially enhanced by an ongoing industrialization.

How can these processes be described?

a. First it must be asserted that *the process of growth of societal systemness is irreversible and directional.* I have already conceded that in the history of societies there are no known cases of a reverse transformation from universality and specificity toward particularism and diffusiveness, from structural complexity toward structural simplicity, from macrostructural systems which are based on a high interdependence of the units toward agglutinations of units which are self-sufficient both economically and socially. Stories of the decay and degradation of societies described what may actually be called moral decay—the evaporation of economic, political, or military power; alienation; a change from functionalism to obsolescence and redundancy; dysfunctional latent consequences; the dissipation and falling apart of existing orders—usually either from impinging external forces or from the strain of overwhelming internal pressures—which usually lead to a new systemness that absorbs the elements of the old development; never a return to earlier existing orders and structures. Societies, political systems, and other systems may persist for long periods of time without tangible major changes, indeed without any transformation into distinctively different system orders. The process of growth of development of an accruing systemness may not be discernible for ages. A socioculture, a structure of systems, or one system may look stagnant and petrified, as though having no factors or forces conducive to change or transformation, as though it is congealed for eternity. Eventually, it either dissipates or develops new orders of a greater complexity and systemness. Sociocultures and system structures are never reborn reconstructed as they supposedly were in the past. I must emphasize here that the propensity for irreversible societal development should not be identified with what some writers regard as inevitability of progress. What is described here is not progress but the process of system development, and I wish to abstain from judgments whether or not it is to be qualified as desirable, progressive, or beneficial for mankind and so forth.

System development implies *continuity*—at least in general. Within it, we commonly, if not inevitably, find discontinuities, anomies, dissipations, or disequilibriums. Development is a peculiar continuity. As a matter of fact, we speak of it as growth because it must be seen as an irreversible process of continuity which produces entities of greater complexity in an ongoing accrual of change.*

The pace of societal development is not necessarily steady, or even rhythmic; in fact, it is rather uneven, sometimes advancing so minimally as to be practically invisible, at other times remaining frozen, at still other times advancing in bursts of transformations and in manifold innovations which generate accelerated transitions. Broadly speaking, the belief is that traditional, preindustrial societies tend to transform themselves rather slowly. Industrial societies, on the contrary, transform at an accelerated pace which increases as new innovations increase. In asserting a continuity in the process of development, we do not concede to *post hoc propter hoc.* Nor is this an attempt to smuggle in the idea of historical inevitability. I merely contend that a sociocultural system is not an abstraction; it is made up of people, groups, agencies, and institutions which carry on the inheritance from the past. Growing societal systemness results from a confluence of factors, forces, cleavages, and exigencies which both come from the past and are inherent or engendered by systemic interdependencies.

Defining societal development as growing societal systemness I do not imply a movement toward an equifinality or predestination; it cannot be explained by teleology. Nor is it a process of the unfolding of a potential capacity of the physical, moral, organizational, spiritual, or any other attributes of the progenitors of humanity, of a given society. At each level of development, at each minute of time in any society, decisions are taken and actions are performed which cumulatively bring about the eventual next step in the growing systemness. Nothing is preordained; it is evident, however, that developing societies are moving toward a greater complexity and toward an increasing systemness. It may be engendered spontaneously in the course of manifold societal interactions or it may be created on purpose in a consciously planned fashion to achieve a greater output of productivity, greater efficiency, or control over society. What is essential and reveals itself regardless of the fortuitous factors and additional characteristics (and this is said without any reistic implications)

---

* Of course, not all changes in a socioculture or system are necessarily directional. Many are not significantly consequent for the growing systemness.

is that self-differentiating sociocultures and societal systems evolve irreversibly and directionally toward, and transpire into, ascending complexity; to make the reflection tangible and comparable in terms of general system theory,[19] we borrow a term from thermodynamics and say that they decrease in entropy.*

* This poses the question of inputs. Some writers on general system theory assume, as von Bertalanffy points out in *General System Theory*, pp. 97-98: "Self-differentiating systems that evolve toward higher complexity (decreasing entropy) are, for thermodynamic reasons, possible only as open systems—e.g., systems importing matter containing free energy to an amount overcompensating the increase in entropy due to irreversible processes within the system ('import of negative entropy' in Schrödinger's expression)."

Ashby (see *An Introduction to Cybernetics,* and his "Principles of Self-Organizing System," in *Principles of Self-Organization,* H. von Foerster and G. W. Zopf, Jr., eds. (New York: Pergamon Press, 1962) strictly maintains this view and proposes to define a system as a "machine with input." Von Bertalanffy raises objections against this, pointing out that "Ashby machines" are special cases of cybernetic model machines. Such machines operate on inputs. In his opinion, Ashby's definition cannot be applied to the most important and obvious forms of self-organization—not to ontogenesis, probably not to phylogenesis, and certainly not to social organization. For instance, on p. 98, he comments: "The differentiation within a developing embryo and organism is due to its internal laws of organization, and the input (e.g., oxygen supply which may vary quantitatively, or nutrition which can vary qualitatively within a broad spectrum) makes it only possible energetically. . . . In both respects, the living organism (and other behavioral and social systems) is not an Ashby machine because it evolves toward increasing differentiation and inhomogeneity, and can correct 'noise' to a higher degree than an inanimate communication channel. Both, however, are consequences of the organism's character as an open system."

Here I disagree with von Bertalanffy. It is true that sociocultures and the systems that organize them are not "Ashby machines," but they are not organisms, either. We cannot say for sure whether or not internal laws of social organization really exist. The argument going on for ages now between (1) those who assume that man's actions are but an exteriorization of historical inevitability, the unfolding destiny of mankind, or that they happen in the realization of self-progressing inherent laws of organization, (2) those who assume that the history of humanity is but a history of chaos, the accumulation of accidental events, congregations, associations, and discoveries, and so forth, and (3) those who think that it is a combination of both has become now very sophisticated indeed, yet it is as unresolved as ever. The harnessing of energy may be regarded as an input which makes the growth of societal systemness possible. However, growing amounts of energy are not put into sociocultures from the outside by external agents. The progressing ability of man to harness energy in accelerated amounts reflects the accumulation of experience, the ascendance of man's knowledge, reflection, and abstract thought in his search for new solutions which will better fulfill the new generation of human needs. I would hesitate to reduce this complex interdependence simply to inputs. Some reflections on need-fulfillment, and especially on the need of security and its general effects on invention and societal development and growth are presented in the next section of this book. Finally, it is worth noting that K. E. Boulding (*The Meaning of the Twentieth Century,* New York: Harper & Row, 1964), pp. 137-55), suggests a different application of the concept of entropy to societal evolution. He states (p. 139): "Entropy can also be thought of as a measure of chaos—which may be defined, oddly enough, as the most probable state of any system. Negative entropy can then be thought of as measuring the degree of organization, structuring, or improbability of a system. Evolution

b. It has been asserted a number of times that growth in societal systemness entails a differentiation which generates more intricate and stronger interdependencies and expanding interconnections. More specifically, it may be said that the growing interdependence reveals itself in the declining self-sufficiency and growing complementation of the units of the systems, and these bring about the *build-up of an increasing density of channels of societal exchange and the multiplication of actual, patterned, recurrent exchanges* of goods, information, and (in some cases) of actors themselves. The ongoing differentiation manifests itself in the proliferation of specialized or specific roles, the institutionalization of specialized, goal-directed organizations, and in the sifting out of new self-articulated subsystems and systems elevated from the earlier existing systemic structures.

These processes have now become subjects of specialized theories and fields of the social sciences. Exchange theory, for example, deals with the process of multiplying exchanges. Role theory is focused on diverse aspects of role differentiation. The theory of organization is concerned with phenomena of organizational growth, with peculiarities of organizational structures, and, to some extent, with the differentiation of specialized systems. Obviously, neither the premises and tenets of these theories nor, as in some cases, nearly separate disciplines (such as the theory of organization) can be discussed here, but I should offer a few comments to relate our discussion to them.

Exchange theory tells us that exchanges are essential components, and carriers of societal interactions instrumental in establishing relations between actors spreading cultural patterns, and advancing the process of learning and communication.[20] *Growing societal systemness implies an increase in interdependencies, interactions—hence also in exchanges within societal structures.* Therefore, (1) More channels open for exchanges. The volume and variety of exchanged commodities (including goods, services, information, and the like) multiply because of both the availability of more commodities destined for exchange and the increased inclination of the actors to conduct exchanges; (2) Each individual, agency, and unit of societal structure depends on exchange for satisfaction of their own needs, desires, or strivings; (3) Most of the process of exchange involves the participation of numerous actors. Exchanges be-

---

moves the world toward less probable and more complicated arrangements, system patterns, and structures, whether in biology or in society. Thus even though the principle of diminishing potential is moving the universe as a whole toward increasing chaos, the evolutionary process operates to create more order at some points at the cost of creating less order elsewhere. This is what I mean by the segregation of entropy."

come more frequently indirect, and between distant parties; (4) Exchanges are conducted in pursuit of gains; rarely solely in fulfillment of reciprocities; (5) The exchange most commonly has the character of market transactions which involve anonymous partners.

Growing societal systemness entails an ongoing differentiation and institutionalization of specialized agencies and organizations which are embedded as units in the network of systemic interconnections. It entails greater organization both in size and in the volume of overlapping units and more specialization in organizational activities. Bureaucracies are built up, simultaneously generating networks of specialized roles and informal relations and stratifying those involved in their structures. Organizations subsequently become divided into branches and segments which tend toward autonomy. This is all the subject of organizational theory. R. Michels's study on the German Social Democratic party[21] can be mentioned here as a classic exploration of such processes.

Organizations are sometimes defined as systems. I prefer to regard them as parts or units of the systems of still larger entities. In any case, this does not seem to be a very controversial issue. Finally, to avoid any confusion, I must emphasize that although they appear to be in sort of an organismic process of growth and expansion, organizational activities which result in an enlargement in scale and expansion of the organization are manifestations of the achievement-oriented activities of their participants. They are neither inevitable nor resulting in organic evolution.

3. As was mentioned earlier, a growing systemness entails not only a differentiation of roles and the institutionalization of new organizations, but also an ongoing process of the *generation of new systems.*

Originally human societies existed as aggregates of functionally similar, relatively self-sufficient units, linked loosely into agglutinations by ethnic and cultural relatedness. Each unit was engaged in collecting or producing means for its own consumption on its own behalf. Exchanges were sporadic. Local leadership came into being because of the search for security and in the pursuit of cooperation and consensus in common actions. Leaders were usually men of prestige. When prestige changed into authority, and authority generated political power over a territory, political systems emerged. At this point, we could proceed with references to the writings of Sir Henry Maine, L. Morgan, and other evolutionists—or, as a matter of fact, to Weber's analysis of the transformation of traditional authority. Since, however, this is an attempt to depict a process different from the one usually discussed by writers of an evolutionist inclination, I wish to direct the reader to Lucy Mair's book, *Primitive Government.*[22] It is a comparative analysis of traditional political systems in precolonial East Africa. Mair compares different types of precolonial systems: (1) Systems with government, but without a state. Here, elders are the natural authorities. The redress of wrongs inflicted by another group is obtained either by feud[23] or through negotiations conducted by "professional mediators"—the so-called leopard-skin chiefs, the masters of the fishing spear, or the elders who act in the capacity of chiefs, priests, and judges simultaneously, and who are obeyed because they have prestige and not because they could coerce the parties involved; (2) Systems with minimal government, because it is government over a very small community, because the number of recognized positions of leadership is small, and because the extent of leadership is narrow. Here a sort of articulated chieftainship is already institutionalized; (3) Systems with diffused government, with a sort of spiritual leadership over larger territories. These are political systems not in the sense that they follow decisions imposed upon them by a higher authority, but in the sense that they all recognize a single man as supreme over them all; (4) Kingdoms, organized as a rule around hereditary monarchies. They appear both from the expansion of a government over a territory and from an expansion "in depth," in the sense that people within it are more subordinated to decisions which come from above. Here the institution of clientship emerges: the king and the chiefs nominate subordinate officers to transmit their messages to the territories under their rule and to receive reports from them. (5) Lastly, the features of African precolonial states are examined. Functional and social differentiation is far advanced there. Mair elaborates upon what Herskovits[24] and other earlier Africanists called the privileged "leisure classes." Kings collect tributes from the territory under their direct rule and from rulers who are subordinated to them through clientship, vassalage, or confederation. Various courts are bursting with intrigues and conflicts. The struggle for power becomes intense. The political system, as it is examined in the case of the Interlacustrine kingdoms becomes multidimensional;[25] it already consists of several networks of interrelated institutions—the traditional chiefs who claim a hereditary right to rule, the king's nominees, the warrior commanders, the queen's (or some other dignitary's) own appointees, and so forth. This is how a complex political system emerges.

Lucy Mair does not claim that the order of her comparative analysis is the actual order of transformation of the less complex structures into the more complex, semistate organization. She states only the following:

> Earlier anthropologists made it their aim to reconstruct the development of institutions in an evolutionary series, from "germs" which were to be found in the simplest forms of society, and some of their conjectures have come to appear rather ludicrous in the light of knowledge gained later. I do not assert that those peoples which now

have hereditary monarchs must once have had a political organization like that of Nuer. Nevertheless, it is reasonable to suppose that they have not had a state form of government ever since the dawn of their existence as human beings.[26]

As a rule, traditional political systems were monarchies. They controlled territories which ranged from small to enormously large. They were either imposed on the population by means of conquest or came as a result of the voluntary association and affiliation of petty chiefs and heads of various kinds of tribal units or other societal agglomerations. The idea of a state separate from the kingdom—and especially the state's formal institutionalization—emerged late in history. If I am not mistaken, it came in connection with the spread of the ideas on social contract. Thus, it may be asserted that traditional political systems were basically kingdoms* "forming a territorial society having the legitimate monopoly** over authorized use and regulation of force in the society."[27]

Let me now say*** that I accept the definition of a system as an aggregate or assemblage of objects joined in some regular interaction and interdependence. When we apply it to traditional political systems, the following can be pointed out: the framework, the boundaries, and, in fact, the actual borders of traditional political systems were often blurred. The meshes of the network of their structural interconnections were wide; the aggregation was relatively loose; the links between the agencies under the command of the central authorities and such centers were tenuous and unstable. Agencies of the system, whether nominated or self-appointed, were functionally diffuse. Actually the aristocrats, the nobility, the elite, the minorities—who were in command over large pieces of territories assigned to them, only participated in the system.[28] The majority of people under their rule continued to live in rather self-contained, isolated communities; they were subject to the whims of their local rulers with little, if any, recourse to the central authority; they were indeed in a very indirect relationship to the political system. Folk-urban and nobility-aristocratic cultures were separated and organized around different codes of conduct and values.[29] Sanctions for the existing order were sought in sacred scripts and in traditions. Above all, in connection with our discussion here, I must stress that such systems were hierarchical and structured of diffuse roles. High specialization, of course, did exist, but

---

* Of course, I realize that there are vast differences among tribal kingdoms, city-states (especially the ancient Greek democracy and a few other cases of small-community democracies), large medieval kingdoms, and great ancient empires. I use the term "kingdom" for convenience.
** As can easily be seen, this description is a modified version of Weber's definition of authority, and Almond's definition of political systems.
*** See the following section of this chapter.

specialized roles were few, and, especially important, they were subsidiary and linked with the diffuse agencies. They were not connected with one another into separate, functionally defined systems or subsystems. Thus, we can say that traditional political systems manifested but a small capacity to generate "daughter-systems" which could eventually grow to maturity as separate yet cognately related entities and assemblages.

Eventually, however, as M. Weber, M. Bloch, R. Coulborn,[30] and other writers on such societies tell us, servants of the rulers and other specialized functionaries of the courts obtained offices within the structure, and these offices tended to grow into bureaucracies which were linked into separate hierarchical orders. Thus prerequisites matured through which new, specialized, semiindependent "daughter-systems" could be emitted from the original structure of political systems.

Eisenstadt[31] characterizes this process of differentiation and formation of such new systems as follows: To maintain the system in efficient operation and under control, rulers had to nominate special personnel to act on their behalf and with their authority. "The rulers would always stress the point that these officials were either their personal servants or the servants of the polity that they wanted to establish, but were not representatives of any groups or strata in the society."[32] They had to have an amount of autonomy and independence to act as efficient "organs." This led inescapably to "a far greater differentiation of political activities, of the roles of the 'ruled' and the development of 'division of power' between the major aspects of the ruling institutions."[33]

The process described above culminated concomitantly with the beginning of industrialization, and, cumulatively with other processes, it led to the transformation of traditional political systems into modern political systems. The boundaries of political systems were then fixed, in the sense that political systems became separated from other systems of the socioculture and from other political systems. The network of political relations expanded, and the channels of political communication proliferated and established themselves firmly. Universalistic, secular, and legal norms of action replaced the particularistic orientations and privileges once granted by the ruler. Citizenship and the principle of legal equality replaced ascriptive status, thus fostering the development of national consciousness and the emergence of nations consisting of citizens. Legally defined freedoms were proclaimed. Elective governments replaced hereditary monarchies. Thus political systems expanded and involved nearly all the population within its scope. They become more complex and integrated. They also become more differentiated.

What I wish to point out here is not only that roles were more strictly differentiated and articulated, but also that specialized systems were generated in that process. This happened when specialized roles of a similar nature and in separate fields were gradually associated and linked into separate system-entities, each with their own structures, their own internal flow of information, and their own separate interests—often in conflict with other specialized systems. In this way, the parliamentary system become separated from the executive system (which is the government strictly speaking), and from the administrative system. The judiciary obtained an independent position from politics—at least formally.* Party, mass media, law enforcement, and so forth, systems become articulated into at least semiautonomous entities. To be sure, such systems are still under the umbrella of politics; they are still linked with the political system, but they are at the same time differentiated, self-articulated, and autonomous. The members of such systems relate to each other not only in the capacity of roles but also in the capacity of representatives of their respective systems. In the middle of the nineteenth century Lorenz von Stein[34] and later other writers, including Marx, were debating about the alienation of the state from the civil society. It can now be maintained that this tendency toward alienation has expanded. Specialized systems tend to alienate themselves from the parent structures, although the intricate interdependence between them—as well as between them and the systems of other societal entities—simultaneously becomes stronger.

Similar trends can be traced in the sphere of economic systems. Self-sufficient economic units, engaged basically in subsistence functions for their own consumption, were eventually absorbed by and embedded into peasant agricultural societies. Peasants lived in a dual economy, producing goods on the fields of the landlords, and also producing goods for their own maintenance on the fields assigned to them.[35] For many centuries, until late medieval times, both the lord and the peasant farmed principally to satisfy their own consumption needs. For the market, they produced only small amounts of commodities. The peasant sold on the market only a tiny portion of the goods he produced in his own household —enough to obtain money to purchase goods that he was unable to make himself. The lord sold larger portions of his goods to obtain all kinds of luxury items. In any case, they were only marginally concerned with production for the market. Only with the beginning of industrialization did what was marginal become principal, and what was principal start to become less important. New avenues to obtain money were opened. The whole value-orientation had to be and was changed. Max Weber tells us that the Protestant ethic emerged in a sense as an expression of that new orientation. Benjamin Nelson[36] examines how the principles of usury

* Class, ideological, and value-oriented connections are disregarded at this point.

based on Deuteronomy were well suited for the needs of subsistence and for an economy directed only marginally for the market, and how they became an impediment and even became obsolete in the new era. He first shows how Luther and Bucer sponsored the break with the medieval interpretation of usury, and how Calvin then took the decisive step, exploiting "the ambivalence of the Deuteronomic passage," and reinterpreted it so as to clear the road for the introduction of new norms. Thus one of the last barricades on the way "from tribal Brotherhood to universal Otherhood" was removed.

New times began. The lords, the owners of the land became predominantly, if not totally, money-oriented. They reset the principles and the organization of their agricultural estates. They transformed them into productive enterprises subordinated to the needs of the market. "Cut off from its roots in the soil, feudalism had become parasitic, deriving its strength from the maneuvers of powerful magnates and the countermoves of the monarch."[37] In England "the sheep became men." The landowners drove the peasants off from their fields to raise sheep. ". . . The chief carriers of what was eventually to be a modern and secular society were at this time fundamentally men of commerce in both the countryside and the towns."[38] "Those who promoted the wave of agrarian capitalism, the chief victors in the struggle against the old order, came from the yeomanry and even more from the landed upper classes."[39] In Germany and all over continental Europe, "toward the end of the fourteenth century, certain changes began that later led to the enserfment of the peasant. The towns declined, the central authority weakened. But most of all, there appeared the beginnings of an export market for grain. Together these forces altered the political balance in the countryside."[40]

In short, these changes and trends, together with the process of industrialization, the development of commerce, and the like, transformed the societies into national economic systems. Differentiation and specialization advanced simultaneously. Specialized branches differentiated themselves within the fields of business, agriculture, industry, and commerce. Each of the differentiated branches gradually obtained systemic features and developed its own interests and peculiar structures. In some cases, such articulated system-branches entered not only into a competition over markets but actually conflicted with other industries. Thus, for example, in the United States, the railroads found themselves in conflict with the airlines and with car manufacturers; oil industries that sought to develop along the seashores came into conflict with the fishing industries. Economic, market-type relations were interwoven into the political structures. In fact, political, social, and the like, interactions obtained a market-value aspect. Not only were systems of industry generated within the sphere of national economies, but so too were special institutions whose function it was to mediate between systems and between systems of different sphere-activities. Thus, for instance, in the economic sphere, pressure groups were founded whose job it was to influence the political decision-making process. In politics, as another example, all kinds of offices were established to deal with the problems of national economy—to plan it, regulate it, and so forth. As we know, the current tendency in all societies is toward more state intervention in economies and other societal affairs and generally toward etatization of the social structure.

On the whole, then, the process of growth of societal systemness accrues in the integration and differentiation of roles, organizations, and systems, and in a mutual interpenetration of such differentiated and separate systems. It entails the incessant generation of new systems and within such systems the simultaneous proliferation, and consolidation of more and wider systemic relations and interdependencies.

(d) As was stated before, industrialization constitutes the turning point in the ongoing process of growing systemness. Industrialization and technological development make the incessant system growth not only more discernible, and more active (if such an expression can be applied), but they also make it more precipitous and in a sense (and this must be stressed) inevitable. As a result of industrialization, the growing societal systemness becomes magnified and intensified and, indeed, proceeds in an avalanche of economic, cultural, and social changes and perpetual sudden abrupt transformation. I have already discussed the consequences of industrialization in other parts of the book. I have also referred the reader to special studies on that topic. I cannot discuss industrialization in detail here. Nonetheless, there is a need for at last a general list of the *major consequences of industrialization which cause the process of growing societal systemness.*

They can be summed up as follows:

1. Industrialization entails a continuous multiplication of the volume of harnessed energy in a society, a mounting prevalence in the ratio of inanimate to animate sources of power, combined with the accelerated application of scientific knowledge which leads to an enormous increase in the effect of work.[41] Standardized goods and objects of daily use in the society are made in great quantities with an increasing complexity in the division of labor and by sophisticated technological methods and means. Production becomes increasingly separated from consumption, and the process of production becomes separated from the family life of the producers and the owners of the means of production. Production for the market becomes dominant over production for one's own consumption. Social interactions become permeated by market relations.

2. Increasing portions of the population live in urban centers. Most of the population becomes urbanized. The proportion of the population engaged in earning its living outside agriculture far exceeds the number of people earning their living through it. The agricultural population dwindles.

3. The whole society becomes transformed into a large national economy and engages all the members of the society in an intricate network of market-type interactions.

4. The mass, uniform, standardized culture of the crowd, spread by mass media communications, prevails over the culture of individual performance.

5. The family unit ceases to perform many of the functions that it performed in traditional societies. Its importance as a unit of the social structure is on the decline. One's job and one's family life are mostly separated. Specialized educational institutions take over from the family a large portion of the socialization functions it once performed. Most of the many specialized roles performed by individuals in social interaction become disconnected with family life, and are part of the activities within groups, agencies, organizations, and so forth, which are organized for the pursuit of narrow, specialized goals and interests.

6. The relations in social interaction are prevailingly instrumental, impersonal, deprived of strong attachments. The links and interconnections which bind groups, agencies and organizations (which are, as a rule, organized for highly specialized activities) are increasingly indirect and intermediate and contain more and more elements of market-type relations as well as more systemic qualities.

7. Systems are emerging in all spheres of life nowadays. These are intermeshed and interconnected into larger systemic units. The entire society becomes permeated by systemic interdependencies. With the spread and build-up of systemic interdependencies, the technological, economic, and political potential of the society, the state which acquires more regulative functions within it, attains a power hitherto unprecedented. Simultaneously, however, the whole structure becomes extremely fragile and vulnerable to any accidental disturbance. Any action affecting a selected unit of the system can cause chain reactions whose eventual consequences cannot be anticipated.

8. Societal development is linked with economic and technological developments. Thus it occurs in conditions in which the ecological environment is increasingly devastated and in conditions of other disastrous consequences of industrialization. Maybe these can be avoided or reduced. In any case, as the situation is today, while people in the industrial societies are enjoying the results of an increased output of productivity, hu-

manity as a whole increasingly experiences a growing impoverishment of natural surroundings. Thus many voices are heard calling for limitation of development in general, technological development especially, or at least greater control of it.

9. Forced into performing an increasing number of roles within the variety of systems in which he has to live, the average member of modern society feels alienated and transformed into a cog of a gigantic machine. Systemic relations generate more enmity than amity. Even within structures of semiorganismic interdependencies where roles are allocated and people act on orders, they have to struggle and compete for any position. Thus the systems engendered by various kinds of macrosocietal developments are torn apart by multiple conflicts and cleavages.

10. People still view societal development as a remedy against their predicaments. Today, however, at least in Western societies, they are no longer satisfied with a development which is primarily directed toward the increase of output of material goods. They are searching for development which will be instrumental in the restoration of community life and allow the individual to retain his identity and autonomy.

There are different ways to industrialize societies. Industrial societies of the West differ from the Soviet Union and the societies similar to it, and both of these differ from Japan. As we know, this is not only because of a diverse cultural background. It is especially due to the differing political orders in those societies, and to the different types of industrialization methods applied. Thus transition from traditional to modern societies differs from society to society. Industrialization entails a growth of societal systemness, but under different ideological conditions and different political climates the essence of similar systemic relations and structures differs considerably.

4. Types of Interdependencies in Growing Societal Systems

Critics have written many times that theories propounding primarily either the vision of a system composed of subsystems of functions in static interconnections, or a paradigm in which the societal system is depicted as a feedback mechanism producing and regulating political decisions only, cannot provide satisfactory explanations for the process of societal development. What is needed for the understanding of societal development is a theory viewing the societal system simultaneously as a structure of systemic interactions which are generated by an intrinsic process of differentiation of specialized constituents within a growing interdependence. Though some writers have proclaimed a need for such a system theory,[42] it is not available at the moment. For a working basis for such an approach, and its eventual application in the discussion of the growing societal systems it would perhaps be useful to look at the way in which general system theory treated the subject, and especially how scholars in this field defined the concept of system. Here are such examplary definitions:

"A system can be defined as a complex of interacting elements."[43]

"A system is a distribution of the members in a dimensional domain."[44]

"Initially we can define a system broadly and crudely as *any* entity, conceptual or physical, which consists of interdependent parts."[45]

"The kind of system we are interested in may be described generally as a complex of elements or components directly or indirectly related in a causal network, such that each component is related to at least some others in a more or less stable way within any particular period of time."[46]

These definitions are not too different. They stress interaction, interdependence, and regular relatedness of elements and components in a complexity of wholeness. Should one begin the discussion of systems in societies with any of these definitions, he would probably have to continue it by characterizing the specific nature of systemic relations in social interactions as opposed to interconnections in other types of systems. Here, I wish to say only a few words on these differences.

Mechanical systems are *assembled,* erected, and constructed. Organismic systems *unfold themselves* into greater complexity in an evolutionary process which is at the same time endo- and phylogenetic. Theoretical, analytical, and logical systems are products of man's mind. They are deducted, abstracted, spun, devised, and *contrived.* Men *discovered* the existence of a solar system, an ecological system, and other systems in their surroundings. They also discovered that they themselves are part of systems. Sociocultural systems in which men live *transpire* in the course of the differentiation of specialized societal roles requiring complementarity and reciprocity of other specializations in a growing interdependence of members, groups, and agencies of society. They become increasingly all-encompassing as these interdependencies proliferate. This is the process of *growing societal systemness.*

It is especially important at this point of our discussion to differentiate within the structure of societal systems three types of macrostructural interdependencies: (1) interdependence of coexistence; (2) complementary interdependence; (3) semiorganismic interdependence.

a. Interdependence of coexistence

Whenever people, groups, or societies have to live together in close proximity they become interdependent by virtue of that very fact. The actors may not wish to interfere with the lives of others, they may attempt to pursue their own goals only. They may isolate themselves, be hostile or indifferent to each other. They may avoid any exchange. But if they live together they are dependent on each other, and they have to take into account what the others do. Intentionally or unintentionally, they are bound to affect each other. They live in proximity, sharing the same local, national, or international neighborhood, and proximity produces interdependence. These are instances of interdependence without functional complementarity, based solely on the necessity of living together in spatial association where the action of one actor affects the possibilities of another. Differentiation in such circumstances can be characterized as the separate and independent development of each actor. Yet all the actors are interdependent since each is a part of the surroundings of the other. Coexistence in a subsistence economy in a close area, or international relations between the Eastern and Western blocs maintaining economic and cultural exchanges at only a small scale, yet dependent on each other (armaments of one incite the armament of the other) are examples of such a case. The effect on our lives of pollution carelessly created by others is another example of how men are related in interdependencies of coexistence. With the increase of population, spread of communications, diminution of the distances between habitation of individuals, groups and nations, the impingement of the interdependence of coexistence upon any member of society increases.

b. Complementary interdependence

This is an interdependence ensuing from division of labor, from specialization and complementarity of units related in mutual exchange either directly or through the medium of other actors. It develops on a small scale in simple cooperation. On a large scale it spreads as an interaction on the market of autonomous yet dependent agents. With growing specialization, it becomes increasingly impossible for the actors to exist without exchanging goods and services. Thus this is an interdependence based on the necessity to sell one's own products and services in order to obtain the services and products of the others. The more one is specialized in such interactions, the more he has to offer, and the more he becomes a part of the structure of intermeshing systems of patterned relations (economic, political, social). Bargaining and competition become involved, relations in which values depending on demand and supply become established. Interactions and interdependencies emerging from such relations can therefore be translated into and defined in economic terms.[47] An old maxim from the times of Justinian, which is also used by Marx in

Capital, reflects the character of complementary interdependencies: *Do ut des, do ut facias: facio ut des, faciout facies*—I give that you may give. I give that you may produce. I produce that you may give. I produce that you may produce. The social, political, and economic systems of capitalist societies, as indeed any structure of voluntary cooperation, provide formidable examples of such interdependencies.* The complementary interdependence of a modern political system relates self-differentiated agencies and units in a variety of coalescing overlapping structures. As examples, the following differentiations can be discerned: (1) differentiation and specialization of the political professions and of a variety of auxiliary specializations (politicians, party bureaucrats, administrators, ideologists, propagandists, mobilizers, advertisers, lobbyists); (2) differentiation of specialized agencies of political representation such as political parties, interest and pressure groups, political clubs; (3) stratification of political participants into professionals, militants, active and passive participants; (4) differentiation and separation of the institutions of the mechanism of political balance (executive, legislature, judicial authorities; local, provincial-state, and general state authorities, party systems). The complementary systems are especially structures of market-type relations.

c. Semiorganismic interdependence

An organismic interdependence is an interdependence of nonautonomous parts of a whole. It arises in an organic process of growth, beginning with an ovule and continuing through differentiation of tissues into specialized organs of complex wholes. Organs are not actors, however. They cannot act on their own behalf or exist independently without other organs or the whole body. Societies do not develop in such a way, though some sociologists tend to apply the organismic model as an explanation of societal growth and development. Bureaucracies, however, do develop along patterns resembling organismic development, through proliferation and specialization of units and "organs" in a subservient relation to the whole structure. Thus I propose to view them as semiorganismic interdependencies. Interdependence in a semiorganismic structure consists not only in complementarity of its units, but of their total subordination to the center. They are not allowed to exist for their own purposes, and they are told that unless they perform orders coming from above in order to implement the functions allocated to them they will be eliminated as dysfunctional, obsolete, superfluous elements. In a society organized into

---

* As Marx writes in *Capital* (Moscow: Progress Publishers, 1965, vol. I, p. 363), "Cooperation based on division of labour, in other words manufacture, commences as a spontaneous formation. So soon as it attains some consistence and extension, it becomes the recognised methodical and systematic form of capitalist production."

a semiorganismic structure the government totally dominates the political system, and the political system all other spheres of life. Economics,
social structure, and culture are regarded as subsystems of the political
order. In characterizing the economic organization of such a system of
interdependencies, W. Brus outlines its features as follows:[48] (1) As a
rule all decisions about economic matters (with the exception of acts concerning individual consumption and employment) are concentrated in
the central apex; (2) The whole economy is encompassed by a hierarchical order. Planning is hierarchical and diverse levels of the economy as a
whole and of its units are bound in vertical subordination. Horizontal
interconnections, if allowed at all, are arranged from above; (3) Decisions from above are transmitted to all units of the structure in obligatory
orders; (4) Planning and the economic calculus are based on natural
(physical) quantities; (5) Money performs only a passive role in circulation in the sphere of state property (between the administration and industries and between industries).

The political and economic organization of the Soviet Union provides
a good example for the analysis of such a structure. Ideally and ideologically it is assumed to form a single organism. Each institution in it is supposed to be an organ of the party-state, and each citizen a cell of the
whole.*

Yet this is the ideal, the model rather than the reality. It is inculcated
in the minds of the citizens, promulgated by the literature and official
propaganda, used in the process of socialization. It is an ideal to which
organizers and ordinary members are urged to strive in order to create a
fully harmonious society. Since, however, the "cells" of that imagined
superorganism are thinking individuals with their own identities and
needs, they act on their own behalf too, and not only as a part of the
whole. They have individual aspirations and personal needs which neces-
sitate generation of conflicts, social stratification, spontaneous emergence
of interest groups and other processes which are dysfunctional from the
point of view of the logic of the system, and of the bureaucratic hierarchy.

Interdependence of coexistence implies respect for the rights of
others though noncooperation with them. Complementary interdependence, on the other hand, is a relationship of voluntary or involuntary
cooperation. At the same time, however, it is a relationship of conflict and
competition. It requires independent action, initiative, decision-making,

---

* In addition to the interdependence of coexistence, of complementary and semiorganismic interdependencies, mechanical interdependencies also exist of artificially
created mechanisms assembled from parts into a whole. If one disregards federations,
political and societal structures do not form such "mechanisms." Durkheim and
Toennies applied this concept in a different meaning.

and inventions. Semiorganismic interdependence is based on the functional rationality of the units for the whole. Units which are not functional are dispensable. It requires subordination, merging with the whole, an absorption into the totality. In return it relieves the individual of the need for decision-making, of the often painful and difficult task of generating one's own opinions and acting on one's own initiative.

One can look at the three types of societal and political interdependencies and their eventual transformation through the prism of the concept of societal development. At first societies consisted of agglomerations of small self-subsistent independent groups occasionally interfering one with another. With their proliferation and the invention of more effective means of production, when men were able to adopt a more active attitude toward their environment, and with other changes discussed in the other chapters of this book, the interdependence of coexistence ensued. The separate units became framed in larger formations of traditional societies, and especially in kingdoms and empires. Independent differentiation within the frame of the dependencies of coexistence advanced slowly, when it was not stimulated by vigorous external factors, such as market competition and need for exchange. Subsequently, however, especially in the course of the variety of processes of overlapping revolutions, the speedily accelerating transformation of traditional societies into the modern followed.

Elements of complementary interdependencies appeared very early in the division of labor in households of traditional societies based on differences in sex, age, and ancestry. With the transformation of traditional societies into modern ones complementary interdependence based on differences in specialization engulfing autonomous actors related in mutual direct and indirect exchanges of services became overwhelming and dominant, determining the whole character of the society.

The state, especially when it is based on a bureaucratic hierarchy, tends to develop according to patterns of semiorganismic interdependence. In the past, empires have manifested tendencies which could be described as resembling semi-organismic developments. Political and social revolutions in the nineteenth and twentieth centuries resulted in the establishment of various systems of democracy. Regardless of their imperfection they produced a variety of institutional structures defending the rights of individuals and interest groups, maintaining in balance conflict and consensus of the interests of the individuals and the total collectivity represented by the state, and curtailing tendencies aimed at total subordination of the individual to the state authorities in a semiorganismic growth. Any political organization, bureaucracy, army, corporation, and, as a matter of fact, any large organization is to an extent based on principles of a semiorganism. Organizations differ, however, in respect to how much they subordinate the individual to these principles and on how much they deprive the individual incorporated in their structure of their individuality and freedoms. Because of the pressure of interdependencies of coexistence, of the need to have constant mechanism-regulating conflicts, because of the growing need of coordinated action, the scope of the semiorganismic interdependencies and engulfment by them of men in society is growing. The semiorganismic interdependencies cannot be simply abolished. Yet one of the basic questions about the current societal and political processes is whether the growing tendency toward semiorganismic interdependence will become completely dominant in society. Will it engulf, permeate, and swallow the interdependencies of the first and second type? Will men become transformed into cogs only? Growing state intervention evident in any social and political order, bureaucratization of all spheres of life, introduction of national planning, the need for concerted organized action in maintaining the environment in a condition in which human beings can survive, the need to control population growth, growing dependence of individuals upon macrostructural systemic structures and institutions, and numerous other symptoms seem to be prodromal of a forthcoming transformation in which the semiorganismic state bureaucratic structure will fully engulf and subordinate, if not eradicate, interdependencies of other types. On the other hand, both in Western societies and in Eastern Europe resistance to the domination of the semiorganism is growing.

Marx devoted most of his writing to an attack on the conflict-ridden capitalist order of society. He wanted it to change into a structure of pure complementary interdependencies in a conflict-free society. Even more than capitalism he detested the semiorganismic state surmounting the structure of the capitalist society. For him, it, like private property, money, the products of work, and religion, was one more aspect of modern life over which man had lost control because of its alienation. Max Weber feared the semiorganismic development and connected it with a pursuit for pure rationality and "wealth stripped of its religious and ethical meaning." Though he was not very explicit in his discussion of it on the last pages of the *Protestant Ethic,* he confronted the iron cage that man builds around himself in pursuit of such targets with opposing principles of what he called humanistic rationalism.

In a "relatively normal" state of affairs the three types of interdependencies overlap and are maintained in a balance. The basic function of the semiorganismic structure is to protect the autonomy of individuals and of the coexistence and complementarity of their interaction. An entirely different situation emerges in what for the sake of convenience may be called a schizophrenic state of affairs. Those in charge of the semior-ganismic structure of interdependencies begin to imagine that they are truly the brain of a real organism. They attempt to subordinate to their will all aspects of life of the other members of the society in the name of higher goals of the totality, of the system, and of the wholeness. Any form of autonomy and of individualism has to be suppressed and if pos-sible eradicated. Men must become merely cells in the tissue of an organ of the semiorganism. The cancer of totalitarianism develops affecting the lives of all members of the society, destroying their freedom, paralyzing grass-roots initiative, killing mutual trust between human beings. The turgidity of the system cannot totally destroy human nature, however. People still behave as human beings, even though as oppressed human beings. Some become fervent servants of the semiorganismic totality either because they do not understand its nature or because they think that such is the nature of life. Others try to hide under the crust of self-isolation. Others rebel. And there are always some who continue to think for themselves.

In societies where all three types of interdependency exist, the deli-cate balance between the interdependencies and the autonomy of the participants can be maintained and defended, even under conditions where the regulative functions of the semiorganismic structures are neces-sarily being expanded.

As characterized above, complementary interdependence whether in economic, social, or political spheres of activities, inevitably includes con-flict and competition. It constitutes a structure of persistent conflicts re-currently resolved and reappearing in new forms, competitions regulated by established rules, cooperation, and exchange intertwined with conflict and competition. Since these interdependencies are based on patterned relations and since they unify the participants into a whole which exhibits some of the common characteristics (of nations) they should be regarded as systems. These are systems of conflicts contained in shells of consensus and covered with other shells of structures of power and authority. Many writers on the subject tend, however, to view the subject differently. For them only the elements of the semiorganismic interdependencies consti-tute systems. They do not necessarily reject the conflict theory as an interpretation of social and political relations. They simply are not con-cerned with it, or with predictions concerning diminution of the auton-omy of the agents and actors in the complementarity of interdependence. They are interested in the suprapolitical organism, on a high level of theoretical abstraction. Groups and individuals, their interests and au-tonomy, their special identity are then at most a variable in an equation. Often the variable is regarded either as unimportant or as constant and, therefore, insignificant for equation. The belief is that real data and facts can be substituted for the symbols after the equation is resolved.

Originally, the concept "development" as applied in the evolutionary theories of societal development was borrowed from biology. It certainly was used by analogy; it was a metaphor, therefore. Defined, however, as a process of differentiation producing growing interdependence through stages of discontinuity, a process of disturbances and social anomie; or as a process of growing societal systemness resulting from changes, yet always inherently conflictual; or as a process of transformation of a one-dimensional *theatrum mundi* role performance into an increasingly broad and complex performance involving varieties of roles or personas assumed by members of society;[49] "societal development" becomes devoid of its original evolutionary content. It acquires then a completely new connotation. It becomes a strictly sociological concept, since only human societies have the capacity of developing in such a sense. In this understanding "societal development" can be applied beside concepts of development with a different connotation. Biological development has to be defined differently from development of projects, events, ideas and, as a matter of fact, societal development. Although it cannot be attempted here, it seems to be possible to introduce some indicative measurements to be applied in its analyses. Such measurements should consist of at least two variables; one for differentiation and specialization, the other for the degree of interdependencies. These variables may also be correlated with assessments of the GNP as applied by economists. Perhaps social role performance, the account of the average number of specialized socioeconomic roles performed by individuals in different societies compared with roles performed in the past, and of the duration in the capacity of roles by individuals, can provide some start for developments of such a scale. I say perhaps, since other criteria and scales may be better fitted to this purpose. A perfect measurement will probably be difficult to find. Economists are not wholly satisfied with the GNP as an indicator of the level of economic development. Then again, criticism could be leveled against the concept of "role." True, it is a concept utilized by sociologists and anthropologists of different schools. True, it was applied by strongly differing theorists such as G. H. Mead, R. Linton, M. Banton, N. Gross, A. M. Rose, T. Parsons, E. Shils, C. Wright Mills, H. Gerth, R. Dahrendorf, R. Turner, W. Buckley, and numerous others. One still can say that "role" is a metaphor borrowed from theatrical terminology. It is a euphemism. It would be better to abandon it in sociological theory. In real life people eat, sleep, have children, attend schools, work, fight, take part in various recreational activities, and do many other things. But role performance? A society imagined as one great theater? Such a society has never existed and is not likely ever to come into being. In real life only a tiny minority of people such as actors and dissemblers do engage in role performances. What can one say in defense of the concept "role" against such critics? Perhaps one should recall Thrasymachus, who said: "You are trying to be funny, Socrates. It's a low trick to take my words in the sense you think will be most damaging."

Comparison of Some Cases of Growing Systemness in Diverse Societies

1. Comparing Different Avenues of Industrialization

Clark Kerr and his associates[1] have introduced a good key by which to differentiate and analyze the varying patterns of industrialization in different parts of the world. They say that a crucial factor in any industrializing society is which elites become the initiators of industrialization, and how they view their role and the nature of the "good society." The universal questions are these:

    a. Who leads the march to industrialism?

    b. What is the purpose of the march?

    c. How is the march organized?[2]

In answering these questions the writers distinguish five types of elites: (1) "The dynastic elite" who engage in industrialization for the sake of maintaining the paternal community; (2) "The middle-class elite" who engage in industrialism in the pursuit of profit on the open market; (3) "The revolutionary intellectuals" who engage in industrialism to implement their vision of a better society, but who, in the course of pursuit of their phantom ideals, develop a highly centralized state which controls the economy and social living; (4) "The Colonial Administrators" who engage in industrialization as a duty for the sake of their "Home Country"; and (5) "The Nationalist Leaders" who promote industrialism to enhance nationalism and national states.

As we know, most of the modern industrial nations were led through the avenues of industrialization by either the middle-class elite or the revolutionary intellectuals. In any case, the writers also say that "all the elites are to a degree and in a way nationalists."

Using the key Kerr furnishes to differentiate the five cases or ideal types of industrialization, I would like to portray especially the two basic cases somewhat differently. There is no need to explain that the middle-class elite industrialization reflects the trend which occurred in Western Europe and in the United States, and that industrialization organized by revolutionary intellectuals reflects the course of industrialization in the Soviet Union and most of the Soviet-type states. Japan may be considered as a case of industrialization started by dynastic and nationalistic elites and subsequently taken over by the middle class. Africa and other new nations, where industrialization is now in the beginning stages, seems to represent still another case.

As was said, industrialization entails some common consequences regardless of the time or manner in which it happens. At the same time, however, it can be organized in different ways, around differing political formulas and ideologies, and—this seems to be most important—it may generate diverse systems and it may be brought about within different systems. I wish first to compare the courses and resulting systems of Western societies and the Soviet Union; and then to proceed to some comments on the course of industrialization and the resulting growth of systems in other parts of the world.

The process of industrialization began in Western Europe about two hundred years before it started in Russia. In both the West and the Soviet Union industrialization began with convulsive, painful societal changes and displacement of people. The poor, the peasants, the populations of the colonies were its victims. They had to pay its price. Many books have been written on the ills and tragedies of the age of transition.[3]

2. Comparing Industrialization in the West and in the Soviet Union

Who were the industrializers? As I have already mentioned, those who accomplished industrialization in the West may be considered a middle-class elite; those who organized it in the Soviet Union may be called the revolutionary intellectuals. More strictly speaking, it was the middle class that started to industrialize Russia. Industrialization was planned on a mass scale later by the revolutionary intellectuals and was subsequently carried out by the new elite of party bureaucrats. In the Soviet-type countries of Eastern Europe industrialization also began originally as a result of middle-class entrepreneurial endeavors. Eventually, after the Second World War, when peoples' democracies were created, it was then carried on under the auspices of the party bureaucracy.

The middle-class elite was and still is an elite of profit-seekers. It has been portrayed as a class of capitalist exploiters, a class of bourgeoisie, a

class of inventive entrepreneurs, and so forth. In theories of social stratification it is distinguished as a class because of its specific position in the
structure of ownership of the means of production, because of the amount
of wealth it controls, and because of its adherence to a particular set of
value orientations and its achievement ethic. Marx distinguished it as a
class because of its position at the other end of the spectrum of class
struggle. Objective and subjective criteria have been applied in its "scientific" demarcation. What is most peculiar about its class anatomy is its
heterogeneity. It is a class only in contrast to other classes. Indeed, it is
internally united (if a common value-orientation and a common ethic are
disregarded) in its competition and conflict over profits, markets, and
money. It is a class which is differentiated but not self-instituted. Hence
it is open, nonorganized. Again, I must repeat that it is a class of individual profit-seekers. Hence, as a class it never promoted something that
could be considered a policy or an ideology of development. It industrialized societies and subsequently promoted economic development, system
growth, and other changes connected with these processes, but it must be
pointed out that it did that not in the implementation of any specific programs of development, but as a by-product of its profit-seeking activities.
It actually became dominant as a class in West European and other societies not as a single elite but as a nosegay of middle-class elites—in business, politics, the sphere of cultural activities, the free professions, and to
an extent even in the armies. These elites occupied the upper scales of the
ladders of social mobility in the capitalist societies and were linked by a
common value-orientation, and, as C. Wright Mills[4] has demonstrated
with the American example, by a multitude of social bridges which united
them.

The revolutionary intellectuals who initiated the programs of organized industrialization in the Soviet Union, Eastern Europe, and in some
cases in other parts of the world were either the impoverished grandsons
and granddaughters of the nobility or the sons and daughters of the middle classes who were concerned with and frustrated by the injustices they
saw. Rarely were they able to recruit a member of the working class or a
peasant into their ranks. They wanted to change the world and introduce
total equality, freedom, and justice. Socialism seemed to be the solution.
Marx and other classic Marxist writers had said that their goal could be
achieved through a revolution which would overthrow the political and
economic domination of the capitalist classes and abolish private means
of production. The result would be economic development and political
education which would simultaneously produce affluence and a high concern for the collectivity. A society would ensue which would be organized
on the principle where "each man works according to his ability and re-

ceives according to his needs." They believed in utopia, and they also believed that it could be achieved through industrialization and economic development. Where they succeeded in getting power, they become the prophets and initiators of organized, planned industrialization. To implement their visions and plans they had to entrust the work to bureaucrats, technocrats, policemen, and to the mass of people in general. These were not utopians, visionaries, or dreamers; they were not concerned with great and high ideals or moral issues. Soon the revolutions devoured their originators and organizers. The revolutionary intellectuals were replaced by accountants, generals, and bureaucrats who had no imagination. True, they proceeded with industrialization. That was their job. They did it in a bureaucratic way, because such were their orders. In some cases chauvinist nationalists have taken over from the revolutionary intellectuals. They, too, have had to rely on bureaucrats. Yet the bureaucrats that we are talking about were not ideal-type bureaucrats. They were men of flesh and, as a rule, with a middle-class mentality and middle-class needs. They have kept the banners of the revolution and socialism flying high. But in their name they have introduced hierarchies and inequality; they have abolished democracy and freedom; they have demanded sacrifices from the masses and downgraded the standard of living of those masses. They have exterminated any opposition and terrorized any potential objectors. Thus they have secured order, subordination, cheap labor, sources for the accumulation of capital, and various privileges and legal and illegal rewards for their own kind.

What were the political formulas for industrialization? The French Revolution, which can be regarded as the symbolic political turning point into modernity, because it legitimized the capitalist order and with it the orientation toward industrialization, erupted under the slogan "Freedom, equality, and fraternity." Freedom became especially dear to the ideologists and philosophers and, indeed, to the middle-class industrial entrepreneurs of the West. It was understood that it was above all freedom for enrichment and entrepreneurship. The revolutionary intellectuals demanded equality. The bureaucrats who had to industrialize the Soviet Union and Eastern Europe then inherited "equality" as a nice slogan to keep as a point in the constitution, on signboards decorating ceremonial places, and as a tourist attraction for the revolutionaries from the West. Fraternity was left for the poor Third World nations.

Freedom became the cherished value-orientation of the West. It was freedom to change one's place of living, freedom of initiative, freedom to invest, to express oneself, to dissent, to elect one's own authorities, to own property, to acquire, to exploit, to buy freedoms, and, above all, freedom to make money. We now know that the answer to the question "Why did

industrialization first occur in Western Europe?" is because of the confluence of factors and events facilitating its generation. Freedom was the
essential factor among them. Without it, achievement orientation, entrepreneurship, and rationality would have shriveled away fruitlessly as they
certainly do in many other parts of the world. Freedom, however, has to
have its limits, and it is evident only in contrast to a lack of freedom. It
has to be limited because of others' freedoms, because it is usually connected with obligations and duties, because it is regulated by authorities,
laws, and norms, and so forth. Freedom is the right to be on one's own,
the right to be different. It implies inequality. The political freedoms and
the freedom to make money as established and exercised in capitalist societies were based on and generated and promoted economic inequality in
the first instance, and social inequality in the second instance.

The Bolshevik revolution was an upheaval against the mounting inequalities of Tsarist Russia, against the feudal order of the past, against
the inequalities generated by the Tsarist state, and against those generated by a rising Russian capitalism. The revolutionary intellectuals leading the Russian revolution wanted it to spread all over the world, believing that it would purge the world of all injustices and establish equality
everywhere. When the Russian revolutionists failed in this, they proclaimed the establishment of a model state, which would guarantee equal
opportunities to all—except former exploiters and enemies of the people—
in fact, those whom they considered to be enemies of their government
and the potential enemies; those that the Party and its leaders thought
would become enemies. Thus the dictatorship of the proletariat became
established.

The revolution was supposed to fulfill a number of functions. It destroyed the corrupt, parasitic Tsarist regime and with it rapacious bud-
ding capitalism. It abolished private ownership of the means of production; it nationalized land, mineral resources, and industries. This was a
means of introducing equality, eradicating exploitation—with it, it was
claimed and expected, any exploitation would vanish forever. It was also
supposed to be the starting point for the process of building socialism.
Marx and Engels maintained that socialism as a system of true social justice—a system of equality which could provide all the conditions for a full
intellectual and moral development for all the members of the society—
could be established only on a high level of development of the productive forces. It was supposed to be a product of moral progress, enlightenment, and of the most advanced technological and economic development.
It was supposed to be a product of an affluent society. Lenin asserted:
"Proletarian socialism sees its ideal, not in the equality of small proprie-
tors, but in large-scale socialized production."[5] Thus what was believed

to be essential to achieve socialism was the maximization of the economic output within an accelerated industrial economic development. It was said (and even believed) that the revolution would not only eliminate the exploitation of man by man but would also make other things possible. It would (1) create a rational organization to increase productivity, based on planning, the coordination of efforts, and the mobilization of the resources, and apply the highest achievements of science, technology, the social sciences, and even art; (2) create a social organization that would subject the interests of the individuals to the common interests of all; it would increase the welfare of all and thus set in motion the social mechanisms of distribution which would generate the submergence of individuals into the common cause, while at the same time providing them (and the community as a whole) with the means to satisfy their basic human needs—means which free man from the degrading "animal conditions of existence." Thus the possibility of achieving socialism was made relative to two scales of reference: (1) the effectiveness of production in the economic system, and (2) the development of egalitarianism as a fundamental condition and element of socialist justice. Those were noble ideas. However, the two aims and the two scales of reference were incompatible, and soon this became evident. The stimulation for production required the introduction of a system of incentives which would reward the innovator's talents, creative thought, and leadership capabilities. Stalin recognized that, and he announced a war against primitive equality and introduced a wide differentiation in rewards for different jobs and for political loyalty. In doing this, he reintroduced the conditions which generate inequality and thus run counter to the fundamental principles of the second scale of reference. In the pursuit of equality, inequality was introduced, and soon it started to grow, reaching monstrous proportions, even though it was not based on private property.*

Socialism and equality in an affluent society were the more advertised and exposed objectives of the industrialization and the organized system growth in the Soviet Union. The less advertised objective was the military buildup. V. I. Lenin once declared: "Large-scale industry is the one and only real basis upon which we can multiply our resources and build a socialist society. Without large factories, such as capitalism has created, without highly developed large-scale industry, socialism is impossible anywhere. . . ."[6] This he repeated on many other occasions. Stalin emphasized other needs. He stressed the importance of industrialization for the military buildup and, generally, to overcome backwardness.

---

* During the so-called "cultural revolution" in China, the alternative course, it seems, was taken. Equality, or at least the outward appearance of it, was maintained and reintroduced at the expense of economic and technological development.

In a speech made before the first All-Union Conference of Managers of Socialist Industry in February 1931, Stalin stated:

> . . . the history of old Russia is the history of defeats due to back-wardness. She was beaten by the Mongol Khans. She was beaten by the Polish-Lithuanian "squires." She was beaten by the Anglo-French capitalists. She was beaten by the Japanese barons. All beat her for her backwardness, for military backwardness, for cultural backward-ness, for governmental backwardness, for industrial backwardness, for agricultural backwardness. . . . They beat her saying: "You are abundant, so we can enrich ourselves at your expense." They beat her saying "You are poor and helpless, so you can be beaten and plundered with impunity." Such is the law of capitalism, to beat the backward and the weak. The jungle law of capitalism. You are back-ward, you are weak, so you are wrong, hence you can be beaten and enslaved. You are mighty, so you are right, hence we must be wary of you. That is why we must no longer be backward.[7]

Now the Soviet Union has become a mighty military and industrial power. Yet the standard of living of its people does not exceed that of Latin America.*

The Bolshevik revolution was a military victory over the White ar-mies. The Red army also crushed the nationalist uprisings in the Ukraine and in Georgia, the uprisings of the nationalist Massavatist movement in Azerbaidjan, and the Dashnak rebellion in Armenia. It suppressed various nationalist movements in Central Asia and in other parts of Soviet Union.

---

* On the standard of living in the U.S.S.R. see J. G. Chapman, *Real Wages in Soviet Russia Since 1928* (Cambridge, Mass.: Harvard University Press, 1963) and M. I. Goldman, *The Soviet Economy: Myth and Reality* (Englewood Cliffs, N.J.: Prentice-Hall, 1968), pp. 50-59. Comparisons on standards of living between the Soviet Union and other countries are difficult to make as the data are not reliable. In my opinion, the standard of living in the Soviet Union or in other East European countries under communist rule could be evaluated fairly and in comparison with the standards of living in other parts of the world only when the consumption of the average worker and civil servant is taken into account. Goldman's assessment seems to reflect well the reality of the standards of living in Soviet Russia. One can get some idea about its present level also from the Soviet literature on the subject. See *Trud i zarabotnaia plata v SSSR* (Moscow, Gos. Izdat Ekon. Lit., 1968). In this collection of articles such data as the following appear: the Soviet citizen who has permission to reside in a major city is entitled to 7-9 square meters of housing. B. M. Sukharevskii in "Zara-botnaia plata i materialnaia zainteresovannost," *op. cit.*, discusses the raise in con-sumption in the U.S.S.R. According to his data, an average person in Soviet Union consumed in 1965: 41 kilos of meat, poultry and bacon; about 250 kilos of milk, cheese and butter, 124 eggs, 12.6 kilos of fish and sea food, 7.1 kilos of fat and oil, 141 kilos of potatoes, 156 kilos of bread, 26.1 meters of all kinds of fabrics (includ-ing materials, cloth linen, napkins, and so forth), 4.1 pieces of underwear, 6.2 pairs of stockings and socks, 2.4 pairs of shoes. For an analysis of the Polish situation, see: A. Tymowski, "Dochody a sposob wydatkowania" *Studia Socjologiczne*, Warsaw, No. 3, 1962.

The Red army introduced and maintained the rule of the Communist Party; Party secretaries were put in command of the army; the commanders of the army were appointed to the Central Committee of the Party. Soviet power has always been based on military rule. After the revolution the Party announced that the country and its people had to be constantly alert because of their capitalist surroundings. Since then the Soviet Union has always considered itself to be in danger. Indeed it has been said that it survived only thanks to the Soviet army. Hence, the army command has great influence on any important political and economic decisions, and the military corps become a privileged stratum in society.

The strength of the army depends on industrialization. Life in the Soviet Union was greatly geared to the needs of the army. The economy, the systems of socialization and education, and the ideology as a whole were and still are subordinated to its needs. The major purpose of industrialization, apart from raising the standard of living and generally building socialism, was and still is to supply the army with weapons and other equipment. Shortages are simply normal in Soviet stores. One may not be able to buy needles, nails, teapots, household utensils, or cloth; butter, meat, or other foodstuffs are often lacking. A car is out of question for the majority of citizens. The means of eradicating shortages in the market have not yet been devised in the Soviet Union. The industry first and above all serves the army. Some experts estimate that about 40 per cent of the national output is absorbed by the army. It is certainly correct in regard of the output of the industries and national income. One cannot make any judgments as to whether these evaluations are correct on the basis of the analysis of the Soviet state budget. Nonmilitary branches of the state and society bear many of the military expenses under different labels. Research on new weaponry is conducted in the institutes of the Soviet Academy of Sciences in numerous agencies of space exploration, chemical industry, and so forth. Prices even on some nonmilitary commodities are below real costs (for instance, radios, transportation, and the like). Prices on weaponry and military equipment could be set by the government practically at will and regardless of the real costs, invested labor, and materials. Industries cannot go bankrupt in the Soviet Union. The product is simply transferred from one governmental department to another.

How was the "march" to industrialism organized? It will be answered by a number of contrasting comparisons.

a. Goal Orientation in Society Interaction

In Western societies goal orientation is toward the primacy of individual achievement. In the Soviet Union and Soviet-like states it is officially and programatically toward the collective achievement of the society. It is claimed that through a general improvement each individual will also improve his own well-being. In practice, however, each member of the society struggles to use his position within the general setup for his own benefit. The higher he is in the social structure, the more he can accomplish in it. On the highest level there are men who can do the most. Stalin's dictatorship, where the whole state and everything in it became practically his own estate, is an extreme case. Yet there are no institutional mechanisms designated to prevent this from happening again.

b. The Political System

The political systems of the two industrial societies—that of the West and that of the Soviet Union and Soviet-like peoples' democracies—are of different kinds. They can be compared by a number of overlapping sets of categories. The Western system is often said to be democratic, pluralistic, and open, while the Soviet system is said to be totalitarian, monolithic, and closed. Using Apter's terminology,[8] we may regard the Western system as belonging to the reconciliation type, while the Soviet system may be regarded as a mobilization system in the process of transition into a bureaucratic system.* Both these systems, as all political systems, are structures of conflict within a setup of consensus. However, within the Western systems, conflict, consensus, and dissent are normal and legitimate forms of interconnection. Hence, Western societies are endogenously open. The Soviet-type systems tend rather to be endogenously closed.** They are developed on the lines of a growing semiorganismic structure. As in the case of other political structures, the Soviet system is bursting with conflicts. In the past the leadership tended to attribute any important conflict to activities of externally inspired subversion. The Party was claiming that causes for conflicts are absent in the harmonious entity of the Soviet Union. Purges were said to be therefore necessary to purge the society from enemies which disrupt the natural harmony. Today, however, differences in opinion and in interests are often coming into the open. Institutionalized agencies to voice divergencies in opinion or

---

* Apter, in "Notes for a Theory of Non-Democratic Representation," p. 306, proposes to differentiate political systems in the following way: "Systems emphasizing ethical (consummatory) values and hierarchical authority result in 'mobilization' systems. Those emphasizing concrete (instrumental) values and pyramidal authority are 'reconciliation' systems. Systems with instrumental values and hierarchical authority can be called 'bureaucratic' systems. Those with consummatory values and pyramidal authority can be called 'theocratic' systems."

** A system cannot be absolutely closed. Conflict appears in it regardless of whether it has or does not have legally institutionalized provisions for dissent and conflict. Where such provisions are absent conflict is clandestine, or it is disguised in the form of purges, a struggle with relics of the past, and so forth.

cleavages in interests are still absent. Party committees, especially in the upper part of the structure, occasionally become arenas of bargaining and confrontation of important interest groups. Binding decisions are still coming down from central authorities. The sphere of local initiative is still limited. The leaders are willing, however, nowadays to listen to the advice of experts. Avenues through which important interest groups, though not masses, can exert limited pressure on authorities seem to begin to emerge. Dissenters are still punished severely, though not as mercilessly as in the past. Potential "enemies of people" are not sent to concentration camps on a mass scale anymore. Shortages in consumer goods are still common in the U.S.S.R. and other communist countries, however, generally the standard of living went up. The table below contains the data (in 1971 dollars) comparing the total output of goods and services of the U.S.S.R. and the U.S. in the last twenty years:

	1950	1960	1971
U.S.S.R.	168 bil.	303 bil.	526 bil.
U.S.	503 bil.	690 bil.	1.047 bil.

On the whole, the system is transforming itself into a more bureaucratic order, into a self-perpetuating administration dealing with the allocation of things and men. The Soviet citizens are nowadays not ashamed to openly voice bourgeois aspirations and, as some experts see it, society is on the verge of a new revolution, this time one of rising expectations.

In Western societies the primacy of economic interest prevails. There is an increase in state intervention and regulation even here. More and more state control and even more state entrepreneurship becomes evident. Greater specialization and differentiation generates greater interdependence and need for concerted action. Thus society on the whole and its units and agencies separately, and structures and groups previously relatively independent become engulfed by all kinds of semiorganismic interdependencies. Until now, however, the spheres of economic, political, and other systems permeate each other but remain basically autonomous and not subordinated to single decision-making centers. Perhaps Western societies will become more semiorganismic in the future; At present still great areas of privacy, free initiative, and decision remain open. Soviet-type systems are based on a primacy of politics—strictly speaking, on Party supremacy.

The Growing Societal Systemness

If we compare system growth, we can say that in Western societies it consists basically of the differentiation and *separation* of roles, organizations and systems which are in an increasing *interdependence*. System growth in Soviet societies consists of the differentiation and *subordination* of new roles, organizations, and systems in a *dependence* on the center. In Western societies the changes which transpire from the growing systemness occur in a natural, continuously ongoing process of change which institutionalizes itself in differentiation. In Soviet societies, differentiation, the articulation of new agencies, and the like, occurs in the implementation of orders which come from the center. Private associational activities (excluding those of marriage, or individual friendships, for example) are practically banned. Some experts assume that the Western system could be improved by centralization and subordination to the state; the Soviet system, on the contrary, would have to be decentralized. Conservatives and liberals in the West rather favor maintaining decentralization, while in the Soviet Union they voice approval of more centralization and stiffening state control.

Both the Western and the Soviet systems are orders of disorder and disorders of order at the same time. However, as I pointed out, the process of ordering and disordering in the West occurs in bargaining, in market-type interactions which generate self-organization and self-ordering in a process of legitimate conflict and competition. Systems, organizations, and agencies come into being, they mesh, overlap, come into juxtaposition, fight each other, and confront their interests on their own initiative. True, again there is more regulation from the state now, but basically the essential features of such structures of self-regulation are maintained. In the Soviet system changes can occur only if they are permitted by the center, coming from the top down. New roles—and especially new organizations and agencies—appear upon appointment from the center.* All important political conflicts are clandestine. The Soviet system is formed like a Russian doll; it is wooden and tough; it contains inside it another doll, which contains another smaller doll, and so on. The Communist Party is the all-embracing great doll. It contains, in declining importance and size, the smaller dolls of the subsidiary subordinate organizations and systems embracing the individual. The smaller dolls obviously cannot encompass the larger ones. The order is set up for eternity. No alternatives are given. The state, the economic, and educational systems are but extensions of the Party system; in fact, any organization is an extension of it.** Depending on who is in control of it at any given time, the Party may allow, in some circumstances, the expression of one's own opinions, especially in professional matters; however, any idea or innovation that is suggested

* Of course, each of the strata of the bureaucratic order has its own sphere of competence in implementing the decisions which come from above.
** The only exceptions are churches.

has to be introduced for the sole purpose of strengthening the system. The Party is supreme.* Thus the Dubčeks and other "reformers" who appear from time to time in the Soviet Union and in other Soviet-like countries are allowed to speak up only because they claim that their programs will strengthen the Soviet system, socialism, and the Party. To come forward with the idea of introducing a competitive Party system is regarded in Soviet-type societies as a crime. The Party permeates all organizations and systems by a network of Party cells. The center transmits its decisions and instructions down to the subordinate structures and units. Exactly as in some theories on political systems, the center is fed with demands and support. The demands are very modest and exactly as programmed by the center; the support is very strong, exactly as required by the center. In either case, the dose is manipulated from the center through the interiorization of proper life attitudes and behavior, and through terror spread by the security agencies. Another input—that of relaying information—is also required by the center. The Soviet system is a mechanism which transforms such delations into decisions. We are told that a system may be jammed with demands, especially if demands do not receive enough support. In the Soviet Union or Soviet-like system such occurrences are practically impossible. Demands are minimized, and support—or at least the visible signs of support—is maximized upon instruction from the center. The mechanism becomes jammed (if such a paradigm is sufficiently explanatory), mostly as a result of the intense struggle for power in the center. Sometimes in such cases, the top dignitaries must seek real support from the comrades in command of the lower levels and strata of the Party but not from the entire population. Such a situation occurred after the death of Stalin and during the rule of Khrushchev, and it has happened on a number of occasions in the Soviet-like states.

Politics in Western systems is the art of recruiting supporters. Politics in Soviet systems is the craft of eliminating and exterminating those who are one's real or potential enemies. Both the Western and the Soviet systems are founded on the basis of representation. Both have a structure of parliamentary institutions, elections, and so forth. From the constitutional point of view the Soviet system is actually a hierarchy of elected councils. Both systems claim to be democratic. The mechanisms of representation of the Western-type systems are mostly not as effective as people would like them to be. The representative, the member of parliament, congress, senate, or other institutions of representation has at the same time to rep-

* In some of the Soviet-like states the system is formally a multiparty one; however, the other parties are subsidiary agencies of the Communist Party. They do not compete with it for power, and their programs are designed as implementations of the ruling Party's platform.

resent his electorate which is as a rule divided on many issues. He has to represent the party of which he is a member, and in Europe the party often tells him what kind of a position he has to take. He is under pressure from those groups and organizations which financed his campaign and rendered other types of support. Yet he also has to express his own views. Critics say that the influence of the average man on the decision-making of governments is very limited indeed. That is true. There are no such problems in the Soviet-type systems. Ninety-nine per cent of the citizens usually vote, and 99 per cent of them usually vote only for the candidates nominated by the Party. A member of the parliament in the Soviet Union does not need to ask his electorate what they are in favor of. He knows that they are for the Party and for its decisions, and so they will continue to be now and in the future. The sessions of parliament are only ceremonial happenings, anyway. All important decisions are made in the narrow circle of the top Party leadership.

d. The Economic System

In both the Western and the Soviet economic systems, the organization of production is, strictly speaking, geared toward the maximization of economic output. The economic system of the Western societies is an arena of action of mostly privately owned corporations, industries, and business enterprises, acting on their own behalf and at their own risk. The production of goods is designed for profit, and it is directed toward the market. The market situation and supply and demand are essentially the major mechanisms which regulate what is produced for sale. Of course, other factors also affect the market situation—for instance, state controls, subsidies, duties, the situation in the labor market, and the like. In short, the economy is an arena of competitive interactions between the many parties which are seeking profits and sources of income on the one hand, and the commodities needed for consumption on the other. In the Soviet economic system, the production is ordered by the state, and it is controlled by the Party. All enterprises are as a rule owned by the state. The state (strictly speaking, the Party) decides what is to be produced, with what quality, and at what price. The state is the sole monopolistic employer. The more important jobs in all fields are under the management of their respective Party committees. The state owns nearly all business enterprises, the wholesale and retail stores, restaurants, coffee houses, and even the equipment of peddlers. It provides the citizens with recreation. Bargaining over prices, wages, or salaries is practically nonexistent. Strikes are banned. The function of the trade unions is to mobilize the workers to increase their productivity. Yet in the Soviet-type societies there is one other, and quite important, secondary economic system. It is semilegal, but mostly it operates clandestinely. It consists not only of the black market, but also partly of the kolkhoz market where agricultural products and all kinds of commodities are on sale that cannot be obtained in government stores. It consists of a multitude of transactions illegally conducted by governmental officials and employees, sometimes even with the object of maintaining government factories and institutions in running order. So-called "deficit" goods—goods on which there are shortages—can be obtained there. Some make millions in such transactions. The prisons are full of people caught while involved in them.*

In Western systems, although economics and politics affect each other, they are still basically separate spheres. If either one is more of a determining factor, it is certainly economics that determines many political situations. In the Soviet system, the economy is subordinate to politics. Not only are industrialization and economic development thought to be means by which to implement ideological aims, but the political elite—strictly speaking, the Party committees on each level of economic organization—are in control of the respective economic institutions: the Central Committee of the Party controls the whole country; regional committees are in the regions, district committees are in the districts, and factory or office committees are in each enterprise or office. Thus the political decision-making center also acts as the economic decision-making center. In fact, the congresses of the Party and the meetings of the Central Committee and the lower committees are busy mostly with economic decisions. However, that does not mean that they are composed of people who are qualified to solve economic problems.

One final important difference between the Western- and Soviet-type economies must be mentioned. Soviet economic development is planned. Plans are set up to specify targets which are to be achieved in all branches of economic life, and to allocate the financial and technical means for their implementation. They are set up as the means for rational direction and management, and for the mobilization of resources and personnel. (I am not going to discuss their effectiveness in this study. This is a topic for more competent students of economics.) What must be stressed here,

* M. L. Goldman, in *The Soviet Economy: Myth and Reality* (p. 102), after some Soviet sources points out: "After all, although they made up only 3 percent of all cultivated land area, in 1964 the private plots accounted for 42 percent of the country's milk and meat production, 73 percent of the egg output, and 60 percent of the potato harvest." Yet it must be remembered that such plots are barely tolerated in the Soviet Union as relics from the past, as a menace to the economy, and as a dangerous source for the regeneration of capitalism. Thus peasants who own them are allowed to work on them only after their work in the kolkhoz. As a rule they are not allowed to maintain more than one cow and a very limited number of chickens and pigs. They are, of course, not allowed to hire laborers or to expand.

however, is that plans are often detrimental to the initiative and flexibility of action which are badly needed to solve the virtually unsolvable problems of the socialist economies of the Soviet type.

The modern capitalist economic system differs substantially and in many respects from the nineteenth- and early twentieth-century system.[9] However, many of the earlier characteristics still remain valid. Schumpeter has written:

> Bourgeois society has been cast in a purely economic mold: its foundations, beams and beacons are all made of economic material. The building faces toward the economic side of life. Prizes and penalties are measured in pecuniary terms. Going up and going down means making and losing money. . . . The promises of wealth and the threats of destitution that it holds out, it redeems with ruthless promptitude. Wherever the bourgeois way of life asserts itself sufficiently to dim the beacons of other social worlds, these promises are strong enough to attract the large majority of supernormal brains and to identify success with business success. . . . Spectacular prizes much greater than would have been necessary to call forth the particular effort are thrown to a small minority of winners, thus propelling much more efficaciously than a more equal and more "just" distribution would, the activity of that large majority of businessmen who receive in return very modest compensation or nothing or less than nothing, and yet do their utmost because they have the big prizes before their eyes and overrate their chances of doing equally well.[10]

Veblen[11] and other writers have asserted that the capitalist economy is wasteful. Many writers have pointed out that both directly and indirectly it "sabotages" production; it is based on injustices and generates injustices; it is geared to the fulfillment of the needs of the privileged few and not of the needy masses. It is an instrument of depreciation and of keeping down the level of the material and the spiritual life of the people. It sacrifices the industrial art to the production of luxuries (and it can be added at this point that it wastes its resources on war equipment and armaments), and it thereby forces both the talented and the mass producers to waste their time and efforts on producing useless things which satisfy the frivolities of the leisure class. It wastes much of the effort and money that are needed on advertising, persuasion, or distribution through a long chain of agencies. It is an instrument for extracting money from the poor in return for useless and often harmful commodities and services which only degrade people. It produces moral devastation, and the like. P. A. Baran and P. M. Sweezy add that the modern monopoly capitalist economy produces much surplus.

The logic of the situation is as follows: if total income grows at an accelerating rate, then a larger and larger share has to be devoted to investment; and conversely, if a larger and larger share is devoted to investment, total income must grow at an accelerating rate. What this implies, however, is nonsensical from an economic standpoint. It means that a larger and larger volume of producer goods would have to be turned out for the sole purpose of producing a still larger and larger volume of producer goods in the future.[12]

On another page they add: "Since surplus which cannot be absorbed will not be produced, it follows that the normal state of the monopoly capitalist economy is stagnation. . . ."[13] It is even worse than that, Baran and Sweezy tell us, because even if production increases, the mounting surplus is wasted on advertising and civilian and military government spending. In sum, a capitalist economy is wasteful, since it is unable to utilize its potential, and most of what it produced is on wasteful ends.

There is a saying in the Soviet Union: "Capitalist societies are based on the exploitation of men by men, and in our society it is just the opposite." Soviet economy is planned. It is said to be geared to the needs of the masses. It certainly does not waste its efforts on advertising. It is concerted and goal-directed. It is centralized and subordinated to the political needs of the Party. It is, however, at least as wasteful as the capitalist economy, although for different reasons. In the first place, it wastes an even greater proportion of its output on military spending and government administration, because its main purpose, after all, is to fulfill those needs. In the second place it produces for the needs of the citizens. It is wasteful because it is inefficient and redundant. Utilizing cheap labor, it produces commodities of a very low quality at an enormous cost, but since it has a monopoly it forces the consumer to buy them anyway. The consumer has no choice. It is wasteful because it is made rigid by planning, by superfluous administration and controls, and by absurd administrative rules based on the principle of total mistrust and the assumption that the society is constituted not of citizens but of big and petty thiefs. It is wasteful because its bureaucratic rules kill any flexibility of action, make any initiative sterile, and kill the will for improvements. It is directed toward the extraction of a maximum amount of work for minimum pay, in a situation where the workers have no recourse to any organizations which can defend their rights. Yet there are also great achievements in such a system. In a short span of time, the Soviet Union and other Soviet-like states were transformed into modern industrial societies. This has been achieved through enormous sacrifices, as a result of maintaining a near subsistence standard of living for the masses. It has been achieved in defiance of the absurdity of the bureaucratic order and the senseless use of the economy to fulfill absurd, often maniacal ideological and political aims and tasks. Centralization destroys much initiative and invention. It may be an extremely effective instrument to harness concerted action, or to mobilize resources and people, but when a decision is wrong, this setup rapidly spreads disaster over enormous territories in a most disruptive, devastating way. It does, however, have the potential to recover, again at the price of enormous sacrifices. The Russian, Polish, Czech, and Hungarian people pay for such experiments and the well-being of the new leisure class.

The Soviet system claims to be socialist—the realization of the vision and theory of Marx and Engels. Yet, in reality, it has nothing in common with either classic Marxism or with humanistic socialism. Neither of these anticipated the rigid centralized states which serve only the purpose of existence for its own sake and for the elite which is in control. Both were theories designed to elevate man to higher levels of humanity, not to degrade him into the status of pawn and robot.

e. Social Stratification

A contemporary analysis of societies cannot be satisfying without a comparison of their social stratifications. It is very difficult, however, to discuss and compare the stratification of the Soviet society with other social structures. While there are many good studies of the class structure and social stratification of Western societies, studies on stratification of the Soviet society and other societies in Communist countries are few and usually not sufficiently exhaustive.[14]

As a matter of fact, such studies cannot be published within the Soviet Union or in Poland, Czechoslovakia, or Hungary. To characterize societies in these countries as stratified is against the ideology of the Party. At most, sociologists writing on stratification there were allowed to indicate that some functional differentiation must inevitably exist under Communist rule as well; that it may have the appearance of a hierarchy; and further, that if this occasionally changes into a hierarchical order with privileges for those who occupy its upper positions, it is a deviation rather than the rule.

The Soviet and other East European societies under Communist rule are stratified in many respects, and by different social, economic, and political mechanisms than by capitalist societies. Therefore, concepts of class and social stratification established in studies of societies completely different than the Communist ones cannot be effectively applied to the analysis of the social structure of the U.S.S.R. The Soviet and other Communist societies respectively are becoming increasingly transformed into huge bureaucratic orders. Positions within these bureaucracies determine the position and status of the individual in the hierarchical order of the society as well. The upper strata of the Party bureaucracy constitute the controlling top level of the hierarchy of social stratification. Some other positions in various hierarchies, such as the army, intellectual life, and science, often involve high incomes and privileges similar to those in the upper level of the Party. Yet the Soviet elite, or upper strata, is certainly not a class in the same sense as the upper or middle classes of the capitalist societies. Indeed, it has its own separate subculture different from that of the working class. As many data indicate, it is a separate strata which increasingly tends to perpetuate itself as such. In the past, membership in the Party and especially holding a position in the Party apparatus were the springboards into the various channels of mobility in society. Today this has changed considerably, and education has become very important in the acquisition of higher positions in society. Thus, one must carry two cards in order to move easily and quickly into the upper strata of the Soviet hierarchies (including that of the Party): the Party membership card and the university diploma.

3. The Case of Japan

Japan is the only country in Asia which is as highly industrialized as Western Europe, the United States, or the Soviet Union. Yet it is still another case of industrialization and of growing systemness, however different from those described earlier.

What is peculiar about Japanese industrialization?* Experts tell us the following:

> The study of the modernization of Japan is inevitably that of the interplay of external and indigenous events; it is compounded of culture change and of culture contact. While on the one hand we may feel we have the advantage of knowing the nature and the strength of modernizing impulses which impinged upon Japan from outside, it is no simple task to identify the interaction between these impulses and the Japanese matrix upon which they played.[15]

The process started after the Meiji restoration of 1868. What followed, though, actually had its roots in the "feudal mentality" and traditions of the past. Three traditions are often mentioned in Japan as being especially important in enhancing and facilitating the process of industrialization and the adoption of modernity: (1) the existence of a central bureaucratic authority above the fragmented feudal polity; (2) the militaristic

---

* The writer has never been to Japan and has never had a chance to study the Japanese society thoroughly.

traditions and aspirations, and (3) the rise to influence and power of the merchant class.

> Since the lines of cleavage in Japanese society were vertical as well as horizontal, they enabled a section of the agrarian ruling class to detach itself from the Tokugawa system and put through a revolution from above. The foreign threat was decisive in this connection. Under its unifying force, the new government acted in such a way as to preserve the privileges of a small segment of the élite, open up opportunities for others, and ensure national survival.[16]

From 1868 onward, the new rulers of Japan, with the support of a great part of the Japanese society, were engaged in the continuous building of a modern centralized state and army. The policy and action were prompted by external threats, originally from China, later from Russia, and at the same time by the advent of the West armed with modern technology. Both the modern national state and the modern army could only have been elevated on the basis of an industrial society. Industrialization became a national task and the government that inspired it found a good response in the various sections of the Japanese society.

> . . . Meiji policy amounted to using the peasant as a source of capitalist accumulation. In turn this required opening the peasant economy even wider to commercial influences and offsetting some of the strains incurred thereby through efforts to incorporate the peasants into a cohesive body politic. Dismounting feudalism from above was not so much an aim or a policy in its own right as a means to other ends.[17]

Education spread rapidly and it was willingly accepted. It further enhanced an interest in learning, studying, entrepreneurship, and invention. The Japanese system of education disciplined and promoted an attitude of "conscious learning," and it produced a citizen who was inclined to respond well to "further training, be it in a conscript army, in a factory, or at lectures arranged by his village agricultural association."[18] Education, religion, tradition, nationalism, and the pursuit of money and wealth were combined together as a service of reverence to the emperor, his state, and his policies. Through industrialization, wide programs of education, and spreading of urbanization Japan become transformed into a modern industrial nation at an unprecedented speed. The goals defined by the Emperor were supported widely as those of the nation in general, and of the citizens individually. Thus modernity became a continuation of a tradition which was rooted in antiquity. Capitalism was imposed on top of the feudal structure. It merged with it and absorbed it as a culture. After the Second World War the principle of competitive interaction which industrialization had established earlier in the sphere of economics was transferred also to politics. Japan became a Western-type capitalist society, but retained the spirit of traditions transmitted from the past.

4. The Case of Africa

Sub-Saharan Black Africa is now in the incipient stage of industrialization. To be sure, industrialization proper has started in only a few places on the continent, and industrial enterprises, especially large and complex ones, are few—mostly in mining. Industries which produce machines have not yet been created at all. Africa must face the consequences of industrialization which have already happened elsewhere before it can properly industrialize itself. In Africa those consequences are of a kind different from the consequences faced by the now industrialized world. In a sense, colonialism was the child of European industrialization. Colonial rule and what is called acculturational modernization[19] followed it immediately, and then came the colonial struggle for independence. European industrialization (including the U.S. and the U.S.S.R.) brought other fruits to Africa: modern science and technology, modern statal organization and administration, modern education, the products of the mass culture, and so forth. They most surely affect Africa, and they change her, they most surely produce new societal, economic, and political structures, and new systems of interaction which overlap, mesh, and grow toward greater complexity. Africa has to adopt the consequences of industrialization in order to start her own industrialization. Who leads the march to industrialism? What is the purpose of the march? How is the march organized in Africa? These questions will be answered in more detail in a later section of this book. At this point, they will be handled concisely, for the purpose of a comparative analysis of the different modes of industrialization and societal systems growth.

Industrialization—and, more generally, modernization—is, broadly speaking, organized from above in Sub-Saharan Africa, by the governments of the independent states. The elite which is leading and organizing the march is composed of the leaders of the nationalist struggle for independence, the intellectuals, and the top civil servants. The indigenous class of entrepreneurs is still extremely small.[20] Industries and businesses are either state owned, or they belong to foreign entrepreneurs. The purpose of the march could be defined as follows: (a) to buttress the political independence through economic development and nation-building; (b) to raise the economic output of each country—starting with agriculture and the mining industries—in order to establish sources of capital accumulation and raise the standard of living on the continent as a whole;

(c) to create "societal infrastructures" for further developments by spreading education and technical knowledge, building universities, and promoting their own scientific research. Some industrialization proper is under way right now, but only implementation of these goals will elevate a springboard for a wide industrialization and transformation of the continent in a later stage. Thus Sub-Saharan Africa is struggling to pass in only a few decades the road of technological transformation and systems growth that took Europe several centuries, while at the same time trying to retain the indigenous values and culture which are deeply rooted in the African tradition.

Africa is seeking to adopt the European, American, and Soviet experience in building political institutions, organizing economies, building industries, developing agriculture, and widening access to education and health services. Even elements from the various ideologies are being borrowed. However, this is not a blind transplantation of European institutions on African soil. As a rule, African countries do not want to become either small Americas, or imitations of France and England, or Soviet-type republics. True, some adopt more from the West, and others from the Soviet Union. On the whole, however, Africa is attempting to combine elements from all achievements and remake them to suit African conditions. Practically any innovation introduced in Africa from Europe is soon permeated by the indigenous culture, as Bronislaw Malinowski described a long time ago. It neither becomes a part of the traditional Africa, nor exactly resembles its model. That is why so many institutions in Sub-Saharan Africa are syncretic. Many institutions are now in the process of remaking themselves. Of course, there are some institutions or achievements which have to be adopted and maintained exactly as they were created and are developed along lines similar to their European parallels. The state, the party, the administration are erected as general, all-encompassing system-frames, to be filled out with a growing systemness from the bottom up. This is the policy of African socialism which is promoted in various versions in most of the newly independent African states. The idea is to enlarge the scale of the traditional communities, so as to transform them into nationwide structures. The slogan is fraternity; the target is a detribalization which still retains the value of traditions. African leaders express the hope that such growth is possible and that it will eventually engulf the ongoing transformation introduced from above. There is a great deal of utopia in such calculations and ideological expectations, yet this is what is now being sought.

Nation-building is being accomplished through the implementation of the above transformations and in other endeavors as well. National histories are being written; pride in African traditions, culture, and values is invoked; a national consciousness is being created which absorbs the tribal loyalties and enhances the spirit of belonging to the new nation. Major efforts are being made to stimulate agricultural production and to spread education. Roads are built; self-help schemes and cooperatives are organized in the pursuit of such developments. In most of the new African nations economic development and the social change which is related to it are subjected to planning. Specially established planning committees, ministries, and other agencies deal with such policies. Great expectations are attached to planning, too. It is thought that planning should be instrumental at least in achieving the following aims: spelling out the direction of coordinated actions (especially in the field of economics); organizing concerted actions, and mobilizing resources and men; and obtaining foreign credits and aid.

The process of organized development in Africa is still in its initial stages. It is an enormously difficult task to erect modern structures and independent systems of governments which generate differentiated and functionally specialized roles and organizations out of assemblages of particularistically oriented, diffuse tribal units, and to do this in a situation where capital is lacking, skilled personnel are scarce, wide experience in personnel management is nonexistent, and many social and political problems accumulated from the past have to be solved simultaneously and in a short time. Never has such a gigantic endeavor been undertaken. No wonder that setbacks and disappointments occur along with achievements.[21]

5. The Perspective of Convergence

We derive a few final comments from the comparative analyses of the societal and political consequences of industrialization in various parts of the world. Industrial and industrializing societies display some common features. A set of basic similar systems, roles, and institutions which perform specific kinds of differentiated and essential societal functions appear to be immanently engendered in societal interactions of any industrial or industrializing society. Thus, all such societies have governments, elections, political parties, parliaments, networks of mass media communication, and so forth. All have national economies. All have at least state bureaucracies and administrations. The more advanced industrially do as a rule have more complex bureaucracies, and, generally speaking, they have more systems, more systemness, and more differentiation within a more complex interdependence. The industrial men who live in such societies (and, in the case of industrializing societies, the men who have already become involved in the modern ways of living) seem to have certain essential common characteristics or qualities, regardless of their nationalities or dwelling places. They are products of standardized similar courses and procedures of education which are similar throughout the world. If cultural and ideological peculiarities may be put aside, these procedures inculcate into modern men's mind a more or less equivalent, condensed societal experience and knowledge no matter where they are. Be it in the Soviet Union, Poland, France, Britain, the United States, Ghana, or Japan, a student in school or in the university learns similar basic facts and methods. An appropriate document certifies that he has learned the facts, methods, techniques, or skills to perform a definite job, and that he has obtained a definite level of education which has an equivalent anywhere in the world. Of course, the education may be better here than there, but generally, a qualification obtained in one society implies that the person will be able to handle a similar job in other societies regardless of the differences in political regimes. Industrial men seem to be alike everywhere. They seem to display similar needs, life goals, and behaviors. (This is, of course, when cultural and ideological distinctions are not being considered.) Industrial, and even industrializing societies all over the world face some similar problems: delinquency, loneliness in mass societies, wide dissatisfaction with the quality of life, impingement of the standardized mass culture on the individual, pollution, and so forth. In short, men are alike in many respects. However, the ordering of systems and the nature of interdependencies within and between systems of industrial societies differ strongly. Societies with similar technologies which to some extent require similar structures of management; societies which have some institutions in common; societies run from a point of view of highly abstract, comparative-functional analysis by similar looking organizations, and hierarchies—such societies can still be essentially different. Similar or identical types of weapons and technologies (and sometimes even similar organizational methods) are used in the pursuit of diverse aims and serve societies which adhere to divergent ideologies and are of a substantively different nature. The assertion seems to be trivial and self-evident. Yet one may ask the following: even though societies differ now, is it not possible that they will not differ so much in the future? People and even experts on other societies often display ethnocentric tendencies—and not only when they analyze Third World nations. So even though it is a trivial point, it still seems pertinent enough to be mentioned—especially in view of recently circulating theories which minimize the importance of such differences.

Some students of modern industrial societies believe that we are approaching the era of convergence[22]—the era when the hitherto differing orders of systems, states, and societies will as a result of industrialization and its consequences become very alike, and hence (they claim) convergent; maybe they will even be fused into one worldwide order of a new society. The argument runs that this will be more rational, more economical. It will eliminate a great deal of useless competition. It will end many of the international conflicts, much of the spending on warfare (especially highly expensive nuclear armaments and related defense), wars, and many other miseries. As a proof of an ongoing process that is bringing mankind into such an era, comparisons are especially made of the development of the Soviet Union and the United States. Many similarities are found. Some ignore the differences or say that these will eventually become less important, and on the basis of the common features of industrial societies they see at least a possibility of convergence.

The contention of an approaching convergence was originally based on the assumption that the Soviet Union, after achieving a high degree of industrialization, would have to bend to the requirements of rationality and hence change its highly centralized, inefficient, economically wasteful order into a more decentralized and democratic one—into an order more like that in Western societies, although private property would probably not be reintroduced in the Soviet Union. Originally such ideals circulated as ambivalent well-wishing for the Soviet and other East European peoples. When a theory emerged out of the hope, the economic, cultural, social, political, historical, and all other differences between the West and the Soviet-bloc countries were minimized. Similarities in industrial management (often rather general), in daily needs, and in the mentality of the average man in both systems were exposed, and the hope obtained the shape of a probability.

Recent events in the Soviet Union and other East European countries have shown that such expectations are indeed premature, if they are at all founded on fact. Attempts to introduce some democratization, decentralization, or liberty in Czechoslovakia were crushed. Not much has changed in the Soviet Union and other East European countries in regard to political and intellectual freedom, economic efficiency, and decentralization even following long discussions. In Poland some degree of leniency toward those who dared to initiate discussions on the need of change was suppressed. In Czechoslovakia purges are currently taking place. The regimes remain stiff and rigid though some changes both in the economic life and the organization of the control of the Party and the state over the life of citizens have taken place. The systems in communist countries remain to be centralized though less by means of political links and more by means of bureaucratic subordination engulfing the entire society.

Some convergence theorists maintain that convergence will still come about, but for different reasons. The argument is that for the sake of rationality, Western societies will have to become more centralized, and eventually their economies will have to become more coordinated. It is said that in the capitalist economy the state already interferes a great deal. In many countries of Western Europe it already owns important enterprises or branches of industries, and the communications and mass media networks. More government control and interference and more penetration by the state into the ways of living of the individual citizens are envisaged, and with it more concerted economies, less competition, and less extravagant individualism. The belief is that the tendency in the world is toward uniformity. People will become more alike, societies and states will become more alike, and thus convergence will be possible, if it is not yet imminent; it will ensue naturally. Some convergence theorists agree that the prospects of living in such centralized states of the future seem to be rather grim.

In such assumptions there is plenty of exaggeration and even more poorly founded speculation. First, even if societies and states become alike, they may still continue to compete and be in conflict. Second, there is a greater probability for the parallel continuation of a number of diverse orders of systems, of differing states and societies on a similar level of industrialization. Is it not true that differing societies in the past also shared some functional similarities and were to a degree alike? For instance, it may be argued that peasants living in similar climatic conditions but in divergent societies, under different rulers and in different structures of social relations, performed similar jobs and were mentally and functionally alike. Certainly there is more intercommunication and exchange now. It is true that modern people are even more culturally alike, that bureaucracies are everywhere, and that the average man could but very little influence the course of important government decisions. Yet, in different countries—and especially in different blocs of countries—the modern man lives in totally different orders of systems and economic, social, and political relations. And why should this change? Considering how redundant, and inefficient the Soviet economy is, and how long it has been unable to solve the many problems plaguing the Soviet population from the onset of the Soviet state, why should we believe that a worldwide, centralized economic and political system, even with the help of all the computers in the world, will do better than a world system composed of member units acting on their own behalf? Besides, let us not forget that many of the convergence theories are designed more as means by which to criticize the world of today than as unbiased attempts to predict the future.

On the other hand, however, it is true that in spite of the great differences in the political and economic orders, countries, secieties, and people are more interdependent now than they were in the past, and in the future they may become even more interdependent. In a sense, they share the common fate of living together and of being destroyed in case of a nuclear war. Yet, should war be averted, the prospects seem rather to be for a multilinear, parallel, divergent development of differing societies which bear some similarities, share some common features, and have some similar and comparable institutions. What seems also to be evident now, and what may also proceed at an accelerated pace in the future, is differentiation within the growing interdependence on the international level. Diverse sociopolitical cultures of the world will probably be increasingly involved in more interactions and intercommunications and more differentiation on overlapping levels will result. Whether the units will differ totally or share some features, they will certainly be more interdependent. Thus growing systemness ensues on the international level and assumes international dimensions. At the moment it is rather an interdependence of coexistence with frequent occurrences of conflict and tension. Some of the participants in that interdependence are related in complementary interaction. It is not, however—at least it is still not—a beginning of the appearance of an international world-wide semiorganismic intersocietal system.

6. Current Trends and Changes in the Soviet Union

Nikita Sergeievitch Khrushchev, the former First Secretary and Prime Minister of the Soviet Union, once said that there is no point in having socialism in the U.S.S.R. if the Soviet worker will not have a standard of living higher than that enjoyed by the American worker. Khrushchev was known as a pragmatic, practical Party boss. Yet he was also probably the last idealist among the ruling élite of the Soviet Union who sincerely believed in the possibility of practical implementation of the principles and ends of Marxism in the Soviet Union. He wanted the Soviet Union to become not only the mightiest military and political power in the world, and further, the leader in space exploration, but also to become the country of the greatest abundance in the world, and simultaneously a society based on truly egalitarian principles with equal rights and access to the abundance for all (except for some national minorities that he personally was not too fond of).

In future textbooks of history he will probably be remembered as the man who delivered the speech against the "cult of personality" in the

Soviet Union, as the one who thereby initiated the process of de-Staliniza-
tion in this country and in other East European societies under communist
rule. He will be mentioned as the man who released hundreds of thousands of prisoners from concentration camps, as the man who suppressed
the Hungarian Revolution against Soviet domination. He will be recalled
as the leader who provoked the confrontation of the Cuban crisis, and as
the one who introduced the idea of coexistence and competition between
the capitalist and the Soviet socioeconomic systems. Khrushchev was the
man who attempted various policies and campaigns in his striving to make
the Soviet Union both abundant and egalitarian at the same time.

He initiated the campaign of settling the virgin lands in Siberia and
Kazakhstan, the aim of which was to solve the problems of chronic shortages of agricultural foodstuffs in the Soviet Union, to increase the output
of the agricultural sector of the economy for industrial needs, and to fill
the areas scarcely populated in the U.S.S.R. (especially those close to the
Chinese border). He was especially concerned with the decline of the
revolutionary morale of the Soviet youth, and he hoped that mobilizing
the youth to settle in the distant noninhabited lands would regenerate this
spirit.

He failed in these efforts. The young people lacked the revolutionary
consciousness expected of them. The idea of devoting their lives to the
conquest of the virgin lands was abhorrent to them. They preferred to
enjoy the comfortable life in big cities. They were mobilized and sent to
the virgin lands by the Party and the Komsomol (the Communist Youth
Organization). This, however, was not an adequate solution since the
settlements established in the virgin lands soon obtained the character
of forced labor camps. The climate and the environmental conditions in
Siberia and Kazakhstan were harsh; rain did not fall periodically, changing these lands into vast deserts. Khrushchev's propaganda and the machinery supplied by the government could neither change these conditions nor bolster the morale of the young Soviet generation. Further, by
this plan of action, Khrushchev enraged the Chinese, who for a long time
had had an eye on these lands, which they had hoped one day would
become theirs.

After his visit to America, Khrushchev decided that the secret to the
abundance of foodstuffs in capitalist countries was found in the extensive
growing of corn. He hoped that by introducing more corn cultivation into
the Soviet Union he would be able to increase the number of cattle and
raise better breeds of them and subsequently produce more milk and
meat, thereby finally solving the problem of chronic shortages of these
products in the Soviet stores. Khrushchev ordered many of the collective
farms and state agricultural enterprises all over the Soviet Union to re-

linquish the traditionally planted crops and instead to raise corn. He was so confident of success that he announced in a lengthy speech that in ten years there would be an abundance of meat and milk in the Soviet Union, and that the standard of living of the Soviet citizenry would excel that of the West. Again he failed, however, in his ambitious undertakings. Instead of increasing the output of agricultural production, his experiments and innovations caused a catastrophic decline in the output of all kinds of agricultural products all over the Soviet Union. There was not enough grain for the coming year; peasants began to slaughter their cows which could not be kept throughout the winter. Khrushchev did not blame the enemies of the people for his failures, and he did not let his people starve and suffer from lack of bread as Stalin did. Instead, he blamed the weather, and bought large quantities of wheat from France and Canada.

As Lenin had been in the past, Khrushchev was annoyed by the growing bureaucracy and inequality in the Soviet Union. He was annoyed by the inability of the Party to eradicate the persistence among the Soviet people of what was regarded as petty bourgeois mentality manifested especially in desires for individual riches and for better living conditions. He wanted to bring to a halt the growth of the new privileged élite strata in the Soviet Union. He was worried especially about the attitudes of Soviet youth, who were prone to imitate the life style of youth in the West, attributing great importance to dress and recreation. He felt that they were not sufficiently serious in expressing their ideological attachment, that they showed too frequently a lack of respect for seniority and for the sacred traditions of the Revolution. Khrushchev felt that the Soviet leaders had to cope immediately with these "dangerous" tendencies. Thus he introduced new rules of recruitment in the universities, which are the entrance ways to the ladders of mobility in the Soviet society. He proclaimed that his aim was to give an equal opportunity to all young people, and to that end he introduced rules which were supposed to equalize the chances of those from the intelligentsia with the sons and daughters of workers and peasants. Young people, after completing their high school education, were supposed to take a job, the best being one that required manual work, and only after a few years thus spent, to resume their education in the universities. Alternatively, they were expected to work while studying in factories and workshops, and the universities were ordered to change their syllabuses accordingly. Factories were ordered to employ and to train students to operate machines. However, Soviet bureaucrats, detesting manual work, abhorred the idea of their sons and daughters becoming factory workers. To factory managers, the students were a menace who did not contribute in any way to the increase of productivity. The students were undisciplined and wasted both a lot of raw materials and the time of the supervisors who had to be especially assigned to them. To operate workshops in the universities was both expensive and wasteful. The university administrations hated the scheme since it burdened them with too many new duties. Experts felt that students should study in order to become good specialists in their own fields, not waste time on training which they would never use later on. Needless to say, Khrushchev also failed in this endeavor.

A number of other reforms were undertaken under Khrushchev. The privileges and enormous incomes of some of the upper groups of the bureaucracy were reduced. Measures were taken to improve the lot of the lowest income group. The kolkhozniks received better pay for their products. Economists were allowed to discuss modest economic reforms of the Soviet economy.

Finally, Khrushchev came forward with the idea of creating a two—instead of a one—Party machine within the structure of the Communist Party. A separate Party apparatus was to deal with the matters of industrial and urban organization. The other one was to be responsible solely for agricultural developments. He believed that such a reform would enable the Party management to become more specialized and efficient. Even though these intentions were not aimed at the transformation of the single party into a two-Party system, the members of the higher Soviet bureaucracy felt extremely endangered by this initiative and its unpredictable consequences.

Khrushchev was removed and his reforms were abandoned. Tough "realists" were put in charge of the leadership of the Party. Conditions, however, have not yet returned to the state of affairs which prevailed under Stalin.

Whatever one may say about the cruelties, wastefulness, irrationality, and unpredictability under Stalin's rule, it is obvious that the Soviet Union attained great achievements at that time. Despite the inefficiency of the centralized Soviet economic organization, the existence and operation of multiple overlapping and crosschecking mechanisms of control terrorizing the society and stultifying innovative initiatives and changes, and the preoccupation with heavy industry and subordination of the production to the needs of the army, the standard of living of the population nevertheless began to improve. The Soviet Union has not yet reached the level achieved in the Western industrial societies. The standard is not as high as that exhibited in the show windows of the Soviet regime in Moscow and Leningrad; yet certainly life improves. To be sure, the wives and daughters of the workers and of the low-ranking administrative staff officers have still to wait long hours in meat-, butter-, and other queues; however, more foodstuffs are now, to a greater extent, readily available.

In general, more commodities are obtainable in the stores, and industries have a higher production output for local markets. Life is still on the average poor, but has visibly improved in comparison with what it was ten or fifteen years ago. More importantly, the majority of the Soviet citizenry can now sleep in their homes without fear of being rudely awakened and sent to a concentration camp without a trial, despite the fact that they are loyal, hard-working citizens and even good Party members. The people in the Soviet Union, however, still live under the rule of terror and enforced politicization wherein the scope of privacy is limited to family affairs. One can neither freely express his beliefs nor associate with others who hold similar beliefs. The system of cross-checking the activities of each member of the society by the Party, the various administrations, the police, and other apparatus is still in operation. Nowadays, however, if one falls into the disgrace of those in power the punishment is not as severe as in the past. The penalty is no longer the concentration camp but more often the loss of one's job. Since practically the only employers are the state and the Party, and hence alternative means of making a living are scarce, the potential loss of one's employment constitutes a very painful threat. Moreover, the terror of the earlier periods is still remembered. Intellectuals are no longer shot on a whim of the Party secretary as in the past. Nowadays, the publication of their works is prohibited if they are not adequately subservient to the Party. They may eventually be sent to the "yellow house," as the insane asylums are called in the Soviet Union. Shooting without a trial is no longer the practice. Soviet heads of state also feel more secure than did Stalin and his associates. They know that a sudden rebellion would no longer be possible. Molotov, Bulganin, Malenkov, and Khrushchev all survived after losing their offices.

Anyone in the Soviet Union, beginning with the First Secretary of the Party down to the average worker, is conscious of the many faults of the existing order. The average man in the Soviet Union, however, does not complain very much about the lack of freedom; it has been his lot from time immemorial. He is more concerned with the inefficiency and wastefulness of the economy, the shortages in stores, the autocracy, despotism, and lawlessness of the petty and the mighty bureaucrats upon whom he depends entirely in everyday life.

The citizenry of the Soviet Union and of other East European communist countries would like their economic and political system changed. What they desire most is the removal of the incredible and obvious redundancies of the obsolete bureaucratic order. They want to be more trusted by the government and feel a greater respect for their dignity from power-holders. Many intellectuals believe that the present system can be changed into "socialism with a human face." They too want more freedom and dignity accorded to them and the average men.

From time to time, especially if a "thaw" comes and the Party is more lenient, intellectuals and experts on economic, political, and social affairs come forward with various proposals for change. I cannot discuss these in detail here; however, in general it can be said that until very recently both in the Soviet Union and other East European countries as well as in the West it was most often assumed that the remedy lay in decentralization, especially in the sphere of economic organization.* It was believed that decentralization would engender grass-roots local initiative and would enable the entire system to become more flexible, efficient, and productive. Proponents of such reforms in communist countries are usually careful to stress that the political system must be kept centralized under single party control. Whenever they dare not to stress this, they are condemned as revisionist, expelled from the Party, and often punished even more severely.

In the structure of the communist regime the economic and political systems are so bound together that it is impossible to change one without affecting others. It is the Party which runs the economy.

There are, however, those who propose changes of an entirely different kind to make the system more efficient and productive. They are indeed concerned primarily with the economic system and their projects are focused on the increase of output of the national economy, but it is evident that the same methods may also be applied in the area of political and social organization. Politics and social interactions are in the same degree factors of the economic structure as the economic system is part of the political order. I would call them initiators and harbingers of cybernetization of Soviet society, even though their initiative is not limited solely to the use of cybernetics and computers.

I am speaking here of a group of leading scientists in the Soviet Union who maintain that the lack of efficiency in the gigantic all-encompassing total system of society is caused by the absence of adequately developed channels of information. Cybernetics, mathematical economy, modern theories of management and administration as well as modern electronic technology and computerization especially can provide the means which will maintain the existing order while simultaneously making it more efficient. They tell the Party that armed with such means, the Center would be able to transmit its decisions more rapidly, have immediate information feedback on their implementation containing

* Examples are the proposals of the Soviet economist Liberman, the proposals of Polish economists Kalecki, Lipinski, Brus, and others; the economic reforms proposed by the Action Program of the Communist Party in Czechoslovakia in 1968.

strict and reliable data, and on the whole achieve a much more effective control. Even previously unmanageable decisions in local affairs could be coordinated, perhaps directly from the Center.

They tell the Party:

> We have acquired a hitherto unprecedented means for collecting, storage, systematization, classification, transmission, transformation, receipt, and utilization of numerous streams of information. Until now, however, we [and they actually mean *you*—S.C.] have not been able to learn how to manage and direct them.[23]

They recommend use of modern theories of management and computers in reorganization of the Soviet economy and adequate deployment of the resources of manpower and technology in order to produce an optimally efficient, productive economic organization of the society. In their opinion computers have to be placed throughout the country in any decision-making center. These must be interconnected with the Central computer. Their aim is to increase economic efficiency and productivity; the social and political implications of such a reorganization, should it really be implemented, will obviously be very great and hardly possible to envisage.

Originally such innovations were associated with the work of the Academicians L. V. Kantorovich, L. S. Sobolev, V. S. Nemchinov, V. V. Novoshilov, and other leading economists. At the end of the 1950's their initiative came under attack from the official Party political economists. Thus Western experts described the situation as a sign of conflict between scientists and politicians.[24] Perhaps that was true for the past. It is obviously not true anymore. The change in attitude of the Party leadership regarding this initiative became evident initially in 1963 when the Central Economic Mathematical Institute (TSEMI) under the directorship of N. P. Fedorenko was established. The Institute became the center for the development of the project of cybernetization of the Soviet Economy. Numerous other institutes, working on similar lines, were created in other cities shortly afterwards. The immediate result of the establishment of these institutes is visible in the numerous articles on mathematical economics and its practical application which appeared in the *Ekonomika i Matematicheskie Metody* and other Soviet journals, as well as in numerous books. The most important of these publications is certainly Fedorenko's master plan for cybernetization of the Soviet economy published under the title *Project of the Optimally Functioning Economic System of the Socialist Economy.*[25]

The Party has now given all its mighty support to the development of the program and the actual implementation of the cybernetization of the Soviet economy. In 1964 the Central Committee of the Party and the Council of Ministers announced a decision to establish a Unified Automated System of Management. Brezhnev devoted a separate section of his speech to these reforms at the XXIV Congress of the Party in March 1971. Numerous conferences were held on various aspects of the implementation of the Plan. In December 1971, the Central Committee of the Party announced a special Resolution "On Methods of Further Development of Social Sciences and of Their Role in the Communist Society." It stresses especially that economists in the Soviet Union have committed a major mistake by devoting not enough attention to mathematical economics. The Party urges both the theoreticians and actual managers to apply more of the achievements of modern science, and especially of cybernetics, mathematical economics, and theory of system management.[26]

What are the essential ideas and the current state of development of the cybernetization of the Soviet economy? The proponents of cybernetization refer indeed to Marxism-Leninism as the inspiring source for their plans and undertakings. Any issue of *Ekonomika i Matematicheskie Metody* begins with an article devoted to the great importance of Lenin's work for the development of mathematical economics and cybernetics. All other articles, however, are mostly on complex and sophisticated mathematical models to be applied in economics both in planning and management. What could be really regarded as a general theoretical framework for these studies is systems theory. In almost Parsonian terms, N. P. Fedorenko,[27] N. Y. Petryakov,[28] L. Kuce, M. Goriakov,[29] and other Soviet experts[30] assert that social structure consists of a number of systems. The economic system is of prime importance among these; it could also be regarded as a complex cybernetic system. It is said that this system in the U.S.S.R. is composed of several interdependent subsystems (a) of perspectivistic planning; (b) of offices dealing with projects and construction developments; (c) of information; (d) of actual production. It is asserted that complex cybernetic systems have a homeostatic nature.[31] The goal of the government and of the central management is defined as optimal development of the organismic balance of this homeostasis, which is simultaneously supposed to result in optimal productivity. Conflict-ridden capitalist societies, according to these opinions, have a centripetal nature. Because of the anarchy in capitalist economy, the competition for profits, they cannot constitute a harmoniously working system. It is asserted that, by contrast, the Soviet system which is organized around a centralized structure and is guided by a monistic ideological principle, is ideally suited to become a perfect cybernetic structure.[32] Stochastic models, linear programming, game theory, input-output schemes, modern theories of balanced planning, theory of probability, various cybernetical paradigms and complex mathematical schemes are utilized in designing models of compositive units and of the entirely cybernetized future Soviet society.

It is not possible here to analyze the numerous complex models and mathematical equations in the relevant literature which are proposed nowadays for nearly all fields of the Soviet economy including agriculture. On the whole, the plan envisages the establishment of a wide network of local automated computerized centers ASUP (*Aftomaticheskaya Sistema Upravlenia Proizvodstvom*) interconnected by wires and through bureaucratic subordination with automatized control and decision-making centers ASU (*Aftomaticheskaya Sistema Upravlenia*) on higher levels. These eventually are to be connected with a national ASU which would deal with central planning and management on a national scale and which would be subordinated to the supreme control of the leadership of the Party. Planning and management would thus be conducted by computerized decision-making, the utilization of other modern electronic machines and through the application of highly abstract mathematical calculations. It is expected that such a system would speed up the transfer and flow of information. It would enable the leadership to be fully in control of the national economy. It would make it possible to obtain at any time the required relevant and reliable data and thus to make the most appropriate decisions speedily. While ASUP's are expected to guide definite enterprises in their daily activities, the ASU are expected to engage in activities on three levels. (a) They would provide operative control and coordination of the daily activities of enterprises implementing the one, five, and fifteen year plans[33] designed by the appropriate authorities; (b) They would solve theoretical problems pertaining especially to the programming of the future and adequately adjust the activities of the first level to those of the second level;[34] (c) They would seek solutions for problems which science has been unable to solve until now and anticipate such problems.

At present the leadership of the Party and numerous institutes of economic management in the Soviet Union are striving to develop both the theoretical framework and actual network of the ASUP and ASU which will deal with the goals of the first level. A central data bank is planned for the implementation of this task. It is assumed that it will store in an optimal way the information available concerning material resources, the productive capacity of enterprises, inventory data, traffic of all possible kinds, as well as information about individuals (their qualifications, and so forth) participating in the cybernetized system, which is practically the entire population of the Soviet Union.

Researchers in Novosibirsk are working on different aspects of optimal planning. They are interested in developing a plan of the most rational territorial allocation of resources, productive units, and the population in correspondence with the location of natural resources.[35] Their problem could be succinctly posed as follows: Mineral resources in the eastern part of the Soviet Union inhabited by the bulk of the population are becoming increasingly exhausted. Siberia and the Far East are still relatively underdeveloped with an enormous potential of mineral resources, water, natural conditions for cheap construction of large electric plants. These are still scarcely populated areas. Hence researchers are working on a plan of transferring the centers of activity and population of the Soviet Union to those underdeveloped areas. Again, cybernetical models and complex mathematical calculations are applied. The government has unsuccessfully for some time urged the people to move to the East, to accomplish the industrialization of that part of the Soviet Union. Now it is hoped that better solutions would be worked out.

The bulk of the great amount of literature available on the subject is concerned with theory and models of cybernetization of the economy. ASUP and ASU are, however, already widely introduced in the organization of the Soviet economic structure. According to some data, three branches—the electric, natural gas, and cement-producing industries— are already managed by an ASU type of semiautomated control. Numerous ASUPs were established in the enterprises of other industries. The current ninth Five Year Plan envisages that by 1975 about 1600 ASUP and as many ASU centers as possible will be in operation. Some literature already exists assessing the effectiveness of the introduction of automated computerized control centers in diverse enterprises.[36]

The organizers of the cybernetization of the Soviet economy encounter numerous "practical" difficulties. Among the most persistent and most difficult to overcome is the absence of computers both in adequate volumes and adequate capacities. Instead of *Minsk 22* and *Ural 14*, belonging to second generation computers, third generation computers are now introduced. Computers are also at the top of the Soviet Union's shopping list in the United States and in other Western countries. Trained specialists to run the numerous ASUs and ASUPs are in high demand. Soviet experts admit that one of the greatest problems that they face in the implementation of their endeavors is the psychological barrier; the hostile attitude of the administrative and working personnel toward their innovation. Effective methods for overcoming such difficulties have not yet been found.

Recently the Soviet government established a new agency to direct the implementation of the plan of cybernetization of the economy and to solve the various problems connected with its organization and supply both of computers, software required by computer users, and the training of an army of 125,000 specialists in five years to operate computers and to program them. The agency operates under the name Scientific Research Institute for Problems of Organization and Management and is headed by the First Deputy Chairman of the State Committee for Science and Technology which is equivalent in its position within the Soviet governmental structure to an autonomous ministry.

It remains to be seen whether the plan of cybernetization of the Soviet economy will be implemented, and especially whether this will solve the persistent problems of inefficiency, wastefulness, and shortages of goods, or whether on the contrary it will produce instead many new, now hardly foreseeable problems. It is a fact, that these changes are not in the direction of decentralization. Many experts on Soviet economics are skeptical about this new venture. They say that in the past the Soviet Union has launched many crash programs, but has been unable to solve the immediate problems stemming from overcentralization. Criticism against the plan of cybernetization has also been voiced in the Soviet Union. A. Y. Boyarsky, a mathematical economist himself, is especially vociferous in his criticism against the presently introduced plan of an optimally functioning economic system.[37] He points out that the current promulgators of systemic cybernetization wrongly assume that the system as a whole is the consumer, while in fact it is composed of diverse individuals and groups with conflicting and changing values and interests. They assume an unrealistic static situation. And what is especially wrong, in his opinion, is that they believe that it is not possible to select the profitable goals of the society and translate them into quantitative volumes, while in fact preferences, desires, interests, and goals differ and change. He writes that the introduction of a pure market economy is neither effective enough nor desirable for the U.S.S.R. The only other way to solve these problems would be to entrust them for decision to a dictator, which, of course, he tells us, contradicts the elementary principles of Soviet Society.[38]

Although all of the consequences of the current attempt to cybernetize the Soviet economy cannot be envisaged, some are already evident. A. A. Modin[39] assesses that the introduction of mathematical methods and computerized automated management of enterprises increased the direct output of productivity by three to eight per cent. It made possible an increase of fifteen to eighteen per cent in the scope of productive tasks resulting in more accurate planning. The efficiency of inventory, storing, and of transfer procedures of materials and part products have improved by twenty-five to thirty per cent. The time consumed for accounting operations in most enterprises under ASUP has been reduced by forty to eighty per cent. In the initial stage of its operation ASUP and ASU actually require an increase of administrative personnel. Eventually, however, the technical and administrative personnel could be reduced substantially. Other writers have pointed out that cybernetization requires a new attitude in work. The most important requirement as a result of its introduction is co-ordinated rhythmic and exact implementation in time and quality of the working tasks, instead of overfulfillment of plans. In fact, mobilization campaigns that urge overfulfillments of productive plans are still waged in the Soviet Union, but not so much in institutions under the control of ASU. Methods applied in the assessment of plan fulfillment were considerably improved with the use of mathematics. Instead of numerous indicators which adversely affected the productivity before, fewer simpler and better indicators are applied nowadays. It is hoped that this will stimulate greater efficiency and eventually increase the productivity. This also remains to be seen.

One may add a few more points. It is quite noticeable that in debates concerning economic problems, priorities, and so forth, Soviet experts refer nowadays less than in the past to quotations from Marx and Lenin as a proof of their righteousness. More often, the proof of truth is sought in mathematics and pure economic terms. Cybernetization and computerization of the society will inevitably provide the state and the police with more information concerning most aspects of the lives of citizens. Simultaneously, the Soviet rulers will be able to afford more of the luxury of allowing the small dissenting groups to voice their opinion. Well-established after so many years in power, secure in their control of the society, they will feel safe enough to allow the opinions of various minorities, which, of course, they may ignore if they wish to do so. In any case, they will know for sure how subversive and dangerous the dissent is. It is uncertain whether cybernetization will stimulate or, on the contrary, quell the grass roots initiative. Notwithstanding assets anticipated from cybernetization and computerization it is badly needed for the improvement of the situation in the Soviet society.

In the 1940's and '50's experts on the Soviet Union developed a totalitarian model of the society and applied it in analyses of Soviet affairs. The works of H. Arendt, J. Armstrong, M. Fainsod, C. J. Friedrich, and Z. Brzezinski are examples of such an approach.[40] Later on, especially when Khrushchev was in power, experts began to apply a different perspective in analyses of U.S.S.R. Developmental and functionalist approaches became fashionable. The works of A. Inkeles, B. Moore, F. C. Barghoorn, recent works of Z. Brzezinski and S. P. Huntington and of numerous others can be mentioned as examples.[41] These writers were mainly interested in what they believed were profound changes within the Soviet political and socioeconomic structure. Nowadays still another trend seems to be prevalent. The proponents of this new model view the Soviet Union as an industrial society under the rule of a modern "mature" bureaucracy. The system, as A. Kassof put it recently, is an "administered society."[42] From such a perspective, the problems of modern Soviet society are those of complexity, size, intercommunication, interdependence of the parts with the whole, of allocation of means and rewards in a most effective and rational way, of regulation of inputs and outputs, and so forth, plus problems of other "normal" industrial societies, such as urbanization and its consequences, mobility, pollution, juvenile delinquency, and the like.*

This last approach is very much in keeping with the vision on direction of current changes in the Soviet Union as seen in this book.

It is not solely the image of the Soviet Union, however, that has changed. The changes in approach reflect to a degree the very real transformation that has taken place within the structure and the ideological inclination of the Soviet Union itself.

Marx viewed the future socialism as a gigantic community of free intellectuals and artists. Lenin, who was primarily an organizer of the Russian revolutionary underground organization, envisaged socialism as a huge political structure, modeled upon the conspiratory Bolshevik Party established and directed by him. It too was to be disciplined and integrated by political means, through education and enhancement of the working class consciousness. According to Lenin's figurative flowery expression: any cook in such a society must have the knowledge, skill, and capability to run the government. Stalin was a military commander and commissar. While he originally tried to follow Lenin's path in building socialism by politicization in an effort to transform the society into a monolithic political organism, whether consciously or unconsciously, he subsequently began to shape it increasingly in accordance with the pattern of army structure and organization. Everything had to be done on command. No opposition to a commander's order could be voiced, let alone accepted. All policies and campaigns were conducted in the manner of military battles. If the price of victory was human life, then this was deemed normal. This is how military battles are won. It was most important to save the commander since the battle had to go on. The economy, the systems of socialization and education, and the ideology were subordinated to the needs of the army. Even tsarist generals were proclaimed

* For a general comparison of diverse models on Soviet society see A. Inkeles, "Models and Issues in the Analysis of Soviet Society," *Survey*, No. 60 (July 1966).

to be heroes of the builders of socialism. Mao Tse-tung, on the contrary, seems to be attempting to shape his socialist society upon the model of a guerrilla peasant organization, composed of an aggregation of millions of small community-type fighting units.

The present leadership of the Soviet Union is composed of bureaucrats and administrators. Instead of placing the primacy on politicization they are literally administering the society. They strive to keep it integrated by bureaucratic means. The problem is that the changes which were described here are never officially disclosed, thereby producing a sort of enormous cognitive dissonance on a collective scale—a huge discrepancy between ideology and the real state of affairs. The ritual is still to quote Marx and Lenin and to claim that whatever happens was anticipated by them. However, the number of naïve people who still believe this is dwindling even in the Soviet Union.

Of course, all the numerous changes and trends of development in the U.S.S.R. cannot be attributed solely to the different personalities of the leaders. Perhaps the personality actually reflected the changes in the situation. Khrushchev had to be dismissed since he did not reflect the actual bureaucratic spirit of the new Soviet élite. He was introducing reforms in an attempt to make the society more egalitarian, while the bureaucrats composing the ruling élite considered it right to maintain it hierarchically. After much suffering the Soviet people have now achieved some relatively better conditions of life. They are, however, envious of people living in capitalist countries and especially in the United States. They are now becoming even more thirsty for the gadgets of middle-class life not available in Soviet life. And the élite has an even greater desire for them than the average person has. The cyberneticized society looks promising in this respect.

In developing from a huge conglomeration of nationalities and groups the Soviet Union is changing from a gigantic political monolith into a prodigious bureaucratic monolith.

7. The Overdeveloped Western Societies

While most of the societies of the world are facing problems of underdevelopment and are struggling to overcome them, and while the Soviet Union has become industrialized and highly developed in certain respects but still underdeveloped in many other fields, Western industrial societies, including Japan, are approaching the threshold of overdevelopment.

At the end of the eighteenth and the beginning of the nineteenth centuries, Thomas Malthus wrote that the population of the earth has a constant tendency to increase beyond the means of subsistence. He explained how this tendency increases in a geometric ratio: while the soil is being depleted, the amount of food supplies can be increased in an arithmetic ratio only. "In two centuries the population would be to the means of subsistence as 256 to 9; in three centuries as 4096 to 13, and in two thousand years the difference would be almost incalculable."[43] Malthus's theory was rejected by many writers. It has been proven that the population does not increase as he predicted, and people have been able to increase the output of consumer goods in much greater quantities and varieties than he expected; hence the problem which Malthus predicted has not begun to occur. Incidentally, Marx was among the earliest and staunchest critics of Malthus, as he believed that human invention could overcome any shortages. He and other writers insisted that because of the great resourcefulness of our planet and the inventiveness of man, one cannot foresee in the predictible future any such situation as Malthus anticipated. And it was, in fact, later pointed out that Malthus completely underestimated the gain in productivity made possible by new technologies, applications of science, and economic development. Many writers have argued that we are entering the era of abundance and have pointed out that some societies are already facing the problems of having a surplus rather than a scarcity of farm products. They are willing to admit that there are regions wherein people do not have an adequate supply of food, but that this is a matter of time—a technicality in distribution and exchange. These shortages are not imminent; they will disappear if the right science, technology, and organization are applied. The belief in the possibility of unlimited increase of abundance was, and often still is, prevalent.

I do not know of any contemporary subscribing to the theory of Thomas Malthus. However, in reading some of the numerous books on social and ecological problems in the Western societies of today, and about the even more gloomy apocalyptic perspectives predicted for the future; driving on the crowded highways of America where breathing sometimes becomes difficult; walking along the shores of the polluted oceans where one becomes oily and dirty after a short swim; listening to the common warnings about radiation, mercury in the sea food, poisoning by nonorganic pesticides—one must, even unwittingly, pose the question: perhaps Malthus is not so totally wrong in the long run. Many writers nowadays seem to be less fascinated by the virtues of development, especially technological development, than was common only a few years ago. Some even say modern industrial societies are becoming overdeveloped and uncomfortable to live in. Again the fear of overpopulation is on the agenda. This time the danger of starvation is not being stressed so much, yet many writers still think that it may become imminent and that we may have difficulties in producing an adequate supply of food. A more strongly emphasized point is the danger of pollution created by industries which are needed to maintain so many people, and by the millions of people themselves, and the dangers of exhaustion of some important mineral resources. Recently F. H. Knelman coined the term "quadrilema" of our future disaster, including within it overpopulation, pollution, destruction by nuclear radiation from either military or civil installations, and a total war for survival because of maldistribution of consumer goods within and between nations. Abundance turns out to be costly, and more and more people believe that it has become too expensive already.

The price has several aspects. Pollution is one, but perhaps it can be overcome both by expensive means of modern technology and by the mobilization of the public in a united struggle against it. The price in social consequences is also high and equally important. Discussing it, one must consider not only the destruction of a community life which has so often been described by earlier sociologists, and the problems of the transformation of our societies into lonely crowds and mass societies.

It has become more and more evident that *the modern industrial societies of today are approaching the point where further differentiation of specialized roles, institutions, agencies, and systems will not produce by themselves a self-balancing cohesion and interdependence resulting from the need of complementarity alone. Roles, agencies, and systems become too specialized, too differentiated, and separated to retain their relative interdependence, and to relate with other complementary units in interaction without any external intervention.* The number of roles performed by each individual constantly increases while the duration of performance of each role and time spent in interaction with other actors while performing it is shrinking persistently. Roles become fragmented and change into part-roles, fragmental roles, incidental roles, or they become fluid. It becomes more and more difficult to set clear limits between roles, units of action, and processes. Systems and processes become two aspects of the same flow of events and action. Highly specialized roles, agencies and processes have to be interconnected in too many interdependencies, in too complex ways, by the medium of too indirect interconnections. Systems of such interdependencies are very complex indeed. Spontaneity and the need for mutuality alone do not generate the necessary links and interconnections. There is not enough cohesion in the system. Complementarity has to be supplemented, if not supplanted, by rules, regulations, bonds, interconnections imposed from above, most often by the state.

Differentiation generating new interdependencies and specializations cannot proceed indefinitely without causing structural changes. The structure of complementary interdependencies has to be placed in the crust of semiorganismic structures. This, of course, requires the relinquishment of some, and the limitation of other freedoms of the individuals, groups, and agencies until now acting primarily on their own behalf, and concerned solely with their own interests. As the principle that the individual will take care of his own affairs and that everything will work out on the whole by itself turns out to be no longer sufficient. Abundance in one respect generates scarcities in another respect. Abundance of clean water, fresh air, green pastures, and forests turns out to be at least as important as the abundance of cars, air conditioners, television sets, houses, food, and recreational facilities. It becomes self-evident that the process of development felt in all spheres of existence has brought us to a point where our life-styles and all the social and political organization governing them will have to be drastically amended or even reorganized so as to fit the needs of the approaching supraindustrial era.

The need for greater regulation of the interdependence of coexistence; the need for interconnection of the self-differentiating specialized units of complementary interdependence; and the greater demand for more social services for the populations require more state activities, and these produce greater etatization. As was said before, acquisition of more functions by the state, introduction of more social and welfare services to the society, self-differentiation into more specialized agencies also of the governmental and para-statal bureaucracies enhance this process even more.

What seems to be plausible as a result is that the semiorganismic interdependencies will permeate to an even greater extent the social structure of Western or capitalist societies. The functions and control of the state over coordination of various spheres of activities will expand, and perhaps capitalist societies will begin to change into state capitalist societies. In any case, we should expect more state interference in the life of individuals, groups, private associations, and business. Many facts indicate that the process is already far advanced. President Nixon's recent economic decisions were just one in a series of numerous manifestations of the growing control of the state over the economic affairs of the society. The national economy of the United States is, for the first time in its history, acquiring a national management. One of the articles in the November 29, 1971 issue of *U.S. News and World* begins with the following words: "Rarely have so many decisions, affecting the lives of so many Americans, come out of Washington in so short a time. Day after day, rulings on pay, prices, profits, rents, dividends and other pocketbook issues pour from the agencies running the Administration's program of economic controls."

Of course it may be said that these are temporary measures. Some of the presently introduced controls will certainly be relinquished, yet this will not change the fact of a constantly growing state interference and control, and thus a greater imposition of the semiorganismic structure of authority over the society.

According to some estimates, every sixth American is employed by diverse governmental, federal, and state administrations, semistatal agencies and institutions (including the army, police, schools, universities, research institutes, air lines, post offices, and so forth). According to other estimates, the number is much higher. If we add to this number those on welfare, who are in a sense maintained by the state the proportion will be still greater. It may be said that they are employed on the taxpayers' money, hence they are maintained by the society. Even this is not exactly the situation if other Western societies are considered. Here also the number of people who depend upon salaries from governments and semistatal organizations is increasing substantially. But another factor is also important. The French and the Italian governments, for instance, not only run the railroad and airline systems but own various industries that employ hundreds of thousands, if not millions, of people.

It is true that until now the state in Western societies has interfered little in the personal affairs of their citizens, or certainly has interfered to an incomparably smaller degree than the Soviet state has done. Employees are organized in independent unions. Some employees use their governmentally paid positions to fight the policies of the state. They can choose to work for private corporations and firms, or organize their business. They have rights and freedoms which by and large are respected by the government. And of greatest importance is the fact that while the individual in the Soviet Union faces the state as an individual alone and is not permitted by law to organize any organization outside the Party-state control, in the West the individual faces the state as a member of various interest groups which are independent of the state. Institutionalized powerful forces defend his rights and autonomy both as a citizen and as a member of various interest groups against the encroachment of other groups and the state.

Simultaneously, Western societies are increasingly permeated by semiorganismic interdependencies. Unions and interest groups are becoming big, bureaucratized, and semiorganismic as well. This is not tantamount with the establishment of a totalitarian state. Semiorganismic interdependencies and structures produced by them may be depoliticized. They may furnish the members of society with many options in their personal affairs, for example, in consumption, in the selection of services and functionaries of authority. These may not be maintained by a system of terror and surveillance and intensive indoctrination. However, more state control may require the relinquishment of some, and the limitation of other freedoms of individuals, groups, and agencies which until now have acted primarily on their own behalf, solely concerned with their own interests. It is quite plausible that most of the current freedoms and rights of Western democracies will be upheld. In the new composition of the balance between interdependencies of coexistence, complementarity, and semiorganism the old rights and freedoms lose much of their previous power. In fact they could be upheld but become sterile and ineffective simultaneously. Western political systems are generally composed of two essential elements, a structure of representative democracy and of institutions of executive, regulative, statal political power. While the first structure did not change much since the nineteenth and the beginning of the twentieth century when it was established, the second has expanded tremendously.

There are, of course new spontaneously developing new attitudes toward politics in general and the growing etatization of societies in particular. While, on one hand, we can see a growing apathy toward politics there is also another trend of growing concern. The issues of concern are not necessarily strictly political but, as a matter of fact, mostly social, such as poverty, pollution, overpopulation, equal opportunity, and so forth, yet precisely because they are the subject of widespread concern they attain a political importance. Political divisions today do not run necessarily in correspondence with class or Party lines. They run across such lines. This is even true for Communist societies. People are divided first into those who are and those who are not concerned; then according to their attitudes connected with particular concerns. There is a strong longingness and attempt to return to community life. The modern communities are not, however, of the old type based primarily on kinship, neighborhood ties, and coexistence, they are linking together people sharing the same life style, similar interests, beliefs, attitudes. They run across borders of countries and societies producing still another network of societal interdependencies within and across nations' political boundaries, linguistic entities. They are primarily cultural affiliations generating social and political attitudes and linkages.

One can read nowadays that freedom is dear, but there is nothing wrong with giving it up in order to live and prolong the existence of humanity. There is a world beyond freedom and dignity too, we are told, but what kind of freedoms are we required to give up? It is true, as some modern writers point out, that our freedoms even in the Western world are already very limited, that we are restricted in a multitude of ways, and that our actions are determined by many factors beyond our control, understanding or even knowledge. It is also said that the residual freedoms of ours are very illusory and that they will be taken away gently so that their loss will not be too painful and that we shall not even know that they are gone. Should we be content with the promises that this loss will relieve us from the burden of searching for solutions and making decisions by ourselves? Is it not worthwhile to recall here Hegel's statement that freedom is the understanding of necessities? Engels extolled it. Lenin and Stalin quoted it. Today one can see how that idea became subsequently interpreted and applied in the practice of the Soviet Union. Let me also recall that many social scientists in the past proclaimed that development, whether economic, technological, scientific, or societal, is a march toward greater human freedom—freedom from the most painful necessities, from scarcities, freedom for creative thinking, and moreover, the freedom to influence the societal decisions which affect our lives.

Social scientists are only now beginning to discern the tendency herein adumbrated. It would be premature to propose solutions to problems that have only now begun to be evident. We do not have the power to arrest ongoing development and progressing differentiation generating new interdependencies. Perhaps our societies need to balance the encroachment of the semiorganismic element engulfing and permeating all spheres of our life with the acquisition of more and greater freedom— freedom generated by knowledge and understanding, as well as the freedom to influence those who master the semiorganismic giant, whether they are politicians or technocrats. The spreading quest for new forms of participatory democracy is proof that this need is now becoming more manifest.

Scholars still quarrel as to what are the most important features of feudalism. They have propounded numerous theories on the transformation of traditional and feudal societies into modern industrial ones. There is little argrement about what are the most important sources, tendencies, and characteristics of that transformation. At present we have not only to continue working on these explanations but also to begin explaining the current accelerated transformation of the industrial societies into superindustrial ones. The past looks different from any new perspective of modernity. In the future, as now, we will have again and again to reevaluate the meaning of the past and its consequences for the present and for a still distant future.

Social scientists, and especially the earlier sociologists, believed that they would be able to anticipate and direct the course of technological, economic, and societal development; yet it seems that development proceeds much faster than our comprehension of it. I am not a specialist on prognosis and prophecies; however, after comparing all the processes of development discussed in this book, I must reluctantly say a few words on its eventual direction.

Personally, I believe that while development is irreversible at any of its points, its further progress depends upon man's decision at each of these points. Complex latent social, economic, and political consequences occur as a result of narrowly oriented strivings for individual gains. The consequences of our actions cannot always be anticipated, wholly predicted, or controlled.

On the whole, however, there are still two ways open for further societal development. The first is complete subordination of men to the systems dominating them, which is the vision promoted by Jacques Ellul, Arnold Toynbee, and earlier writers such as Ortega y Gasset, and numerous others. They say that our freedom and options have and will become even more limited. A possibility of a suprarational totalitarian society is not only a fantasy. It can really be imposed on us, and not only under communist rule.

There is, however, a second option still open. Supertechnology and superproductivity can open unprecedented options of freedom and choice in the future for mankind. Some writers tell us that our future problems will not be the lack of options but rather a plethora of choices. Will these, however, be real choices or fictitious ones as between two brands of toothpaste, two kinds of cars which actually are not too different, or two political parties which pursue the same or similar policies? In situations of abundance options do not seem to have the same importance as in situations of scarcity.

A few things are now clear, however. Man in a superindustrial society will have much more free time at his disposal. The time spent on education will probably be expanded. It is plausible that after completing a university education the people of the future will spend some years in self-programmed individual creative activities. Perhaps the men of the future will have more time and more facilities to think, to create unique things, and to be unique themselves. Bureaucracies will be reduced and replaced by computers and by other adequate technological means. Man could be made a robot subordinated to the needs of machines and systems elevated by himself. He could also become a free creator in any field in which he had personal inclinations.

In this hypothetical future, problems of underdevelopment in the Third World nations will probably be solved. Mankind will not be able to afford having underdeveloped areas on the planet. Poverty in its current guises will most probably be eliminated. Many other plagues besetting our societies of today might be removed. Perhaps the future super-industrial society will be called socialist, or supreme, or paradise on earth. And yet the solving of present conflict and problems will probably produce new ones, as well as new inequalities, injustices, and expectations; however, today we must struggle to solve the current ones.

8. Why System Perspective?

We live in systems. We travel on the freeway system, by railroad or air-line systems. We communicate with other people through telephone, mail, or radio network systems. We use the energy of the electric distribution system. We are educated and educate our children in the institutions of the educational system. We work in various organizational systems and obtain our food, clothing, and any goods that we consume in stores and supermarkets of the distribution systems. We elect our government through the party system. We are part of numerous other overlapping and intermeshing sociocultural systems. We depend on systems of hundreds of thousands or millions of people and they, the millions, depend on us as part of their system. In any country in the world more systems are in operation today than there were ten, twenty, or one hundred years ago, or at any other time in the past. An individual who lives in the United States is more dependent on and more involved in systemic interactions than one who lives in Britain, and the person who lives in Britain more than one who lives in Africa. Life constantly becomes more systemic. And individuals and groups, participants in systems benefit increasingly from this process which makes more goods and services available. Yet at the same time they become more dependent, and painfully so, on other people in depersonalized relations and the anonymous systems involving them.

Systems are constituted of standardized, replaceable, exchangeable constituents interacting with other standardized, replaceable, exchangeable elements in patterned, repetitive, regular interactions. In the past people lived in kinship groups, villages, towns, and cities. They, too, were linked in systemic interaction. Then, however, there were fewer systems, they were less dense and not so far-reaching, and they did not regulate, standardize, and impinge on men's lives to the same degree that they do now. The sociocultural systems in which we live are not fairy-tale monsters. They are created and generated by men, in some instances as intentional goal-directed activities in order to make life more efficient, to produce more, or to communicate more easily with other people, in other instances as by-products of the innovations or developments pursued by men in order to improve their individual lives.

Men are growing increasingly aware of being and becoming part of systems. This is especially evident in the direction of the development of many scholarly disciplines. Science of any kind is an attempt to systematize knowledge. Today it has become increasingly a knowledge about systems, systemic interactions and interdependencies. New, specialized disciplines such as general systems theory, exchange and organizational theories, set and game theories, cybernetics and others studying abstract systemic interrelations and systems as wholes have emerged in the last ten or twenty years.

Reflecting this interest of growing systemness which is evident in any sphere of life, the social sciences have also begun to change their orientation. Earlier they were concerned with individuals or groups at the most, with man in relation to other individuals and groups. This is still their basic interest. Now, however, one can also note a growing interest in the systems in which men are involved, in the whole, in the interdependencies between parts and the whole. In the past, there was some indication of interest in systemic interactions, yet system itself was not the topic. Societies were viewed as assemblages of individuals, functioning without a background of systems. Toennies, Max Weber, Durkheim, and Cooley acknowledge the inadequacy of such a sociological perspective. They called attention to the fact that man is not only an individual and a social being, but part of groups and larger social structures. They wrote that with the progressive division of labor, specialization, urbanization, bureaucratization, and rationalization, and with the continuation of other processes, men become increasingly involved in the *Gesellschaft*, in rationally organized societies, organismic solidarities, secondary groups. They become increasingly dependent on large-scale societies around them, more and more involved in complex far-reaching binding structures and interdependencies. Yet even though these writers called attention to the ongoing process of engulfing men in networks of more complex interdependencies, their emphasis was not on the systemic nature of these processes and of the structures and complexities generated in these processes. They and other writers of their time were still concerned with the problem of what happens to man as a result of these processes. At least a great many modern functionalist theorists in sociology and certainly most political systems theorists have adopted the opposite approach. Man has disappeared from their perspective. They are not concerned with his aspirations, plights, or individual features. Their subject is the system alone, and they attempt to present it in a form most purified from human imperfection and individualisms, as a pure model of a system—a model in the sense of an abstraction, in the sense of an ideal type, and scheme of all societies in the past, present and future.

Do societies actually have a systemic structure? If so, can and should we attempt to explore it? Do we need system approaches in social sciences? What are the advantages and disadvantages of the use of system approaches in the analysis of societies? I believe that societies are constituted of systemic relations and, therefore, have to be explored as systems. This is not to say that all other approaches have to be replaced by a system approach. I will agree with those critics of system theories who point out that numerous societal phenomena cannot be explained by means of a system approach. Yet numerous questions posed to the social sciences by current or ongoing processes of change, societal structuralization and development can best be answered by means of a systemic approach. If Parsonian theory is not good enough, perhaps other system theories are more satisfactory, such as the general system theory, n- person game theory, or models based on the adoption of cybernetic schemes into social sciences. Perhaps only in the complementarity of many systems theories will the right answers be found. In any case, a comprehensive system theory of society is urgently needed for the understanding of general interdependencies emerging and persisting in societal interaction and structures which cannot be explained satisfactorily by theories viewing the phenomena only from the vantage of an individual or the perspective of a group. Systems and systemic interdependencies are increasingly impinging upon individuals as members of society. They play an ever more important role in our lives. They have to be explored and understood better.

The strength of any system theory of society lies in the same feature as its greatest weakness. It can provide an interpretation of the most general, persistent societal interconnections, of the most recurrent aspects of common societal interactions. It does not explain the actions or the motives of specific individuals or groups or cases, and it is not concerned with the peculiarities of specific courses of events. It provides a wide, far-reaching perspective. From its vantage, however, all details of the analyzed phenomena are missing. "One cannot see the woods for the trees," says the proverb. Application of a system approach is an attempt to explain all woods at once. Critics say that from such a perspective one cannot see the trees at all, yet that is not necessarily correct. Trees have to be explained as part of the wood and woods as constituted by millions of trees. It requires a sociological imagination, a *Verstehen*, a sociological empathy.

Man, especially modern man is engaged in numerous societal roles in diverse societal interaction. He is simultaneously *homo sapiens, homo faber, homo oeconomicus, homo politicus, homo sociologicus,* and *homo systemicus.* He also acts in other capacities. He belongs to numerous groups and participates in overlapping structures of interdependencies and interactions constituting the society. Universality and uniqueness are both aspects of any process; they are separable only in abstraction. "Rationality, taken generally and in the abstract, consists in the thoroughgoing unity of the universal and the single."[44] The patterned universal element present in any action composing the structures of societal systems is only apparent in a multitude of unique individuals, actions which cannot be repeated spatially or temporally. Unique persons constitute unique groups and societies. They act in self-interest yet in doing this they are the bearers and producers of the patterned interconnections which constitute lasting systems.* System approaches reflect the pattern found in universality absorbing uniqueness. Though one can speak of systems of cultures, much if not all of the cultural context has to be left out in considerations based on system theory, yet societies are never culture-free. Man is a vehicle of the culture which produced him and cannot be totally purified of his cultural identity. Thus pure systems are and have to be abstract.

Acknowledging the limitations of system theory one should also see its utility: (a) System theories are intended as interpretations of wholeness and universality. They relate individual cases. They characterize the general, the repeatable, and the regular. (b) In comparative analyses of societies they extricate a standardized, universal, common pattern from unique, peculiar, individual factors, and thus provide a frame of comparison for the unique factors. (c) They explain development processes, as I attempt to demonstrate in other chapters of this book. (d) They do not produce answers to the numerous social questions and problems besetting men, but they help to pose such questions.

Three general methods of constructing system theories of society have to be distinguished: (1) A system can be elevated as a logical construct based on pure logical propositions. (2) It can have the character of an analytical system. In such instances its premises are usually constructed of variables abstracted from societies. These are interpreted and linked together by means of conjecture. Proponents of system paradigms of the above two types as a rule do not claim that the social systems described in their theories exist in exactly this form anywhere in the world. Such systems are models which are helpful in the discovery of patterns in the immense agglomeration of facts and data of social reality. (3) System theories of the third kind are expositions of the societal interconnections which have a systemic character and which together with other systemic elements constitute a skeleton of the structure of social

---

* This is indeed only one of the numerous cases of the dualist nature of societal and human phenomena which man constantly has to consider in his incessant striving for understanding of himself and the society.

reality. Again diverse aspects of reality can be exposed in diverse ways. Numerous system theories on the same subject are possible.

When I discuss societal systems or the growing societal systemness in this book, I am interested in all kinds of interactions resulting in transpiration and organization of societal systems and especially in the processes producing societal systemic interdependencies listed here under number three.

9. The Growing Systemness in International Relations

The field of international relations seems to be a very quaggy land for a nonexpert. However, in order to complete the overall picture of the growing societal systemness, I have to attempt to sketch its manifestations at the supralevel of international relations. The topic of conflict and consensus in international relations, though pertinent here and related to preceding chapters, will be omitted. The discussion will not be concerned with the international systems as balance-of-power, and I do not feel competent enough to prescribe the means by which such a balance can be maintained in international relations. In short, what I am concerned with here are only the manifestations of a *growing differentiation within expanding interdependence in the worldwide sphere, with the growing systemness in international relations.* The discussion will, therefore, be limited to (a) the concept of international system; (b) differentiation and integration in the sphere of international relations; and (c) the vision for the future of international systems.

a. The International Systems

When we switch the discussion from the level of entities within national and state boundaries to the level of international relations, we are neither lifting the analysis to a more abstract meta-level, nor dealing with augmented units of the same kind as in studies of national sociopolitical or sociocultural structures. The sphere of international relations is simply not composed of the same kinds of interactions or not even of similar kinds of interactions as a national macrostructure. Besides, we know from sociology that rules and theories on small groups cannot be mechanically applied to macrostructures and even less so to supra-macrostructures, and vice versa. In the field of international relations, nonetheless, many theories which were developed for state or even smaller units are applied. This is so because in the first place, international relations have always been a part of political theory; in the second place, it is difficult to draw a clear line between foreign policies of states and international relations; and in the third place, it is difficult to delineate strictly the boundaries of the subject. One has to accept the rules of the game if one wishes to play the game. And the rules are, as I said, that many students of international relations either directly apply the theories and models of political systems of national states or tacitly accept the assumption that the sphere of international relations is in a sense a gigantic political system. How much, then, from the point of view of an outsider, does the sphere of international relations resemble a political system?

International relations is a superstructure, not so much of roles but of competitors and partners who are in a huge, ongoing game for gains. The units of it are nations, states (sociopolitical structures of systems), agencies which represent the diverse interests of those states and groups within them, and international associations, plus the agencies (or organizations) of the unique structure of the United Nations. Within that superstructure the units relate to each other in conflict, competition, cooperation, exchange interactions, and in continuous bargaining, and these are all occasionally interrupted by war. It is worth noting that the relations which entangle nations in international politics are classified as political, economic, and sometimes as cultural, but not as social. This is not accidental. Although representatives of nations may maintain social relations, the nations themselves are never described in terms of social relations, because that is a different level of relations. Apart from foreign policies and trade, which constitute international relations, such relations have recently become a basis for generating a superstructure of institutions and organizations beyond the nation states,[45] with a unique center at the United Nations.

The units of international relations—especially states as opposed to units in a political system within national boundaries—are not subordinated to any central authority. The charter of the United Nations contains provisions for imposing the decisions of the Security Council and the United Nations on fellow members in specific instances, yet the United Nations in practice has little power, especially when it comes to enacting general decisions.* Some students of international relations have recently

* If one attempts to compare the structure of international relations with different types of political systems, one has to look for a model in which the leadership, the authority, and the center has very little power to impose decisions on any member against his consent. Then, paradoxically enough, the only model derived from an actual political system which well fits the present state of the superstructure of international relations is that of a tribal African society with a minimum of government. The Nuer provides an excellent example for such a model. [See E. E. Evans-Pritchard, *The Nuer* (1965).] The tribe was divided into numerous segments: "Each segment is itself segmented and there is opposition between its parts" (p. 142). Specific sections were uniting for war with other, usually adjacent sections: "Law operates weakly outside a very limited radius and nowhere very effectively" (p. 169). Among the Nuers certain persons and families are more respected than others (that is, the big powers), "and people will wait to see what they do and then follow suit" (L. Mair,

even coined the term "international stratification,"[46] thus implying that the superstructure of international relations is actually a hierarchy of nations. Yet is it? Of course, there are big powers, and there are rich and poor nations; but there are also blocs, and a model of class struggle applied to international relations simply distorts its real constellation. It seems that if a model of political systems has to be applied to international relations, it has to be a model of a system without a government. Is it not true that at best the United Nations, its center, provides no more than a table for negotiations, with a sort of ordered anarchy around it? Its officers, with all due respect, are in fact no more than go-between chiefs, mediators, and their assistants. It is the member states of the superstructure, and not the center, who have political, economic, and military powers; some of them have great powers. Occasionally, they support the center when it imposes decisions on smaller states, but they do so only when it suits them.

The institution of the United Nations is undoubtedly a major step forward in the structuralization of an interdependent superstructure of international relations. Prior to its creation, the various states were settling their quarrels on their own, often through wars. The invention of nuclear power now deters them from entering into war and strictly speaking, into a major war.

The United Nations was established primarily as a device to keep peace, and as a forum of negotiation to prevent large wars.* Its offices

---

Primitive Government, p. 63). The Nuer attach importance to the maintenance of peaceful relations, but they do not seem to attach importance to any concerted action at all, except perhaps in warfare: "When the Nuer dispute, it is usually not a clear issue between right and wrong. Indeed, it would be correct to say that, usually, both parties are to some extent right and that the only question which arises is, 'Who has the greater right?' " (Evans-Pritchard, p. 171). It is further said that the Nuer live in an ordered anarchy. They do not have any central authority except *kuaar twac*—the leopard-skin chiefs, whose political significance consists of settling feuds: "He, the chief has no judicial or executive authority, he has no means of compelling people to pay. . . . He is simply a mediator who persuades by exhortations and threats." (Evans-Pritchard, pp. 171-75). The interactions in the Nuer society are very complex. Indeed, a model of political system where a strictly differentiated authority presides over a given territory and makes compelling decisions which are sanctioned by its possibility to apply physical power does not fit the case of the United Nations of today. For a more elaborate comparative analysis of world and traditional primitive political systems, see R. D. Masters, "World Politics: A Primitive Political System," *World Politics,* Vol. XVI, July 1964.
* The preamble of the charter of the United Nations, written in 1945, states that the aims of the United Nations are as follows: "To maintain international peace and security by taking measures to remove threats to the peace and suppress acts of aggression, and by adjusting or settling disputes and situations which might lead to a breach of the peace . . . ; 'to develop friendly relations among nations based on respect for the principle of equal rights and self-determination of peoples, and to take other appropriate measures to strengthen universal peace'; 'to achieve interna-

have gradually become engaged in other activities as well—for instance, assisting in the economic development of developing nations and helping poor nations in their education and health services. Since 1950 the United Nations Economic and Social Council (ECOSOC) has undertaken discussions on the progress of economic development in the world and the problems related to it. Timidly it has advised that one per cent of the national income of the prosperous industrial nations be used to support the economic development in the poor nations. To perform the numerous special functions of the United Nations, specialized agencies or organizations were established, such as UNESCO (United Nations Educational Scientific and Cultural Organization), FAO (The Food and Agriculture Organization), and others.

Neither the United Nations nor its Security Council is a superstate.[47] The charter of the United Nations denies it any right "to intervene in matters which are essentially within the domestic jurisdiction of any state" (Art. 2.7). I have indicated that the Security Council has the right to enforce its decisions by various means, including warfare if it is considered necessary. The member states must in that case provide the necessary means and power.

Until now I have shunned the use of the term "system of international relations." In the relevant literature on international relations, one can learn that the concept "system of international relations" is a model, a derivative from the actual relations in the international sphere. Ernst B. Haas, whose work is widely regarded as a classic study of international relations, wrote that

> . . . the system consists of the relationships among the *patterns* of trade, war, migration, and subversion as they impinge upon one another in the confines of international organizations. . . . Systems may either stress or slight the empirical world; what matters is that the empirical world need not be aware of the system. . . . This said, another distinction is immediately in order. A *concrete system* is a pattern of relationships that can be specified with reasonable certainty and accuracy—as defined by the purposes of the scholar or observer—for a given historical period or a given empirical setting. An *analytical system* is a pattern of relationships that may or may not exist in actual life. It is designed by the observer for purposes of

tional cooperation in solving international problems of an economic, social, cultural, or humanitarian character, and in promoting and encouraging respect for human rights and for fundamental freedoms for all without distinction as to race, sex, language, or religion'; and 'to be a center for harmonizing the actions of nations in the attainment of these common ends.' " See L. M. Goodrich and E. Hambro, *Charter of the United Nations. Commentary and Document* (Boston: World Peace Foundation, 1946.)

projection, or for comparison with actual behavior patterns. Analytical systems can even be used for purposes of prediction. . . .[48]

As I said before, analytical systems are not of great interest for this study. Haas characterizes the present "concrete" international system as a "heterosymmetrical multipolarity." He assumes that in the future the polarization will increase even more, and will become evident not merely with respect to military and security questions, but also in trade, economic development and planning, and other fields.[49] Rephrasing his statement one can say that he is concerned with differentiation within the growing interdependence in international relations. This is especially evident in the different answers Haas gives in his writing to the question "Why cast integration into a systemic mold?" The answer is: because of the virtues of the systemic approach.[50] In one other instance, because participation in systems is a "learning process" as a result of which actors "learn" how to redefine their objectives in order to make them "rational."[51] Still another answer given by Haas is because "units engage in policies which are based on a systemic referent."[52]

While Haas views the nation-state as an "environment" of the international system, as a source of input or at least a "prism" or "screen" for the feedbacks of the international system, Deutsch takes an opposite view. His interests focus on nation-building, which eventually transpires into intra-national and international integration. Deutsch views the sphere of international relations as predominantly an arena of foreign policy. The question in which he is most interested, even when discussing the sphere of international relations, is "What are the relations of a nation to the world around it? . . . And how do they (nations) relate to international organizations and to the international political system?"[53] Thus he discusses previous efforts to unify Western Europe, and he asserts that regional organizations are the path to general integration. Although he analyzes the functions of the United Nations, of the Security Council, and other organizations with an international status, he shuns using the concept "international system." What exists in the international sphere, in Deutsch's analysis, is a constantly changing assemblage of units which lead to amalgamation only in rare cases. As for the subject of international systems, Deutsch poses questions rather than answering them: "Is there more amalgamation toward single peoples or single markets in particular regions of the world, or has there been a sharpening of differences?"[54] "The United Nations: World Assembly or World Governments?"[55] Much of his writing is devoted to explanations of why such questions become current. Objectively, however, Deutsch is preoccupied with two tendencies: the differentiation of nations in their process of nation-building, and their integration in supranational structures. In a sense, Haas and Deutsch present complementary analyses. Haas views the process from the level of the superstructures of international systems, while Deutsch views it from the perspective of state-units which are engaged in a process of wider integration.

Morton Kaplan is known in the field of international studies as a student of models of international systems.[56] He distinguishes six such models: (1) the "balance of power" model; (2) the loose bipolar system; (3) the tight bipolar system; (4 and 5) the hierarchical system (in directive and indirective forms); and (6) the unit-veto system. Only the first two are said to have respective concrete counterparts in the modern world.[57] All six models are analytical devices of divergent states of equilibrium which are abstractly imagined. The entire endeavor is an exercise in speculation, which is expected to be instrumental in comparative analysis.

b. Differentiation and Integration in the Sphere of International Relations

The international system is composed of units which are systems in themselves. It encompasses not only states and international organizations (which are obviously systemic structures), but also various systems of international exchange: trade, achievements in science and technology, cultural patterns, beliefs, and other products of human activity and creativity, and all kinds of societal experience. So the sphere of international relations is not only a sphere of political activities. The writings discussed here are primarily concerned with international political interactions, and it is true that these are of primary importance when international systems are under consideration.

Second, in the literature on the subject, the discussion is most often on growing integration. I prefer to speak of growing interdependence. Integration is a form of interdependence which, apart from the dependence of the units on what is going on within and around other units, presupposes a degree of cohesion or cooperation among them. While it is true that some units of the international system become integrated, what seems to me to be more important (and in a sense more primary—occurring all over, and in a sense conditioning the endemic or general integration) is the proliferation and growth of interdependence of systems in international relations. Interdependence may consist in subordination, cooperation, competition, a steady flow of exchanges, the balanced autonomy or sovereignty of the units—in short, any situation where events and processes in some units affect events and processes in other units, even if they are highly separate and quite isolated. Complementary interdependencies in international relations develop especially as a result of industrialization and international trade. Most of the international relations belong to the type of interdependencies of coexistence. As a matter of fact, people and leaderships of countries became aware of their importance only quite recently.

The growing interdependence in the world is evident not only in world politics but also in all kinds of small facts of daily life. The stock market on Wall Street reacts to crises in Europe or between African states. The devaluation of the British pound and the American dollar affected many currencies in the world, even though they did not belong to the sterling area or have close financial dependencies on the American dollar. Changes in the prices of important commodities in one country sometimes affect the whole international market. The fate of a Ghanaian cocoa grower or a Kenyan or Brazilian coffee grower depends on the tastes of an American, British, or French housewife, and on the current course of the Soviet Union's policy—that is, whether in the effort to strengthen its influence in Africa or Latin America the Soviet Union decides to buy the local coffee, cocoa, or other products. President de Gaulle's actions to buttress the value of the French franc caused a chain reaction which affected the dollar earners. In turn, the fall of de Gaulle affected the position of both the franc and the German mark.

News, ideas, cultural patterns, innovations, and fashions today spread rapidly throughout the world by different means and channels of communication and exchange. Even iron curtains cannot effectively withhold enough of this spread of interconnections. True, the Soviet citizen somewhere in Siberia may be quite isolated from the outside world, but even he finds an increasing number of foreign goods in his store today; he more often uses foreign tools and operates foreign machines in his factory. Even he occasionally listens to a foreign radio broadcast and watches a foreign movie.* The bamboo curtain is, of course, less penetrable, but who can claim that what has happened behind the bamboo curtain has no bearing on events in the United States or in other parts of the world. The recent development of relations between the U.S.A. and China shows that mutual influences may even increase in the future. It is not just that everything is interconnected. The volume of interdependencies encompassing the entire world has become wider and denser, more articulate and institutionalized. The world is split by a multitude of conflicts but even they contribute to its interdependence. Growing systemness and interdependence in international relations, of course, does not imply

* Some time ago I traveled from Tanzania throughout the Middle East, Western Europe, and Great Britain to the United States, and later to Canada. The trip lasted about two months. During that time, as I stopped in various places, I had a chance to watch on the televisions of different countries the same serial programs made in the United States.

greater unity of the world or between states. In the atmosphere of enforced coexistence it allows only settlement of some differences and conflicts by peaceful and political means, through negotiations, and indeed attempts to organize some cooperation for the benefit of all.

Within growing interdependence there is more differentiation. Let me examine some of its manifold facets. First, the *differentiation and articulation of nations* must be discussed.* In some cases, it was a lengthy process which lasted many centuries. In other cases, it was a process of eruption. Some nations evolved their national identity; other nations were built.[58] In Europe nations evolved in a lasting historical process of cultural transformation and amalgamation; kingdoms became states, and former subjects, through emancipation, became citizens and acquired freedoms and rights. The American nation emerged from a federation. In Africa the party came first, and the state was next; now the process of the amalgamation of tribes, often an extremely difficult one, and the generation of national identities is under way. In Asia one can find all these courses and other more specific ones. National differentiation is actively progressing not only in new nations but also in Europe. One constantly hears of national aspirations to separate identities, autonomy and even complete independence of what hitherto were at most separate ethnicities. Ideologies, cultural differences, myths, economic interests, ambitions of leaders, and so forth, are all instrumental in this everlasting and continuous process.

Second, there is the differentiation of *regionally and ideologically oriented blocs or communities of nations*. In the past, in the era of kingdoms, blocs were established on the basis of dynastic connections and intermarriages. Nowadays blocs are established principally on the basis of ideological affinities. While nations institutionalize their differentiated identity by proclaiming independence, blocs announce their separation and establishment in formal treaties. They subsequently erect specialized agencies and organizations to implement their aims. Six West European states, united on a regional basis and by ideological affinity, formed the Common Market. Then it became extended when it was joined by Great Britain and other nations which before were united in a separate constellation. The Common Market is affiliated with a number of other countries that to an extent share its ideological and economic orientation. Some leading European politicians view the Common Market as a beginning of new general European integration. Until recently, however, it reflected more the growing interdependence and systemness of the European economic structure. It established a number of subsidiary agencies, such as

---

* The topic will be discussed in detail later. See Chapter V, part 2.

the EURATOM, ECSC (European Coal and Steel Community), CCC (Customs Cooperation Council) and others. NATO (North Atlantic Treaty Organization) is an example of a military bloc. It was called into existence by the United States, Canada, and a number of European states sharing in anticommunist orientation. The United States is a member of still other regional organizations which cover other areas: the OAS (Organization of American States), SEATO (South East Asia Treaty Organization), and a number of others.

The Soviet-bloc countries are organized by the defense treaty of the Warsaw Pact; for economic cooperation they have COMECON (Communist Organization for Economic Cooperation). They, too, have established a number of subsidiary agencies. In addition, they are unified through alliances among the communist parties.

China is struggling steadfastly to establish her own circle of satellites, yet up until now she has been rather unsuccessful (with the exception of Albania).

Out of a spirit of African unity the OAU (Organization of African Unity) was established. Cooperation within it, however, is not very effective. A number of additional regional African organizations can also be listed: the EAEC (East African Economic Community), OCAM (Afro-Malgasy Joint Organization), and OERS (Organization of Senegal River States), and some others.

Arabs—apart from the Arab League, which is an arena for the internal struggles of the Arab world—are united in their hate for Israel. They have established a number of agencies and organizations to promote their cause, yet except in the United Nations, they have been unable to act as a bloc.

In addition to a number of other bloc-type organizations not mentioned here, still alive is the British Commonwealth, which, on the basis of tradition, holds together a number of states now of different ideological and political organization. There is also a sort of a unity of formerly French countries which are bilaterally related with France.

Third, there is *differentiation of what may be called the channels of specific exchanges:* trade, cultural affinities, or a common language, and so forth. These are not explicit societal or political structures, though the exchange activities are performed by specialized agencies. Each country has agencies to promote trade with foreign countries, conduct the exchange of information and cultural activities, explore the possibilities of cooperation, and the like. Such channels and agencies overlap, mesh, and pervade each other, and constitute a complex network of channels for international exchanges. Exchanges take place in the implementation of policies, and each state has its definite patterned policies as to what kind of exchanges it seeks, and with which partners. Exchanges may be direct or mediated by other partners. They may reflect the economic complementarity of countries: one is industrial, the other is agricultural; one has industries which produce commodities needed by the other; one is a natural market for the other. They may be based on certain predilections developed over time—common past, language, culture, and so forth. Thus the African and Asian countries previously under British rule still remain in the Commonwealth, and tend to maintain lively trade and cultural relations with their former metropolis. Poland and Rumania have persistent inclinations toward alliances with France, and Czechoslovakia leans toward Austria and Germany, in spite of the fact that Poland, Rumania, and Czechoslovakia belong to the communist bloc. One may say that these are natural inclinations, and so they are.

Conflict and consensus are mutually conditioned. Association implies dissociation, and vice versa. What constitutes differentiation in one respect reflects integration or growing interdependence in another. Nationalism is a process of differentiation within nations; it is also a process of internal integration and consolidation within the structures of transpiring systems and role structures. Blocs differentiate one group of states from another. On the one hand, they unite, while on the other, they generate animosities, conflicts, and cooperation. As I have pointed out on many occasions, differentiation and growing interdependence are two aspects of the same process.

Another process of differentiation which creates interconnections (and thus interdependencies) is the emergence in modern times of the manifold *international voluntary associations*. Traditional societies basically knew only two types of international relations (apart from trade relations): those under the domain of the church and those under the domain of the king and aristocracy. The first type was institutionalized through religion, the second, in dynastic colligations of aristocratic families. In modern times numerous international voluntary associations developed, due to the universality and specificity of orientations, the professionalization, the development of a multitude of economic, cultural, and political interconnections, the technological buildup, and the spread of communications and exchanges. They serve to link the interests and specific objectives of particular states into larger networks. They constitute a separate network of international systemic relations.

c. Visions for the Future

There is a saying: an optimist today is a man who thinks that the future is still uncertain. Such a reflection could also be derived from the various contemporary visions of the future of mankind.* Contrary to their nineteenth-century predecessors, the twentieth century visionaries are rather gloomy, dejected, and in despair about the prospects for our future. As I have indicated, convergence theorists have now taken a course to predict a similar trend of increased, accelerated bureaucratization in the Soviet Union, the United States, and other societies. They assume that a single, worldwide system will eventually have to be established for the sake of functional rationality and efficiency. It is described as a kind of supra-Third Reich totalitarian society, or an Ingsoc as imagined by Orwell. Some see the spring of such inevitability in technological development; others see it in militarization; still others, in bureaucratization, in the growing systemness, or in a combination of these and other factors. Thus J. Ellul writes:

> Finally, technique causes the state to become totalitarian, to absorb the citizens' life completely. I have noted that this occurs as a result of the accumulation of techniques in the hands of the state. Techniques are mutually engendered and hence interconnected, forming a system that tightly encloses all our activities. When the state takes hold of a single thread of this network of techniques, little by little it draws itself all the matter and the method, whether or not it consciously wills to do so.
>
> Even when the state is resolutely liberal and democratic, it cannot do otherwise than become totalitarian. It becomes so either directly or, as in the United States, through intermediate persons. But, despite differences, all such systems come ultimately to the same result.[59]

True, Ellul emphasizes that the future totalitarian state and society will also be totally rational, which means it will not be racist, brutal, or a reign of arbitrary dictators.

> In such a state nothing useless exists; there is no torture; torture is a wasteful expenditure of psychic energy which destroys salvageable resources without producing useful results. There is no systematically organized famine, but rather a recognition of the pressing necessity of maintaining the labor force in good condition. There is nothing arbitrary, for the arbitrary represents the very opposite of technique, in which everything "has a reason" (not a final but a mechanical reason).[60]

After reading these paragraphs I had a number of questions: What will these systems do with the useless people—those who will not be able

* The literature on the subject is extensive, and this fascinating topic cannot be discussed here broadly enough. Only a few selected prognoses will be briefly confronted here.

to work or will not have work? Will they allow useless recreation? What will they do with philosophers and artists? What is the purpose of building such a state? A few pages further, there is an answer to the first question: There will be no useless people in such societies. The "thinking machines" will calculate exactly how many and what kind of people are needed. Ellul tells us the following: "Artificial insemination will be employed. This according to Muller, will 'permit the introduction into a carrier uterus of an ovum fertilized in *vitro*, ovum and sperm . . . having been taken from persons representing the masculine ideal and the feminine ideal, respectively. The reproductive cells in question will preferably be those of persons dead long enough that a true perspective of their lives and works, free of all personal prejudice, can be seen.' "[61] It may be added from other sources that a highly developed technique of "xeroxing" will be invented to reproduce the selected patterned men and women, and not only hearts but other parts of the body will be transplanted as well. Who knows? Maybe the brain, too, will be transplanted, or at least a way will be found to transfer the accumulated knowledge and experience from one mind to another. People will be made happy and maintained happy throughout their lives by drugs which will keep them in a state of constant and instant happiness—all, of course, under the control of the government. Perhaps to be sad or unhappy will be a capital crime. Ellul mentions that "The orientation of this Humanism may be Communist or non-Communist, but it hardly makes any difference."[62]

Brzezinski and Huntington assume that it does make a difference.[63] Disregarding all established schemes, they have undertaken a comparative analysis of the changes, transformations, mechanisms of decision-making, structures, and so forth in the United States and the Soviet Union. They have discovered a parallelism between the two countries. They assume that "The Soviet and American political systems, each in its own way, have been highly successful."[64] They assume that in the future the political system of the Soviet Union "will be characterized by greater rationality, less coercion, increased reliance on social control."[65] It will be a system of "affluent collectivism." They say that the Soviet system has many advantages over the Western system, yet "All the strong points of the Soviet system—in ideology, in leadership, in policy-making—would be impossible to duplicate in a society which protects the liberty of the individual."[66] They express the opinion that convergence theory minimizes and ignores the differences between the two cultures, structures, and political systems and exaggerates the importance of other factors. Their conclusion, then, is that eventually both societies will overcome their current problems and continue to evolve in their own way and will not converge.

The official Soviet view on the perspectives for the future can be summed up as follows: For the time being, and in the immediate future, for the sake of avoiding a destructive war, the capitalist and socialist (Soviet) systems have to coexist, evolving collaterally. Simultaneously, the "ideological struggle" has to be intensified. This means two things: (a) "Revisionism" (that is, any deviation from the official party line) and "bourgeois ideology" have to be suppressed in the Soviet Union and the Soviet-type states; and (b) Efforts to increase the external domain of influence have to be maximized by different means, especially in regard to "countries that have chosen the noncapitalist road of development."

Semischolarly or scholarly Soviet literature on the prospects for the future (I discard science fiction altogether), can be divided into three groups: (a) Books with ideological formulas on "problems of building scientific communism";[67] (b) Advice for Third World nations on how to attain affluence in a noncapitalist way;[68] (I will not discuss this kind of literature here); and (c) Some literature which opposes the official Party view. Two such publications are especially known.[69] The first is by the leading Soviet physicist, A. D. Sakharov, who is also a leading advocate of convergence. In his opinion, only a combined effort by all mankind can solve all our problems. "Only universal cooperation and the lofty moral ideals of socialism and labor, accompanied by the elimination of dogmatism and pressures of the concealed interests of ruling classes, will preserve civilization."[70] He believes that in a converged society which encompasses at least the Soviet bloc and the Western countries under a socialist government respecting intellectual freedom, the wasteful efforts previously invested in developing armaments will be utilized in productive activities for the benefit of all.

Amalrik undertakes an analysis of the present state of the Soviet Union in order to derive conclusions as to what its future will be. It is a very grim picture, with little hope for improvement. In his observation, the whole society of the Soviet Union is but a huge prison. Its leaders are just prisoners of the first order. It is a stagnant, inefficient, eroded, gigantic state, ruled by terror and a mindless, mediocre bureaucracy. "Freedom there is synonymous with 'disorder.' " True, the terror has now become more selective, and mass persecution more lenient. Amalrik argues that it is a state dominated by a bureaucracy which pays lip-service to an ideology of socialism, but which, in fact, has only one aim: self-preservation. "The only thing it [the regime] wants is for everything to go on as before: authorities to be recognized, the intelligentsia to keep quiet, no rocking of the system by dangerous and unfamiliar reforms."[71] What the bureaucracy fears most are innovations. Subsequently he envisages that the regime will become increasingly weaker and more self-destructive, although its military potential may even increase. Eventually, it is bound to clash, and the war this time will be with China. After a protracted war, he predicts the disintegration and dissipation of the Soviet Union, followed by a long period of anarchy.

Both Sakharov and Amalrik belong to those Eastern Europe thinkers who believe that a huge, centralized system of political power which controls all the spheres of life without democracy is inefficient, wasteful, redundant, absurd, and inhuman. While Sakharov believes that it must change because it is irrational to keep it running and growing, Amalrik says: "It is possible that we will indeed have a 'socialism' with bare knees someday; but not likely one with a human face."[72]

The question is: do men have a choice or is everything predetermined? Most proponents of the convergence and evolution theories seem to think that there are no options. Clark Kerr,[73] on the contrary, argues that the future is a matter of choice, and that "The coming struggle for power is over how far communism and capitalist pluralism may be drawn away from their coordinated and managerial forms towards syndicalism."[74] He thinks that the future is not in a centralized system but in decentralized plural collectivities,* and he points out that there are many ways in which individual freedom can be increased within modern industrialism, thus making industrialism more humane. It has to be a "free choice society," based on liberal pluralism, the decentralization of large organizations, and a diversification of opportunities allowing a wide latitude for life styles off the job.

E. Haas is a proponent of a realistic approach. Looking over the threshold of the new era of postindustrial societies, he predicts:

> . . . Culturally, the world will be more and more sensate, preoccupied with empirical perception, secular, humanistic, utilitarian, and hedonistic. People will be less and less willing to deter gratification; they will be bent exclusively on immediate enjoyment of whatever they value. Elites will tend toward both egalitarianism and meritocracy. Scientific knowledge of all kinds will accumulate even more rapidly than it does now. Society will change faster and more universally in proportion to the application of this scientific knowledge through technology and its diffusion. Industrialization will be worldwide, though its benefits may not be; both affluence and leisure will increase in proportion, but population will also continue to burgeon, thus giving us a continuing race between food supply and people.

---

* It is worth noting that Kerr's approach is to some extent congruent with the concepts of African socialism and other similar concepts in Third World nations. There, too, the stress is on collectivism in smaller units which mesh together into a large society. And there is hope to the extent that the role of centralization can be kept under control by small corporate groups.

Primary occupations will decline even more in importance, and secondary occupations will begin a downward trend. Education and literacy will spread more evenly throughout the world, and so will the capability for mass destruction through war. Urbanization will reach the point of the megalopolis, if not the necropolis.[75]

It is a projection of the present into the future, accounting for the ongoing trends without wishful thinking. Such ongoing processes as described above will be worldwide. They will proceed in a parallel manner, at different paces, within a worldwide interdependence. Hence Haas also anticipates that the current multipolar heterosymmetrical system in international relations will produce a multi-bloc, asymmetrical state of relations. Thus, more differentiation within a growing interdependence will ensue. The West will retain its imperfect pluralism, in which although the masses are unable to make important decisions, the leaders still depend on them and have to bargain for their support.[76] The Soviet bloc countries will remain authoritarian. China will be able to increase its economic output, and in its search for mutual exchanges with other states, it will stabilize its internal situation. In the Third World nations, where the pace of industrialization and agricultural improvements does not match the spread of education or satisfy the rising expectations and aspirations, one may expect some convulsive political upheavals. Subsequently, however, with further increases in production and as a result of the next stages of industrialization, the situation will become stabilized. The role of international organizations and interdependencies will simultaneously become greater, especially to hold together a world which is divided into many blocs and differentiated on many levels.*

How remote the contemporary visions of the future are from those of the old man Karl Marx, who dreamed that society in the future would become a sort of worldwide community of philosophers and artists like ancient Athens, but, of course, without slaves.

* Herman Kahn and B. Bruce-Briggs (in *Things to Come, Thinking About the Seventies and Eighties*. New York: Macmillan, 1972) present a similar vision of the future in the next twenty years. In their *Surprise-Free Projection for the Seventies and Eighties* they predict that we will continue to live in *La Deuxième Belle Époque*, in which, in their opinion, we live already. They forecast a relative loss of power by the two contemporary superpowers and raise in power of Japan to the second position after the U.S. They tell us that we should expect a worldwide "green revolution," but also intensification of environmental predicaments in connection with further technological developments. They hope, however, that international environmental controls will be introduced eventually. Sustained growth will continue and the ratio of the world's GNP will be kept within 3-15 per cent limits; the gap in wealth between the already developed countries and the rest of the world will not change significantly. Multinational corporations will become even bigger and more powerful. New/old turmoils will continue in Africa and the Middle East. The world will become more interdependent. Cultural and ideological patterns will spread rapidly from one area to others.

10. Man: Master or Slave of Systems?

a. Ancient Arab tales tell about powerful genies imprisoned in bottles. When they are found and released, they become either great servants to the finder or menaces to people. The Greek poet Hesiod wrote a marvelous story about Pandora, the beautiful girl created by Hefaestus at Zeus's orders, for the purpose of punishing the people. When possessed by Epimetheus, Pandora opened the jar containing the treacherous evil gifts sent by the gods, thus releasing the miseries and troubles which have beset and harassed us to this day. Only one worthy gift, the spirit of Hope, was left under the lid. Medieval Jewish tales speak of Golems—artificial homunculi created by rabbis. One Golem is especially famous: he was made of clay and brought to life by the incantations of Rabbi Löw of Prague. When he escaped from the control of his creator, the Golem became destructive and dangerous and had to be destroyed by the rabbi. According to ancient Ghanaian beliefs, thoughts released from the human brain become powers. They roam around the world, materialize into beings, work for people or harm them, or become spirits. In any case, as soon as they are released from the brain, they can no longer be controlled; they live on their own.

From the onset of human existence man has faced the problem that he might release forces which he would not be able to control. And he actually does release them. He creates objects, invents mechanisms, and organizes systems which he is unable to master—systems that absorb him, make him a part of them, and are thus dominant over him. Man recurrently finds that he is in a trap. He wants to free himself from dependency on nature, on society, or on the systems which surround him. He invents, creates, builds, organizes, and discovers that he is a captive of his creativity, of the norms he has established, of the systems he has expanded, and of the structures he has erected.

The topic reappears frequently and in various versions in literature. Engels argued that man can never wholly anticipate all the consequences of his actions, especially the consequences of his inventions. Robert K. Merton used similar observations for a framework for his theory of manifest and latent functions. He tells us that "numerous other sociological observers have, then, from time to time distinguished between categories of subjective disposition ('needs, interests, purposes') and categories of generally unrecognized but objective functional consequences ('unique advantages,' 'never conscious' consequences, 'unintended . . . service to society,' 'function not limited to conscious and explicit purpose')."[77] Numerous examples are then listed. True, this is not exactly the same problem that I am posing here, yet these observations are variations on the same theme.

Lorenz von Stein writes that in the middle of the nineteenth century the negative equality of the classes and estates which had been in existence until then was replaced by a positive equality institutionalized in citizenship. Civil society, encompassing the citizenry, generated the new modern state to deal with its matters, to act on its behalf. Soon, however, the state developed its own interests and imposed its will over the society.[78] The description can continue: as a result of a long, precarious process of class and group conflict, the society finally institutionalizes a system of representation. Parliaments and political parties are established to express the will of the people, and specifically the interests of various groups in regard to the state. Soon, however, political parties acquire new functions which are often no longer derived from the nature of the association. So they become channels for recruitment to political authority; they become agencies which mold public opinion; they become avenues for political careers; they acquire institutions to perform these and many other functions, and they are subsequently gradually incorporated into the structure of the state. They are still representative institutions, yet they also perform other functions which are often incongruent with their original aims.[79] R. Michels points out that in order to perform all these functions and to cope with the extended membership as well, parties established bureaucracies. Soon, however, the bureaucracies developed their own interests and their own bureaucratic codes and patterns of behavior which differed from those originally proclaimed by the party. Subsequently, they looked upon the party as their subordinate domain. Since then, a multitude of studies has been published on bureaucracies, showing again and again how systems of bureaucracies differentiate themselves from the original structure, develop their own interests and structures, and impose them on the original structure that they were intended to serve. The function of rule and service is fused. Rulers and bureaucrats call themselves servants of the society.

W. G. Sumner,[80] and later J. O. Hertzler, made use of such observations to construct a general theory of institutions. Hertzler tells us that any society, any association emanates numerous institutions.

> The specific institutions are the numerous special and concrete forms of social apparatus by means of which the multiplicity of needs are met. But the specific institutions fall into major groups and fields. Such combined institutions in a particular field constitute an order or a system, that is, a segment of the functional activities essential in any society. We can speak of institutions as "systems" of human activities or behavior "clustering" around functions. Thus the economic "sys-

tem" consists of an array of specific institutions which have to do with economic needs, activities, functions and mechanisms; the political, religious and all of the other major institutional systems, are similarly constituted and have parallel blocks of individual and social needs to satisfy.[81]

Societies in general, and associations as fractions of societies in particular establish institutions as mechanisms to fulfill certain functions. Institutions grow into systems and alternative structures which engender subservient institutions.

Systems in societies are *made of men*. Man cannot live beyond systems. He struggles against the fetters of the systems in which he finds himself. To liberate himself and other people he invents and erects new systems which are more efficient and engulf and subordinate him even more.

b. As I have indicated, modern life would not be possible without a high degree of systemic connections and many overlapping, enmeshed systems. Growing systemness and economic development are mutually interdependent. Communications within and between societies expand by means of spreading system interconnections. There is a proliferation, extension, and advance in intersocietal and worldwide exchanges of ideas and beliefs, experiences, commodities, and cultural achievements in the course of and by means of the growing systemness. System growth implies and materializes in higher specialization, greater differentiation of roles, increased efficiency, better organization, and, as was said many times, greater interdependence. These results are generally regarded as desirable. Yet there is still another side to the growing systemness. Industrialization, social change, development, and growing systemness also produce uprootedness. They cause alienation among men. They pervert the social character of human interactions and deprive them of individuality. As both Marx and Toennies (and many other writers afterwards) asserted, they result in the transformation of life into a huge market. Traditions and attachments to traditional ways of life are destroyed in their course. Life, production, consumption, recreation, joy, sadness, and even the people themselves become standardized. With them come the widely known phenomena of the crowd of lonely people, the mass society. Could we have the first without the second, the desirable without the undesirable, the abundance without the mass production and standardization?

There are those who believe in the rule of the inevitability of events —in fate, predestination, Kismet, Karma, and so forth—those who assume that everything is preordained; they believe that what happened did so because it was inevitable, and what will happen will do so again in the implementation of inevitability. In their opinion, systems are teleological, and move toward their equifinality. If the equifinality is a totalitarian communist, or fascist society, or one similar to them, what can we do? Is it not better to adjust ourselves to it—to float with the stream? Besides, such systems will functionally be more rational than those of today. True, they say that the Soviet economy and the economies of the totalitarian states have until now been wasteful and inefficient, but with the recent introduction of computers, linear programming, and various modern techniques, this can be changed. Central planning, the so-called command economy, and with it, social policies, can now be rationally managed and conducted. Why can it be done with computers and why was it not done without them? It is supposed to be self-evident—but why? What in my opinion is evident is that this logic contains a tacit expectation (if not hope) that the rulers and leaders of such perfect future totalitarian societies will not need to think and will not make decisions. Computers will do that for them. The leaders' tasks will be merely to maintain order. Will they struggle for power or for influence? Will they imprison their opponents? Should we assume not? Since computers and linear programming will decide who should have power, influence, and prestige; who gets what, and what is wrong and what is good, there will be no opponents. Should we assume that when someone seeks a position in such a perfect state, he will just have to file an application on a punch card containing information on his qualifications to the Department of Allocation of Roles, and he will automatically be allocated? Mayakovsky, a Russian poet at the time of the October Revolution, already envisaged such a mechanism, even prior to the invention of computers. In his play *Bath,* the computer forecast and imagined by him, has the habit of always responding: "Request denied."

On paper, systems can be abstracted from men, from their concrete societal reality, from human ambitions, aspirations, striving, from culture and civilization, from daily conflicts, and so forth. On paper they can be made perfect without any problems. However, culture and civilization apart from technology are constituted of traditions, norms, conventions, rituals—seemingly useless refined games and patterns of behavior. In the abstract pursuit of logical thinking, one can forget about the specificity of individual cases; one can abstract from that element of reality, or assume that it is constant. But it is not. A system which is not a construct of variables, a concrete system of a real society purified from such elements, would be either a system of mammals or a system of robots. Sane systems which encompass human beings have to be systems of irrational beings pretending that they are rational. Man is not a master of the systems in which his life takes place. Yet societal systems do not exist prior to men or without men. They are the products of historical processes, and the past cannot be changed. The systems of tomorrow depend on what man does today, and at each step numerous options are open. Perfect societal systems, especially systems without conflict, competition, or social problems cannot be envisaged. Yet there is an option as to which of the imperfect systems to choose. To be more exact, about 20 per cent of the people are lucky enough to live in societies where some options are still possible. Man is not a master over the systems he creates, yet only in those societies where he has the right to dissent, to express his opinion, to disagree, to be in conflict with other groups and with the systems—only in those societies is he not a slave of the systems. Two courses are open in the future: (1) more systemness and less choice, or (2) more systemness and more choice.

The Third Approach: Development and Innovation in the Search for Security

This section is organized around theories which focus primarily, if not exclusively, on causes of development. More strictly, it concerns psychological attitudes assumed to precede and accompany modern rapid accelerated economic development, and which may be regarded as causing that development. After a brief review of the discussion around Max Weber's work, *The Protestant Ethic and the Spirit of Capitalism,* my attention will be directed toward an analysis of a variety of approaches to the motivations which, in action, produce the effect of economic development. Theories of status withdrawal and achievement motivation will be reviewed. A number of propositions concerning other motivations which presumably affect the process of economic development and behavior in the course of industrialization will be presented and examined. Such theories as a rule do not engage in explanations of what is economic or societal development; they are not concerned with explorations of the effects and courses of development and growth processes. They take for granted that development is desirable, and attempt to answer the questions: "Why did development occur at the time and in the place it did?" "Why did it occur in Europe first?"

Undoubtedly, these are important and stimulating questions which have provoked prolific reflections and illuminating theories. Yet the questions themselves already contain a number of implicit presuppositions, and hence are presumptive if not presumptuous.[1] First, such questions presuppose that development is unique rather than common, everlasting, and continuous. It occurs in some societies under specific conditions, it does not occur in others. Second, the questions concern modern eco-

nomic development, and they imply the understanding that such development occurs in consequence of industrialization. Third, they are not
concerned with problems and aspects of evolution and societal growth
discussed previously.

It is known that people in parts of the world other than Europe—in
China, India, in what later became the United States, and in many parts
of Africa—have in the past, during the medieval ages preceding the industrial era, lived in civilizations and states of not a lesser complexity than
that existing in Europe at the same time. Thus theories answering the
question: "Why did it happen in Europe first?" begin with the assertion
that though other people founded highly sophisticated and magnificent
cultures, though they applied in their productive activities (in harnessing energy) technologies and organization comparable to or even "higher"
than those in Europe at that time, *it was not fortuitous* that industrialization happened first in Western Europe, and that so many discoveries and
inventions instrumental to the subsequent appearance of affluent societies
were made there first. This is an important point: all the theories which I
will discuss now exclude a view that modernization happened in Europe
first by accident. They exclude, for instance, the probability that one important invention such as the steam engine or a number of coinciding inventions and events happening fortuitously in Europe triggered off a subsequent avalanche of other inventions, discoveries, and technological
innovations producing concomitant social and economic changes, cumulatively bringing about the birth and growth of modern industrial societies. To be sure, no one has ever put forward such a guess, and since
there is no ground for it, it is not implied here either. Instead, the popular belief is that something was in the air or in the quality of the people
to make Europe distinctive and special, to make Europe the cradle of
modernity. The question is what.

Both this and the earlier question "Why did it all happen in Europe
first?" were answered at least in two different ways. Such questions were
instrumental in provoking racist responses and were used rhetorically in
a wide spectrum of theories which promulgated racist ideas. They were
specifically used in theories attempting to prove the racial, intellectual,
cultural, and general superiority of the white race. At the minimum such
theories embarked on explanations of the exclusive character if not of
European people themselves then of the stimulating climate in which they
live. Subsequently the argument was refined by pointing out, for example, that the climate was more stimulating in one country than in another.

Books on European superiority over people of other continents were
written long before the era of industrialization and modern times. However, colonial conquests and later the spread of fascism produced condi-

tions especially facilitating the spread and promulgation of such theories. Especially in the nineteenth and the first half of the twentieth century European white racism flourished exuberantly. Many of the racist theorists, starting with A. Gobineau, A. H. S. Chamberlain, V. Lapogue, and ending with the most fervent and prominent Nazi ideologists, have exploited various versions of the question. "Why did it happen in Europe first?" has been used both as a rhetorical question and as an answer in such theories. It was a basic point in their argument, a shield in defense of their chauvinistic pride and a trick to avoid all complex and important problems involved in such a discussion. Such theories are irrelevant to our discussion, however, and will not be considered here.

Our concern will be with another kind of theory, with the specific approach which attributes the beginning of industrialization, its subsequent overwhelming spread and all changes related to it, to a specific motivation and behavior. In short, it attributes development to a specific way of thinking and acting which spread over Europe in accelerating intensity from some time in the sixteenth century and was transplanted later to America and other continents of the world. It may be called a psychological factor, or a restless spirit incessantly forcing people to act, to push forward, to invent, to discover, create, acquire, build, expand. Some call it the spirit of capitalism, others an achievement-orientation, still others a striving for modernity. If this factor was the cause or at least a facet of industrialization and development of Europe, if it is instrumental in producing development, it has to be known and understood in order to apply it in other parts of the world where industrialization and development is required. The first man to propose such an approach was Max Weber in *The Protestant Ethnic and the Spirit of Capitalism*.

1. Weber's Protestant Ethic and the Spirit of Capitalism

As a rule, great works in the social sciences have the peculiar quality that they not only contain great ideas but can be read many times and interpreted differently each time. Apart from the idea intentionally expressed by a great man, such works usually contain a wealth of other thoughts prodigally and carelessly left to successors for pondering. Interpreters dig in those mines of ideas, occasionally discovering new precious stones to be polished into shining gems to the glory of the discoverer as well as to the source. Today, even the most fervent admirers of Weber do not claim that development or even capitalism was generated solely by the Protestant Ethic, but that does not seem to be the main point made by Weber himself. He spoke about the capitalism of his time, about modernization before the First World War. Asserting that economic development in

Western Europe occurred only when the society became psychologically ripe to produce it, he argued that Protestantism facilitated and stimulated its psychological maturation. Though Weber does not mention Marxism at all in *The Protestant Ethic and the Spirit of Capitalism,* his argument is obviously a polemic against Marx. It could read as follows: it is not true that capitalism sprang from the development of "productive forces" of technological development. On the contrary, capitalism and technological development were possible because of specific mental conditions occurring after the sixteenth century in Western Europe which were especially due to the spread of the Protestant ethic. He does not tell us why at that particular time conditions became ripe for such a drastic change in psychological attitudes. Historical explanations are available for that. Marxism also provides an answer—again a controversial one—to this question. In fact, Weber's argument is directed against the insufficiency, the exaggeration, and the one-sidedness of Marxism; it is not a repudiation or an attempt to disprove it totally.

I do not intend to add a new interpretation of *The Protestant Ethic,* to the ones already in circulation. I am merely presenting its basic ideas with special emphasis on the points relevant to the forthcoming discussion.

Weber begins his reflection with an appreciation of European culture. He sees far away in the past the seeds of what he calls "Occidental rationalism," a characteristic of capitalism found in many spheres of life in Western civilization. He devotes much attention to the spirit of capitalism, telling us "that development of the spirit of capitalism is best understood as part of the development of rationalism as a whole, and could be deduced from the fundamental position of rationalism on the basic problems of life."[2] The spirit of capitalism is evident where man is dominated by the making of money, where acquisition and action in pursuit of more acquisition become the ultimate purpose of life. Those under its spell cannot stand waste of time in idle ramble or even in the spontaneous enjoyment of life. Life is to be spent in achieving. The pursuer of acquisition is hence restlessly and constantly in action to achieve the maximum in the shortest time possible. He advocates greater efficiency, since this leads to more results in his incessant fervent striving. He acts systematically generating and building systems of action in calculation and anticipation of others' actions. He is under a constant urge to rationalize his enterprise, the organization under his control, and the capitalist organization in general. Credibility, punctuality, honesty, inventiveness, adaptability to new circumstances are prized by him, since such qualities are instrumental in efforts of achieving. ". . . Capitalism is identical with the pursuit of profit, and forever *renewed* profit, by means of continuous, rational, capitalistic enterprise."[3] The man under the spell of capitalist spirit has no regard for anything which holds him up or impedes his urge. Weber especially tells us that such a man has little regard for traditions, which often look to him as fetters impeding his climb to wealth, and from there to still greater wealth. "The most important opponent with which the spirit of capitalism . . . has had to struggle, was that type of attitude and reaction to new situations which we may designate as traditionalism."[4] Hence the capitalist, the acquisition-seeker is an innovator by nature. Action and profit-making become a *calling* for him. Yet it is not greed which drives him. Weber argues that in fact ruthless unscrupulous greed for money without calculation becomes a hindrance in capitalist entrepreneurship. It is irrational, and rather typical for tradition-oriented, backward societies. The capitalist spirit requires that both the acquisition and the spending of money be strictly calculated and directed toward the goal of progressive optimal accumulation.

Weber asserts that the spirit of capitalism which permeated and engulfed the societies of Western Europe and America, the spirit which produced the modern Western civilization, were engendered by the Protestant Ethic. Since he omits other factors which may have facilitated its birth or enhanced its growth, one has to assume that in Weber's opinion the Protestant ethic was at least one of the most important of the conducive and generating factors. In his portrait of the Protestant ethic, Weber emphasizes its attitude of respect for work. He points out that "the God of Calvinism demanded of his believers not single good works, but a life of good works combined into a unified system."[5] Work from this point of view was not only a means of living, but a purpose, a calling and a way of prizing the glory of God. It implied that man should not waste his time in idleness or on enjoyments. Wealth itself was not reprehensible but the use of it for enjoyment of the temptations of the flesh was declared a great sin. The Protestant ethic, says Weber, sanctified work and especially business entrepreneurship. It promulgated puritanism and asceticism within mundane occupations, an asceticism of an entirely different kind from that promoted by Catholic monasticism. The Protestant Ethos required: "(1) repudiation of all ascetic practices which were irrational . . . (2) repudiation of the attitudes of contemplation, and (3) especially, and above all, the practice of asceticism in the inward mundane, in self-realization of family life, and in (ascetically comprehended) calling."[6] In short, Weber contends that in contrast to earlier types of asceticism Protestantism promulgated a new *rational* active asceticism without ostentation directed toward maximization of productivity combined with a modest use of the produced wealth. It promoted a code of self-restraint instrumental for the continuous progressive accumulation of capital.

Attention must be called to one more point. Weber attaches great importance to the concept *Beruf,* which is generally translated into English in the current edition of *Protestant Ethic* as "calling." He himself occasionally adds the English word "calling" in parentheses.* He also writes about both politics and science as *Beruf* which is, in that case, translated into English as "vocation." In the present work he asserts that the Protestant ethos inculcated in the minds of its followers a sense of calling. On some pages he even suggests a sense of predestination for an active life and productive work. Combined with puritanism, modesty, self-restraint, and with mundane asceticism in general, this sense of calling generated the right atmosphere for the spread of the spirit of capitalism.

I said that great theories not only present great ideas but can be read and interpreted differently by different readers. They may also divide the world of their readers, and their greatness is reflected in that division. They inevitably generate followings of true believers and admirers; they unavoidably have great enemies. Eventually heretics and revisionists appear among the ardent followers too. This is true for great religions and ideologies. It is true for Marxism and great philosophical theories. And it is true in regard to *The Protestant Ethic and the Spirit of Capitalism.* Books have been written to disprove it; some students spent their entire lives fighting it. It became nearly a profession to criticize it, yet it remains a classical study inspiring new generations of social scientists. Its importance today may not consist so much in what it actually says about the influence of the Protestant Ethic on the spread of the spirit of capitalism as in its indispensability to an understanding of what has been written on industrialization and development in Europe. The discussion of it, which has lasted half a century, is well reflected in the papers of S. N. Eisenstadt and E. Fischoff.[7] Without attempting to recapitulate all the arguments, let us glance at a few of the opponents' views.

H. M. Robertson focuses his criticism especially on Weber's concept of "calling."[8] He argues that the spirit of capitalism was not the creator but the creation of the class of businessmen. According to Robertson, if the calling which Weber speaks about has any function at all, it is not in achievement orientation or even in the generation of a capitalist spirit. It is not a stimulus toward great wealth, invention, and exploration, but rather an invitation to live orderly lives and to perform the duties imposed upon men by God. Hence the calling has no message of a capitalist

* See M. Weber, "Die protestantische Ethik und der 'Geist' des Kapitalismus" in *Archiv fur Sozialwissenschaft und Sozialpolitik,* vol. XXI, 1905, p. 82. The translation used the term "calling" also for *Berufsidee; Berufasarbeit* is sometimes translated as "labour in calling" (p. 108) and other times as "worldly activity" (p. 112).

nature. "Men do not need to be 'called' to riches to devote themselves whole-heartedly to their pursuit without stopping to enjoy them."[9] Weber is mistaken when he unhistorically assumes that "calling" as a code of conduct meant the same thing to everyone between the sixteenth and the twentieth centuries. In fact, its meaning changed. Robertson adds that Catholicism required asceticism of the same kind and to the same extent as Protestantism. "And so ordered life which would be recommended by a Puritan by virtue of the doctrine of the 'calling' was also recommended by the Catholics."[10] Robertson feels that Weber exaggerates the importance of Protestantism as a factor generating capitalism, and that he ignores cases of Catholic, Jewish, or merely secular capitalists.

Kurt Samuelsson undertakes a review of the discussion around *The Protestant Ethic* to use in his own attack the arguments of both the opponents and those who agree with Weber.[11] He agrees with those who say that the capitalist spirit existed long before the Reformation. He argues that the Catholic outlook underwent great changes as a result of debates and internal struggles lasting many centuries, and he too claims that the ethic promulgated by Catholicism was not very different from that of Protestantism. On the other hand, neither in its Puritan nor in other Reformed guise did the Reformation involve any sudden ideological break with the past. Weber attributes the changes in the ideological, intellectual, and ethical climate solely to Protestantism, while in fact Protestantism was itself a product of a number of changes occurring in the European culture at that time. The decisive factor in the spread of the spirit of capitalism must lie in something other than religious reorientation. The seventeenth and eighteenth centuries were times of great enlightenment. Is it not true, Samuelsson poses rhetorically, that physiocratic and early liberal philosophies promulgated an antireligious or at least a secular orientation? "This new spirit of creativeness, of protest against the old order, of inquiry and widening horizons, was a feature shared in common by economic progress, political and cultural trends, and the break with Catholicism."[12] In Samuelsson's opinion, the spirit of capitalism did flow from Puritanism, but it was very different from its source and even contradicted it. He examines some data on the economic development of England, Holland, France, Germany, and other West European countries to find support for his belief that, though some relationship seems to exist between the prosperity of these countries and Protestantism, it might well be the converse one of prosperity leading to Protestantism. He too concludes on the basis of that examination that Protestant states have no position of pre-eminence over Catholic, nor Puritan states over the rest of the Protestant group.

Mercantilism, the Enlightenment, Darwinism, economic liberalism—all these systems of thought in which a central role was played by economic expansion and the belief in a better future for nations or men through the increase of capital and the raising of standard of welfare—cut across all religious creeds, or went over or around them.[13]

Thus he asserts that all the evidence contradicts Weber's theories.

Herbert Lüthy argues that neither Weber nor those who support his approach know enough about Protestant and Catholic theology or about the complex financial relations of the time of the Reformation to talk about them as profoundly as they do.[14] He feels that Weber employs his two key concepts, Protestantism and capitalism, in an ambiguous and cloudy way. Historians who follow Weber's path, and even those who oppose him, have added to the confusion by including in the discussion new ambiguous concepts such as feudalism. Weber speaks about Protestantism as an ethic and not as a theological dogma. However, he actually limits it to a peculiar kind of Calvinism, not found in reality but of an ideal type constructed by himself. Lüthy follows a similar argument about Weber's understanding of capitalism. Weber does not discuss capitalism but the spirit of capitalism. He points out,

> We should avoid in any case casual declarations that the Reformation was this or that, a bourgeois, feudal, peasant, proletarian, national or nationalistic movement. It was all that and much more than that, since it was an all-engulfing crisis of the essential beliefs marking the beginning of a new era. What the Reformation was and wished to be cannot be discovered in retrospect and by examining what became of the individual Protestant or reformed churches and sects. These are the *outcome of a disaster* breaking the movement of the whole Western Christianity.[15]

Lüthy continues: assuming that Protestantism and capitalism have a more strict connotation than the vague one implied by Weber, one can, of course, examine the interconnections between religion (and especially the Reformation) and economic behavior. Yet such relations are very complex and indeed indirect. Weber might better have called his book: *Protestantism and Modern Society* or *The Reformation and the Spirit of Western Civilization* instead of employing euphemisms as he does. Lüthy, Trevor-Roper and other contemporary critics of Weber in agreement with earlier opposition say that Weber is wrong; Protestantism cannot be defined strictly.[16] Even if we agree with Weber on what it means, still we cannot agree about the degree of influence which it exerted on the factor that some people call capitalism.

The position of the defenders of *The Protestant Ethic* is well expressed by Julien Freund. Weber specified that the causal relationship between Protestantism and capitalism must not be taken in the sense of a mechanical relationship. The Protestant ethos was one of the sources of the rationalization of life which helped to create what is known as the "spirit of capitalism." It was not the sole nor even a sufficient cause of capitalism.[17] Raymond Aron takes a similar attitude.[18]

While critics attempt to expose the weak points in Weber's study, defenders disregard them and expose those elements which remain valid, elucidative, and inspiring. Thus Aron sees the importance of Weber's analysis in the questions he asks, even if his answers are not totally satisfying. He finds value in Weber's emphasis on the influence of religious thought on modes of action and orientations of economic activity; in his establishing, on the basis of events in Western Europe, a comprehensive correlation between religious ways of thinking and attitudes in economic action; and in his demonstration of the kind of orientation which was instrumental for the generation of the spirit of capitalism. In Aron's view, these factors greatly contributed to an understanding of why Western capitalism did not develop originally anywhere outside Western civilization.

Accepting and promulgating a similar assessment of Weber's work, Reinhard Bendix adds another point. He contends that a part of the importance of *The Protestant Ethic* consists in the demonstration that, *in spite* of religiosity, *in spite* of the seeming incompatibility of religious devotion with intense economic activity, the latter expanded overcoming limitations, stiffening norms and rules and traditions which seemed to congeal any attempts to introduce profound innovations. Bendix writes,

> According to all experience, religious devotion was usually accompanied by a rejection of mundane affairs, while men who were engrossed in economic pursuits tended toward religious indifference. Why, then, had the rising commercial classes embraced Protestantism when the medieval Church's control over daily life had been so notoriously lax that few real obstacles had been put in the way of the rising economy? In place of Catholic tolerance, the Protestants had introduced a thorough-going regulation of private and public life; yet the bourgeoisie had risen to the defence of this "unexampled tyranny of Puritanism . . ." Indeed, the middle classes, which have rarely been characterized by either heroism or intense religiosity, developed heroic qualities of character in their acceptance and defense of an ascetic way of life. . . . Thus in the Age of the Reformation the rising middle classes deviated significantly from the simple acquisitiveness, religious indifference and more or less outright hedonism usually characteristic of social groups engaged in the development of economic enterprises. The purpose of *The Protestant Ethic* was to explain this paradox.[19]

Apparently, Bendix feels that Weber succeeded in this attempt. In addition, he describes Weber's work as an exalted prize eulogizing the triumph of advancing rationality.

This is also the core of Benjamin Nelson's interest. This writer, a great admirer of Weber's work and defender of Max Weber against Samuelsson, Trevor-Roper, and Lüthy, has published much on themes related to the Protestant Ethic.[20] In earlier writing he especially exposed Weber's theories of societal transformation as a process of striving to overcome the dualisms in intergroup and intragroup moralities, in man's belonging to a collectivity and his own individuality. He insisted that the Weberian Protestant Ethic should not be interpreted narrowly, as a local event in Prussia in the sixteenth and seventeenth centuries. It has to be regarded as a manifestation of general existential and cultural forces which spur men toward new images, as a force which breeds a new *conscience* and generates a need to act continuously and relentlessly "in impersonal service on behalf of an impersonal goal . . . in interest of God's mastery."

Weberian theory characterizes the historical process as an ongoing trend toward higher rational organization of societies. Nelson exhibits another aspect of this tendency and defines it as a transformation of parochial brotherhoods into universal otherhoods. (This expresses excellently the idea of growing systemness.) Yet Nelson's analysis of Weber's writing is not a mere eulogy. He portrays Weber's work as an incessant search for understanding the undercurrents of socio-political processes. He describes it as a drama in which Weber sees in the rationalization of life the solution to man's struggle to overcome the dualism and dichotomies of his life, only to discover that rationalization cannot ever be fully accomplished and that the bureaucratic rational order is even more conflict-ridden and bursting with dualisms. This is especially evident in Weber's own retrospective analysis of his work. Nelson acknowledges the weaknesses of Weberian writing. Weber remains too much a son of his time—he points out—but are we not all guilty of this? He asserts that Weber has "failed to stress strongly enough the extraordinary many-sidedness and resilience" of what Nelson calls "rationales of thought and action, especially as these come to be elaborated within the cultures of conscience."[21] He argues that the present Mathematics-Science-Engineering-powered twentieth-century World-Revolution can be understood only through an appraisal of the past, and especially of the two sixteenth- and seventeenth-century upheavals of (1) the Protestant Reformation and (2) the Scientific and Philosophical Revolution. Both were a challenge to what he calls "The Court of Conscience of Christendom." Both these revolutions generated a process of growth of "new rationale systems, structures of reasons, explanations, procedures establishing requirements in respect to truth, virtue, legality, fittingness."[22] Nelson indicates that from our perspective the revolutions of the sixteenth and seventeenth century look very different than from Weber's perspective. "Weber's images of rationalization everywhere reflect the mammoth machinery of the Age of Iron and Steel. It is no wonder that he did not foresee what we have hardly begun to understand ourselves, almost a half-century after his death."[23]

Almost in defiance of the many warnings, confutations, and criticisms, Weber's thesis has recently been tested in a most peculiar way. His theory is used in a number of researches on the development of Asian societies, and it turns out to be a most fruitful methodology in many of these undertakings. Inspired by Weber's contentions, Robert N. Bellah finds that the Japanese religion's promotion of diligence and frugality made it instrumental in generating the spirit of entrepreneurship and the activity fruitful in Japanese industrialization.[24] Clifford Geertz finds that the leaders of the reformed Moslem community in Modjokuto and also in other parts of Java displayed a remarkable genuine bourgeois ethic. Similar to the phenomena described by Weber, Geertz writes that "By purifying Indonesian Islam of Hinduist and animist mystical and ritualistic accretions and focusing attention on dogma and morality, by severely criticizing the traditional aversion of the Moslem community to formal organization of any kind, and by substituting a progress-oriented self-determinism for the creed's classical fatalism, it injected a new dynamic into the *pasar* context."[25]

Looking at the numerous volumes written in support of and against *The Protestant Ethic,* and considering the fact that the other superb works of Weber have not provoked comparable disagreements, one must ask: Why is there so much fuss about that particular book? Although many books written by German sociologists prior to the First World War are forgotten, why has this one provoked, and increasingly continued to provoke, so much passion?

A partial answer is that the study leaves great latitude for interpretations. Weber's assessment of the Protestant Ethic and its effect on other processes of development in Europe seems different at different times. The book poses highly important questions such as, "Why did it all [industrialization] start in Europe?" But, as usually happens with important questions, the book does not provide answers satisfying the broad spectrum of students interested in the question. Further passion has been aroused because Weber's ravishing admiration for acquisition-seekers and his lack of sentiment for the past and profound uncompromising veneration for ascending functional rationality sound offensive to conservative and radical critics of capitalism. With some exaggeration, it may be said that the debate around *The Protestant Ethic* looks like a debate between liberals and conservatives, with most of the conservatives arguing against Weber's contentions. Today it is difficult to determine whether Weber contended that the "capitalist spirit" was the only spirit generated by the Protestant Ethic, but it is certainly difficult to agree that only the ethos of Protestantism generated capitalism. The theory and analysis set forth in *The Protestant Ethic* contains implications and elucidations which are perhaps imprecise but which extend far beyond the thesis that the Protestant Ethic spreading during the sixteenth and seventeenth centuries engendered an atmosphere conducive to the rise of entrepreneurship and the spirit of capitalism in Western Europe. The importance of Weber's work consists in begetting and establishing a new illuminative approach to societal growth and development; in posing a most fertile contention that religious, psychological, and general motivational factors must be accounted for in economic development and industrialization. Weber introduced a new approach and a new theory to explain the fascinating process of the origin of modernity. Perhaps Weber was not totally right, yet his theory cannot be disregarded by those who write on development. Thus most of those who are concerned with Weber's theses now are often not interested exactly in the Protestant Ethic; yet surely if they are interested in problems of development, they must consider Weber's assertion that the degree and intensity of modern economic development and industrialization depends in part on the magnitude of the striving for achievement. Some interpret his concept as the impulse for acquisition, others say in diverse cases of industrialization the motivations differed. Weber describes it as a *calling to achieve*. To these two key concepts of the Protestant ethic—*achievement* and *calling*—we will have to return later in our discussion.

Weber's work instigated interest in a number of other, more distantly related topics and had a great bearing on many kinds of research: on innovators; on the role of the "marginal" people, on the role of variant and deviant personalities in development; on the role of minorities in the growth of national economies; on the role of dissent and initiative in promoting entrepreneurial activity; on achievement motivation. To all interested in the above problems, *The Protestant Ethic* is a manual. In the course of the birth of the many new nations after the Second World War, new questions were posed: "How can we make it happen again faster and better?" "How can we generate industrialization or general economic growth in the new countries of Asia and Africa?" "What can be learned from the development of the Western nations, of the Communist states, of Japan to induce development in other parts of the world?"

2. Status Withdrawal

One of the few attempts to answer these questions by pointing in the same direction as Weber did, by demanding the creation of psychological conditions first, is Everett E. Hagen's theory of status withdrawal. Following Adam Smith and later Karl Marx, economists were concerned primarily with the issue of capital formation and its consequences. Max Weber called attention instead to the men who make the capital. Hagen follows Weber's path, even though he insists that he is not writing under the inspiration of the *Protestant Ethic*. In fact he states that this work is now obsolete.[26]

Because of their emphasis on capital formation, most economists claimed that with money any, or at least most, of the problems could be solved; poor nations were underdeveloped because they were poor. Economists of that inclination considering the underdevelopment of new nations and their lack of economic growth were primarily concerned with real or illusory barriers which they thought prevented or grossly impeded capital formation and hence economic development in such countries. Numerous theories of overlapping vicious circles were propounded: a vicious circle of low income and inadequate saving; a circle of low rates of industrialization and inadequate markets; one of an insufficient infrastructure because of insufficient capital and low level of investment because of insufficient infrastructure; of a preponderance of consumptive spending because of poverty (in accordance with Engel's law) and of poverty because of an antiaccumulative attitude. Though no one said that the new nations were doomed, the crust of backwardness and underdevelopment looked unbreakable. The debate has not produced generally accepted answers. The prospect began to look even worse when it was discovered that the gap between industrialized and underdeveloped nations was actually widening. Yet the new nations had just obtained the most important instrument for development—their independence, their fate in their own hands.

At the outset of the last decade, however, a new attitude toward the problems of the economic growth of new nations gradually started to emerge. It was said technological creativity precedes capital formation. Was this not true for Europe? Why should it not be valid for new nations? Thus the springs of economic development were spotted outside the sphere of pure economics. Some economists became increasingly interested in the social and psychological factors of economic development, their impact on economic growth and on capital formation. They were joined in that pursuit by sociologists and psychologists, who devoted much attention to the cause of innovation and to innovators as a distinctive type of personality. Though the approach was often very different from that of Max Weber in *The Protestant Ethic,* the questions were still, "What generated the entrepreneurial spirit in the past? How did entrepreneurial behavior spread and become dominant? Would an entrepreneurial attitude be generated on a wide scale in new nations? Would that suffice to start an accelerated economic growth?" The new hero was not *capital* but the entrepreneur, the innovator, the *modernizer.* The remedy was no longer to seek capital, but to transform people, educate them, inculcate in their minds a desire for raising their standard of living, teach them to apply modern knowledge and technology; then economic development would come by itself. Advisers from Communist nations preached the same thing in another version: the development of a socialist consciousness and the education and training of the people is most important for speedy advancement on the noncapitalist road of development. The efficacy of such remedies will be discussed later. Now I shall merely look at a number of theories which appeared on the wave of that new attitude.

Hagen presents his theory within a framework of contrast between traditional and modern societies. He maintains that each of these societies is composed of and produces a different type of personality. Traditional society is dominated by *authoritarian* personality, which avoids anxiety brought about by independent, critical, and innovative thinking. The authoritarian man makes decisions which exactly follow the patterns established by tradition and authority. The world in which he lives looks to him as an agglomeration of mysterious unexplainable phenomena, put together without causative interconnections by arbitrary external and often willful powers. Men are embedded in such phenomena, if not by sheer whim of those powers, then to "serve their own purposes and disregard his unless he submits his will to theirs."[27] Their ways cannot be understood by human beings. Hence the authoritarian man fears to demonstrate any opposition and initiative which might offend those above him. He is submissive, highly in need of dependence, obedient to superiors, and uncreative. He expects that his subordinates will be the same and will behave in accordance with the established patterns. A traditional society dominated by such people is stagnant and hostile to innovations. As a rule, it lasts without significant changes for ages. It forms a sort of self-perpetuating equilibrium which persists because people must be content with it.

On the other end of his extrapolation Hagen poses the *innovational* personality. Its main traits are creativity, openness to experience, restless curiosity. The man with an innovational personality believes that worldly phenomena are set in interconnection, that they are logical and coherent and hence may be understood and explained. He persistently searches for new solutions and does not take for granted generally accepted evaluations. Though he has doubts, he is confident that he can evaluate the order of things themselves and solve problems. He wants to understand and interpret in his own way. He feels a pleasure in solving problems and a duty to pursue achievement. He feels "a personal responsibility to transform the world that far transcends a profit motive." The man with an innovational personality is not necessarily a happy man. He may be driven to creativity by an incessant anxiety which causes him to feel satisfaction only when he is striving, only when he is searching and changing. The world of innovative personalities is in constant flux. It is a world of self-perpetuating changes and innovations which constantly generate new standards of living, evaluations, techniques, values, and aims. So far Hagen is not very different from other writers who have employed the model of extrapolation.

Then he poses the question: How can the self-perpetuating equilibrium of traditional societies be broken? How can a traditional society dominated by authoritarian personalities be transformed into a modern society incessantly changing under the instigation of domineering innovational personalities? Hagen answers that this happens in the circumstances of *status withdrawal*.

He tells us, "In a traditional society in which social disruption has not occurred the purposes, values, and activities of each group are respected. Each group in the society has its accepted place and feels that it is valued. To each group, therefore, not only its own status but also the structure of the society as a whole is good. Since the existing relationships are satisfying, changed ones have little attraction."[28] In some circumstances, however, a group may be dispossessed of its awarded status. In other cases a group may discover that it is not so highly regarded as it feels it deserves to be. Several cases of such status withdrawal are examined: when a traditional elite group is replaced by another group; when symbols and beliefs which a subordinate group considers vital are depreciated or even prohibited by a superior group; the case of inconsistency of economic and other statuses; the case of nonacceptance of a migrant group in a new place of residence; the derogation of institutional activity without change in the power structure.

Status withdrawal means disregard for one's role in society or disregard for one's beliefs and aspirations. It is painful to be disregarded, argues Hagen. People without a role in society become alienated and frustrated. Groups without a status or groups forced to accept a status much below their expectation lose their purpose for existence and become discontented with the established order. The harbored resentment is then transferred to their progeny. Frustration and rage continue to be accumulated from one generation to another. Now Hagen applies Merton's model of individual adaptation to his scheme, putting "new wine in Merton's bottles." Anxiety and resentment cumulated and bred from generation to generation produce a series of generational personalities: first, the retreatist, followed by the ritualist, the innovational, and finally the reformist personality which, in his view, is typical for modern changing societies. How does this transformation occur?

Hagen attributes great importance to child rearing, viewing it as the decisive factor in the transformation of societies. In a true Freudian spirit he assumes that the childhood determines what men will become and how they will react to values and events. A sense of what is right and what is wrong inculcated in one's mind in childhood remains for a man's entire life. Assuming that, there is reason to expect that the male part of a group which loses its status or which claims a status which is being denied to it suffers more than the female part of it, Hagen argues that men will despair because of loss of regarded status and become weak; they adopt an attitude of retreatism. Women, on the other hand, resenting the weakness of their husbands, will do everything to instill in the minds of their sons an anguished desire to be better off than their progenitors. Hagen assumes that the mothers will educate their sons (nothing is said about daughters) in a spirit of self-reliance, in a yearning for achievement and fervent aspiration to prove their worth to others. He speculates that these lessons should in due time inspire the sons to become innovators and reformers. They will acquire and establish new roles, challenging the actual elite. (The anticipation that those who have withdrawn the status from fathers may also prevent the sons from establishing new roles is not taken into account.) This happens in Hagen's opinion when two conditions are fulfilled: "a requisite for economic growth in a traditional society is not merely that upward social mobility by new means is possible,* but also that upward social mobility by traditional channels is not possible."[29]

---

* It is interesting to note that this stipulation resembles Lenin's famous saying on conditions necessary for a successful revolution (See " 'Left-Wing' Communism—An Infantile Disorder" in V. I. Lenin, *Selected Works* (1967), vol. III, p. 392): "The fundamental law of revolution, which has been confirmed by all revolutions and especially by all three Russian revolutions in the twentieth century, is as follows: for a revolution to take place it is not enough for the exploited and oppressed masses to realise the impossibility of living in the old way, and demand changes; for a revolution to take place it is essential that the exploiters should not be able to live and rule in the old way. It is only when the *lower classes* do not want to live in the old way and the *upper classes* cannot carry on in the old way that the revolution can triumph."

In some respect Hagen's theory resembles Vilfredo Pareto's ideas about the circulation of élites. Parallels between residues and derivation in one theory and types of personality could be easily drawn. The description of the ambitious and rebellious sons of those who lost their status looks similar to that of the contraélite in Pareto's paradigm. Of course the two theories differ profoundly too.

Hagen illustrates his theory with case studies of Colombia, Japan, Burma, the Sioux, with occasional reference to the situation of the blacks in the United States. He is most elaborate in a case study of English history. He points out however that the British history is longer and more complex than that of any other society and that it is, therefore, more difficult to make firm statements concerning causal links in it. Thus in that case he wishes to make only tentative statements.[30] It is not clear why British history is said to be more complex than Japanese, but this cannot be pondered here. Neither can we examine his study of Britain or other case studies. However the reader can be referred to L. Kasdan's article which examines Hagen's theory in application to Colombia.[31] Kasdan asserts that one should not regard whole populations, whether Parsees, Jews, Samurai, or Basque as an undifferentiated entity. Such groups contain individuals of diverse talent, and are constituted as social structures in which, in accordance with established norms, individuals occupy different positions (and roles, it may be added). Discussing the case of autonomous economic growth in Colombia, Hagen calls attention to the fact that the group of entrepreneurs in that country is comprised of a great proportion of persons of Basque origin, who are, in his view, the progeny of men who lost their status. Kasdan points out that the case is not so simple. In the Basque rural community the family usually owns a rather small piece of land. It is regarded as inviolable and is inherited patrilineally (often regardless of the sex of the heir). The male-youths who were deprived of land inheritance and who subsequently could not easily find partners to marry tended to emigrate to America. The social structure was thus constantly producing people who could acquire a status only if they could succeed by their individual initiative. Certainly not all Basques and not even all those who could not inherit land were smart enough to amass wealth and become entrepreneurs. Kasdan discusses similar cases of rural societies with a great output of emigrants and tells us that he cannot find evidence in the examined cases to support Hagen's assumptions. Besides he expresses some general views about Hagen's theory.

First, there is too little attention paid to social structure features which modify the manner in which socialization impinges upon different members of the same society. Secondly, the model he uses of a traditional (peasant) society is overtly static and social structure is seen as deriving from psychological phenomena.[32]

Some other doubts in addition to those posed by Kasdan may be raised too.[33] Hagen embeds the authoritarian personality in traditional society and the innovational in modern society. Yet one does not need to refer to Nazi Germany, prewar Japan, or other fascist regimes to show that authoritarian personalities and regimes are not necessarily traditional. In fact Hagen's characterization of the authoritarian personality could admirably fit any typical bureaucrat, a person who avoids the anxiety of independent, creative, innovative thinking. Such a person makes decisions in accordance with rules prescribed by a superior authority. He is submissive, obedient to those in command, and uncreative. It may be also said that talented and innovational personalities appear in any society, yet not all societies are ripe enough to accept their unfolding. Innovators are needed to provide the spark for development, economic development especially, yet development and modernization occur only there where the requisite material conditions (not necessarily the abundance of capital) can be found and where the society as a whole and the individuals in it have a burning need for change and innovation.

Hagen assumes that those who lose their status or are unable to attain the status to which they aspire are bound to become retreatists. Their wives will not share their attitudes and will hold their husbands in contempt or generally resent their lack of achievement. This is a very ethnocentric appraisal of the women in traditional societies. True, in some traditional societies, for instance of the Ashanti or the Yoruba in West Africa, the women were active and full of initiative, even in the past. In most traditional societies, however, women are passive and conservative. One can hardly imagine women in such societies unanimously changing on their own the pattern of education established by tradition. Hagen does not provide enough evidence to support an assertion such as this, which contradicts the usual understanding of the subject. It is worth noting that today retreatism has become a well-established ideology in the United States and Western Europe. A wide array of its prophets can be heard daily chanting and professing on any campus. Those who adhere to it are not the sons and daughters of the minorities or of those who have had their status withdrawn. On the contrary, those who worship it are the offspring of the successful middle class. Thus, retreatism does not necessarily result from status withdrawal, and status withdrawal does not necessarily produce retreatism and subsequent innovation. The graveyard of history is full of tombs of groups and classes who lost their status without remarkable descendants who became innovators, entrepreneurs, and rebels. Where are the innovators and rebels descending from former

nobility and aristocracy? It is true that minorities, some socially or culturally marginal groups tend to produce innovators, entrepreneurs, and
rebels above the average proportion of a given society. However, this is
true only for some marginal groups and in conducive circumstances.
(a) It is quite easy to give examples, especially of ethnic marginal groups
that encapsulated themselves in retreatism for ages. Some such groups
are still that way. (b) Numerous marginal groups vanished in isolation
or became slowly and invisibly absorbed by the core groups of society.
(c) In modern times, especially in Europe and the United States, when
societies are in flux, values are changing and the principle of egalitarianism has become widely approved, in case such separate groups should
adhere to a value-orientation which does not inhibit them from coming
out with initiative, members of the marginal groups become involved
either in revolutionary or entrepreneurial activities. Illustrations for such
cases are obvious. They seek to become a part of the society and they
grab any opportunity available for this. The third instance which is
clearly considered by Hagen is too complex to be explained only by a
change in child-rearing. Hagen views the change in the attitudes of
descendants of those who had their status withdrawn as the result of a
husband-wife and father-son conflict during the socializing process. He
does not take into account that agents other than those belonging to the
narrow family circle exercise profound influence on the process of education. Indeed, the importance of those other agents in generating interest and preparing a child of a cultural or social marginal group for
subsequent action and entrepreneurial activity in the larger society cannot be overestimated.

Hagen wrote his study anticipating that it would help to understand
the problems of new nations and provide a remedy for these problems.
The question is then: what kind of advice can one take from Hagen's
theory for those who are organizing economic development in new nations? Certainly not that they should breed innovators by withdrawing
status from selected groups.

While it is difficult to take Hagen's theory as a guide for policies of
new nations, I think it poses some stimulating hypotheses for historians.
In differing circumstances people may engage in entrepreneurial and innovational activities for different psychological motives. I will try later
to outline some differing motivations and causes which result in innovational activities in divergent situations. Certainly, however, Hagen's point
that in specific circumstances in many societies many innovators come
from cultural and social marginal groups is valid. His contribution is important also because he belongs to the few who seriously attempt to
examine factors of economic growth beyond the economy. His study

shows how complex the relations between the purely economic and other factors are. And certainly Hagen is right when he tells us that psychological factors and the rearing of a new generation in general are important elements in promoting economic development, in some situations more important than the disposition of capital.

3. The Achievement Syndrome

Though some of the writing in the 1930's on the psychology of motivation could be regarded as precursory to modern theories of achievement motivation, in fact it was so meager and inconspicuous that it probably would have been forgotten were it not followed by the glamorous writing in that field today. Most of what has been done in psychology in both the theory and field research on achievement motivation is connected with the name of David C. McClelland and his associates.[34] McClelland's interest in achievement motivation theory was sparked by Weber's *Protestant Ethic.** "Since Freud psychologists have accepted the fact that a simple act may be variously motivated . . . a man doesn't buy a car just because he 'needs' one in a rational sense, but because the possession of a particular kind of car may satisfy other motives—for power, prestige, or even sexual display."[35] He was inspired by Weber's theory. McClelland and his colleagues compared data on Protestant and Catholic entrepreneurs both in the United States and Germany. Some arrived at inconclusive results, but many, including McClelland himself, found that Weber's contentions were greatly justified.** They write that in 1950, Prot-

* Achievement-orientation theory is both an explanation of economic growth and a framework for psychological explorations in motivated behavior, vocational aspirations, expectation of success and failure, risk-taking, and so forth. Only those aspects of the theory and data of research which are related to explaining economic and societal development are in the sphere of our interest.

** See D. C. McClelland, *The Achieving Society,* pp. 50-55, 146-48, 356-62. H. Heckhausen, *The Anatomy of Achievement Motivation,* states on p. 31 that it has not been possible to prove whether Protestants show more pronounced achievement motivation than Catholics. On p. 160 however he states, "The influence of the religious milieu, as suggested by Max Weber (1904/1905), has repeatedly been found to be important (e.g., McClelland, Rindlisbacher, and De Charms, 1955; B. C. Rosen ["Race, Ethnicity, and the Achievement Syndrome" *American Sociological Review]* 1959, vol. XXIV, pp. 47-60; R. E. Carney and W. J. McKeachie ["Religion, Sex, Social Class, Probability of Success, and Student Personality" *Journ. Sci. Stud. Religion,* 1963, III, pp. 32-42]). The Catholic developmental milieu appears to be less fertile for developing high achievement motivation. Although Catholic parents in Germany as well as in the United States do not demand independence from their children any later than do Protestant parents (W. W. Wendt, "Points of Origin for Infant Ecologies: Religion and Purchase of Devices Affecting Pre-Verbal Mobility" *Psychological Report,* 1965, XVI, pp. 209-10 cited in McClelland, *The Achieving Society,* p. 360; Feld, cited in J. Veroff *et al.,* "Achievement Motivation and Religious Background" *American So-*

estant countries were more economically advanced than Catholic countries; on the average, Protestant parents educated their children more in a spirit of self-reliance and thriftiness than Catholic parents did. Why? How was the Protestant entrepreneur motivated in the past? asked McClelland. What were the motivations of entrepreneurs at any time in any country in the world? Is it possible to find a kind of universal motivation preceding intensive economic development in general? Is it possible to motivate people consciously and purposely to generate economic development, especially in underdeveloped countries? In the study by Marian R. Winterbottom of the attempts of 29 middle-class families in the American Midwest to raise their sons to strive for achievement, McClelland found some clues to the direction in which his research should move in pursuit of answers to those questions.[36] The working hypothesis was that Protestant parents in accordance with the ethic of their religion bring up children in a spirit of self-reliance, independence, observance of certain principal rules, and striving for mastery. Such an education is instrumental in generating a strong sense of responsibility and above all a strong desire to achieve in competition with others. Over time and in large scale, this eventually becomes what Weber called the spirit of modern capitalism. McClelland focused his interest primarily on investigations of what he called Achievement motivation (later abridged to n Achievement and subsequently to n Ach. for "need for Achievement").

McClelland asserts that economic development at any time and at any place in the world did and does result from a preceding spread of n Achievement. The higher and wider the spread of the n Achievement, the more likely that economic development will be intense. He and his associates developed numerous methods of examining and measuring the n Achievement in civilizations of the past and, for cross-cultural comparisons, in currently existing societies. Hence the discussion shifts from causes of industrialization in Western Europe to a more general issue. It sounds simple, though its implications are of great magnitude: ". . . high n Achievement will lead a person to perform better when achievement in the narrow sense is possible. . . . If the n Achievement

ciological Review, 1962, XXVII, pp. 205-17), they are more restrictive in their child-rearing practices (Wendt, 1965; cf. McClelland, The Achieving Society, p. 361); they place more value on obedience, orderliness, and cleanliness (Veroff et al., 1962); they punish more vigorously and provide more material rewards (D. R. Miller and G. E. Swanson, "The Study of Conflict" in M. R. Jones (ed.), Nebraska Symposium on Motivation, 1956, pp. 158-77). All this does not seem to favor the development of highly generalized self-reliant value attitudes. The more individualistic and more activistic the religious ethos of an environment, the more strongly achievement motivation is fostered, as McClelland has demonstrated with many separate findings. (Titles in brackets and initials were added where it was possible to find the work cited in the text.)

level is high, there will presumably be more people who behave like entrepreneurs, acting to produce more than they can consume."[37] Even at the primitive level, higher n Achievement is responsible for greater inventiveness. At the beginning McClelland cautiously announces only that *achievement motivation is in part responsible for economic growth.*[38] Later, however, in the fervor of his own achievements and research and discussion, the hypotheses change to: "a society with a generally high level of n Achievement will produce more energetic entrepreneurs who, in turn, produce more rapid economic development."[39] The lesson is obvious: If you wish to have economic growth, induce achievement motivation on a wide scale. McClelland also discusses the impact of other motivations on economic growth. In particular he finds that high n Affiliation has either little connection or is negatively correlated with economic growth, and that "a combination of low n Affiliation and high n Power is very closely associated with the tendency of a nation to resort to totalitarian methods in governing its people."[40] Neither McClelland nor other writers on the topic are clear enough on the effect on economic growth of a high n Affiliation or n Power, either considered separately or in combination with a high or low n Achievement.

Any society, whether primitive or highly developed economically, has its own set of standards of excellence. Having many wives or many children may be considered as a great achievement in some societies, a high position in the power structure in others, popularity, prestige, intellectual proficiency, knowledge, bravery, or simple seniority in others. James N. Morgan tells us that

> This motive is defined as a tendency to strive for success in situations involving an evaluation of one's performance in relation to some standards of excellence. A person with a strong motive to achieve tends to derive satisfaction from overcoming obstacles by his own efforts. He takes calculated risks, rather than playing long shots or being overly cautious. Compared with the need for affiliation—to give and receive affection—or for power—to control the means of influencing the behavior of others and not be under their control—the need for achievement seems most likely to be associated with upward mobility, long hours of work, desires to accumulate capital and educate one's children, and entrepreneurial activity.[41]

In fact, however, when McClelland discusses the n Achievement he is not implying that it means mere striving for the attainment of any of the above listed standards of excellence. Neither is he referring to the satisfaction derived from overcoming obstacles such as obtained in climbing mountains, solving puzzles, or jumping through barriers. Nor is he speaking about self-sacrifice in pursuit of collectivistic achievement such as the pursuit of victory for one's nation in time of war or the ardent pursuit of a collectivistic goal without expectation of rewards. He makes clear that the n Achievement under consideration means individual economic achievement which in general scope produces economic growth. As Weber has also emphasized many times, it is not greed for riches. It is action ". . . on the basis of rigorous calculation, directed with foresight and caution toward the economic success which is in sharp contrast to the hand-to-mouth existence of the peasant, and to the privileged traditionalism of the guild craftsman and too of the adventurers' capitalism, oriented to the exploitation of political opportunities and irrational speculation."[42] McClelland is speaking about accumulation of money, but not about money for its own sake. He tells us that for the n Achievement seekers money is but a measure of success.[43] It gives them "the concrete knowledge of the outcome of their efforts that their motivation demanded."[44] Thus achievement motivation as viewed by McClelland can be described as a latent disposition to compete for a high standard of excellence rewarded in money. Yet it is more than that. Other parts of the study and other writers on the subject assert that a person with a high n Achievement will not only strive for success and the rewards of it in money but will usually seek to establish a steady source of ascending profit. In order to implement this, he will spend less money than he receives. Hence this is an achievement through accumulation. What is such a man trying to accumulate and maximize? Money only? Power? Prestige? Influence? the Good life? Or maybe *security*?

McClelland and other psychologists tell us that achievement motivation is manifest in entrepreneurial behavior characterized by (1) preference for tasks with moderate difficulties; preference for moderate "calculated" risks and aversion for risks containing alternative possibilities of accidental great reward or eventual ruin;[45] (2) energetic innovative activity, especially when it counts for personal achievement;[46] (3) individualism, especially evident in a high sense of responsibility;[47] (4) tendency of prospective planning of individual action combined with a better performance if there is a knowledge of the results of action and an evident probability of success.[48] It is said that men with high n Achievement are highly mobile, like to travel, are businesslike, inventive, do not like to waste time, and have a preference for somber colors.

Numerous projects have been undertaken to examine various aspects and manifestations of n Achievement in societies of the past and of the present. McClelland and his associates have analyzed ethnographic accounts of numerous cultures in an attempt to determine the percentage of adult males engaged in entrepreneurial activity. They coded the content of folk tales of more than forty tribal cultures and of 1,300 children's stories of twenty-three nations, which were scored in terms of their inducement of n Achievement and collaterally in terms of the degree of achievement-orientation of the cultures to which they belonged.* Ancient Greek literature

---

* Though this work is impressive and generally seems to be trustworthy, though the theory derived from these researches seems to look sound and deserves great appreciation, one does not need to be either a psychologist, nor to undertake special research to see that some of the results of such researches are wrong. For example, p. 66 of *The Achieving Society* contains Table 3.1, "Estimates of Percentages of 'Full-time' Entrepreneurs, of Income Based on Low-Level Technology, and of Income-Producing Property which is Individually Owned among Preliterate Cultures Varying in n Achievement in Folk-Tales." The criterion of "Individually Owned" seems to be ill-selected. In Africa the land is even today most often used either in a complex land tenure or in semi-individual group ownership. Any score scale could hardly account for this. The picture created by the table is also wrong in another respect. It contains the names of forty-four tribes in the order of decreasing n Achievement. The Yoruba are positioned in the 4th place, the Masai in the 6th place, the Kikuyu in the 31st place, the Chagga in the 37th place, the Ashanti in the 39th.

I wish to comment only on tribes that I know from my own personal experience. I think, however, that I will be in congruence with the relevant literature. The Masai are indeed a tribe of handsome, brave, magnificent, seminomadic, pastoral people. Even now they rarely engage in farming and not at all in entrepreneurial activities. In both Kenya and Tanzania where they live they are regarded as very conservative people, reluctant to accept innovations. Recently President Nyerere of Tanzania has tried with great difficulty to force them to wear trousers. In Kenya, President Kenyatta allows them to go their own way in order to attract tourists. The Kikuyus are the most businesslike and entrepreneurial people of Kenya. The same applies to the Chagga, who live on the slopes of Kilimanjaro in Tanzania. Both of these people impatiently search for innovations and entrepreneurial possibilities and for opportunities to educate their children in order to achieve a higher standard of living. It is surprising that they and the Ashantis, who are also great freedom-loving, entrepreneurial people, turn out on the bottom of McClelland's list.

Actually McClelland himself is uneasy about the Ashantis. He tells us (p. 68) that "the Ashanti appear lower in n Achievement than they really are, because they avoid making statements of affect or desire." This is not true, however, as anyone who has been in Ghana knows. He also explains that the researchers encountered difficulties in scoring the activities of the common hero of Ashanti folk-stories, Ananse the spider. This is regrettable. Anansi, as we are told, is not an ordinary spider; he is in fact the spinner of worldly social relations. True, he is not so fierce as a lion or so conspicuous as an elephant, but stories say that at one time he served in God's court in the capacity of prime minister. God himself is sometimes addressed as Ananse Kokroko—the greatest of spiders. It seems that the card of Ananse has been punched in the wrong place. He should have been considered as prime minister instead of as an insect. Then the Ashantis would probably find themselves higher on the list.

Some doubts also have to be cast on the findings of the Polish manager (McClelland, *The Achieving Society*, pp. 261-300). McClelland tells us that the psychological situation of a manager working for a very large company like General Electric and that of a Polish manager who works for the state is not very different. Hence both could be questioned in the same way. In my opinion, this is a wrong assumption. The Polish manager cannot change his employer, he has to demonstrate his affection for the Party and solve many problems which a manager at General Electric cannot even imagine. Unfortunately the literature on that subject is scant even in Polish. Nonetheless some publications are obtainable (see for instance A. K. Koźminski, "Rola zawodowa dyrektora przedsiebiorstwa w aktualnym systemie zarzadzania gospodarka socjalistyczna" in *Studia socjologiczne*, No. 1 (24), 1967; A. Wakar, *Morfologia*

from different periods was examined. The result proved that such literature written prior to periods known otherwise as of prosperity of Greece,
as a rule contained stimulation toward entrepreneurial activity. It has
been established too that persons with high n Achievement tend to doodle
in multiple or diagonal waves and "S" shapes. Thus the ceramic patterns
of different cultures at different times were compared from that point of
view. Numerous other examinations were made; special psychological
tests were designed to evaluate n Achievement, and people in various
countries were tested. Recently research interest in the comparative analyses of n Achievement of various African ethnic groups has become quite
significant. Robert A. LeVine has published an excellent study in which
he compares the achievement motivation of the Yoruba, Hausa, and Ibo
tribes of Nigeria.[49] A number of studies of the achievement motivation of
ethnic groups in Eastern Africa are under way now.*

Why is it that achievement motivation appears in waves throughout
the history of nations? As McClelland asserts, it precedes the period of
economic growth. What are the causes of its appearance and spread?
How could achievement motivation be induced?

To this question McClelland and his associates and other psychologists, and recently many experts in the new nations as well, reply: by
learning. McClelland and his associates believe that motives are learned
in reference to both external and internal cues. Since most of the motivations are learned in early childhood, the kinds of motivations learned at
that time, the cues experienced during childhood, are of utmost importance for later behavior. The intensity and the extensity of a learned
motive reflects the frequency, persistence, pleasurability or unpleasur-
ability, continuity, strength of the exposition to definite cues and, of

---

bodźców economicznych, Warsaw: PWN, 1963); S. J. Rawin, "The Manager in the
Polish Enterprise: A Study of Accommodation Under Conditions of Role Conflict,"
British Journal of Industrial Relations, Vol. III.
The Polish manager is indeed well skilled and manifests a high achievement
motivation. However, he is very often a frustrated person because he constantly must
suppress this motivation. Not only is he often prevented from making use of his
skills, but he is poorly paid; even when he has money there is not much to be bought,
or the prices are so high that a person living on a legal salary is unable to afford them.
He is not allowed to express dissatisfaction and the only recourse that he has is to
drinking vodka and telling funny stories. Thus he lives in a completely different psychological situation from his colleagues working for General Electric. Sociologists and
economists have to take into account psychological situations, but psychologists have
also to consider political and economic factors.
For some other valid and interesting criticism of the application of McClelland's
views to traditional societies, see George M. Foster, "Peasant Society and the Image
of the Limited Good," *American Anthropologists,* Vol. LXVII, 1965.
* For instance, while in Tanzania I had a chance to read a formidable paper by J.
Ostheimer, *Achievement Motivation among the Chagga People of Tanzania.*

course, to some extent, the level of intelligence of the person. In short, desired motives may be elicited by properly selected cues; achievement motivation could be inculcated in training of self-reliance, high praise for hard work, persistence in goal attainment, interest in excellence for its own sake. Education and child-rearing which stresses such values are instrumental in reintegrating the expedient motive of achievement desired for its own sake, producing on a large scale the effect of general economic growth.

What are the views of critics of the achievement motivation theory? M. Brewster Smith, who approached McClelland's work with "skeptical approval," maintains that "n Achievement cannot seriously be accorded the dubious status of prime mover (as instinct was), even by the most imperialistic psychologist."[50] On the whole, this is not the royal road to truth, he says. Some studies in McClelland's work are based on rather small and dubious samples. He adds that the time lag of causation between periods of high n Achievement and subsequent presumable economic response is so far stretched (fifty and sometimes more years) in many of the historical cases discussed by McClelland that the whole story seems to look very speculative.

Warren E. Ilchman and Norman T. Uphoff[51] say that this is not accidental. Indeed, there could be no certainty of any causal connection between a high n Achievement and economic growth. Instead of economic growth and entrepreneurship high n Achievement may generate political aspirations, conflict, or social unrest. A regime would have to wait at least a generation for the payoff of the activities inducing n Achievement. They are right that high n Achievement may generate high aspirations, conflict and even political unrest, but one may argue that that is a part of the process of change and economic and societal growth.

In the recently published book, *Motivating Economic Achievement*, McClelland reaffirms his belief that achievement motivation is the major stimulant of economic growth.[52] He marshals evidence that even adults who were educated in a spirit of respect for traditions can acquire a strong desire for modernity and indeed can achieve in economic endeavors if they are properly induced in that direction by external agencies. He tells us that when conducive conditions are introduced to raise people from the torpor of obscurantism, when people become relieved of, or at least partly able to squirm free from, the inhibition of the traditions imposed on them from the past, when it is possible to attract them with a profuse payoff in their own reach, they change their attitude. They change especially when they are put under special training which rewards their prowess and stimulates a desire for acquisition in them. They soon start to behave as modern entrepreneurs; they promote economic activities which cumulatively produce the effect of economic growth, creating more jobs and subsequently raising the general standard of living. The book discusses the activities and the results of special courses in raising achievement motivation organized in India. In his conclusion, McClelland reiterates his earlier advice: Sow achievement motivation to harvest economic development.

It is probably not always possible to implement such a program, and certainly it is neither a panacea nor even a satisfactory remedy for many underdeveloped societies. Yet I do believe that this is good advice for countries where it can be applied and where it can work effectively. In fact many of the governments of the new states struggle in one way or another, in some instances with full consciousness, in others without it, to promote and spread the *n* Achievement. They provoke and support the entrepreneurial activities of their citizens, and they create conditions conducive to such activities. Most modern systems of education using European and American experience are instrumental in catalyzing and solidifying strong achievement-orientations and aspirations for better living.

I said, "where it can be applied," and this is the crux of the matter. (a) Certain cultures and political systems promote value-orientations not conducive to eliciting individualistic achievement aspiration. These are not necessarily traditional cultures and political systems. On the contrary, some such systems are highly oriented toward modernization and have attained a high level of economic development by other means than individualist achievement motivation; (b) In certain conditions which completely lack the other factors making economic development possible, such as natural resources, markets, and capital a plethora of achievement motivation generates a highly tense situation. Instead of economic development, it produces mass frustration; (c) Other motivations than that of achievement, and of achievement in McClelland's terms, might also be instrumental in triggering prodigious courses of economic growth.

George A. DeVos has pointed out that an atmosphere dominated by achievement-orientation of the type described by McClelland could be instigated only in a fairly complex society in which there is ample room for mobility, which is flexible enough to absorb and approve innovations, in societies which attain a high enough level of diversification and specialization of roles to offer a choice in role alternatives and in which higher status can be granted for acquisition and achievement in entrepreneurial activity.[53] In his opinion, "There is no doubt that McClelland's model well suits American culture, but is less applicable elsewhere."[54] This is indeed evident. That Western, and especially American, society is oriented toward achievement, that such an orientation was and is part of American culture is common knowledge. Bernard C. Rosen, Harry J. Crockett, and Clyde Z. Nunn have published a monumental book on achievement in American society, but in fact any book on American society must touch the problem of achievement-orientation.[55] It permeates all spheres of American life, it is part of the American ethos and by many it is regarded as the driving power of the society. What is puzzling is that today a great part of the young generation, the offspring of the wealthy and middle class, the sons and daughters of those who have achieved, adopt a denigratory attitude toward achievement and achieving. They were educated in families which taught them self-reliance and were proud of their own achievement and of the achievements of American society as a whole, they were educated in a spirit of respect for the self-made man, in the ethos of admiration for success. In their homes and in their schools they were taught to evaluate roles on the basis of the opportunities for excellence. In short they were reared in the traditional American spirit, yet they turned their backs on those values. Why? Because Americans have become increasingly other-directed, as some sociologists claim? Yet McClelland has written that other-directedness is part of the achievement syndrome. Out of boredom? Out of abundance? Out of an aggrandized sense of security? Or as Bruno Bettelheim puts it: "I, for my part, doubt whether life was ever less of a rat race than today. But it only became a *senseless* rat race when more and more people came to feel that they were racing after goals that were not really worthwhile or urgent, since survival seemed so assured by the affluent state."[56] Is that the cause?

DeVos asserts that Japanese society was never achievement-oriented in the way that McClelland understands it. In his opinion none of the theories explaining personality, behavior, or motives as individualistic ventures is applicable to Japan. The Japanese is, before anything else, a member of his family.[57] He is reared to feel this way and even when in modern times he becomes an industrial man, he remains that way. To understand the motives of his action, the pursuits of his life and behavior, one has to study Japanese family life and socialization within it. The individual is taught here to be dedicated to his family and, as an extension, to the community, and eventually, to the nation. He is raised in relationships which glorify subordination and even sacrifice of his own needs, interests and desires to and for the needs of the family and of the common cause.* He is taught that selfishness, success only for oneself,

---

* There are also other differences between the Japanese and West European attitudes toward work and the course of industrialization on the whole. Some of these differences were pointed out earlier (see pp. 94-98). J. C. Albegglen in *The Japanese Factory: Aspects of its Social Organization* (Glencoe, Ill.: Free Press, 1958) describes factory relations in Japan as family-type relations (though he assesses them as similar

even individualism is wrong and immoral. DeVos describes also how the Japanese family is permeated by a sense of guilt, self-restraint, and day-by-day hard work. He attributes the greatest importance to these values and especially to the fact that Japanese family life internalizes constantly in the minds of its members a feeling of guilt that one is unable to match the highest standards of excellence, guilt that one does not live up to the behavior ideally expected from him, guilt that unintentionally one may have hurt a fellow member, guilt for transgressions committed and un-committed. The Japanese mother takes the blame for her children's or her husband's bad conduct and performance. The child becomes aware of his mother's self-sacrifice and responds with a desire to compensate her. The propensity toward self-blame and expiation in women is not neces-sarily limited to the role of a wife and mother. It is often so strong and dramatic that one can view it as a "moral masochism." Virtuosity, attain-ment of excellence, and achievement in any field become as a result a form of self-sacrifice, an action aimed simultaneously at pleasing other members of the family and invoking their pride, and at relieving oneself of painful feelings of guilt.

DeVos assumes that this phenomenon of guilt and its resulting en-trepreneurial and other activities is so common that it should be regarded as the psychological underlayer of Japanese entrepreneurship. In addi-tion to such idiosyncrasies DeVos points out a second factor: "cooperative, concerted efforts of many embued with a relatively high sense of mutual trust and a sense of social responsibility distributed throughout all ranks of a rigidly stratified society." The two factors were mutually supportive in the advancement of the Japanese development. At this point, we must distinguish motivations for individualistic achievement from collectivistic achievement-orientation.

In the *Communist Manifesto,* and on many other occasions, Marx and Engels condemned the bourgeois morality and with it the striving for acquisition. Abolishing private property as a means of production, the

---

to those existing in the West in the first decades of the twentieth century). On the whole he asserts that Japanese factory grouping parallels other social groupings. David S. Landes, in "Japan and Europe: Contrasts in Industrialization" in W. Lockwood (ed.), *The State and Economic Enterprise in Japan* (Princeton, N.J.: Princeton Uni-versity Press, 1965) finds very interesting parallels between the Japanese and Ger-man course of industrialization. He also points out that "these aberrant courses of development had roots that went back before the period of industrialization" (p. 182); Yasuzō Horie, in "Modern Entrepreneurship in Meiji Japan" (*ibid.*), points out that "While I would hesitate to say that Confucianism helped to breed the entrepre-neurial spirit as actively as did the Protestant ethic in Europe, it certainly provided an intellectual and moral climate that favored the emergence of this new leadership" (p. 196). There seems to be a change in Japanese attitudes today. As some writers have pointed out, people in Japan have become increasingly more individualistic.

Communist Party in the Soviet Union and later in other East European states under communist rule proclaimed war against bourgeois achievement orientation, individualism, and relentless striving for acquisition. Profit-seeking, except by the state, was declared evil and abhorrent. Profit-seekers were ordered exterminated or re-educated. It was said that individualism leads to impoverishment of man's inner world, it produces a feeling of moral emptiness, it destroys the affection of man for fellowmen, it generates selfishness and finally, isolates and alienates him from the society, leaving him alone "with a divided personality."[58] In a speech to the Communist Youth League in 1920, Lenin declared ". . . our morality is entirely subordinated to the interests of the proletariat's class struggle."[59] It was not difficult, he said, to drive out the landowners and the capitalists, what is difficult is to get rid of the bourgeois consciousness of individualism, entrepreneurship, acquisition, and of money-oriented aspirations.* "To prevent the restoration of the rule of the capitalists and the bourgeoisie, we must not allow individuals to enrich themselves at the expense of the rest."[60] Hence, the Soviet people were directed to other goals. They were told to seek collective achievements of the nation as a whole.** They were told that a man has to work for the good of all people and not just for the satisfaction of the selfish desires of his own

* In another speech Lenin condemned capitalism as an order based on the wolfish law of individualistic striving for profit and acquisition, as a society in which ". . . anyone cares for himself, and only God cares for all." A. S. Makarenko, the classic writer on Soviet ethics and commonly recognized founder of the Soviet principles of education has argued in *Vospitanie w Sovietskoi Shkole* (Moskov: Prosveshchenye Publishers, 1966) that what is typical for a capitalist society is the absolute lack of concern of separate individuals for the interest of the whole society. All moral problems, and indeed all solutions for such problems, are solely based on individual striving without consideration of the interest of others and the society as a whole. He argued further that individualism was inherited by capitalism from both the Christian and Judaic religions and partially even from Islam. It is difficult to change habits and attitudes lasting as long as two thousand years, yet this is the important task of the Soviet education. "Only a man educated in the spirit of a collective ethics, a man whose interests are totally subordinated to the interest of the collectivity could simply and very easily understand the meaning of the famous formula: 'From each according to his abilities, to each according to his needs'" (p. 29). Though it is known that the repudiation of individualism, acquisitive entrepreneurship and other elements of what Weber regarded as the spirit of capitalism belongs to the basic principles of communism, some writers still imply that industrialization in the Soviet Union resulted from individualistic achievement motivations similar to those in the West. See also on this subject Urie Bronfenbrenner, *The Worlds of Childhood: U.S. and U.S.S.R.* With the assistance of John C. Candy, Jr. (New York: Russell Sage Foundation, 1970), pp. 37-62.
** The text of the new *Program of the Communist Party of the Soviet Union* contains twelve commandments of collectivism. It is said to be the moral code of the builder of communism. See *The New Soviet Society: Final Text of the Program of the Communist Party of the Soviet Union*, with Annotation and Introduction by Herbert Ritvo (New York: The New Leader, 1962), pp. 207-8.

ego. Collective achievement will bring abundance to all and not only to the very few. Thus men have to work not to raise their own or their families' standard of living, but that of the whole society, of all the two hundred million Soviet citizens. The people were told that a high standard of excellence and of socialist consciousness and behavior consist of deep dedication to the Communist cause, to the Party and later to Stalin as its leader personally. It must be manifested by high standards of performance in any assigned duty, in hard work, in rejection of all relics of the bourgeois morality, of individualism, and especially of acquisitive striving.

All means available were put in the service of eradicating what was regarded as bourgeois morality, the ingrained desire for individualistic economic achievement, the spirit of permissiveness infiltrating Soviet society from the West. The law, school, theaters, movies, the press, literature, the Party, trade unions, youth, women, children's organizations; all were given the task of inculcating in the minds of the Soviet people contempt for individualism and bourgeois morality. Instead, they were to inculcate a collectivistic achievement-orientation, to educate the masses in the spirit and belief of a common goal of the Soviet people and of the higher value of the new socialist morality.[61] Patriotism was invoked and intertwined with socialist ideals. To make this process of socialization and orientation to socialist collectivistic achievement more effective the party adopted a policy of rewards for those who demonstrate their dedication to the cause in their daily work and in behavior and in speeches.[62] Not only would they help to bring about an improvement in the general quality of life but they would benefit personally and immediately by higher salaries, better housing, numerous privileges and prizes.*

---

* The turn from the principle of maximal equalization to the new policy of incentives and diversified rewards in order to increase productivity was culminated in Stalin's speech at a conference of business executives on June 23, 1931. He declared then "We cannot tolerate a situation where a rolling-mill hand in a steel mill earns no more than a sweeper. We cannot tolerate a situation where a railway locomotive driver earns only as much as a copying clerk. Marx and Lenin said that the differences between skilled labour and unskilled labour would exist even under Socialism, even after classes had been abolished: that only under Communism would this difference disappear and that, therefore, even under Socialism 'wages' must be paid according to work performed and not according to needs. But the equalitarians among our business executives and trade union officials do not agree with this and believe that under our Soviet system this difference has already disappeared. Who is right, Marx and Lenin, or equalitarians? We must take it that it is Marx and Lenin who are right. . . . In order to get skilled workers we must give the unskilled worker a stimulus and prospect of advancement, of rising to a higher position. And the more boldly we do this, the better; for this is a principal means of putting an end to the heavy labour turnover. To economize in this matter would be criminal, it would be going against the interest of our Socialist industry. But this is not all. In order to retain the workers in the factories we must still further improve the supply of products

This is not to say that individualism and acquisitive motivations were let in fully through a back door. Yet people were allowed to have a small private aspiration to improve their own conditions of living, provided it did not reach the point of amassing wealth or acquiring property and they did not engage in individualistic entrepreneurship. Thus provisions were made for an achievement-orientation entirely different from that in the West. The capitalists are dead in the Soviet Union, with no prospect for their rebirth, yet the ghost of capitalism still roams there. Sometime it appears as the spirit of an allegedly terrible past, helping the Party by scaring people and by taking the blame for a present lack of successes. It became dwarfish and it learns to hide in the filing cabinets of Party and State officials, but most of all it loves their homes.

What are the motivations for excellence in work among the Soviet people? The answer can only be tentative without reference to any studies or research on achievement motivation there. A minority of people are motivated by a true and strong belief in the ideals of socialism as they are presented officially by the Party. Such people work for the implementation of the ideals and tasks without regard for the amount of reward. Another minority behaves similarly but is motivated by the spirit of nationalism or patriotism for the sake of great Russia. Still another minority strives for excellence and virtue for its own sake. These are the kinds of people that will behave in the same way under any régime. The majority of people are to some extent motivated by the ideology of the general cause, although it is mainly worn as an ideological armor to present themselves to the society as fighters for the right cause, for socialism and social justice, or to present to themselves a rationalization of their poverty and of the meaninglessness of their life. Practically speaking, they do their work and try to do it better to obtain a means of living and if possible more and better means. Still another minority is inspired by entrepreneurial achievement motivation. They take great risks in forbidden or semilegal activities to release their painful desire for acquisition, their need to act as entrepreneurs and simply to get more money.

In general the n Achievement based on individualism cannot be credited with economic development in the Soviet Union. It would be naïve, however, to conclude that economic development resulted in the Soviet Union from the collectivistic achievement-orientation of the

---

to the workers and improve their housing conditions. . . . The worker today is not what he was before. The worker today, our Soviet worker, wants to live as to have all his material and cultural needs satisfied: in respect of food, housing conditions, cultural, and all other requirements. He has a right to this, and it is our duty to secure these conditions for him." See J. V. Stalin, "New Conditions—New Tasks . . . ," pp. 363, 364.

masses. It was organized from above by the Party leadership and executed with the use of coercion at the cost of great sacrifice by the masses. The leaders made a gigantic effort to elicit a widespread manifestation of collectivistic achievement motivation as a rationale for their action, as they sought support for their program of complete and rapid mobilization of man and resources. What motivated those who organized that enormous complex activity which in a relatively short time made the Soviet Union a mighty military, and great industrial world power? Lofty ideas of building socialism? A desire to implement the immemorial dreams of the Tsars to make Russia great? A wish to raise the standard of living of the Soviet people? A feeling of insecurity because of the hostile surrounding capitalist world? A great need for power? McClelland tells us that "a combination of low n Affiliation and high n Power is very closely associated with the tendency of a nation to resort to totalitarian methods in governing its people."[63] Using McClelland's terminology, one can say that in the Soviet Union a minority with high n Power organized economic development by means of physical and economic coercion and through inculcation of a strong n Affiliation while allowing manifestations of some individualistic n Achievement.

As a matter of fact, this was not an entirely new method in Russia. Peter the Great had no concern for his subjects' achievement motivation or lack of it. As their Tsar he thought he knew what was good for them. After spending eighteen months in Holland, England, and Prussia, where he studied achievements in organization and technology and personally worked in shipyards and in smithies, he returned to Russia to start a broad wave of modernization. He ordered his courtiers and the rest of the nobility to cut their beards and long hair and imposed taxes on others who wore beards. He stripped his officers and dignitaries of their uniforms and attire made of traditional Russian cloth and put them in French lace suits and powdered and perfumed wigs. He ordered them to smoke pipes and to study modern court dancing, and their sons to study modern navigation, engineering, and methods of organization. He replaced the old aristocracy with a new élite, a "nobility of service" capable of handling the new military, administrative, and industrial institutions. Peter the Great also established numerous industries throughout Russia in order to supply his newly organized army and fleet with modern weaponry. He established a new academy of sciences. He won many battles and expanded the rule of Russia over many foreign lands. He hanged and decapitated (sometimes personally) thousands or tens of thousands who opposed his reforms or were slow to accept them. In the swampy outlet of the Neva River, Peter the Great founded his new capital. Since building stone was scarce there officials who wanted to visit the Tsar were allowed to come only if they brought a heavy stone in their coaches. The Russian aristocracy and the officials were ordered to build their palaces in the new city. Hundreds of thousands of peasants were brought to the swamps to build the new capital.*

Though McClelland asserted "that achievement motivation is in part responsible for economic growth," he never considered those other factors or parts which cumulatively bring about the effect of economic development. Does a high level of n Achievement necessarily and always translate itself into economic growth? What about situations when high need achievement spreads and grows, when people crave change and modernity but the country is poor with no available capital and no natural resources? When the government has adopted a policy of suppressing individual entrepreneurial activity? In short, what happens in a situation where needs for achievement are plentiful but the outlets for its translation into enterpreneurship are absent or blocked? These are not rare instances. In many of the new nations this is now the situation. It is said to produce a crisis of aspirations and of expectations. Yet, the phenomenon is not peculiar to new nations. In any modern society one can witness daily the painful anxiety of those who cannot live up to their aspirations, to the level of achievement to which they are motivated.**

4. Calling and Duty

The comparative analysis of the cases of industrialization in the West, in the Soviet Union and the Soviet bloc, and in Japan allows one to extract the important lesson that activities producing national economic development, either accidentally or intentionally, can be sparked by diverse motivations*** and in some cases by a number of motivations. Though usually one can speak in such cases about a prevalent motiva-

---

* This is how Russia was modernized by Peter the Great without any achievement motivation of his people. Of course, one may argue that Russia did not then become a truly modern society, and that this was why industrialization did not continue at an accelerated pace.

** It seem that a discussion of achievement motivation, deviant behavior, and violence would be relevant here. However, I wish to limit myself to only one comment. Widespread high n Achievement in situations where outlets for translation of it into what a given societal order will regard as positive action are blocked might, and very often does, generate tension and violence. Deviant behavior does not necessarily have to be destructive. On the contrary, it can produce important productive changes leading to growth and development. Some aspects of the crisis of expectation and aspirations will be discussed in Chapter 6 of this book.

*** A strong stipulation must be made here that this is not a discussion of the nature and psychological mechanism of the formation of motivations and needs. Motivations are regarded as an imminent factor in action. This is only an attempt to demonstrate the diversity of such motivations in actions generating growth.

tion, it is obvious that different people taking part in a common action are directed by the major kind of motivation in diverse degrees. What is more important, they may engage in similar activities and be directed by different motivations. In his well-documented book on innovations, H. G. Barnett has shown how diverse the motivation for change can be.[64] Apart from situations described by him as "the deprivation of essentials," he lists diverse wants motivating men in action such as preferences, creative wants, relief and avoidance wants (relief from boredom, relaxation from constraints, distaste, and so forth), the desire for quantitative variations, and what he calls vicarious wants (altruistic concern). It is worth noting that Barnett does not enumerate any needs, wants, or motives resembling what McClelland calls achievement motivation.

There seems to be enough justification to argue that while economic development in the West has been sparked and expanded primarily as a result of achievement motivated people, in other societies it was different. Soviet industrialization and economic development was evidently strongly motivated by a need for power, at least by the leaders of that country. DeVos tells us that in Japan it was the feeling of guilt which motivated people to engage in productive activities and strive for achievements. In addition, a number of other motivations, such as a sense of duty, altruism, the need to satisfy one's own curiosity, the need for security, can be regarded as instrumental in sparking innovative, entrepreneurial inclinations. While such motivations as the urge of duty, altruism, curiosity will be touched on only briefly, the need for security will be discussed somewhat more fully.

In *The Protestant Ethic* Weber does not employ the concept of motivation or motive. Nonetheless it seems to be possible to discern in his writing three collateral mutually supportive motivations which he attributes to the makers of capitalism. The first of such "motivations" listed by Weber is *making money*. Though Weber admired the makers of capitalism and described them as highly rational men, he points out that this was an absolutely irrational and transcendental motivation. Weber comments that his hero Benjamin Franklin quoted the Bible in response to the question, "why should 'money be made out of men'?" If it is not greed, and Weber claims that it is not, then it is the fulfillment of a calling.[65] The fulfillment of *calling* or "one's duty in calling," or in still other terms one's moral obligation, is the second of the motivations listed by Weber. Third, he asserts that Protestants, and even other entrepreneurs, and the makers of capitalism in general act from an *urge to achieve a high standard of excellence*. I do not feel that the motivation "to make money" has to be discussed here. The motivation n Achievement and the calling have been discussed already. Nonetheless I wish to devote a few more lines to a discussion of the calling, mission fulfillment, and the implementation of duties.

Weber discusses with great emotion the "calling" as the fulfillment of a mission imposed on men from above. Calling is more than fulfillment of duty. Weber tells us that though the fulfillment of a calling such as making money for its own sake, out of purely eudaemonistic self-interest, is irrational; it is not only the most characteristic element of the capitalistic culture but it motivates men to the most consequential and rational performances. Weber writes further that though the concept of calling is derived from the Bible, it represents the spirit of the translator rather than the spirit of the Bible itself. He stresses that it is not in his opinion a specific product of Germanic culture. He also contends that for Luther the concept of calling basically remained traditionalistic and that only in the Calvinistic interpretation did it obtain its full power. Weber emphasizes: "The conception of the calling thus brings out that central dogma of all Protestant denominations which the Catholic division of ethical precepts into *praecepta* and *consilia* discards. The only way of living acceptably to God was not to surpass worldly morality in monastic asceticism, but solely through the fulfillment of the obligations imposed upon the individual by his position in the world. That was his calling."[66]

Though I cannot enter into a detailed discussion of that subject and demonstrate enough arguments in support of my views, I would like to say that Weber does not seem to be right in this. The concept of calling and even more so of duty is very much a product of German culture. If it is emphasized so much in the Protestant ethic, it is because that ethic too is partially at least a product of the German culture. Of course, any religion or any code of conduct or norms extols the importance of fulfilling moral obligations. Yet in the German culture the focus on duties and moral obligation is profound, highly pathetic, and explicit. In other cultures too, it is the fate of men to fulfill duties. But, in the German culture a greater weight, at least in the past, has been attributed to the function of duties. The belief was that duties generate a feeling of belongingness. Their implementation is a transformation of the present into eternity. They give the man the inner power for great action. Numerous works of German philosophers, many German poems and literary works praise the fulfillment of duties, often not even particular duties but duties in general. From that perspective it often looks and sounds as though the whole purpose of living consisted of the implementation of duties, and as though God created duties first, and then had to invent men to implement them. In the dispassionate voluminous writing of Immanuel Kant one paragraph is full of emotion and overwhelming passion. It is about duties. "Duty!"—exclaims Kant—

Thou sublime and mighty name that dost embrace nothing charming or insinuating but requires submission and yet seekest not to move the will by threatening aught that would arouse natural aversion or terror but only holdest forth a law which of itself finds entrance into the mind and yet gains reluctant reverence (though not always obedience)—a law before which all inclinations are dumb even though they secretly work against it: what origin is there worthy of thee, and where is to be found the root of thy noble descent which proudly rejects all kinship with the inclinations and from which to be descended is the indispensable condition of the only worth which men can give themselves?[67]

All statements containing the form "I ought to do so and so" and hence expressing the feeling of duty, of a moral obligation, and of readiness to implement the command Kant singles out as imperatives (drawing a distinction between categorical and hypothetical imperatives). Kant was not alone in this concern. Fichte, Hegel, and numerous other German philosophers* while opposing in one way or another Kant's views, told the world that they felt personally to be in calling, that the German nation had a great mission to fulfill, that each member of that nation and perhaps of other nations had moral duties. They were great lovers of truth, human dignity and freedoms and were laudable for what they considered to be positive values. The cult of duty and fulfillment of mission was built into the theory of German mysticism. It became a part of the German *Volksgeist*.**

As have numerous other writers, Kuno Francke points out that the Prussian state was the living embodiment of Kantian principles of duty. Not that Kant's views on politics affected directly the shape of Prussian

---

* R. H. Lowie in *The German People: A Social Portrait to 1914* (New York: Farrar & Reinhart, 1945) (p. 103) points out ". . . the great achievements in German science, literature, and art are largely linked with the names of Protestants . . . Kant, Fichte, Hegel, Goethe, Lessing, Hebbel, Schiller, Humboldt, Helmholtz, Mommsen, were all Protestants."

** For a Nazi interpretation on the same topic see for example, F. Schnell, *Volk und Gesellschaft* (1942). W. Hellpach in a modern study on the German national character (pp. 174-75, 202-5) lists as its characteristic qualities: urge to creativity; thoroughness; love for order; strangely enough, lack of good manners, rudeness and even coarseness; stubbornness; sentimentalism. Obedience and what could be regarded as a sense of duty is treated as another side of either the urge for creativity or coarseness. See Willy Helpach, *Der Deutsche Charakter* (Bonn: Atheneum Verlag, 1954), especially pp. 171-229. Some modern German writers tend to discuss the German sense of duty and what may be regarded as action in calling as an attitude toward authority. See C. G. Schmidt-Freytag (ed.), *Die Authorität und die Deutschen* (Munich: Deutsche Verlagbuch Handlung, 1966). The literature on the German character, spirit, soul, mission, fate (*Schicksal*), etc., is immense indeed. Some of the writers on the subject believe that industrialization in Germany was organized by men with authoritarian personalities.

legislation, but men who were inspired by him and followed him, such as Stein, Hardenberg, Wilhelm von Humboldt, Fichte, and Hegel "have been official exponents, so to speak, of the mission of Prussia for a regenerated Germany." Francke tells us also that

> By the side of Kant's stern doctrine of duty there must be placed, as another of the great legacies left to Germany by her classic writers, the Goethean gospel of salvation through ceaseless striving. It is Goethe who has impressed upon German life the Superman motif. As his own life was a combination of *Wilhelm Meister* and *Faust* in their undaunted striving from experience to experience and in their ever-renewed efforts to round out their own being, so it may be said that there is something Faustlike and something Meisterlike in most of the representative men of German literature in the nineteenth century, above all in Heinrich von Kleist, Hebbel, Otto Ludwig, Richard Wagner, Nietsche. None of these men were religious formalists; to all of them life was an experiment of deepest import; all of them found the value of life in wrestling with its fundamental problems. And this whole tradition of striving has been imparted even to the average German of today. . . .[68]

One may argue that any theory of ethics is based on the concept of duty. Plato, Aristotle, and scores of other philosophers in different nations wrote on the duties of citizens. Any African tribal prophet claims that he is an embodiment of a Spirit, and hence the tool of a great mission. The crux of the matter is not in the general insistence that duties have to be fulfilled, it is in the reasons given for their implementation and in the elevation of duty fulfillment to the level of a mission, calling, and purpose of life. In the end of the nineteenth and in the beginning of the twentieth century the concern with missions, calling, and duties became so widespread and intense in Germany that it achieved the magnitude of a national obsession. Marx was caught by it too, proclaiming to the world that the proletariat has a mission to fulfill, and that some intellectuals are the mouthpiece of that historical mission. Not only university professors, but teachers in schools, corporals and generals in the army, and nearly anyone who was teaching and telling others what to do was preaching about missions, callings, and duty, what a good German ought to do in their implementation, and how he should be obedient to the calling and the orders coming from above. There is no need to elaborate on how this was exploited later by the Nazis.

I do believe that this stress on calling and duty was more pronounced in Germany than in other Protestant countries, than in Anglo-Saxon, Scandinavian, or even Dutch societies. Even if only a matter of degree, it seems to be a very important difference, and it seems to have produced a different style of entrepreneurship.* It also constitutes an important element of the political culture, since it reflects an attitude toward authority. I feel that to invoke a sense of duty and calling is as important for economic development as is the invoking of high n Achievement. We know well, for instance, that people in Africa and Asia usually display a strong attachment to their families and with it strong feelings of obligation and responsibility for them. Yet they tend to be parochial and communalistic (family, tribe) rather than individualistic or collectivistic (in respect of the whole society and state). How can a strong sense of duty toward general society and its agencies be induced in these people? How can they be inspired with a feeling of responsibility for that general society? What is involved is something more than patriotism displayed occasionally against strangers or national consciousness displayed in general declarations. I believe that research on dutifulness and on the sense of calling ought to be organized parallel to that on n Achievement. Until now this was not a topic of great interest for students of sociology, psychology, or culture and personality. It was basically of interest in the field of ethics.

A supposition has been put forward before that diverse motivations such as need of achievement, need of power, need for altruism (helping others), sense of duty, calling, need of balancing the feeling of guilt, need of security, are instrumental in economic and societal growth. This is not the place to indulge in a general theory of needs and their expression in action. And I would not like to depart too far (if I have not done so already) from the basic line of our discussion, that of societal development. I think that the motive of attaining greater security is especially important in engendering entrepreneurial and general economic activities producing subsequently economic and societal growth. I would like

---

* This is not to say that the German entrepreneur was not motivated by profit seeking or individual achievement. Apart from the writing of Weber and Sombart numerous other publications on the personality of the entrepreneur appeared in Germany between 1915 and 1935. The German entrepreneur is mostly the hero of such publications. The writers very often stress that the German entrepreneur was motivated by a sense of mission that he has to perform. See W. Hofmann, *Stellung und Bedeutung der Unternehmer-persönlichkeit in der modernen Wirtschaftsorganisation* (Leipzig: G. A. Gloeckner, 1933). Wiedenfeld, "Das persöliche in modern Unternehmertum" in *Schmollers Jahrbücher,* vol. XXXIV (1910); Lujo Brentano, *Der Unternehmer* (Berlin: Leophold Simon, 1907). The writer argues that capital is just an instrument of the entrepreneur. His social function is production of goods. He is primarily an organizer. S. von Lorenz, *Die Entstehung des Unternehmergewinnes* (Vienna: Ostreichischer Wirtschaft Verlag, 1936) (pp. 180-81) distinguishes between the function of capitalist and entrepreneurs. The entrepreneur, he tells us, is acting in the interest of the industry, not purely in pursuit of money. J. A. Schumpeter's interest in entrepreneurship is related to the above tradition. From a modern perspective, the activities of the German entrepreneurs in the nineteenth and the beginning of the twentieth century may be assessed differently. This does not change the fact that the entrepreneurs believed that they accomplished a mission.

to focus the discussion now on some aspects of that subject and on the role of the insecurity within security. But first, let me make just a few more comments on the other motivations possibly influencing economic growth that will not be discussed here more fully. For example, widespread sense of duty and the feeling of guilt can also be interpreted in some cases as altruistic motivations. And there are altruistic motivations of another kind such as the supplying of assistance in economic development.

Thorstein Veblen introduced a number of concepts which are relevant here. He wrote about the instinct of workmanship (manifest in industry), the instinct of predation (manifest in business), and the instinct of idle curiosity. He wrote at a time when the theory of instincts was in fashion in psychology and when instinct theories were influencing other disciplines. From a modern perspective, what Veblen called the instincts of workmanship and predation could be equated with the characteristics of achievement motivation. In *The Higher Learning in America* Veblen contrasts those two instincts with the instinct of idle curiosity, defending the latter and insisting that though idle curiosity does not seem to produce immediate pecuniary gains it is still useful.[69] However, the case of idle curiosity and curiosity in general has to be defended in much stronger terms. Where would mankind be today were it not curious in the past? Curiosity is one of the important faculties which made man human. Without curiosity, culture and knowledge would not have appeared. Joseph A. Schumpeter writes that "The capitalist civilization is rationalistic 'and anti-heroic.' "* He points out that ". . . it is highly significant that modern mathematico-experimental science developed, in the fifteenth, sixteenth and seventeenth centuries, not only along with the social process usually referred to as the Rise of Capitalism, but also outside of the fortress of scholastic thought and in the face of its contemptuous hostility.[70] Capi-

---

* Schumpeter regards the entrepreneur as the major agent in promoting economic development. He contrasts entrepreneurial creativity with the work of both the capitalist and the working-class man. Like Weber (and indeed there are many other parallels between them), Schumpeter argues that the entrepreneur is motivated not primarily by the desire to raise his standard of consumption but by other motives, such as joy of creation, conquest of market, striving for victory in the competitive battle with other entrepreneurs, and in some cases a wish to establish a dynasty or a lasting business firm. He also asserts that with routinization of the entrepreneur's activities and the diminution of his role because of the growth of big, often monopolistic corporations, a society enters into an era of economic stagnation. Thus a "creative" destruction of the equilibrium ensues. Since, however, capitalism still retains a potential of growth, recovery, and even improvement of the economy follows. Some writers on entrepreneurship have voiced the opinion that in connection with the development of big corporations the role of the entrepreneur is declining. However, nowadays one can read also that within the general bureaucratic order of big corporations there is an ongoing resurgence of a new kind of entrepreneurship, and that in the future the role of the entrepreneurs will increase even more.

talism, industrialization, economic growth are as much products of men motivated by curiosity as of achievement- and acquisition-motivated men. Both constitute the propelling forces in the ongoing process of change and societal and economic growth. The restless curious, those who are never satisfied with what they know, who are passionately willing to ponder, to explore, to penetrate the unknown even without pecuniary rewards and even at the risk of their lives, are usually a minority. But would economic growth be possible without such a thoughtful minority?

5. Insecurity Within Security

Discussing what he calls the most important psychic needs motivating men's action, Ralph Linton states,

> Thanks to the human ability to perceive time as a continuum extending beyond past and present into the future, present satisfactions are not enough as long as future ones remain uncertain. We are in constant need of reassurance, although the same time sense which makes it possible for us to worry about what may happen also makes it possible for us to postpone the satisfaction of present needs and put up with current discomforts in the expectation of future rewards. This need for security and for reassurance is reflected in innumerable forms of culturally patterned behavior. It leads the primitive craftsman to mingle magic with his technology and men at all levels of culture to imagine heavens in which the proper behavior of the present will be properly rewarded. In the light of our very limited knowledge of psychological processes it seems idle to speculate as to the origins of this need. It is enough to recognize its importance as a motivation of forward looking behavior.[71]

In these few sentences Linton presents one of the most important motivations of human action. Man is in constant quest for security. He devises the building of shelters, housing, the storing of food and other commodities in an attempt to be secure now and in the future. In his quest for security he provides for law and order, organizes state and multitudinous societal institutions. In his search for spiritual security and protection from transcendent forces he develops religions. He organizes armies, the police, insurance companies; he establishes complex norms of behavior, of traffic, of interaction. He establishes the Security Council of the United Nations to guard his security in international relations. From the onset of his existence man has been searching for protection, greater security, physical, spiritual, economic, social, military, and political securities. He builds new systems to increase the existing security, to discover new dangers, to find out that he is still in a precarious situation.

188
188 Societal Development

Abundance, freedom, equality, knowledge, stability, consensus, economic achievement are sought not only for their own sakes but because they are viewed as sources of greater security. The quest for security seems to be a common, widespread, and important enough motivation to be regarded among the motivations latently inspiring economic growth and development.

What is security? Numerous difficulties are encountered in any attempt to answer this question. (1) Security is subjective. It depends more on feeling than on being.[72] The same situation could be assessed from one point of view as secure and from another as dangerous. It is very difficult to design a method of measuring security or insecurity. (2) Individual and group security have to be distinguished, and as well as the security of structures on different levels of social organization and social order. Then the question of how individual security and group security interact on different levels of societal structure could be asked. (3) Almost any activity can be interpreted as bringing about greater security. Diverse securities are more or less important to people in different situations. In quest of physical, spiritual, and social securities, men engage in almost every kind of military, political, and economic action. It is also often difficult to establish a direct connection between the objective of security and the means employed in its attainment. A man desiring greater economic security may engage in innovations and in entrepreneurial activities, or he may pray to God, join a gang, or engage in a multitude of other activities. The same applies to almost any kind of desired security. The topic is so important, contains such a great explanatory capacity and has been neglected so long that regardless of the difficulties that one has to encounter it is worthwhile examining.

What is security? Let us compare a number of answers to that question found in the relevant literature. Harold Lasswell and Abraham Kaplan define security as

> high value expectancy, position, and potential: realistic expectancy of maintaining influence. Security involves, first certain perspectives (the "sense of security"): demands and expectations as to the future value position of the self. The perspectives must be realistic—the expectations be in fact likely to be fulfilled—or there is only a false sense of security. And the actual value position must be comparatively high: the locus of security is in the present as well as the future.[73]

Psychological research has shown that the things people say they care most about tend to be the things about which they feel most insecure.[74] At a symposium organized at the University of Nebraska in November 1965 on the topic, "Man's Quest for Security," this was most evident. Experts in different disciplines were invited to present papers on the subject, and each of them spoke about different things. The philosopher Sydney Hook asserted that though man now has tremendous power he feels alienated and insecure, and his anxiety over his uncertainty and insecurity has developed "almost *pari passu* with the growth of human power." He attributed today's sense of insecurity to fear of a nuclear war. But that is not the only reason why man feels insecure, Hook explained. Man is a risk-seeking and risk-enjoying creature. The taste of achievement depends very much on the degree of risk-taking. He concluded that "The world will never be completely safe for man, because so long as he has the power of thought and choice he may choose not wisely but disastrously."[75] The sociologist Kingsley Davis pointed out the differences between individual, group and national security.* Security breeds insecurity, and at any level of achieved security another type of insecurity is bred. He then related the problem of security and insecurity to underdeveloped nations, to the antipoverty campaign in the United States, and especially to the problems of population growth. The psychiatrist Howard P. Rome wrote on the parallel quest for security in wishful thinking and fantasy and the endless pursuit of goals in the world of reality. Expressing an economist's point of view, Charles E. Walker was concerned with scarcity of goods and with obtaining economic security by increasing the output of production and efficiency. General Thomas S. Power expressed the opinion that "the decisions to build the hydrogen bomb; to build the B-47, the B-52, and the B-58 strategic bombers; and to build the Atlas, the Titan, the Minute Man, and the Polaris ballistic missiles . . . are the decisions and actions that have given us our security."[76]

Though it is commonly believed that the concept of "security" has wide use in psychiatry and psychology, in fact very little has been written on it even in these disciplines. There too the whole issue has been treated only marginally. Theorists of the "cultural school of psychoanalysis," who stress the importance of the interpersonal factors in the etiology of neurosis, have applied the concept of security as a euphemism for "neurotic" needs of the craving of the alienated personality.[77] Erich Fromm warns against confusion between economic and emotional securities. He argues that "the psychic task which a person can and must set for himself is not to feel secure, but to be able to tolerate insecurity, without panic and undue fear. . . . Free man is by necessity insecure; thinking man by necessity uncertain."[78] Fromm argues that man can tol-

---

* The Daily *San Francisco Chronicle* of June 15, 1971 conducting one of its O'Hara interviews asked a number of people "What is your idea of security?" The answers were: "being married," "clear conscience," "people caring for you," "having no problems," "if you aren't questioning what's happening around you."

erate such insecurity by being rooted in a group, by discovering his "true self" as he relates to his fellow man on the basis of love and brotherhood. He argues that the "schizoid self-alienated" person seeks security by compromising and becoming as similar as possible to his fellowman. On the whole, it has to be said that there is not much to embark upon in the literature if one wishes to regard security and insecurity as important motivations in generating economic growth and societal development.

I must admit that I am unable to define the concept of security satisfactorily. I think, nonetheless, that the topic could be discussed at least hypothetically. McClelland does not bother to define achievement motivation though it could be understood in terms other than his. He rather describes it operationally as a manifest behavior. This seems to be a common way of discussing other motivations too. The closest that I am able to come to defining in a concise cogent way the understanding of security which appears in the following pages is: a consistent impression of being under lasting providential, institutional, or economic protection against the activities of external harmful agencies. *"I feel secure" means I feel that no one, or nearly no one, can willfully put me in a position which I consider to be dangerous or harmful to my interests, in which I may be deprived of my status* or of objects related to its holding.* The subjectivity of the feeling of security has to be emphasized since different societies and indeed different points of view within one society interpret the requirements of security differently. When the feeling of insecurity or the need of greater security provokes and evokes action, it may be regarded as a motivation. Thus the underlying assumption of the forthcoming reflections is that man has a natural propensity for seeking, obtaining, and maintaining his conditions of living on a level which he believes will provide him with a combination of both life satisfaction and security. In any society wants, needs, and actions are greatly determined by the feelings of security and insecurity of its individual members, its corporate groups, and the society as a whole. The feeling of great security may stem from possession of political power, prestige, popularity, wealth, physical coercive power (military power), stability of the situation, belief in supernatural protection, or even inconspicuousness. While people sometimes aim at power, wealth, prestige, or popularity for its own sake, and at other times in pursuit of greater security, possession of wealth, prestige and power may by itself become a source of insecurity and may motivate people into action in quest of greater security. Social organization established in pursuit of institutionalized interactions and

---

* Thus, in partial corroboration of Hagen's theory, status-seeking in definite circumstances is an important vehicle for promoting innovations generating economic and societal development.

interconnections are supposed to provide each of its participants with a degree of societal protection (even prisoners have societal protection in that sense). Societal protection as any other object of scarcity is distributed in any society unevenly. Often, though not always, the vulnerable enjoy more protection than the others. However, the greatest protection in any societal order is accorded to those who occupy the key positions in its structure. Though designed to produce more security, strong societal protection and control over a great share of desirable goods does not necessarily generate a feeling of strong security. The most protected persons are often very insecure subjectively. The degree of internal security of an individual and of a group reflects both the integrity of the man and his or the group's ability to cope with the consequences of life and the degree of dangers encountered from the encroachment of external agents. Individual security is greatly dependent on group security, and conversely a group composed of alienated insecure personalities not only develops a consciousness of insecurity but most often becomes objectively insecure.*

Here again the distinction between being and feeling secure and insecure have to be recalled. A person may be objectively insecure but not be conscious of the dangers surrounding him. In this case he will feel secure. On the other hand, people living in objective security may feel extremely insecure. Even with a corresponding low degree of objective security, low social status does not necessarily produce a feeling of insecurity and especially does not necessarily translate itself into action. Thus Hagen is right in asserting that the person or group that is in danger of losing or had already lost its status may feel insecure, people occupying positions of low status may actually feel very secure.

In his quest for greater security, man changes both the natural and societal environment of his action. He introduces innovations and establishes new institutions in pursuit of conditions which will provide him with more security. Thus the quest for security may become, and as a rule is, a highly effective motivation generating economic and societal development either directly or during pursuit of other objectives. Security and insecurity affects development in a number of ways. These will be discussed now in the form of several hypotheses.

HYPOTHESIS I.   *Societal and political orders producing objective conditions generating feelings of great security for the society as a whole, for all its members, and generally speaking for each of its members individually have as a rule a low capacity for stimulating social change and*

---

* A somewhat similar definition of security has been proposed by Christian Bay (*The Structure of Freedom*, Stanford, Calif.: Stanford University Press, 1970, pp. 74 ff). He discusses subjective and objective security as conditions of freedom.

economic development. A strong feeling of individual and group security becomes a demobilizing and vitiating factor in social and economic action. It especially impairs any inclination toward innovative action.

Traditional societies are a good example of such cases.* Here little room is provided for vertical and horizontal mobility. Positions (and roles) are allocated principally in accordance with traditionally established rules of ascription, where each individual and each group feels secure in a fixed position which can be neither lost nor changed into a higher one. Competition is limited, and its rewards are neither too diversified nor too tempting.[79] In short, societies in which members enjoy a high feeling of security (though they may be poor and accorded with little protection against unexpected happenings) tend to be passive and stagnant. Of course, a high feeling of security is not the sole cause, but one of the mutually reinforcing factors producing an effect of lasting passivity. It may be observed that in accordance with observations of Vilfredo Pareto, Robert Michels, and other writers, this also pertains to the group behavior of élites. Highly dynamic groups, after obtaining a high sense of security, may become passive and stagnant, congealed in their acquired level of development. Without challenges, or without a capacity to respond to challenges, they degenerate into passivity and, as Pareto and Mosca pointed out in the case of aristocracy, into decadence.

HYPOTHESIS II.   *A person or group under the stress of a persistent feeling of insecurity which he or it believes cannot be overcome is bound to be either (a) depressed, apathetic, passive, resigned; or (b) highly frustrated, alienated (or, as some prefer to call it, neurotic), and hence often overactive.* Psychologists tell us that much fear leads to utter withdrawal, or else to violent and destructive actions. A person or group motivated by strong feelings of insecurity (regardless of the objective conditions of security provided by the state and political system) may engage in some cases in highly risky endeavors but rarely, if at all, will he engage in complex calculated innovational activities ultimately producing the effect of economic development.**

---

* On security in traditional societies, see A. Kardiner, *The Individual and His Society: The Psychodynamics of Primitive Social Organization* with a forward and two ethnological reports by R. Linton (1965); especially Chapter IV, "Security System and Basic Personality Structure."
** The above hypothesis accounts for an ideal type situation. In reality, in some societies the conditions could be described as tending toward or approximating the cases depicted in the above formulation. It is pertinent also to point out that responses to danger, uncertainty, and situations in which people not only feel subjectively insecure but in which they obviously are insecure are not solely determined by the agent producing danger and insecurity. Many factors such as the integrity of the person involved, experience in similar situations, familiarity with risk, knowledge of the causes of uncertainty and of danger and of the prospects of overcoming it, other

Paradoxically, traditional societies also provide examples for these cases. The extended family is the source of all security available in such conditions. Beyond the extended family is a sphere of total insecurity. One of the great problems of new nations, especially in Africa, is that the pace of modernization opens the seclusion of the traditional extended family, bringing out individuals who are extremely sensitive to the insecurities of the outer world. The growing supratribal societies contain but a limited capacity to substitute a new source of security for that previously provided by the family. Semitribal cultural, religious, self-help, and other associations bridging the old and the new are quite common in all African urban centers.[80] Among other functions, they provide a palliative form of security, if not real protection, which reduces the feeling of insecurity and tension generated by living in a foreign, often hostile environment.

In most of the new nations the situation is in constant flux. The political system is unstable. Little protection is accorded to innovators and entrepreneurs. Their position is uncertain, their efforts are rarely rewarded with an attainment of positions which will produce strong feelings of security. The political system does not create conditions for long-range calculations and actions producing slow but sure accumulation of profits in wealth, and prestige.

The implications of our second hypothesis are very wide indeed, and to discuss them means to enter into a discussion of the broad range of theories of motivation. This is not our topic, however. In posing the above two hypotheses, I wish only to point out that high security and high insecurity both are thresholds of conditions not very conducive to innovations, entrepreneurship, and general activities generating economic development.*

---

motivations, such as striving for achievement, individual or collective, the belief system cumulatively determine behavior in such situations. O. J. Harvey in *Motivation and Social Interaction Cognitive Determinants* (New York: The Ronald Press 1963) (p. 15) says as follows: "The value of stimuli is . . . not . . . absolute in their facts but dependent upon the base line or internal standards to which the receiving subject compares them in the process of evaluating them and responding to them. Different ones of us treat such base lines differently, both in terms of what they are conceived to be and the effects of events deviating from them."

* Some conservative writers argue that modern mass society, whether capitalist or communist, is tantamount to the end of any security for the individual (see W. Martini, *Das Ende Aller Sicherheit*, 1954; and J. Ortega y Gasset, in all his writing). They contend that the only solution is a strictly institutionalized societal hierarchical order providing his own place to anyone. E. Fromm and other writers who either share his belief in humanistic communitarism or promulgate similar solutions generally share the criticism of the conservatives of capitalist and communist societies. Their solution is "thousands of small face-to-face groups, which are well informed, which discuss, and whose decisions are integrated in a new 'lower house' " (E. Fromm,

HYPOTHESIS III. *In a situation where the society and the state provide at least minimal protection and security for everyone, the feeling that one's own situation is not so secure as one would like may be called stimulating insecurity.* Whether a man is motivated to active or passive behavior by a feeling of stimulating insecurity depends on a number of factors, primarily on the content of the dominant beliefs of the society in general and of the individuals capable of influencing the course of events and on the capability of others to interact with him in his endeavor.*

It has been pointed out previously that the value of stimuli is not absolute. In different societies diverse motivations have to be aroused in order to organize action toward similar goals. A limited insecurity may provoke an inclination toward better adaptation to the existing order; in other words, it may provoke attempts to rectify the state of one's own security by "giving in." Or it may induce innovational activities aimed at changing the conditions which arouse the feeling of insecurity; it may induce actions intended to change the environment. Arthur H. Cole asserts: "Even if economic and social conditions may be generally favorable, and at least some entrepreneurs are willing to battle the hazards, not all such promoters of economic change turn out alike. There are, and always have been, certain forces that condition the character of such bearers of the entrepreneurial role."[81]

Innovations may occur in any society, yet the industrial societies of

---

The Sane Society, p. 361). Still other writers argue that the insecurity now common in contemporary societies stems from a lack of belief in God. They argue that religion provides the answer. See A. W. Watts, *The Wisdom of Insecurity* (New York: Random House, Vintage Books, 1951); H. C. Link, *The Way to Security* (Garden City, N.Y.: Doubleday, 1951).

* Cultures promulgating beliefs that situations are mastered solely or predominantly by powers beyond men's control, by spirits, Fatum, fate, order of things, Supreme Being, anonymous political order, in short cultures which promulgate beliefs that nothing or very little can be done to change a situation incline their members to passivity. Cultures promoting beliefs that man is but a tool of predestination, that man is but an embodiment of fate could inspire their members into fervent and incessant action aimed at implementation of that fate. On the whole, however, they produce fanatics and fatalists, people oriented to narrow immediate goals. Both these types of cultures rarely produce people oriented toward action organized in expectation of distant but steady growing rewards, action based on far-flung calculations. Beliefs of man's total dependence on external agencies generally act as an impairing factor on initiative and even more so on interest in introducing innovations. Only cultures which promote beliefs that man's destiny depends primarily on his own actions generate societies of active and innovative entrepreneurial individuals. Beliefs in one's own ability to anticipate the course of events and in one's ability to change it combined with trust in man's capacity to rectify situations to his own benefit are instrumental in transforming a feeling of stimulating insecurity into motivations generating goal-oriented activity, changing the state of affairs into another which can reduce the feeling of one's own insecurity.

today are the first in history in which people engage in innovations daily on a mass scale. Only in industrial societies do innovations become a way of living. In general it may be stated: Men are inclined to engage on a mass scale in innovational activities directed at the attainment of far-flung goals and steeply but slowly growing rewards in the distant future in situations combining the following factors: (a) People are in a state of stimulating insecurity; (b) The belief system motivates them to reduce their feeling of insecurity through engagement in functionally rational activities; (c) The state of knowledge in the society is on such a level as to provide the means for such actions; (d) Innovational and entrepreneurial activities especially are rewarded and protected; (e) The society in general, and the political system especially produces an atmosphere of general security and provides a minimum of protection to all members of society.*

HYPOTHESIS IV *(conclusive). A motivation of stimulating insecurity within a situation providing conditions of general security is most conducive to the spread of innovational entrepreneurial activities generating economic development.* Limited insecurity within security is common in highly competitive societies maintaining a stable order as a basis of common security, and profusely rewarding achievement in the implementation of socially approved goals.

This hypothesis is of a very general nature. Stressing its generality, I wish to acknowledge that in specific instances the response of a person or a group to the interdependence described above of objective security and subjective feeling of insecurity, due to other factors, may differ from what is considered here as a hypothetical rule. Such factors as personality in individual behavior, or culture in group behavior, may cause in some instances other responses than those assumed herein. Human action is determined to a certain extent by will and consciousness, and not solely by motivations produced by the surroundings, whether naturally or artificially. Accepting exclusions, I propose to view the above statement at least as a hypothesis, if not yet as a valid paradigm.

In general the effect of the factors of being and feeling secure or insecure on the prevailing modes of action could be presented in the following scheme:

---

* As Arthur H. Cole has pointed out in *Business Enterprise in Its Social Setting* (p. 77), "Of primary importance for the proper functioning of an entrepreneurial flow is a beneficent climate of social opinion, a changing climate, to be sure, but one that does not discourage the flotation of new enterprises that can reasonably anticipate an expanding desire for their goods or services, and climate that still attracts talent into the area. Desirable also, of course, is relative freedom from government intervention in the form of favorism of government monopolies, and the like, even freedom from major monopolistic conditions within the private sector."

Hypothetical Modes of Action in Diverse States of Objective Societal Security and Diverse States of Subjective Feeling of Insecurity

Subjective Insecurity of Individuals

Objectively the state of security in society is	Limited	Low	High
Low	Tendency toward adjustment to existing conditions.	Cases happen very rarely, and usually pertain to a minority within a society.	Passivity, withdrawal.
High	*High innovational and entrepreneurial mode of action.* *	Hedonistic careless behavior.	Manifest alienation and frustration. Withdrawal or violent actions.

Exclusions from the rule due to culture or personality

* Provided means for innovational activities are available and such activities are rewarded rather than punished, and the belief system is oriented toward self-reliance and functional rationality.

Schemes always distort the social reality. Accentuating and exposing one aspect which is important from a given point of view, they ignore other aspects. They serve better the purpose of presenting ideas which cannot be properly "whipped into shape" than of depicting concisely the subject of discussion. Yet if their limitation is taken into account, they may help in displaying complex ideas and abstract interdependencies. The above scheme is not so much to explain the diverse forms of actions resulting from the juxtaposition of objective conditions of security and subjective feelings of insecurity (which cannot be accomplished satisfactorily in a scheme anyway), but to expose the case of limited insecurity within high security in contrast to other juxtapositions of objective security and subjective insecurity.* It seems correct to say that the spirit of incessant insecurity within a fair security, although with occasional disruptions, prevailed in Western societies for at least the last two centuries. It germinated long before, and slowly accreted to become dominant. Groups with a higher sense of insecurity, minorities deprived of the average degree of security accorded to the majority, uneven distribution of security, were indeed imminent in such accretion.

Insecurity within security, as it will be called here, thus constitutes an important factor which in some cases by itself, in others in combination with other mutually supporting motivations and factors, generates activities producing economic development. Attempting to look at it pragmatically one can say that widespread economic development stems from grass-root entrepreneurial initiative, and from a common orientation toward modernity manifest both in consumptive preferences for novelties and frequent profuse inclinations to introduce productive innovations (either in anticipation of higher profits in the long run, greater productive output, or just because of the preference for modernity). It can be generated, enhanced, and spread by (a) solidifying and expanding the base of objective security in combination with (b) maintenance of a competitive structure of action which contains institutionalized mechanisms highly rewarding and protecting prowess, innovation, and invention. This is not a prescription for a panacea for new nations. Creation of the above listed conditions in many newly independent states seems to be at the minimum a formidable task. Often it seems to be beyond the possibilities of societies beset with problems, poverty, tribal struggles, illiteracy, and lack of capital.

The four hypotheses concerning insecurity within security presented in this section constitute a set of propositions for a theory rather than a

---

* The attribution of "security" to objective conditions and "insecurity" to subjective feelings as applied here is arbitrary; it could be done the other way around without affecting the essence of the ideas.

comprehensive, wholly elaborated theory on the subject. At the moment I am not able to buttress these propositions either with results of specially designed research or with sufficient sustaining material from other researches. Though much more work has to be done in this field, even in their present form these contentions contain enough material of an elucidative and explanatory quality and some pragmatic value as well. The paradigm of insecurity motivation within conditions of security is not a substitute for and does not exclude other explanations of motivations generating economic development. The variable insecurity within security together with other variables discussed here (those of conflict within consensus, differentiation within growing interdependence, and change within continuity) provides an overlapping set, by means of which new aspects of societal development can be portrayed.

The explanatory capability of the concept of insecurity within security will now be examined in a concise application in two exemplary case topics: (a) The origins of industrialization in Western Europe;* (b) The role of marginal people.

6. Insecurity Within Security: The Case of Western Europe

The modernity of today is deeply ingrained in the past, especially in the European Middle Ages. Historians tell us that to understand how modernity originated, it is not enough to probe its roots. One has to comprehend the seeds and the facilitating factors that in confluence produced the process of subsequent growth. We learn also from the works of the medievalists that to single out one factor as the sole cause of what hap-

* The characteristic of the security/insecurity in the Soviet Union and other East European societies cannot be fitted exactly into any of the boxes of our scheme. The state takes great care to heighten the security of the political and economic systems and the established bureaucratic order. As parts of these systems, citizens perform in the capacity of functionaries of the state. Nearly all employment is in that capacity. They enjoy a degree of security accorded to the office or job that they hold in the system. Their loyalty is constantly retested, and they may lose their position even if they themselves are loyal if they personally, or the group to which they belong within the society, is regarded as no longer trustworthy. A negligible amount of security is accorded to members of the society as individuals. By and large, it may be said that the subjective insecurity is either high or limited, and many innovational activities are punished rather than rewarded. However, certain categories of innovations and loyalty are rewarded highly. Thus there are groups of people in such societies who enjoy the illusion or even a real feeling of security (low insecurity). The amount of coercion is high, and activities producing the effect of economic development at least in certain branches are elicited by small rewards granted to people maintained on a low standard of living. This, with a number of other mobilization means, allowed the Soviet Union and other East European countries to attain their present level of economic development. This is also a basic factor impeding its more intensive development.

pened later is wrong. Since, however, the later historical development resulted from a confluence of factors and processes which all together
produced the later results, it is permissible for some purposes to discern
a factor and discuss it separately, not as the cause but as one of the important *contributing elements* considerably affecting the course of events.
What will be done now is just this, a discussion on one such factor.

Until the beginning of the sixteenth century Western Europe was not
unique. It was different, but not outstanding because of its technological
and economic development, or its political and social organization. Beginning from approximately 1500, Western Europe became the scene of a
series of overlapping revolutions. As Benjamin Nelson asserts, "Ours are
times of runaway revolutions. No less than a half dozen are now in progress across the world.* Some of these revolutions are in anguished end-
phase; others are ominously scattering detonated fragments in all directions; still others are now silently coming above the surface, big with
prospects yet beyond our ken."[82]

Historians disagree about the way in which these revolutions should
be discerned, their timing, mutual causation, and interdependence. Many
historians nonetheless insist that later economic development was set in
motion by events and factors of much earlier times. Treating the matter
liberally, without arguing that some revolutions necessitated the coming
of others, or that they only preceded one another, using the most common
pattern of presentation in history, one can enumerate the overlapping
revolutions as follows: *The commercial revolution.* It started with a
change in the consumptive patterns of the nobility in Western Europe
either, it may be argued, as a result of expanded trade, or as a result of
the development of productive forces, or for other reasons. It subsequently affected the consumption patterns of the population at large.
This coincided with an increase of money (gold) in circulation, and together they produced the multiplication of money transaction and expansion of the sphere of trade. Another factor in that revolution was the establishment of joint-stock business companies and location of the world
trade centers in ports and cities of northwestern Europe (both, because
of conducive facilities and good locations for trade and strong protection
of the merchants by the rulers). The prototypes of the modern economic
systems originated in this way as a result of the expansion and proliferation of market relations, the spread of their network over Europe and
later other continents and the engulfment by them of isolated units of
subsistence economies in an ongoing process of differentiation within a

* Most often two kinds of overlapping revolutions are distinguished: (a) The industrial (including the scientific achievements) and (b) The political. Reformation is
regarded as a prelude to the later revolutions—S. C.

growing market interdependence. Thus the commercial revolution subsequently changed into an *economic revolution*. As E. J. Hobsbawm puts
it, "the shackles were taken off the productive power of human societies,
which henceforth became capable of the constant, rapid and up to the
present limitless multiplication of men, goods and services. This is now
technically known to the economists as the 'take-off into self-sustained
growth.' "[83]

It all started in the era of absolutism. In England, Henry VII of the
Tudor dynasty won the crown (1485). In France, after the religious wars
and interruption of absolutism during the sixteenth century, Henry IV
of the Bourbon dynasty, came to power and restored it (1594). Spain
became unified into an absolute monarchy under Isabella of Castile and
Ferdinand of Aragon (1469). The Swedish and Polish monarchies were at
the apex of their greatness.

Territorial unification under the absolute monarchs created a framework for the later spread of nationalism. Some of the kings, especially
in the northwestern corner of Europe, were enlightened despots, who not
only protected the merchants, the entrepreneurs, the innovators and generally promoted trade and manufacturing, but who also had the courage
to tolerate and support and even keep non-conformist thinkers and philosophers at their courts. The enlightened kings of Western Europe also
developed an interest in art, literature, and philosophy, and supported
scientific exploration. This was the atmosphere in which, under a growing
interest in the natural sciences, logic, and empirical research, the rivulets
of philosophical thinking arising in the Renaissance turned into the
formidable philosophies of Bacon, Descartes, Spinoza, Leibnitz, and
Locke. The blossoming of the philosophies of the French Enlightenment,
of the physiocrats, of classical English economic thought, and of classical
German philosophical thinking followed. The great European *philosophical revolution* was in progress. It was interwoven and connected in
various ways with the concomitantly ascending *scientific revolution*
(Copernicus, Galileo, Kepler, Newton, Boyle, and later Linnaeus, La-
voisier, and countless others). All these revolutions occurred in times of
widespread religious dissent. Condemned by the authority of the Catholic
church, earlier manifested occasionally in theological debates on scholas-
ticism in the form of chiliastic doubt, in the sixteenth century it erupted in
the *Protestant revolution*. Peasant rebellions and religious wars were its
vehicles. New Protestant churches were established spreading the Puritan ethic. It had numerous consequences. Among others, the monopoly
of the spiritual control of the Roman clergy was wrecked. Combined with
the spread of new philosophical ideas and orientations toward empiricism
and scientific exploration, it created the conditions for disseminating

skepticism and freethinking liberalism. Thus it enhanced both the progress of scientific thinking and the drive for freedom manifest in the nineteenth- and twentieth-century upheavals.

All these revolutions were intermeshed; they cumulatively produced not only the propulsive spirit of modern capitalism but also men possessed by that spirit, both the capitalist entrepreneur and the working class. Peasant rebellions and the abolition of serfdom furnished the human material for it. New revolutions engulfing the earlier ones followed: the *industrial revolution* based on modern technology, totally changing patterns of living, production, and consumption; the *educational revolution* introducing literacy; the *social* and *political revolutions,* both those of the nationalist variety and those which were directed at the expansion of rights, democracy, and social justice. The social and political revolutions were the most dramatic, invoking the greatest passions. Often, such revolutions were regarded as the revolutions of the modern age. They occurred in waves; various struggles ensuing simultaneously were interwoven in their advancement.

Among other results, all the above revolutions produced a tangible increase in the state of universal objective security. It was a substitution, and a most dramatic one. In the course of its growth the new security obliterated an older one which was based primarily on dependence and protection created by the family, the kinship system, and the local community, estate, guild, and other societal groups; it replaced the security based on the principle of status allocation based on ascription. Here the writings of Cooley, Toennies, Marx, Durkheim, and numerous others could be recalled. The new security emerging and solidifying in the course of tormenting revolutionary transformations was, however, of an entirely different nature. It was based primarily on two pillars: *the state's protection of citizens' rights, and the freedom available for private individual initiative.* True, it also included some elements or institutions which had furnished security in the past, such as the immediate family, religion, and ethnicity. These, however, were retained either in a residual state, or without their previous determining importance. The new security was also based on the growing societal systemness, differentiation within interdependence.

Some aspects of that new security—the growing interdependence of people, institutions, organizations, systems, and societies—have been discussed earlier. Reinhard Bendix asserts that

In the nation-state each citizen stands in a direct relation to the sovereign authority of the country in contrast with the medieval polity in which that direct relation is enjoyed only by the great men of the realm. Therefore, a core element of nation-building [and, I will main-

tain, of articulation of the new structure of societal security—S.C.] is
the codification of the rights and duties of all adults who are classified as citizens. The question is how exclusively or inclusively citizenship is defined. Some notable exceptions aside, citizenship at first excludes all socially and economically dependent persons. In the course
of the nineteenth century this massive restriction is gradually reduced until eventually all adults are classified as citizens.[84]

Bendix writes further that Western European citizenship expanded on
two lines after the French Revolution. The principle of *functional representation* was extended to the "fourth estate," to those previously excluded from citizenship. Implementation of the *plebiscitarian principle*
advanced as well.* "According to this principle all powers intervening between the individual and the state must be destroyed (such as estates,
corporations, etc.), so that all citizens as individuals possess equal rights
before the sovereign national authority."[85] Bendix next quotes Thomas H.
Marshall, who formulates a threefold typology of citizens' rights: (a)
Civil rights: Here freedom of expression and belief are included together
with others such as the right to own property, to conclude valid con-
tracts, and the right to justice; (b) *Political rights:* Includes the franchise
and the right of access to public office; (c) *Social rights:* Here rights to
benefit from social services and social security and from sharing in the
"social heritage" are listed. Corresponding institutions are enumerated:
the courts, the local and national representative bodies, and the social
services.**

It is possible to discern from what Marshall calls "civil" rights a
separate category of *economic rights.* Here, apart from the already listed
rights to property and justice, rights to engage in entrepreneurial activity
could be included. In each category a number of other rights might be
added, too (for instance, the right to privacy in the category of civil
rights).

These rights compose the Western European and United States concept of citizenship. Citizenship in other parts of the world does not necessarily include the economic rights which were mentioned here or even
many of the civil and political rights. Hence the *security benefits of diverse
citizenships are indeed different.* It also has to be observed that the rights
listed above are formal; they define only the limits of a wide gamut of discrepancies possible within them in practice. They are designed to provide

---

* Bendix then discusses the conflict between those two principles and elaborates more
specifically on a number of liberties.
** Citizenship gives security but it also presupposes some collective responsibility, and,
as one of the discussants of this chapter pointed out, in specific instances (e.g., war)
it actually may put the citizen in a very insecure situation.

citizens with a degree of objective security, with protection against unlaw-
ful encroachments by the state and other authorities and other citizens
and by groups of citizens and organizations; against practices endangering
their property, against limitation of their initiative in legally recognized
fields of activities; against imposition on them of a government contrary
to the will of a legally defined majority of the citizens expressed in
election. These and other rights generate a fair amount of security, and
people in many parts of the world crave similar rights. Yet, on the other
hand, it would not be revelatory to state that today people in the Western
societies feel highly insecure in spite of these rights.

The sources of that incessant feeling of insecurity are manifold.
People fear a new war which may be started at any time by a crazed
general. They feel uprooted and lonely. They become increasingly dependent on a growing number of painful systemic dependencies. They feel
what the existentialists call an ontological insecurity.[86] The anxiety of
insecurity is also caused by involvement in constant competition.* Contrary to the widespread belief, expanding equality does not reduce the
number of conflicts in society. Neither does it reduce the tension of the
competitive atmosphere permeating all units of social organization. On
the contrary, the more a society becomes egalitarian, the greater is the
number of competitors for all positions and roles in it. If, as is the case in
our societies, there are ample supplies of goods and personnel to allow
competition, any status or office constantly faces new contestants who
feel they are equally qualified and more deserving of the status or office.
Increase in scientific knowledge, ongoing specialization, wider and better
education procures better qualifications, new higher competence, new
outlooks, modern and more effective modes of action. There is always
a better way to succeed, and there are always people who try to do it
better. Experience is important, but it too is under challenge. This state
of affairs and social relations generates not only development but also the
tension of insecurity. People are not sure whether their security is secure
enough. Holders of positions and statuses, and of wealth, power, and prestige have to be on constant alert. Both the holders of positions and
statuses and the challengers, both the defenders of the old and of the
new values have to be innovative, apply the most modern techniques, inventions, practices, advertising and propaganda, the newest ideas and
names. In short, modern egalitarian and populistic societies, especially
those of the West, are competitive and become more competitive with

* S. DeGrazia in *The Political Community: A Study of Anomie* (1948) (Chapters VI
and VII, pp. 51, 103) wrote that the three principles of capitalism, competition, im-
personalism, and rationalism generate a persistent state of simple anomie which occasionally lapses into a state of acute anomie.

the spread of egalitarianism.* The rights of citizenship provide the basis for a common societal security, yet because of high competitiveness people are insecure. *Insecurity within security breeds innovations,* searches for new solutions, new ideas, and new technology. It is instrumental to change. It motivates people to act and to achieve. It generates economic development and growing societal systemness.

People belonging to ethnic, religious, social, or cultural marginal groups which are deprived of a status within the basic body of social structure do not enjoy the whole amount of security provided by the citizenship institution. They may not be the most insecure but certainly they most often feel insecure. They are the most maladjusted and disgruntled in society. Sociologists tell us that minorities produce numerous deviant personalities.[87] And marginal groups as a rule have provided in numbers disproportionate to their sizes all kinds of nonconformists, revolutionaries, inventors, innovators, reformers, and entrepreneurs.** Revolutions dispossess the minorities holding wealth, power, prestige, and status. On the other end of the spectrum, however, they also produce groups dissatisfied with the pace of revolution, disillusioned with the mag-

---

* Technological development in Western societies, while generating affluence and producing a high level of general political and to an extent economic security, has detrimentally affected both the natural and social environments. People feel, therefore, endangered by the coming results of further technological development. A new kind of insecurity is spreading, and Western societies are again in quest of a new security to be meshed with the previously established one. The concern about the environmental crisis is growing and becoming the most urgent issue of modern times. People are, however, divided in regard to answers to the environmental predicaments. Some believe that in order to reduce or to eliminate the negative consequences of currently employed technologies new technologies have to be designed and put in action. Space exploration, among other means, is viewed as instrumental in finding some solutions of maintaining the natural environment intact or at least inhabitable. It is worth noting that Soviet experts also tend to express similar opinions. Others fear that such changes will not be efficacious enough; this in their belief will result in greater etatization of the society and will produce institutions and technological means by which the individual will be more controlled by the state and other centers of power. They urge us to restrain ourselves, and reduce economic and technological development in order to keep it more or less at the level presently attained. This, they hope will allow mankind to survive longer than it would should the economic and technological growth proceed at the current rate. While sympathizing with the second approach, I am doubtful as to whether it could be practically implemented.

** A very good analysis of the concept of "marginal people" has appeared in Polish. See E. Neyman, "Typy marginesowości w społeczeństwach i ich rola w zmianie społecznej," *Studia Socjologiczne,* No. 4 (23), 1966. Among other things, the writer points out that at least two different understandings of the concept "marginal group" are in circulation. The first emphasizes *social* distance. According to it (Thrasher, S. Czarnowski), marginality consists of relatively large groups of people without a social status, hence regarded in the society as dispensable. The second (R. E. Park) emphasizes rather the *cultural* aspects of marginality. It regards as marginal a group differing from the society on the basis of adherence to a diverse set of values. Most often such a group is also distinctive ethnically, if not racially, from the main body of the society. Usually it engages in specific occupations, too.

nitude of change, those who are eager to start new revolutions. This is true for all the diverse revolutions mentioned before. Thus revolutions multiply the number of marginal groups. On the other hand, revolutions produce new value systems and orientations, new societal structures and roles, new ways of action, new symbols. Most importantly, they destroy the barriers which kept aside the hitherto marginal groups. In the revolutionary era the marginal men, who even in the most stable secure conditions live with a constant feeling of insecurity, rush to the fore to acquire positions which will enable them to become part of the society. Until then marginal people often engaged in marginal entrepreneurial activity. Now they either become the leading revolutionaries (whether political, religious, or social) or engage with fervor in entrepreneurial business and productive fields. They invent, innovate, and disseminate modernity.

Western Europe between the sixteenth and nineteenth centuries was full of diverse groups of marginal peoples.[88] The cities and towns overflowed with emancipated peasants and jobless town-dwellers. Especially after the series of political upheavals of the eighteenth and nineteenth centuries, numerous impoverished and degraded members of the nobility faced the social abyss. Some of them followed the examples of those aristocrats in England and later in France who joined the ventures of entrepreneurial occupations. The Calvinists, as Weber and other writers have pointed out, were originally and sometimes later regarded as a marginal minority. The industrious, skillful, freedom-loving Huguenots made Holland wealthy, and contributed much with their capital, knowledge of crafts, and education, to the prosperity and economic growth of Switzerland, Prussia, England, and later the United States and Canada. Especially after the revocation of the Edict of Nantes in 1685, they were hunted and persecuted in France as well as in other countries of Europe.*

---

* J. Grant in *The Huguenot* (London: Thornton, Butterworth, 1934) (pp. 163-79) describes the persecution of the Huguenots as follows: "From 1679 the attacks on the Huguenots became constant. Between that year and the withdrawal of the Edict of Nantes in 1685 there were more than a hundred and twenty-five documents of different kinds dealing with the Huguenots, and all of them curtailed their liberties or inflicted on them penalties of some kind. They were not blows struck in blind hatred of heresy, but reveal a carefully thought-out system and almost a science of persecution. . . . Privileges were withdrawn; means of livelihood were taken away; the stigma of social inferiority was attacked in every way; the Huguenots became almost untouchables. When finally the Edict was withdrawn it was nominally the wiping from the statute book of provisions that were no longer needed because the Huguenots had practically ceased to exist." The Huguenots had to run for their lives and to emigrate. In their new locations they had to obtain means of living and to prove their worth by engaging in innovations, inventions, entrepreneurial activities, in industries, free professions, and craftsmanship. On the persecution and industriousness and entrepreneurial activities of the Huguenots, see also J. Pannier, *L'expansion française outre-mer et les protestants français* (Paris: Société des missions évangeliques, 1931).

Members of other Protestant churches were also discriminated against.[89] As Wellman J. Warner characterizing the entrepreneurial activities of the members of the Wesleyan Church, points out, "Few influences were more potent in the eighteenth century than the oppressive sense of insecurity which the fear of death and the general interest in other-worldly safety, so universal among the poorer groups of the period, makes graphic. The diminishing fear of insecurity was both a symptom and a cause of an emerging class."[90]

Then there were the Jews. As Jean-Paul Sartre writes,

> the Jew remains the stranger, the intruder, the unassimilated at the very heart of our society. Everything is accessible to him, and yet he possesses nothing; for he is told, what one possesses is not to be bought. All that he touches, all that he acquires becomes devaluated in his hands; the goods of the earth, the true goods, are always those which he has not. He is well aware that he has contributed as much as another to forging the future of the society that rejects him. But if the future is to be his, at least he is refused the past. . . . The Jew, because he knows he is under observation, takes the initiative and attempts to look at himself through the eyes of others. . . . He absorbs all knowledge with an avidity which is not to be confused with disinterested curiosity. He hopes to become "a man," nothing but a man, a man like all other men, by taking in all the thoughts of man and acquiring a human point of view of the universe.[91]

"But *the man* does not exist; there are Jews, Protestants, Catholics; there are Frenchmen, Englishmen, Germans; there are whites, blacks, yellows."[92] The Jews were and are the classic case of insecure people within security. Werner Sombart, a contemporary of Max Weber, argued that Jews generated the spirit of capitalism and that "those parts of the Puritan dogma which appear to be of real importance for the formation of the spirit of capitalism, are borrowed from the realm of ideas of the Jewish religion."[93] Jews belonged both to the ethnic and cultural margins of European societies.*

In each of the West European countries there were also numerous other small ethnic groups which remained outside the main stream of the national formative process of those times. Some of them have retained their ethnic identity and separateness until now.

Another marginality has to be mentioned too. The Western European

---

* See P. Siegelman, "Introduction" to W. Sombart, *Luxury and Capitalism,* Translated by W. R. Dittman. (Ann Arbor: University of Michigan Press, 1967), for an interesting comparison of Weber's view of the Protestant Ethic with W. Sombart's accentuation of the role of the Jews in the development of capitalism and on the controversy of the two leading sociologists of their time on the problem.

cities were shelters for all kinds of refugees from political persecution. Monarchists, socialists, anarchists, and later communists, frustrated revolutionaries who failed in their endeavors, all sought asylum within their walls.

With the political system, the state, the institution of citizenship providing the frame for a general objective security, security for all seemed to be in close reach. All the people on marginalities welcomed new possibilities of acquiring a status which incorporated them into the main body of society. They became the propelling force of the revolutions pushing Europe and with it other parts of the world into the new era of modernity, into the age of sustained growth.

The ongoing process of runaway revolutions has lasted several centuries and is now spreading all over the world. New and newer dispossessed, oppressed, persecuted, exploited people, those without rights, and those without appropriate means of living come forward, raising their grievances and offering their talents and their skills and demanding their share of rewards. Today the national minorities who were deprived of a fair share of the benefits of the society and the people of former colonies are on the move. Simultaneously, however, especially in the Western societies but partially also in Eastern Europe, another drive has become articulate, a centrifugal drive toward the fringes of the society, toward the marginality.

In the course of the fulfillment of needs, new needs are born. A growing number of sensitive young people do not feel secure enough in the societies built by former generations. They feel superfluous and obsolete.[94] They are repelled by what is called the military-industrial complex, by the dehumanizing systems of the industrial societies of both the Western and the Communist states, and they do not want to be part of it. They reject the culture based on market relations.[95] They abhor bureaucracies, authorities, and authoritarian structures, established patterns of behavior, the values imposed upon them. They express disgust with the contradictions of life and the double standards of the law, morality, and the realities of life. They do not want to be engaged in the rat race of competition for insecure or illusory achievements, as their parents were. They demonstrate their disgust and their protest in various ways, in dress, experimenting with sex or drugs, searching for new religions and ideologies, in all sorts of activities that become known as the counterculture, in manifesting contempt for incessant action and all the other values so prized by Weber and other sociologists and philosophers of capitalism, rationality, and even socialists statism. Such people and the versatile frustrated intellectuals who are joining them are prone to take part in any protest movement against the establishment, the rich, the developed industrial states. They reject the security of the establishment. Charles H. Turner, who describes the attitudes of such people, asserts that "trust is not a naïve belief that a specific person will not beat you with his billy club, it is a determination to create a trustful relationship through 'holy insecurity' and an attempt to persuade the authoritarian conscience that his fear of you is groundless. . . . It is across this 'abyss' between man and man that each must make his 'existentialist leap' to reach others."[96]

Though these people call themselves revolutionaries, they neither belong to, nor are supported by the working class. They do not have a program for the future; they do not agitate and mobilize. They just express their frustration and pain about the present order and the course of its development. Such groups cannot be classified as "bohemian." They are too numerous for this. Though there are writers, painters, actors among them, they mainly constitute simple young men and women without any predilections. History, tradition, the culture and problems of the past are said to be irrelevant. Though they claim to be romantics and existentialists, apart from some exceptions they do not read classic romantics or existentialists such as Stendhal, Flaubert, Faulkner, Hemingway, Caldwell, Kafka, or Dostoyevsky.* Though they claim to be socialists, they do not read Marx or Engels, except for extracts from *The Communist Manifesto* in introductory courses of political science and sociology. The drive is toward marginality. Some say that these people are a maladjusted minority who will come to their senses if we wait. Others say that young people have to express themselves. They used to strive for the conquest of the world, but now everything has been conquered. With no field for action, they drop out. Still others say that these people are the Luddites of the technotronic age. Since they cannot stop progress, they will fade away. And others say that these are the brightest, most sensitive, searching young people, to whom the future belongs. They are in quest of new values, of a higher sense of security based on love and mutual trust instead of constant fighting and competition. The questions are: is this a transient phenomenon or the birth of a new, hitherto un-

---

* Douglas Perez, a student in Berkeley, California, conducted a seminar-paper in my class on the topic, "The ideology of Berkeley" in May 1970 A survey was made of a randomly selected small group of 36 (one Black, four Orientals) students, ages seventeen to twenty-two, fairly representing a cross section of the undergraduates. He asked them to "List the five most important books which you have read since you came to college. They do not have to be books which you agree with, nor do they have to have significantly changed your opinion on any issues. Simply list five most *important* books of any kind." The books which a majority of the students felt were significant were: *The Autobiography of Malcolm X*, Eldridge Cleaver's *Soul on Ice*, Joseph Heller's *Catch 22*, John Hersey's *The Algiers Motel Incident*, Claude Brown's *Manchild in the Promised Land*. Other choices were John Griffin's *Black Like Me*, J. H. Skolnick's *Justice Without Trial*, Henry D. Thoreau's *Walden*.

known marginality of self-made superfluous people, a marginality which will subsequently become dominant? Is this a fashionable social masochism which will be succeeded by another fashion or the beginning of a new important overlapping revolution? Man needs meaningful intimacy with other men to generate a sense of security in sharing and belonging-ness. Nostalgia for such lost security and the insecurity of loneliness could undoubtedly provide explosive fuel for protest movements. It certainly could also provide a bond to unify small groups of rebels emotionally involved in protests. But, could it generate a sense of high security of sharing, and trust, and brotherhood on a nationally and even internationally wide scale, especially in situations of scarcity? Let us not forget that conflict, struggle, and competition begin within brotherhoods. Let us not forget that man hates uniformity and needs recognition for his individuality. Even when he contemptuously discards wealth and power, he is in quest of recognition, of self-imposed sacrifice, of inner power, of existentialist abnegation. He wants prestige. The new security required has to be built out of prestige, and prestige is again stratified. We are too many, and in the modern world we cannot live without authority, and authority has to have power. Bridges could be built of shared emptiness, of self-inflicted suffering and pity because of the suffering of others, but such bridges are not substitutes for productive and market relations needed for men's physical survival. To solve its problems the world needs more development. How can it be produced by an anti-developmental, antiachievement, antidutiful orientation? It is true that "the power of the negative,"[97] whether as a quality of thought or of action, could be a powerful weapon. But what is the struggle for? Between the two, the one-dimensional positive totalitarian state and philosophy and its shadow, the power and philosophy of the negative, there is still a gamut of options, there is still the possibility of being neither totally obedient nor totally hateful, rational and irrational, of believing and disbelieving at the same time.

V

The Fourth Approach: Economic and Political Development

Among the various fields in the social sciences, two disciplines are particularly concerned at present with the theory of development. These are economics and political science. Historians often retain a traditional aversion to the developmental approach. To be sure, one no longer hears such emotional and outspoken attacks as were put forth in the 1950's by historians like Isaiah Berlin and Herbert Heaton. Yet today, as in the past, very few historians feel that development is a legitimate concept which can be adopted and discussed as a historical process or as an undercurrent of a chain of events or an interpretation of what has happened. Sociologists often work on developmental problems, but after their perplexing disappointments with earlier attempts to interpret it, they have obtained a sort of idiosyncratic aversion to it and often give "development" the widest possible berth. Sometimes they explain that its implications are dangerous and that it is better to use other "less dangerous," though also less heuristic, concepts such as social change or modernization. Some anthropologists, for example, A. L. Kroeber and L. A. White, still adhere to a belief in the growth and development of cultures. That, however, has also become rare.

Only in economics and political science is the theory of development in the center of scholarly interest. And though these interests are focused on diverse aspects of societal activities, in economics about economic developments, and in political science about political ones, they share a common attitude. In both cases development is more narrowly defined than in the previously discussed approaches, treating only one of several possible kinds of development in a specific sphere of human interaction. In both understandings or disciplines it pertains to a goal-oriented activity. In both cases such theories are aimed at solutions to problems of the organization of resources and people for specific targets in spheres of increased output of productivity, nation-building, institutionalization, or education. These theories all seem to share a common approach. Economic development is regarded as the attainment of increasing national income, greater output of productive activity, and the proliferation of market relations, specialization, and multiplication of economic exchanges. On the other hand, according to some theories political development strengthens national identities. In other cases, it is said to be attainment of higher levels of democracy. In still others, it is a process of institutionalization and the elevation of more efficient decision-making structures and organizations.

1. Economic Development

One does not need to believe in economic determinism to acknowledge that economic development constitutes the heart of the general theory of development. Most writing on the development of social relations, structures, and functions in definite societies, a great part of the discussion of social and political change, or even many of the theories concerning the substitution of civilizations have necessarily to account in one or another way for the economic factor of economic development. Of course, a specialist in fields other than economics does not need to explain economic development in order to apply the concept as one of numerous concomitant factors surrounding the phenomenon and process under his consideration. This is the job of the economist, and the student in other fields has to rely on his explanations.

a. The Content of the Concept

Excellent books on economic development have been written without an attempt to define the concept.[1] Henry J. Bruton asserts that economic development is a multidimensional concept. "But it would appear unnecessary to insist on a multidimensional measure. In almost all instances, per capita output is an effective surrogate for any identifying characteristics of development ever mentioned, and in those cases where it is not, that fact is well known and the reasons are easy to discover."[2] This is a prevailing view, and many economists consider it so obvious that they do not bother to define the concept. Gerald M. Meier and Robert E. Baldwin, however, are more elaborate. They state that "economic development is a process whereby an economy's real national income increases over a long period of time. And, if the rate of development is greater than the rate of population growth, then per capita real income will increase. . . . And the general result of the process is growth in an economy's national product—in itself a particular long-run change."[3] They explain that in this way we are taking a comprehensive view of the "end result of the development process." If we wish to examine economic development in more detail we must consider changes in fundamental factor of supplies and in the structure of demand for products. It seems to be pertinent to list them here. The

> particular changes in the structure of supplies comprise: (1) the discovery of additional resources, (2) capital accumulation, (3) population growth, (4) introduction of new and better techniques of production, (5) improvement in skills, and (6) other institutional and organizational modifications. Particular changes in the structure of demand for products are associated with developments in (1) size and age composition of the population, (2) level and distribution of income, (3) tastes, and (4) other institutional and organizational arrangements.[4]

This not only brings us to the heart of the theory of economic development but also demonstrates the complexity of the problem and exposes the problem of the dependence of economic development on numerous noneconomic factors.

Various objections have been raised to the use of national income or per capita real income as the criterion or content of the definition of economic development.[5] Critics argue that such concepts as national income and per capita real income are ambiguous. Both can be measured differently. Since in different societies the value of diverse products and services must be included, in each case development means something different. Then how can such criteria be used in the comparative analysis of diverse stages in time and of diverse socio-political and cultural systems?

Witold Kula compounded a list of the basic problems that have to be taken into account when national income is regarded as the content of economic development.[6] His list includes the following points: (1) Change in the range of the marketing products and relations. How does one estimate what is and what is not a marketing commodity? (2) The problem of services. Should services be included in the national income, and if so, which ones? (3) Difficulties of accounting for the dimensions, sizes, yields, and value of productivity of small-scale market production (craft, small farming, and so forth). (4) Absence of uniform market prices. Similar commodities are valued differently depending on marketing conditions, culture, and availability of the product. In many societies not one but several markets with differing prices function collaterally. (5) The importance of nonpecuniary and even noneconomic elements in marketing transactions. The same product may be sold at a different price to diverse purchasers depending on the character of the social relations involved. (6) The absence of market in many societies in the past (in the case of comparisons in time), and the fact that the gauge of national incomes has to take into account the agricultural production (dominant in many societies) which changes from year to year depending on the actual harvest. (7) Lack of standardization of commodities. In addition, Kula points out other problems, chief of which is the absence of data for many nations. Leibenstein, who is also concerned with these problems, concludes that "concepts like income, productivity, investment, etc. involve a very high degree of aggregation, and as a consequence a problem of translating the individual entities into some common value unit."[7]

Other problems could be listed also. How does one treat a situation in which the aggregate national income increases while per capita income declines? Or a situation in which the production of a basic commodity (for instance cocoa) has doubled, the number of persons engaged in employment on a wage and salary basis has increased, the volume of market exchanges in the national economy as a whole has increased, yet the value of the national product and the average standard of living has remained the same or even declined as a result of a decrease of prices on the basic commodity produced for the international market by that nation? And if the preceding situation also faces an increase in the population which has affected the level of national income and the income per capita? Is a society developing economically when it produces more, when more people are engulfed within it by market relations, while the per capita income or even the national income of the country remains constant? Joseph Schumpeter and François Perroux proposed to distinguish between economic growth and economic development.[8] Perroux wrote that economic growth consists primarily of a rise in per capita real income. Economic development, on the other hand, consists of the build-up of national economies, discovery of new resources, technological advancement, organization of new industries and fields of productivity.

Some writers propose to regard national income as an indicator or index of economic development rather than as the development itself.[9] This is not generally accepted, however; other experts propose alternative indices. McClelland, for example, suggests that the amount of electric power produced be applied as a single index of economic growth.[10] Proposals have also been made to use data on capital investments, and the number or percentage of wage and salary earners or a combination of these. E. E. Hagen, for instance, applied a combined measurement of eleven indexes in discussing economic development and the political structure of Latin American countries at the end of the 1950's.* However, these suggestions have been criticized as inadequate in one way or another.

Finally, economists tell us that we cannot take a perfectionist view. We have to accept the opinion of the majority of economists, and they say: "An increase in national income . . . is the most relevant, as most convenient, single measure of development for both poor and rich countries."[11]

Since my intention here is to discuss the concept and theories of economic development for comparison with other approaches only, that opinion will be the guiding one for further discussion. But I must make a few comments on other elements of the understanding of economic development.

b. Characterizing the Process

Theories of economic growth and development originally emerged as theories concerned with the progress of wealth of nations.[12] This is still their major concern. Even when they consider attitudes and behavior of individuals or groups, it is only with respect to the contribution of these factors to *the advancement of the well-being of nations as wholes.* If economics is a science of numbers, this is only partially true with regard to theories of economic development. Although they have one foot in the field of the science of numbers, the other must be in the field of the sci-

---

* E. E. Hagen, "A Framework for Analyzing Economic and Political Change" in R. E. Asher and others, *Development of the Emerging Countries* (1962) (pp. 4-5). Hagen writes "The eleven indexes of economic development . . . are the following:
Welfare:
1. GNP per person in 1957.
2. Doctors per 1,000 persons in about 1956.
Communications:
3. Vehicles per 10,000 persons in about 1958.
4. Telephones per 10,000 persons in about 1958.
5. Radios per 1,000 persons in about 1957.
6. Newspaper circulation per 1,000 persons in about 1956.
Industrialization:
7. Energy consumption per person in about 1958.
8. Per cent of labor force employed outside agriculture and service sectors, latest census year.
Urbanization:
9. The per cent of population inhabiting urban centers of more than 100,000 inhabitants at a date within or close to 1950-1960.
Education:
10. Per cent of population literate at a date within or close to 1950-1960.
11. Ratio of enrollment in primary schools to population of school age.
For a similar scheme see G. A. Almond and J. S. Coleman, *The Politics of Developing Areas,* Conclusive part (1960). For still another scheme, see I. Adelman, *Theories of Economic Growth and Development,* pp. 4-5.

ences of social and political interaction. And this is why they are of concern here.

Whether they are introduced as theories of the growing wealth of nations, theories of the increase of real national income or real per capita income, or interpreted as theories of the expansion of market interdependencies and thus of the development of economic systems, theories of economic development revolve around an analysis of the process of increase in volume and of qualitative differentiation in the *output of technological productivity.*

Except for Marx, writers on economic development do not imply that they are dealing with a process which advances inevitably. Neither is economic development steady and continuous. On the contrary, most writers on economic development acknowledge that economic development occasionally becomes disrupted for some time, that it may become congealed or stagnant or even change into a decline. Notwithstanding these interruptions, such development is assumed to be generally sustained and persistent, producing increased productivity and ascending national income. The concept of economic growth does not entail either a potentiality unfolding itself in a preordained way in institutions and structures, or a teleological finality to which the process aims. It is not an organismic or semiorganismic process. It is manifest in concrete productive outputs which can be measured, and thus it cannot be regarded as a metaphor.

Bert Hoselitz has pointed out that the various paradigms for stages of economic growth are devices either for the study of progressive development in a given economy or for comparative analysis of concomitantly existing or succeeding economic systems. On the other hand, they are either "ideal" constructs or "abbreviated and somewhat schematic presentations of actual historical developments."[13] In any case, they are models, analytical systems, heuristic constructs.

As a rule theories of economic development are not explicitly defined as theories dealing with consequences or with causations of organized action generating industrialization. In practice, however, such theories have to, and usually do, *revolve around the topic of industrialization,* why it does or does not occur, what determines its pace, what impedes it, and what facilitates its spread and growth. Even if they treat agricultural societies and view agriculture as the basic springboard for economic development and increase of the national income, they include the factor of industrialization at least as a market for increased agricultural production, and as a source of innovations stimulating the process of modernization in hitherto underdeveloped areas.

In general, theories of economic development focus on the interplay of expanding technology and the accumulation of scientific knowledge with changing attitudes and behavior of both producers and consumers within an environment of socio-political and cultural factors. Until the Neo-Keynesian period theories of economic development were essentially concerned with an analysis of the development of capitalism; causes of its crises, predictions for its duration. They searched for solutions to problems generated during its development. Since then, the theory of economic development has undergone a split. It now has three separate branches: (1) Centered on problems of maintaining a steadily growing output of productivity and national income in an equilibrium rate of growth year after year; of keeping the volume of the output generated by investment on a steady rate of accelerated accretion and simultaneously increasing the economy's capacity for absorption of further investment. This branch is concerned with the maintenance of a steadily expanding capitalist economy. (2) Centered on problems of maintaining a high rate of economic growth in the planned centralized Soviet and East European economies; of eliciting more efficiency and flexibility, and removing retarding consequences of overplanning in an economy subordinated to political goals; of resolving chronic shortages plaguing both the people and industrial enterprises from the onset of such economies. In short, this branch is concerned with the designing patterns of successful planning and conduct of the economies of the Communist countries. (3) Centered on problems overcoming the "vicious circles" of underdevelopment in postcolonial economies and putting the new nations on the track of accelerated economic growth.

Earlier theories of economic development were concerned with explaining the past and with prophesying the future, while modern theories of economic development are more concerned with programming policies. If they are projective at all, it is only for the purpose of suggesting alternative possibilities and policies in attempting to resolve the current problems of societies of today.

The three branches of contemporary theory of economic development are bridged by the need to include the growing worldwide interdependence. Problems of today's national economies cannot be solved on the basis of internal situations in the separate countries of the West, the Soviet bloc, and the new nations alone, nor solely in the sphere of pure economics. Economic policies must depend on conditions of war and peace, on the degree of affiliation of a country with other countries of similar ideological proclivity. In addition, the separate fields of the theory of economic development are beset by the growing variety of perplexing problems of humanity as a whole, such as: the maintenance of the pace of economic development in individual areas and in the world in general in order to balance a growing overpopulation; the spanning or at least the control of the hiatus between rich and poor nations; the stabilization of world prices and their transformation into an incentive for development in underdeveloped areas. These are problems common to all three branches of theories of economic development.

c. Variables of the Variant Theories of Economic Development

Looking at the topic from another angle, one can characterize the theories of economic development and economic systems as paradigms constructed around sets of selected dependent and independent variables such as capital, labor (including its quantity, quality, and economic orientation), equipment, credit, land and natural resources, markets, distribution of wealth, and other social and political factors.[14] Economic theories differ over the number of such variables to be taken into account, the selection of variables regarded as leading, dependent and independent, and the relationship of the variables in the paradigm which are regarded as "given" and which are regarded as changing.

In most cases economists regard social and political conditions as "given." From such a perspective developing economic systems are said to be nonequilibrium systems in constant flux due to changes of variables and partially changing interdependencies between them, as opposed to the equilibriums or quasistable subsistence equilibriums of underdeveloped areas. Modern economic theory tends to translate the factors of economic development into quantitative data. Yet the economist often suggests that this cannot be fully accomplished, since a number of factors which economic theory inevitably has to take into consideration, such as the quality of labor, the causes of change, policies, the changing attitude of consumers, the effect of inventions and of innovations, and other social and political factors, cannot be translated into quantities. Many of the variables taken as constant are constant only in abstraction.

Theories of the stages of economic growth have to be regarded as special instances of the theory of economic development.[15] The most widely known and applied is the theory of stages of economic growth suggested by Walt W. Rostow.[16] He distinguishes five basic stages of economic growth: the traditional society, the situation establishing preconditions for the take-off, the take-off, the drive to maturity, and the age of high mass consumption.

Rostow assumes that the stage of the take-off is crucial for change from traditional into modern societies. It begins the lasting sustained accelerated process of growth. He discusses various cases of it and also points out that as a rule it is also the stage of the industrial revolution. The situation for the take-off becomes ripe when science develops and a "leading sector" (food, wool, cotton, rubber, oil) of production emerges in the economy. Fulfillment of other preconditions is essential too. Thus resistance to change has to be removed, a class of entrepreneurs has to emerge, agricultural productivity has to increase. The society has to acquire an attitude of accepting as normal the regular flow of high-rate innovations. Then the take-off begins. It can be traced by a particular sharp stimulus which may have the shape of a political revolution. It may come about first as a chain of technological innovations and social consequences resulting from them. A necessary, though not a sufficient, condition for the take-off is an increase in the ratio of savings and investments of the national income from between five to over ten per cent. Thus it is said that economic development begins with a sharp rise in real output per capita and continues where a sustained growth of it is being maintained.

Historians of economic thought usually portray the history of theories of economic development as a chain of paradigms. The links of that history are theories characterizing the course and causes of economic development and describing the basic variables of the interdependencies in national economic systems.

Mercantilists and physiocrats were harbingers of the discipline. Their ideas are regarded as the prelude and first link to the ensuing continuity. Then come the classical economists. Adam Smith was the founder of the school and its most formidable representative. He was first to construct a theory in which both systemic and developmental approaches are combined. The basic variables of his theory are: the size of the labor force, the stock of capital (made of savings), and the amount of land (including supply of resources). He assumes that capital formation is the driving force of the technological progress, and that saving and investments applied to resources and labor generate technological advancement. Once put in motion technological progress becomes cumulative requiring newer and newer investments for ever faster and greater technological progress. In a sense Adam Smith can be regarded as a proponent of the concept of growing systemness in economics. Economic growth accelerates in the course of division of labor and continuous specialization stimulated by the interaction of demand and supply on the market. Its results are increasing volume of commodities on the market, reduced time necessary to produce commodities, better technical means, and growing social complexity. There are, however, numerous factors which limit and impede growth. Division of labor may be limited by the extent of the market. Land and the supply of economically useful resources may become scarce. The rate of savings may be affected by prodigious spending or by governmental and private action hindering the free display of natural competition and the investors' security. Adam Smith was a staunch defender of free market competition. Like Malthus, he views economic development as a race between technological progress and population growth. He predicts that the development of capitalist societies would soon reach its apex. Economic progress swamped by overpopulation would eventually turn into a sustained downward slide ending in stagnation. Growth, he argues, cannot last for ever. In short, he views *economic development as homogeneous sustained process of accumulation* turning after a downward trend into stagnation. *The rate of capital formation* was the leading variable in his theory.

Marx's theories of societal and economic development are two parts of one whole. He appraises capitalist *economic growth as a spasmodic agony progressing in convulsions* of economic crises, social and political upheavals and accumulation of overlapping conflicts between productive forces and productive relations. It is described also as a widening polarization between the wealth and poverty of the capitalist and working classes and of imperialist and colonial nations. It fosters a concentration of capital and an intensification of the competition among capitalists. And it brings about a decline in profit on single items due to the development of better techniques of production, yet at the same time increases the mass of profits of the capitalists. Marx characterized capitalism as beset with inherent contradictions especially stemming from the fact that in a socioeconomic system based on private property the means of production are used solely in pursuit of profit in order to accumulate more capital for its own sake and not for the benefit of the society of producers. At its onset, he wrote, capitalist development is directed toward its own destruction; inevitably it will be succeeded by socialism. The variables of Marx's paradigm are (a) *capital* consisting of the wage bill (capital), constant capital (the means and materials utilized in production), the surplus value or absolute amount of profit—the product of exploitation of the working class; (b) *productive forces* consisting of labor, skills, resources; (c) the *productive relations* constituting the essence and frame of capitalism.

The list of economists belonging to the neo-classical school is long. Only a few will be mentioned here: Alfred Marshall, Leon Walras, John B. Clark, Vilfredo Pareto, Eugen von Böhm-Bawerk, Knut Wicksell.

Economists of the neo-classical school have basically focused their interest on micro-economic problems. Theirs was an attempt to work out a short-run micro-maximization formula. To the theory of general economic development they addressed themselves only in an indirect way, treating it as an aggregate of micro-economic problems. The times were different from those in which the classical economists lived. Contrary to the predictions of the classical economists and of Marx the economy of the capitalist world neither collapsed nor slid into a stationary, stagnant trend. Recessions and crises occurred but in general the economy showed a capacity to recover and expand again. It also showed deviations from the basic model of purely competitive structure. Thus the neo-classical economists worked with microstatic models of economic equilibriums and attempted to define the "stabilizing and destabilizing factors" affecting the free competitive conditions in it.[17]

Their models rest on the assumptions that (a) the capitalist economy is stable and tends to grow and expand proportionally; (b) The rate of interest and the level of income determine the rate of saving. These too are growing gradually and continuously; (c) Marshall and other members of the school adhere to the belief that all income tends to be spent; and they assume the existence of nearly full employment conditions; (d) The state is not an obstacle to economic development. The negative effects of "the bigness" of some firms tending to monopolize the market and hence unbalance the competitive system can be eliminated or rectified; (e) Population growth is moderate, and the average member of society has an inherent inclination toward improving the conditions of his living by striving for an increase in his and his family's income. Thus the level of skills is gradually increasing; (f) Development stems from the process of an ongoing "progress and diffusion of knowledge." (g) Since capital can be substituted for labor, a country could develop economically even in conditions of scarcity of labor. *All variables are characterized either as fixed and constant or as tending to increase gradually and proportionally.*

In literature discussing the neo-classical theories, these variables are sometimes divided into exogenous (such as the government) and interrelated indigenous (such as profit-seeking, thrift, spread of knowledge) variables. On the whole to the neo-classical economist, economic development is self-propelling and spreading in a harmonious, continuous, gradual, self-reinforcing process of growth.

According to some writers, Joseph A. Schumpeter was a neo-Marxist, even though he opposed Marx; others say he was a neo-classical economist. Though both are probably right, the sociologist and economist Schumpeter is in a class by himself. Schumpeter's model includes at least the following interdependent variables: (a) productive forces comprising both such "immaterial things" as labor and attitudes, and such "material things" as land, resources, and "producer goods" ("each good matures into a consumption good through the addition of other goods");[18] (b) technology; (c) social factors; (d) *growth*—the effect of ascending changes produced by the combination of productive forces (a); and (e) *development*—the effect of cumulative reinforcing changes of the technological and social factors (b) and (c) and to an extent of growth (d).[19] *Growth and* *development are characterized differently.* To a degree, growth generates development, but it is one of the less important factors of its causation. Growth is steady, continuous but slow. Development* is characterized as discontinuous, disharmonious, uneven, cyclical, unstable. It starts when, in anticipation of profits, innovators engage in entrepreneurial activities introducing new goods and new methods of production, when they open new markets, find new sources of raw materials, or reorganize the industry. New productive factors are thus released demanding new investments and yielding higher profits. The innovators seek credit; since the prospects of development look good they easily get credit from banks, which enables them to expand their activities even if they do not have savings. As price levels rise the money supply expands still more. Productivity expands. The taste of consumers is changed by the action of producers, thus the market expands. Firms and industries grow. Then the process of "creative destruction" begins. Small firms are swallowed by the giant ones, and the giants are too redundant to be efficient. The economy collapses to rise again on a higher level. The cycle then repeats itself on a higher level. Schumpeter asserts that technological change is the determining factor of development. Social factors are conducive or impeding, however, and they too rank as important. The entrepreneur allured by prospects of profits and of fulfilling other ambitions and desires is regarded by Schumpeter as the propelling force of development. Like Marx, Schumpeter predicts a decline of capitalism and its succession by socialism.

I have just compared four visions and four different theoretical per-

---

* J. A. Schumpeter writes in *The Theory of Economic Development* (pp. 63-65): "By 'development,' therefore, we shall understand only such changes in economic life as are not forced upon it from without but arise by its own initiative, from within. Should it turn out that there are no such changes arising in the economic sphere itself, and that the phenomenon that we call economic development is in practice simply founded upon the fact that the data change and that the economy continuously adapts itself to them, then we should say that economic development is not a phenomenon to be explained economically, but that the economy, in itself without development, is dragged along by the changes in the surrounding world, that the causes and hence the explanation of the development must be sought outside the group of facts which are described by economic theory. . . . Nor will the mere growth of the economy, as shown by the growth of population and wealth, be designated here as a process of development. For it calls forth no qualitatively new phenomena, but only processes of adaptation of the same kind as the changes in the natural data. . . . Development in our sense is a distinct phenomenon, entirely foreign to what may be observed in the circular flow or in the tendency towards equilibrium. It is spontaneous and discontinuous change in the channels of the flow, disturbance of equilibrium which forever alters and displaces the equilibrium state previously existing. . . . These spontaneous and discontinuous changes in the channel of the circular flow and these disturbances of the center of equilibrium appear in the sphere of the wants of the consumers of final products. . . . It is . . . the producer who as a rule initiates economic change, and consumers are educated by him if necessary."

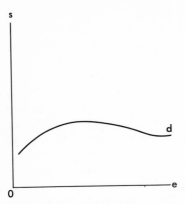

The perspective of the classical
economist

s — savings
e — Labor and resources
d — *development*

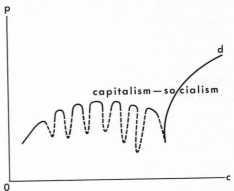

The Marxist perspective

p — productive forces (new technology
and skills)
c — accumulation of social conflicts
d — *development*

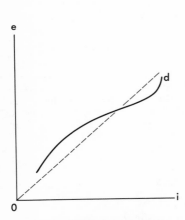

The neo-classical perspective

d — *development*
e — exogenous factors
i — interrelated indigenous factors

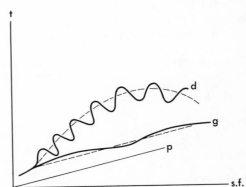

J.A. Schumpeter's perspective

t — technology
p — productive forces
s.f. — social factors
g — *growth*
d — *development*

spectives on the subject of economic development, emphasizing diverse aspects of this process, exposing different variables as leading and determining its ratio. For a mnemotechnical purpose that comparison could be visualized as above.*

d. Economic Development in Capitalist Societies from Post-Keynesian Perspective

In an elegant essay on contemporary theories of economic development and growth, Henry J. Bruton says, "There are writers who believe that all a theory of economic growth can hope to achieve is establishment of a loose framework consisting of a number of general propositions, held together by intuition and *ad hoc* theorizing; and there are those who feel it may be possible to devise a theory of growth comparable in elegance and precision to, say a modern short-run theory of income determination."[20] He discusses what he calls the Capital Stock Adjustment theory and the sources and nature of structural and institutional changes. He describes "the long-run behavior of short-run parameters" such as the population, the saving-income ration, the capital-output rations; referring to models like that of Harrod-Domar Hansen he outlines the problems of "aggregate demands." Bruton writes that fairly reliable conclusions can be reached with respect to the requirements for consistent growth in a short-run period. This is true whether one applies the model of a neoclassical economist like Walras or a Keynesian model. "When however the period of time is lengthened—as it evidently must be, if the formulation of a growth theory is the aim—difficulties multiply rapidly."[21] A discussion of continued growth over a long period has to include such variables as population, its behavior, and the ratio of introduced innovations. Precise specifications (as opposed to truistic generalities) for the behavior of such "variables" cannot be construed. When one attempts to relate a theory with such "variables" to the time factor the problems become even more difficult and unpredictable. Thus, from a strict point of view of economics the model of economic growth and development has to remain "incomplete." Bruton concludes, "This leads us to an exceedingly important conclusion. It must be recognized that in a long-period analysis the distinction between economic and noneconomic factors loses significance, and it becomes necessary to acknowledge that *economic growth must be seen as a special aspect of general social evolution,* rather than as a process which can be factored out of the social system and studied in isolation.[22]

* For a graphic presentation of the visions of economic development, see also B. Higgins, *Economic Development,* pp. 131-34; I. Adelman, *Theories of Economic Growth and Development.*

The Harrod-Domar model is often considered the most appropriate example of post-Keynesian theory for countries that have achieved considerable economic development (that is, capitalist industrialized countries) and which now face the problem of expanding development while retaining a state of equilibrium. This is a theory of development for already developed economies. It focuses on the exposition of diverse probabilities revolving around a steadily accelerating rate of investment which simultaneously generates higher incomes (to be reinvested) and increases the productive capacity of the economy. It assumes full employment and a static state of a number of other parameters. Meier and Baldwin characterize the idea contained in the model as follows: "Investment is at the center of the problem. . . . According to Domar, this equilibrium rate of growth depends on the size of the multiplier and the productivity of new investment. It is equal to the propensity to save times the inverse of the accelerator. Income must increase, therefore, at a compound interest rate if full employment is to be maintained."[23]

The writers list a number of weak points in the theory, especially since it includes, and has to include, a number of key parameters, which in reality are not constant and "whose behavior" is not fully predictable and not static either. Among such parameters are population growth, capital accumulation, the propensity of people toward maximization of profit and toward improvement in general of their conditions of living (inclination toward greater economic and other security), and the international situation. Meier and Baldwin assert that it is impossible to express quantitatively many significant characteristics of the productive factors, and it is impossible to account for the myriad of social, political, and economic forces. Economists have to rely here on theories from other social sciences. Yet they take a somewhat more optimistic view than does Bruton.

> That other forces affect the crucial economic factors should not be interpreted to mean that these theories are irrelevant. They are limited, but they are extremely valuable within their limits as a foundation upon which to construct more elaborate and complete explanations of this complicated social problem. Most important, not only do they answer many economic questions in their own right but they also suggest many questions to ask of other subjects. Indeed, without these theories it would be much more difficult to know what contributions the other disciplines might make to a more adequate understanding of development.[24]

One more point should be added. Modern theories of economic development acknowledge that the actual course of economic development depends on the juxtaposition of numerous decision-making factors: politicians, entrepreneurs, investors, banks, advertisers, stockholders, consumers.

e. Economic Development in Communist Economies

Soviet and East European theories of the development of economies under communist rule emphasize even more the importance of decision-making. "In socialist society the national economy is an integral organism, directed by a single will. To ensure harmonious coordination and maximum integration of all parts of the country's social production mechanism becomes under these conditions the chief economic requirement. This is expressed in the law of planned proportional development of the national economy."[25] Two factors mentioned here are intended to work together to bring about steadily advancing proportional development: (1) the laws of development (apart from the law of planned proportional development, other laws are listed too) and (2) the will which takes shape in decisions. It is implied that these elements are more than congruent. In fact, Soviet economists often assume that decisions are but vehicles of inevitability for the laws of development. At the same time they say that development is a goal-oriented activity in pursuit of maximization of economic productivity. They assume then that both materialization of laws and implementation of decisions are indeed achieved in national planning.

Oskar Lange lists four types of "laws" operating in "socialist economy." (1) *General laws* "in the sense that they operate in every socioeconomic system. These are the laws of production and reproduction."[26] Here he includes the most general principles of organization of production such as division of labor both in society in general and within a plant or productive unit, and such as the principle "that one cannot accumulate if one consumes." (2) *Specific laws of the socialist mode of production.* These laws determine the purpose for which production is organized and the basic mode of organization, for instance whether it takes the form of competition, monopoly, or planned direction. "Thus socialist relations of production which consist in the social ownership of the means of production have two consequences. One is that production and all economic activity is done for satisfaction of the needs of society. The other is that the basic mode of social interaction in economic activities is planning, by which I mean a conscious guidance of economic processes by organized society."[27] (3) *Laws of an intermediate nature, specific to more than one mode of production,* such as the law of value and laws of monetary circulation. (4) Laws not connected with the socialist mode of production but *"resulting from the particular types of superstructure of management. . . .* Different methods of managing socialist economy which change histori-

226   Societal Development

cally and also from country to country produce their own particular economic laws. They produce specific economic laws because they produce specific incentives of action and opportunities of action."[28]

What Lange calls "laws" some East European economists regard as parameters within which economies in the Soviet Union and Eastern Europe operate, and within which planning and decision-making have to take place with regard to both the general direction of development and specific modes of action.* Lange and other economists in Eastern Europe assert that economic laws under socialism do not operate spontaneously "but that organized society shapes in a conscious purposive way the circumstances which determine the operation of economic laws. In consequence the economic laws can be made to operate in accordance with the human will, just like man through modern technology can utilize the laws of nature and make them operate in a way which conforms to his will."[29] This brings us back to the issue of decision-making and planning as the mechanisms of generating development in Soviet-type economies.

National planning in communist societies includes decisions on various aspects of the functioning of the economy. (a) Decisions about priorities. Whether to concentrate more on the development of industries or of

---

* Lange and others apply the concept of economic laws to emphasize that leaders of East European states have to take into account that "they cannot do whatever they wish." Their decisions bear consequences. To be effective and produce a high rate of economic development, he writes, economic laws require the application of incentives. Lange and other economists sharing his views advocate the idea of separating economic management from political government. Referring to Marx's theory of the "withering of the state," Lange asserts that "the process of gradual separation of economic management from political government thus prepares the institutional conditions for the 'withering away' of the State. The gradual reduction of political guidance of economic processes is an essential reflection of the process of maturation of socialist society" (ibid. p. 15). This writing pertains also to the discussion going on between East European economists in the last ten years or so on the possibility of applying diverse models of socialist economies and diverse roads toward socialism in different countries. The debate was sparked by the Twentieth Congress of the Communist Party in the Soviet Union. Advocates of the idea of different ways to socialism argued that the basic principles of socialist economics, such as abolition of private property of the means of production, and direction of the economy by central planning do not exclude the possibility of economic organizations different than the one in operation in the Soviet Union. They were especially for greater decentralization of economic decision-making, which in their opinion could stimulate more grass-roots initiative and eliminate some of the stagnating consequences of over-bureaucratization. See I. Kronrod (ed.), Zakon stoimosti i iego ispolzovanie v narodnom hoziaistvie SSSR (1959); W. Brus, Ogólne Problemy funkcjonowania gospodarki socjalistycznej (1961); S. Strumilin, "Zakon stoimosti i planirovania," Voprosy Ekonomiki, No. 7 (1959); C. Bobrowski, "Modele gospodarki socjalistycznej" and M. Kalecki, "Z zagadnien teorii dynamiki gospodarki socjalistycznej" both in O. Lange (ed.), Zagadnienia ekonomii . . . , Ekonomicky ústav ČSAV (Prague, July 1969); G. Grossman (ed.), Essays in Socialism and Planning in Honor of Carl Landauer (1970).

agriculture, and if on industries (as is the case all over the Soviet Union and Eastern Europe), how much to invest in industries producing raw materials, in industries producing means of production, military equipment, or commodities for consumption by the population. (b) Decisions about the division of the national income between accumulation and consumption. (c) Decisions about the ideological interpretation of the above decisions. These are very important decisions since they serve not only to rationalize policies but also to mobilize the population and aid in the ideological and political struggle going on both within and outside the Party. (d) Other decisions of central planning, such as on long- and short-range targets of production, the rate of growth of the national income, and decisions concerning the mobilization of men and resources and allocation of tasks within the national labor structure. Planning, as it operates in Eastern Europe and the Soviet Union includes not only anticipating the directions of proposed activity, a list of targets, and allocation of tasks and means, but also control over the implementation of plans and correction of the targets and tasks in the course of implementation of plans. It is a continuous process and consequently is often defined as one of the facets of economic development or even as the institutionalized form of economic development. What seems evident is that both Soviet and East European economists view development as a goal-oriented action. It does not mean, however, that the plans necessarily lead to targets or that they are always or usually implemented.

f. Economic Development of Economically Underdeveloped Areas

Turning to theories of economic development of the underdeveloped areas one has to discern two basic cores of problems around which the whole debate revolves. These are: (a) explanations of the causes and factors of underdevelopment, and (b) theories of perspectives and prescribed remedies. Among explanations of the causes of underdevelopment, those using the concept of vicious circles have to be mentioned first.* Ragnar Nurske has described it as follows: A country is poor because it is poor.[30] With regard to supply, the real income of the population is low, and it has but a small capacity to save and to accumulate capital, hence its productivity is low; hence, in turn, the low level of real income is maintained. With regard to demand, the country is poor, and it has but a small buying power; thus, it cannot attract capital; hence its productivity is low; therefore, its real income is low, which discourages investment. Each of the links of the circular chain is both the cause and the consequence of the other links. Other vicious circles overlap or are

* Theories of achievement motivation explain the underdevelopment as resulting from lack of achievement-orientation.

intermeshed with the above. They all result in the same explanation: a country is poor, and its people are poor because its economy has not developed; its economy cannot develop because the country is poor and cannot attract capital. Critics point out the lack of historical approach in such an explanation. The chain must have started somewhere; it must have developed into a spiral rather than a semicircle. It does not explain much, since each of the variables involved could develop independently without necessarily affecting other variables. Some critics of vicious circles theory argue that underdevelopment resulted from capitalist and imperialist exploitation.[31] Others maintain that underdeveloped countries are poor because capitalism did not advance enough there and the entrepreneurial activities promoted by individual entrepreneurs or by the state have not become widespread enough. Leibenstein proposes instead of the vicious circle theory his own explanation of "quasi stable equilibrium." He argues that "a certain minimum per capita income level has to be achieved in order for the economy to generate sustained growth from within."[32] However, what this minimum is and how it is generated is not explained. Numerous other explanations of the causes of underdevelopment and of the impediments for development have been voiced.[33] All these theories seem to contain a grain of truth, but the phenomena of underdevelopment are undoubtedly complex and only a composite explanation of a gamut of theories could provide a satisfactory answer.

Proposed solutions to the problems of underdevelopment are even more numerous. These will not be discussed at this point, partially because they are too numerous, partially because they seem to pertain more to economic policies than to the theory of economic development. Some of the experts regard it as most expedient for new nations to embark on the development of agriculture in order to create a basis for capital accumulation. Others argue for human investment (education) as a key to a complex, yet promising solution. Still others view self-help schemes of small communities as the springboard for wider development. There are also those who propose state development of an infrastructure in order to attract foreign and local investment.

Other issues within the theory of economic development are also controversial. Yet there is a body of points on which some sort of general agreement seems to be evident: (a) Economic development is visible in a growing national income. It is not a sufficient characteristic of economic development yet an inevitable aspect of it. (b) Economic development depends strongly on noneconomic factors such as political systems, attitudes, and culture. (c) Economic development is not unilinear. In diverse economic, social, and political conditions the problems of economic development differ considerably. Hence diverse theories have to be applied both to explain and to promote perspectives of economic development in each of the major differing socio-political systems of the modern world. (d) Economic development is not necessarily consistent and homogeneous and does not progress at a uniform rate. Though the process is generally sustained and expanding, within a general continuity stagnations, regressions, slow-downs, and occasional lapses are quite possible. (e) Development depends greatly on developers, on decisions, and on goal-oriented action whether in fulfillment of individual or group goals and tasks.

2. Political Development

"Political development" is a term coined in political science probably no more than ten years ago, yet it already has a substantial literature. Writers on political development do not confine themselves to phenomena or situations which have recently emerged or were recently discovered. In fact, the issues under this heading have always been in the center of political theory. What is new is a new approach to problems and processes explored earlier in a different way. The concept belongs to the theory of political systems the tenets of which need not be discussed here.[34] It attempts to view politics in abstract categories, garners diverse political occurrences into a coherent model-structure where political inputs are constantly transformed into outputs (thus, it is similar to other cybernetic models and some of the modern models in economic theory). Political development is one of such abstract categories. The long list of the literature in which "political development" is used makes it apparent that we are not talking about a merely glamorous terminological shell designed to cover up baffling discourses on meaningless issues. We are dealing with an important concept already in wide current circulation. At the same time, however, it is evident that we are dealing with a concept which has different meanings for different writers.

Lucian Pye sees that this variation in interpretations has to be scrutinized and that analysis has to lead to a coherent theory of political development. Such a theory could be instrumental both as an explanation for processes and as guidance for the practice of new nations. After a review of a vast array of literature in which he discerns at least ten variant interpretations of the concept of political development, Lucian Pye proposes to recognize three dimensions lying at the heart of the process of political development: *equality, capacity,* and *differentiation.* All three, he writes, have a natural tendency to increase. In addition he finds that the process of political development includes six crises "that may be met in different sequences but all of which must be successfully dealt with for a society to become a modern nation state."[35] These are: (1) The Identity Crisis, which has to be resolved in attainment of a common sense of national identity; (2) The Legitimacy Crisis, which has to lead to recognition of the authorities and their right to undertake binding decisions; (3) The Penetration Crisis, which means the build-up of channels of downward communication; (4) The Participation Crisis, which refers to the emergence of interest groups and the resolution of problems of mass participation in the political process; (5) The Integration Crisis, which consists of problems and solutions related to the organization of the entire polity into a system; (6) The Distribution Crisis, which is a code for the variety of problems stemming from allocation of power, prestige, offices, wealth (goods and services). Though Pye does not say explicitly that the theory of political development is designed for new nations, the selection of crises and the propounded solutions are tailored especially for such cases. The theory assumes that should it be possible to resolve all these crises in orderly sequential stages, political development and stability will eventually ensue. However,

> In most of the new states the crises are all appearing simultaneously, and governments are, for example, striving to use the distribution crisis to resolve the identity problem. The effort to raise the standards of living in these cases are in large part related to creating feelings of basic loyalty to the nation, and this procedure raises the question of how stable such states can become if their citizens' sense of identity is tied too closely to the effectiveness of particular policies.[36]

This writer has no quarrel with a theory propounding that the resolution of conflicts—in this case specific political conflicts—as part of a process of development. It is worth pointing out, however, that some of the "crises" listed by Pye are chronic in any society. Which society is free from constantly recurrent conflicts on the issues over the distribution of goods and offices and over participation in the structure of power and decision-making? These "crises" have many faces, and in each system they apear in the form of an accumulation of different problems. Thus, it is obvious that today industrial nations too are facing the integration crisis: Canada, Britain (Ireland), the Soviet Union, and even the United States are examples. Problems, like the drive toward marginality, the generation gap, differences in value-orientation which are sometimes described as manifestations of societal anomie and at other times as a reflection of inherent conflict, could certainly be regarded as a form of the identity crisis.

Lucian Pye is proposing a theory of political development to suit the new nations. He focuses his interest on the specific form which these crises manifest in Asia and Africa. He gives the impression that he is contrasting nations which have such crises with nations which overcame them long ago. He considers political development as an ultimate goal producing stability and with it a rise in the standard of living, resolving many, if not all, of the social and economic problems of the new nations. Broadly speaking Pye is right in asserting that some political stability and integration, and a greater amount of legitimacy, more developed channels of communication and wider participation in political affairs are important for transforming the new into modern nations. However, development cannot be equated with stability or even with a striving toward stability. Pye introduces a number of concepts around which wider theories were organized later. As he acknowledges, some of these concepts were elaborated in a collective endeavor of a group of scholars specializing in the field of new nations.[37] From the vantage point of an observer in 1973, the world, its problems and perspectives, and theory of political development look differently than in 1966, as discussed by Pye.

The concept and the theory of political development as it appears in numerous publications still reflects a wide variety of opinions. In some writing it encompasses a number of collateral formative tendencies. In others, one aspect of political life is especially exposed as reflecting political development. Discussion of political development may pertain to (a) Generation, solidification, maturation, and actions of self-established separate *political entities.* Here theories of the birth or *building of nations* and of nationalism can be included. Sometimes this is interpreted as a process of political integration. (b) *Growing systemness of political interaction.* Theories of the building of political systems can be included here. However, "building" can be understood differently; for some writers it is primarily a process of wider participation of the members of a society in political life. Thus in discussing political development they are especially concerned with enfranchisement, articulation of interest groups, their ability to affect the process of decision-making, and other aspects of participatory democracy. Other writers view the growing systemness as a process of institutionalization of political organizations and procedures.[38] Still others define political development as a process of growth of capabilities of the political system.[39] (c) In some cases formation, maintenance, and self-differentiation of *political cultures* is regarded as a process of political development. But this could also be related to the formation of nations.

a. Differentiation of Self-established Political Entities: Formation of Nations, Nationalism

The problems which one has to encounter in attempting to view political development as a process of the formation of nations are multitudinous indeed. The modern world is divided into nations occupying definite territories. Most people living in that world know approximately what the word "nation" means, but practically all attempts to define it seem to be unsatisfactory. In a lecture delivered at the Sorbonne in 1882, Ernest Renan said:

> I intend to analyse with you an idea which seems simple and clear but which lends itself to the most dangerous misunderstanding. . . . In our day one commits a serious error, one confounds nation and race and one attributes to ethnographical or rather linguistic groups sovereignty analogous to that of real people.[40]

Now, as in 1882, the same could be said.

To be a member of a nation does not have exactly the same meaning in all languages. In the German and Slavic languages, for example, belonging to a nation and having citizenship are entirely different. Nations are differentiated on the basis of combinations of diverse criteria, in each case differently, on the basis of a common language, origin, distinctive national character, common religion, residence in a common territory, common culture and social organization, common interest manifest in national consciousness. A macrostructure, a large group of people sometimes numbering millions, exhibiting all the above characteristics and aspiring to a separate nationhood may still not be regarded as a separate nation by others. There are clearly nations which are not recognized as nations by the international community. Only if a group which is distinguished from other similar groups by its sharing of the above characteristics establishes itself under a separate independent government does it obtain the full status of a separate and recognized nation.[41] Thus some nations do not have the recognized status of a nation, and many states encompass a number of nations.

Some students attribute the apearance of European nations to the destruction of the political order of feudalism, the promotion of all or nearly all people within a society to the status of citizens, and with it acquisition of rights to participation in the political life of the country. Reinhard Bendix's *Nation Building and Citizenship* discusses political development in this sense.

Some writers attribute the birth of the European nations to the emergence of national economies. They believe that the links of the all-embracing capitalist economic systems have cemented the cultural and ethnic unities which had come into being in the European states earlier, bringing about the birth of modern nations. National consciousness emerged then on the basis of common interests of the society unified by various integrative processes, among which the economic one played the decisive role.[42] Such views were especially promoted by Stalin and the Marxist writers employing his theory.* The concept "nation" is defined in such literature too rigidly, and many of the new nations, especially in Africa, are not nations from the strict standpoint of such definitions. Yet the idea seems to be valid that nationwide economic systems coalesce, solidify, and bring to maturity modern national entities. Reflecting on theories like the above, one can say that one aspect of political development is a complex process of *self-determination, establishment as a separate national political entity, enfranchisement, ongoing integration especially as a result of economic development.*** Nationalism is the propellant force behind that kind of political development. And nationalisms, like nations, exhibit diverse characteristics.

Kenneth Minogue writes that nationalism begins as Sleeping Beauty and ends as Frankenstein's monster.[43] He distinguishes three stages in that process. The first, labeled stirring, is a period of awakening, of revulsion against foreign rule, culture, and ideas. Then comes the stage of the struggle for independence, followed by the third stage of consolidation. Beyond that lies the "integral nationalism" or totalitarianism. Yet, in reality, not all nationalisms change into totalitarianism. Minogue's description is not a rule. True, in some cases nationalism buttressed colonialism and imperialism. In others, it just became the foundation of national existence alongside other nations. Indeed, especially in European history, nationalism has often had an ugly side. Yet, from this one cannot gauge that the ugliness was inherent, and that any nationalism will become transmogrified into a Frankenstein monster of totalitarianism. Nationalism in Asia and in Africa may not be a Sleeping Beauty, but it certainly is the driving power of modernization. There are also not yet signs of change into a monstrous variety.

Nowadays nations are said to be built, and nation-building, national integration, modernization, and political development are diverse sides of the same process of transformation of traditional into modern political entities.[44]

---

* J. V. Stalin in "Marxism and the National Question," *Works* (Moscow: Foreign Languages Publishing House, 1953), Vol. II, p. 307, states: "A nation is a historically constituted, stable community of people, formed on the basis of a common language, territory, economic life, and psychological make-up manifested in a common culture. It goes without saying that a nation, like every historical phenomenon, is subject to the law of change, has its history, its beginning and end. It must be emphasized that none of the above characteristics taken separately is sufficient to define a nation. More than that, it is sufficient for a single one of these characteristics to be lacking and the nation ceases to be a nation."
** It must be pointed out that enfranchisement in many cases does not lead to democracy.

b. Political Development as Growing Systemness of Political Interaction

Political development can be regarded in a sense as a process of growing systemness of the societies with an emphasis on the development of political linkages and institutions. In fact, diverse aspects of the growing interdependencies of both the complementary and semiorganismic variety have been defined by political theorists as political development. Some students of the subject feel that phenomena of the growing functional complementary interdependence have to be regarded primarily as political development. They focus their attention on the transformation of the interdependence of coexistence into the complementary interdependence. Their interest is manifest in studies of change of the "agraria" into "industria";[45] on the growing democratization and complexity of political participation;[46] on expanding enfranchisement; on the changing structure of political representation;[47] on differentiation of interest groups and their impact on the political process.[48] In most of these studies political development is portrayed as generated by increasing mass participation on political affairs, as a process of institutionalization of the equality and freedoms of democracy. Recently, however, there has been a declining professional interest in the above-mentioned issues.

Attention is now focused on another point of departure and other processes, as concern centers more on growing interdependence of the semiorganismic type. The issues are bureaucracy and political development, institutionalization in the process of political development, and increasing capabilities of political systems.[49] What could be extracted from these theories is an interpretation of political development as a process of coordination and subordination under a center.

Interpretations in terms of institutionalization and increasing capability have achieved particular currency in the definition of political development. A. F. K. Organski defines political development as "increasing governmental efficiency in utilizing the human and material resources of the nation for national goals."[50] He views political development as a unilinear process ongoing in time and parallel to similar unilinear processes of economic development.* Samuel P. Huntington proposes a different approach, viewing institutionalization as political development. He explains that "institutions are stable, valued, recurrent patterns of behavior" and asserts that institutionalization produces stability.[51] In his opinion, the goal of political development is stability. It is achieved in the

---

* He distinguishes four stages of political development: (1) the politics of primitive unification; (2) the politics of industrialization; (3) the politics of national welfare; and (4) the politics of abundance.

course of greater institutionalization of political organizations and procedures. To measure institutionalization he introduces four polarized pairs
of evaluation: adaptability-rigidity, complexity-simplicity, autonomy-
subordination, coherence-disunity. The more a political organization is
adaptable, complicated (constituted of multiple organizational subunits,
hierarchically and functionally), autonomous (differentiated and separated from other spheres of activity), and coherent (and unified), the
more it is institutionalized and the more it is considered developed. He
applies this theory to new nations and finds that most of the contemporary problems of these nations stem from insufficient institutionalization.
As the solution to these problems he recommends the introduction of a
strong party organization which will become a key to stability.

However, institutionalization could be defined differently. Since competition and conflict may be part of a stable order, they are often as institutionalized as stability itself. What seems even more doubtful, however,
is the assumption that a single party provides stability and that stability
necessarily provides development and solves all problems. Several years
ago I wrote a paper which, while not so elegant or so far-reaching as Professor Huntington's, contained a similar belief in the instrumentality of
single parties in building a stable, integrated, and developing political
and economic system.[52] I am no longer sure that this was right, that the
single-party system by itself could provide the solution. True, a single-
party system in an economically underdeveloped country can provide the
means of mobilizing resources and masses, and this is important. Then,
however, the problem becomes the utilization of these resources and potential capabilities. A single-party system in a small economically underdeveloped country under a dictator fearing criticism and change and destroying grass-roots' initiative transforms itself from an instrument of
development into an instrument of retardation. Like the multiparty system, the single-party system is a tool and tools can be utilized for diverse
purposes. Huntington cites the Bolshevik Party of the Soviet Union as an
example. Though he is not entirely clear, he seems to suggest that the
Party was able to achieve a balance between organization and mobilization, on the one hand, and development and stability on the other hand.
This is a misunderstanding however. The secret police, the Cheka, NKVD,
MVD, KGB, and not the Party, has to be credited with the maintenance
of "stability." The troublemakers, the initiators of instability, like Trotsky,
Bukharin, Malenkov, and Khrushchev all come from the Party leadership.
Stability as well as instability can be productive or sterile.

Gabriel A. Almond characterizes the political system as a mechanism
which transforms political inputs into outputs. He points out that the political system not only generates such transformations, but compels the

obedience and performance of those encompassed by the system.[53] The performance of the political system itself can be evaluated by testing the changing range of the internal and international capabilities of the system. He lists five categories of capabilities: (1) extractive (drawing material and human resources); other writers discuss the same topic under the heading of mobilization; (2) regulative (control of the behavior of individuals and groups); other writers refer to this as regulation of conflict and consensus; (3) distributive (allocation of goods, services, and statuses); (4) symbolic; (5) responsive (relationship between inputs and outputs).

Unlike his earlier writing, in recent publications Almond attributes great importance to dysfunctional inputs as the "cause" of change and subsequent political development. He tells us that when all the flows of output—extractions, regulations, allocations, and others—obtain a level of magnitude which the political system can cope with, then we may speak of the political system as being in equilibrium.[54] This is a somewhat different understanding of equilibrium from that found in functionalist theory. Dysfunctional inputs contain innovations. In whatever forms they appear, whether orderly petitions or violent demonstrations, they affect the capabilities of the political system and change it. Such dysfunctional inputs come from other systems of the society where new roles and new attitudes are born. They change the political system and by a feedback change the system's adaptation, recruitment, and socialization. Dysfunctional inputs vary according to (a) their source, (b) intensity, (c) subject matter, and (d) quantity (they may be incremental). In such an interpretation political development becomes related and interdependent with social change and economic development. It focuses on the generation and transformation of the structure of the semiorganismic interdependencies impinging upon the society from above. The political process is viewed as in interplay with the grass roots and with other systems.

Almond's writing on political development can be interpreted variously. He may be considered (especially on account of his earlier writing on political systems) as a writer discussing the impinging paramount semiorganismic system. One can read him differently too, though I am not sure whether this was the message that he wished to transmit. Here is the multiheaded dragon, the Leviathan with his numerous capabilities, approaching. Can you, dwarfish creature Man, stop him from swallowing you? Can you control him? One can draw on the metaphoric and contradictory meaning of categories applied by Almond (as one can on any theory) and reject his theory as imprecise and confusing.[55] Or one may see his theory as a perspective interpretation containing an opulence of heuristic possibilities. Certainly he offers a better interpretation of some aspects of the processes regarded as development of political systems than do other writers. He himself characterizes his theory as probabilistic and tells us that he regards it as a first step toward constructing a theory of the "development of political systems." This is worth emphasizing: His theories, as well as those of other writers in this section are more theories of the development of political systems than theories of political development in general.

One more theory on the subject of political development seems to be expedient to recall here. It is just generally adumbrated by Karl W. Deutsch.[56] He proposes to apply six criteria for evaluation of the diverse aspects of growth of the decision-making system. These are: (1) the degree of growth of the manpower encompassed by the system and its potential capability for action; (2) its economic strength with a special consideration of the rate of the economic growth; (3) the growth of operational reserves, or the availability of material and human resources capable of introducing relevant changes in response to new challenges; (4) the rate of growth of autonomy of self-determination; stronger cohesion, expanding network of internal channels of communication producing a better steering performance of the system; (5) the ability of the structure to overcome internally its problems of enlargement in scale through self-transformation; (6) goal-changing ability. It is further said that the growth of "decision system" in all these aspects has to be balanced by a growing autonomy of the compositive units of the whole generating within the society or state an "integrative behavior" based on the awareness of existence of an internal multiple autonomy. These criteria have to be considered as instructive and availing. To my knowledge, unfortunately, they were never applied in a concrete case of an analysis of political development. My own ideas on the subject partially correspond with those listed by Deutsch.

Some new features of what may be regarded partially as political, partially as general societal development have recently become evident. Early in the twentieth century, sociologists focused their attention on transformations of the agglomerations of communities into a wider network of associational bonds of society, in the course of which the structure became permeated by impersonal market-type relations. These processes are still in progress spreading over new territories which include the new nations, and they become more acute in earlier industrialized countries. Yet nowadays these processes are becoming engulfed by a new tide of semiorganismic interdependencies imposed upon and permeating modern societies. The Soviet Union and other Communist countries were developed as semiorganismic structures. Today, however, Western societies as a result of a complex process of etatization have also become in-

creasingly subordinated to a semiorganismic organization generated by
the state. The process consists primarily of acquisition by the government
and the state of more regulative and coordinating functions in the society.* Applying the derivative from the French word *état*—the state, I call
it etatization.

Originally the modern state, at least as it was characterized by earlier
Liberals, was supposed to be endowed with a minimum of functions. It
was structured in such a way as to perform only functions of defense
against foreign encroachment and maintenance of law and order within.
The belief was that people protected by society will manage by themselves to handle their affairs and regulate their relations with others. Subsequently the state had to interfere increasingly in the interactions between groups and individuals and to organize various public services
earlier either nonexistent or run on a small scale by private institutions
and the Church.

Three factors at least can be listed as causing the described process
of etatization or acquisition of new functions by the state and permeation
by its agencies of the society. These are economic, technological, societal,
political development requiring coordination between extremely complex
interdependencies in societal structure; growing demand for various
forms of public services; the natural propensity of any state as a huge
organizational bureaucratic structure to expand and grow.

From an institution of rule, the state has changed into an institution
of public representation and government. Today, however, it is increasingly changing into an institution of administration and management of
societal affairs. This is a tendency of development in political life.
Whether it is a desirable development is another subject. It will certainly
produce more standardization, depersonalization, and shrinkage of the
autonomy of individuals, even if democracy remains intact. It will also
considerably affect the state of privacy in society.[57]

c. Development of Political Culture

Although obviously an important topic about which political behav-
iorists and social psychologists have produced a wealth of data, this data
has not been utilized either in the construction of a comprehensive theory
of political culture or in studies of political cultures in diverse societies.
Among political scientists there appears to be little interest in problems
of political culture. At most, they have paid lip-service to its importance
as a factor in politics. Anthropologists whose interests were strongly focused on culture did their work most often on traditional societies and
only rarely ventured to explore the political culture of industrial nations.

** See pp. 117-23, Chapter III.

In addition, in studies of traditional societies they often viewed political culture as identical with political systems.[58] This is justified by the lack of pronounced differentiation in traditional societies of diverse spheres of activities, among others of politics from social, economic, cultural, and religious life and organization. To be sure, various aspects of political cultures were occasionally discussed either in connection with culture in general or with specific nations, in historical analyses of politics or in general books on selected societies.*

Studies specifically focusing on the theory of political culture are rather rare, and Almond's and Verba's work has to be regarded as a classic introduction to the subject.[59] The writers not only introduce the concept but also present a typology of political cultures. They distinguish between three models of pure political cultures: (a) parochial political culture; (b) the subject political culture; and (c) the participant political culture. In addition they differentiate three types of mixed political cultures: (a) the parochial-subject culture; (b) the subject-participant culture; (c) the parochial-participant culture. The writers imply that in the course of historical development these cultures become superimposed one over another in the order mentioned here. They are not only diverse types but also stages in a directional sequence of the historical development of political culture. The writers assume that political culture may or may not be congruent with the structures of political systems. At that time Almond was basically concerned with the values of participatory democracy, and what he defined as the civic culture was viewed as the superb efflorescence of that stadial historical superimposition. The writers state, "The 'citizen' is a particular mix of participant, subject, and parochial orientations, and the civic culture is a particular mix of citizens, subjects and parochials."[60] Actually an assumption is made that such cultures allow individuals to act simultaneously in the diverse roles of parochials, subjects, and citizens. Since it requires rational participation of individuals (positively oriented toward the system) within the input of politics, the civic culture is an allegiant-participant culture. It is culture "plus something else," a rather well-balanced, stable culture in which citizens are fairly competent to participate in politics, and "in which the political culture and political structures are congruent."[61]

Almond and Verba present a comparative analysis of five democracies—the United States, Great Britain, Germany, Italy, and Mexico. These societies are evaluated by means of structural-functional characteristics, and cultural, subcultural and role-cultural units within them are differ-

---

* Alexis de Tocqueville's studies *Democracy in America* and *The Old Regime and the French Revolution* could be regarded as examples of brilliant work on specific political cultures.

entiated. The United States and Britain are regarded as model democ-racies, and other societies tend toward the model structure. Though the study discusses conflict on various levels of social organization, and be-tween various sections and groups in these societies the focus is on con-sensus. The writers assume that conflicts are subordinated to "higher, overarching attitudes of solidarity," and that the balance is maintained through the flexibility of the system and cultural set-up which provides room for apparently contradictory demands. Consensus is not only main-tained but is steadily growing through learning, socialization, and edu-cation. In short, civic culture develops parallel to a democratic structure of society. Cases of what in the writers' terms would be regarded as civic cultures put under control of an authoritarian political regime (for ex-ample, Czechoslovakia or Greece) are not taken into account. Thus one can draw a conclusion that if a society does not have a democratic order it is because it has not attained the level of civic culture.

J. P. Nettl has suggested a somewhat different conceptual view of the subject.[62] In his opinion, the more the political system differentiates itself as a separate entity, the greater the "specific crystalization of politi-cal culture." He proposes to distinguish four thresholds of the develop-ment of political cultures reflecting the degree of institutionalization of the political authority. The more the authority is institutionalized (here institutionalization is similar to Huntington's concept) the more a politi-cal culture is developed. Thus, the first threshold of the development of political culture is reached in a society when it becomes aware that an institutionalized authority exists. The second threshold is reached when a structure of political roles (tax collector, policeman, ruler) becomes embedded in the societal structure. The third step is the emergence of a consciousness of the existence of a system to which individuals belong, either of their own accord or because of coercion. This is a level of institu-tionalization not only of separate roles but of systems. Finally, the fourth threshold "is where evaluation matches the level of internalization, so that there is little disparity between cognition as such and meaningful evaluation of some sort."[63] The four thresholds are said to differentiate four levels of acculturation.* Nettl promises to analyze the political cul-ture in terms of pattern variables and suggests a distinction between con-stitutionalism and elitism as the two basic patterns of political culture. All other political cultures he proposes to locate on the axis of these two ideal type extremes. Political culture he analyzes in juxtaposition with what he defines as political mobilization.

Although Almond and Verba place the United States and Great Brit-

---

* Thus, the concept of acculturation is defined differently here than in other fields, for instance in anthropological literature (e.g., by M. J. Herskovits).

ain in one group, in one Anglo-Saxon political culture, this does not seem to be justified. Both are democracies, in both societies politics is a sphere of competition and bargaining, and both have two-party systems. But the structure of the two-party systems differ, traditions differ, and attitudes toward authorities and politics differ. Nettl's treatment of the subject is even less justified. He puts together both Britain and the Soviet Union in "the elitist culture category in terms of subsystem differentiation and institutionalization of authority."[64] The United States and Canada are placed in the constitutional category and Communist China is said to have a constitution- (or institution-) oriented culture.[65]

The studies of both Almond and Verba and of Nettl attempt to delineate the boundaries of the political culture by separating it from general culture and from the political structure.* While this seems to be justified when the subject of discussion is political culture by itself, from any other point of view the problem must be posed differently. Political culture is a part of both the sphere of culture** and the sphere of politics and must be discussed as a bridge between the two, as a product of overlapping of the two spheres, rather than as a separate entity. As a part of the general culture political culture engenders social interaction and as the general culture it develops through transmission from generation to generation in a cumulative process. It includes institutionalized patterns of behavior, attitudes, symbols, and beliefs. It can be learned, and as a rule is inculcated, through a variety of means of socialization such as family life, schools, the state, and specialized agencies and organizations which care about its maintenance and spread, often in combination with the promotion of a corresponding ideology.

Anthropologists characterize culture as ideational. This is especially true for political culture since it revolves around conceptualized ideal norms and patterns of behavior.[66] It is cumulative and continuously changing. Yet, at the same time, it provides continuity. The culture of a definite society can be developed and enriched either indigenously or by adoption of foreign elements into it. In either case, it cannot be entirely replaced by another culture either voluntarily or through imposition upon a society by foreigners. Thus, it could be said that man is only partially free in his acceptance and choice of culture and cultural patterns of behavior. Culture is inherited and man is part of it. Of course, any culture could be remolded in the spirit of new times and adjusted to

---

* Nettl in *Political Modernization* engages in a long discussion on the importance of measuring the political culture, which leads him to the conclusion that "culture is altogether the most difficult aspect of politics to measure" (p. 58).
** I am speaking of cultures of nations, tribes, and similar units, not of the culture of mankind.

values promulgated currently. Even when old values are rejected and new ones are deliberately chosen, however, the new culture must be built on the foundation of the pattern behaviors, values, and beliefs generated in the past. This is true for culture in general, and especially true for political culture. Thus, political culture as a rule contains diverse traditions and experiences. According to the requirements of the times, certain elements of tradition and of the political culture are available for use, while others are "stored" until needed. Thus diverse interpretations of the same elements of political culture are possible in different societies, and one can say that a culture is "stable and constant" and "flexible" at the same time. In general, political culture tends to change more slowly than the political system or the social structure related to it.

As an element of politics, political culture is reflected especially in attitudes and pattern behavior concerning authority, political power, and the rights and freedoms of individuals and groups. It is manifest in predispositions common in society to be either submissive or hostile, or to treat selectively decisions coming from "above." It is found in inclinations toward active or passive participation in political life or abstention from it, in the degree of emotional involvement with political and social problems, in the character of conflict and competition over political issues, in the inclination to cultivate traditions, in stereotypical attitudes toward national and other groups. Developed in the course of history, political culture is composed of an organized body of political pattern behavior and attitudes which are to varying degrees rational or irrational.*

Though it is not certain whether political cultures can be measured, they surely can be evaluated qualitatively. An analysis of a political culture could account for the following (1) *The congruence* of the political culture with other elements of the culture in general (for instance, whether a competitive orientation in politics reflects similar orientations in economics or social living). The congruence of political culture with the pace of social and economic change, and with the political structure of the society in general. (2) Its ability to change; the flexibility of the political culture. Its capacity for absorption of innovations both from other political cultures and from other spheres of social activity. (3) The efficacy of the political culture as a transmitter of beliefs, values, norms, and pattern behavior from the past. (4) The institutionalization of a political culture. This includes an assessment of how much norms and values promoted by a culture are implemented by specialized

---

* Thus, a much wider range of pattern behavior and attitudes is included here in the concept of political culture than proposed by Nettl. He wrote, "A political culture may be said to exist when political authority, and the process relating to that authority are effectively internalized by members of the society" (p. 57).

institutions and how much such institutions permeate the social order of the society. (5) The content of values, norms, pattern behavior, and attitudes promoted by a political culture, especially its characteristics within a set of overlapping extrapolated orientations such as: authoritarianism versus democracy; collectivism versus individualism; tolerance for dissent, competition, and conflict, or rejection of them; emphasis on subordination of the individual to the collectivity or the opposite promotion of individualism; respect or disregard for traditions. These orientations also affect the next variable, (6) The integrative capacity of a political culture (how much it contributes to the general political integration of society).

Such an evaluation of a political culture takes into account the character of its functions (and the assumption is that though some functions of political cultures are identical in any society, others are peculiar to one) and the content of the values promoted by it. Since too many varied traits and qualities must be considered I do not think that it is possible to find an objective common denominator for the evaluation of the development of political cultures, without viewing such development selectively and omitting some aspects of it. For example, a political culture could be regarded as highly developed when it is rich in long-standing traditions, or when these are well institutionalized. Or when it contains allowances for a degree of dissent and provides an amount of freedom to the members of society. Or when the political authority is well internalized, or when the culture provides conditions conducive to the elevation of a complex hierarchical structure of authority. Or when it is highly integrative. On the whole, political culture, like general culture, is continuous yet the above listed individual qualities may be more or less salient at different times. Since it is continually and cumulatively strengthening and expanding its sphere, political culture can be characterized as ascending at an accelerating pace.

The character of a social and even more of a political structure is only partially determined by the level of technology and harnessing of energy in the productive process. To be sure, a good typology of societies may begin by differentiating diverse societies in accordance with the level of harnessing of energy applied in them; this is important, especially in the comparison of diverse societies throughout history or of different areas. But this should be regarded only as the beginning of a typology. Within such "types" one has to differentiate societies and political orders in accordance with their peculiar social and political traits. Thus, under headings such as traditional, modern, industrial, feudal, capitalist, and socialist a great diversity of political regimes, social structures, cultures, and political cultures can be included. The comparison of political cultures within such categories is often very fruitful heuristically. David E. Apter's comparative analysis of political cultures in traditional African societies can be used as a good example of such a comparison.[67]

Examining the diversity of traditional African political cultures through the prisms of functional, behavioral, and normative evaluation, Apter extrapolates two prevalent value orientations: the instrumental and the consummatory. This is confronted with three types of authority and of the political organization: hierarchical, pyramidal, and segmental. Thus, six types of political cultures are distinguished: the instrumental-hierarchical, exemplified by the Baganda; the instrumental-pyramidal exemplified by the Hausa-Fulani; the instrumental-segmental, by the Ibo; the consummatory-hierarchical by the Fon in Dahomey; the consummatory-pyramidal, by the Ashanti; and the consummatory-segmental, by the Nuer. Such or similar schemes can be applied in constructing typologies of political cultures in industrial, capitalist, Communist, and other groups of societies.

The basic traits of a society are inevitably mirrored by its culture, but social structure is only one of numerous factors affecting the character of the culture. A good typology of cultures cannot be based solely, or even principally, on variables pertaining to the social structure of society.[68] A typology of political cultures cannot be derived simply from comparative analysis of political regimes and current structures of authority and political power. Although unceasingly continuous, at the same time political culture is constantly changing as a result of the influence of the political system as well as the impact of other factors of the general culture and social relations. It is simultaneously new and old. Old pattern behavior persistently reappears in it, and new social experiences become incorporated into it as a part of the storehouse of collective political memory.

Political systems grow, or have to be built and imposed, on a ground of a definite political culture existing in society. The character of the political system and regimes change much faster and more drastically than political cultures. New social and political orders gradually transform the political culture making it more congruent with their own altered characters. In the course of that process, however, the new political system becomes more and more saturated by the culture in which it is embedded. As a result of such osmosis the old pattern of behavior in the guise of new political offices, roles, and symbols reappears as a part of the new political culture. Thus history repeats itself. Parallels between situations and characters in past and present politics can be drawn. The continuity of political cultures also reflects the persistence of the national psychological traits commonly regarded as national character.

d. Political and Economic Development Compared

The three elements of the political reality—the entity (nation), the system (including the structure of authority), and the culture—do not develop in full congruence. But, during the growth of political integration, they do produce at least one common result: an increasingly strengthened common consciousness of belonging to a macrostructure of society. Correspondingly, within the sphere of politics one can distinguish three types or levels of mutually supportive ideological, organizational and cultural integrative processes* buttressed by integration in other spheres of social living, in generation of a common culture, in economic development, and in general by the growth of secondary interdependencies within national boundaries.

How interdependent is economic and political development?

Theories of economic development began to appear much earlier than theories of political development. In spite of the fact that problems pertaining to what is now regarded as political development were studied by the ancient philosophers, it was not until recently that writers on politics attempted to place them within a frame of developmental perspective. The systemic and developmental approach to politics are of recent origin.

Within the general process of economic development a number of mutually related trends are distinguishable: expanding market interdependencies increasingly engulfing all members of society; growing productivity; growing national income; growing income per capita. These trends are not precisely correlated, and for short periods of time some of them may appear without affecting or causing the others. On the whole, however, they produce a common effect, and most economists agree that Gross National Product is the leading measurable indicator of economic development. Political development is composed of many trends and threads too, but it is difficult, if at all possible, to discern a single leading indicator of it. Certainly, none is acceptable to most writers on the subject.

Economic development is goal-oriented, and the goal is generally regarded to be objectively desirable. The process and the goal are practically identical and the goal of economic development is unquestionably inextinguishable and inexhaustible. However, it might be debated whether such development is worth its social price, whether its course, and the means used in its attainment, are good enough. Political develop-

* Diverse forms of political integration could be classified in a different way. Thus M. Weiner, "Political Integration and Political Development" in *The Annals*, Vol. 358 (March 1965), proposes to differentiate national, territorial, value, élite-mass integrations, and integrative behavior. See also C. Ake, *The Theory of Political Integration* (Homewood, Ill.: The Dorsey Press, 1967).

ment cannot be characterized in the same way. If it can be considered goal-directed at all, its goals sound nebulous, whether defined as institutionalization, increased capability of the system, or greater integration. Defined as the growth of democracy or of nation or nation-building, it must envisage a point of satiation when the desired democracy has been achieved, when the nation has acquired independence and a separate identity. After a point of satiation further development leads to something entirely different (from democracy to anarchy or totalitarianism, from nationalism to imperialism or chauvinism).

Parallels can be drawn between economic and political development when both are characterized as differentiation within a growing interdependence, but that is not the usual way of viewing the problems. However, theories of economic and political development do share at least one trait. They both envisage diverse possibilities of implementation depending on the involvement of the participants. Both presuppose planning for the future of the society. Both anticipate an element of freedom (in some interpretations an element of freedom within a general necessity) which may be variously exploited, producing diverse conditions and leading to further developments.[69]

Political development and diverse arrangements of political organization open and stimulate or block and impede the process of economic development. An inverse proposition cannot be asserted in the same degree. The effect of economic development on political organization and on individual aspects of political development seems to be rather more indirect and less determining. It is much easier to predict the effect of political changes and transformation on economic development than the effect of economic development on politics. At times one reads that a high level of economic development and industrialization necessitates the organization of democracy, or a higher level of individual freedoms or complex political institutionalization. At other times, lack of democracy is attributed to the low level of economic development of a country. Such beliefs seem to sway on doubtful arguments. Differing political systems based on diverse degrees and structures of authoritarianism, oligarchy, limited democracy, and general democracy exist side by side in any period of history, often resting on similar levels of economic development. Economic development affects the character of political systems and the course of political development* in various ways, but it does not determine directly the structure of institutionalization of political authority or its hierarchization. It affects the structure of political freedoms of a society but it does not determine their degree and scope wholly and directly.

* One can refer here also to exchanges between the political and economic systems. See T. Parsons and N. I. Smelser, *Economy and Society.*

Political systems and development seem to have a more immediate and direct effect on the course of economic development. At least three basic lines of shaping economic development by political means can be demarcated: (1) In the first instance political authorities create conditions generally conducive to economic development without interfering much in the actual course of economic activities. Governments support trade, business, entrepreneurial, and innovative activities, implying a system of security defending private property, accumulation of capital, investments, and the rights of the owners. This occurs in the early stages of capitalism. (2) In the second instance political authorities interfere with economic activities and provide some regulation for economic development. They eliminate tension which cannot be eliminated in spontaneous competition. They pave the way for certain economic developments. They defend to a degree the rights and well-being of the working class and of the farmers. They build an infrastructure on which economic development can be set. They introduce laws defending economic development. In short, political authorities develop a frame for economic development, but economic development progresses on its own. This is the case of advanced capitalism. (3) In the third instance political authorities engage directly in planning and implementing economic development. They become the owners of economic enterprises. They define the targets of economic development, its direction, and the rate of capital accumulation, mostly by diminishing consumption. They provide the resources and organize the political mobilization of men to implement the economic targets. This is the case of the Soviet Union and other East European nations. This is also to a degree becoming a tendency in modern Western societies.

3. The Case of Socialism with a Human Face

In 1956 Arnes Naess published a book in which he presented 398 definitions of democracy extracted from various writings from the time of Solon, Plato, and Aristotle up to Stalin and Truman.[70] Should one wish to write a book about the concept of socialism in the same way, one could not collect nearly as many definitions as Naess did, but there would be no difficulty in collecting more than fifty. Let me begin with a few of these divergent understandings.

In all of Marx's and Engels's writing, in *Poverty of Philosophy, Communist Manifesto, Critique of the Gotha Programme, Critique of the Erfurt Programme*, in *Anti-Dühring*, the opinion is expressed many times that socialism begins with the withering away of the state, when classes disappear in connection with the abolition of private property which they believed was the source of all conflicts, of the class struggle, and of many forms of alienation, including especially alienation of the state from society. The whole autonomy of the civil society could be reinstated in their opinion, "only when the actual, individual man has taken back into himself the abstract citizen and in his everyday life, his individual work, and in his individual relationships has become a *species-being*, only when he has recognized and organized his own powers as *social* powers so that social force is no longer separated from him as *political* power, only is human emancipation complete."[71] According to Marx and Engels, socialism would come as the result of economic and social inevitability. Since they believed that the inevitability was real and unavoidable, Engels wrote that the Marxist theory is scientific, contrary to other theories of socialisms which they regarded as utopian. The Marxist vision of socialism was utopian too, however, though in another sense. Marx and Engels believed that the impossible could become possible simply if people became conscious enough and wished for it strongly. They argued that it was possible to master a socialist society which would be at the same time highly industrialized and affluent, with a complex division of labor and advanced specializations, yet basically conflictless and without social stratification. In short, they envisaged socialism as a worldwide comradeship of workers emancipated from economic, political, religious, national, and other dependencies, who were highly educated and thus practically intellectuals.

Joseph Stalin inaugurated socialism on December 6, 1936 when the Constitution of the Soviet Union he had drafted was proclaimed.[72] It was then that the single Party-state became absolutely dominant in Soviet society, permeating all its units, transforming each individual into a mere atom of the semiorganismic system. Stalin claimed that the Soviet system was socialist since (1) it abolished private ownership of the means of production and proclaimed the state the owner and the master of the economy; (2) it was based on such principles as "from each according to his abilities, to each according to his work," and "he who does not work, neither shall he eat." It was a concept of socialism, if not diametrically opposed to that of Marx, at least considerably divergent from the original Marxist one.

The Syndicalists and Guild Socialists believed that in a socialist society the industries would be run by syndicates of workers or by all employees, and that industries of the whole society would be directed by a coordinating center composed of delegates of syndicates, unions, and possibly bourses.

The Russian Narodnicks, diverse groups of Social Democrats, and the Fabians promulgated still other understandings and principles of organization of socialist societies. The book recently published by George Lichtheim is a good manual for comparing such ideas.[73]

Today socialism has become fashionable in Asia and Africa. Especially in Africa many leaders claim to be building socialism. Some say that socialism existed in Africa in the precolonial period and that the task now is to resurrect it. Léopold Sédar Senghor explains,

> In our understanding socialism . . . is a rational organization of the human society as a whole based on the highest, most modern and efficient methods. Its aim is in accordance with the definition of François Perroux striving "from good life to higher forms of life" or more strictly "development of all people, perfection of the human kind in each individual" (F. Perroux, *L'Économie du XX° siècle*, p. 195). This means that socialism begins with freedom and equal opportunities for all men.[74]

In another publication he tells us that "Socialism is essentially *politics,* that is, an art of governing men of a given society by organizing their relations harmoniously."[75] At the other end of Africa Julius K. Nyerere looks at the issue somewhat differently. In his opinion socialism is an attitude of mind. It is a family based on the inclination to share. It is a brotherhood and the application of the principle of human equality to the social, economic, and political organization of the society.

"Socialism with a human face" is still another interpretation of the issue. The concept itself was coined during the short-lived Dubček regime in Czechoslovakia. What meaning is attached to it, and why is it discussed here?

Socialism with a human face is rather a collective vision than a comprehensive theory. It is a vision of "revisionist" philosophers, sociologists, and economists in Eastern Europe. It cannot be defined strictly yet but can be described. It is a belief in the possibility of transforming the semiorganismic mass society where individuals are deprived of their right to a separate identity into a society where human dignity is restored and the atoms and molecules of the all-encompassing body of the Party-state, the millions of human ants of the gigantic ant hill built over a fifth of the earth, will become men again possessing individual consciousness. It is, therefore, a vision of a socialism with millions of faces rather than with one face.

Since it is a vision of a society, not of angels, spirits, and pawns, but of human beings and groups of individuals, it foresees a society with conflict and with social stratification, yet with conflicts and social stratification different from those in already existing societies. Those who believe in it assume that the three basic items of scarcity, consumptive goods, political power, and prestige, will still be desired and will continue to be objectives of competition. However, they believe that because of increased productivity, raised standards of living and social reform the distribution of economic rewards will become more even. As a result of expanded participation in political activities and the institutionalization of numerous overlapping agencies of representation of diverse interests, political power and the authority and process of decision-making on the whole will be more under the control of the various interest groups of the society. Prestige will become the leading value-orientation. Political power and economic rewards will depend on the degree of its acquisition. Since this is a vision of the transformation of the sociopolitical and economic order of societies in Eastern Europe, the issue of abolishing the private property of large industrial and business enterprises does not need to be considered. The proponents of variant versions of human socialism usually favor leaving small industries and businesses including some peasant landholdings in the hands of private owners. Experience has shown that the state cannot cope efficiently with small industries and small retail business.

Most of the basic economic, social, and political problems of societies under Communist rule can be put under the following three headings: (a) Stagnation and inefficiency, hence low productivity of the economy as a result of rigid centralization, suppression of initiative under bureaucratic direction, and subordination of the economy totally to political goals; (b) Overgrowth of the semiorganismic Party-state. Destruction of privacy and deprivation of freedom and the rights to express group interest and to form organizations and agencies outside the sphere of control of the Party and state; (c) Subordination of all East European societies under the control of the Soviet Union.

Proponents of the socialism with a human face assume that within it the spheres of economic and political systems will become more separate and autonomous. At the same time they will be subordinated to social, rather than to state, control.

Relieved from impeding subordination and control of the state and the political order, the economic system will be put on the track of work on the basis of profitability and principal economic rationality. It will remain as a planned economy but the plans will be flexible and based on consultation with the population. Diverse political parties promoting diverse directions of economic development within a general socialist frame will be allowed. Thus, the economy will become considerably decentralized, which will lead to increased productivity as a result of the stimulation and rewarding of initiative both by prestige and economic gratifications. Political democracy will be introduced, and it will be based on a multiparty-system buttressed by a complex network of representatives of various interest groups. Freedom of expression and of organization will be established, and it will become the source of initiative and development. Nations and national states will regain political independence, and thus the lines of development and of structuralization of diverse societies will differ considerably.

This is a vision not of a perfect society, but of a society which will differ both from the capitalist and Communist states and societies, of a society which will provide more chances for anyone. The problem is that the ways leading to it have not yet been discovered.

Some say that it is not worth the effort since it will be a society with conflicts and social stratification; thus, it will still resemble capitalism. Others say that the people of Eastern Europe and other parts of the world are so weary of experiments with socialism that it is not certain whether they would choose such a socialism even if they are offered the choice. The question is whether they will ever have the choice. The case of socialism with a human face is discussed here as an example of a program of liberation of the economy from the domination of the political system and of the political system from the semiorganismic stiffening order of the Party-state.

vi

The Fifth Approach: Modernization

Factum abiit, monumenta manent—The event is past, the memorial of it remains. So says an old Roman saying. Thus the huge body of modernization theories will remain for posterity as a monument of a collective effort by social scientists to respond to the pressing needs of modernization and the development of new nations. It is certainly more a monument to an effort than to a success, but as another Latin proverb says, *Nihil est enim simul et inventum et perfectum*—Nothing is ever invented and brought to perfection at once.

Modernization is a peculiar form of societal development. It is not a new phenomenon, although the term was not used in the past as frequently as it is now.* To be sure, it was used more to discuss the introduction of new technology and new organization and less in regard to nations and social processes. The interest in new nations sparked the interest in the theory of modernization. Thus the concept was coined first. It provided a convenient vehicle by which sociologists and political scientists could return to problems and discussions on societal development which had been abandoned earlier, without at the same time creating a need to use the devaluated ideas connected with an earlier understanding of the process of development. In any case, "modernization" does not contain any organismic implications such as "development" and "growth" could have.

At the end of the 1960's numerous studies appeared propounding various retrospective and perspective theories on the process of moderni-

---

* In some parts of this chapter I am exploiting ideas expressed by me before in several articles.

zation, announcing that modernization is actually omnipresent and ever-lasting, but that in spite of this fact, in some societies and under certain conditions, it does not proceed as fast as would be desirable. Conclusions from these works were meant to be instrumental in the formulation of prospective theories of development for new nations and were meant to generate policies which would accelerate the spread of modernization. The interest in the topic became so widespread, and so many articles and books were written on the subject that separate volumes of bibliographies are now published on the subject.[1]

1. Modernization: The Concept

In conventional usage, "to modernize" means to "render something old fashioned up to date" or "to reshape something out of date to suit the requirements of modern times." Thus people speak of modernization as characterizing all efforts to bring technology, ways of life, social organization, art, modes of production, and even fashion up to date. The scholarly understanding of the concept, however, does not necessarily correspond to this meaning. Thus, problems of modernization are most often treated descriptively, and the concept is defined projectively and arbitrarily.

In his lengthy work, Marion Levy, Jr., assumes that modernization is a phenomenon that may appear in a more or less intensive form, and that it is therefore gradeable. "A society will be considered more or less modernized," says Levy, "to the extent that its members use inanimate sources of power and/or use tools to multiply the effects of their efforts. Neither of these elements is either totally absent from or exclusively present in any society."[2] While he declares himself unable to suggest exact criteria by which to measure the continuum of modernization, Levy postulates that one can safely distinguish between the relatively modernized countries (the United States, the Soviet Union, England, and France) and those which still have a long way to go in this respect (Burma, India, Ceylon, and some Latin American countries). He, therefore, introduces a division of all societies into the "relatively modernized" and the "relatively nonmodernized."

It was only the last half century which witnessed the emergence of societies which (1) base their manufacturing technology to a greater extent on inanimate power than on animate power, and where even the social organization is based on technical facilities, and which (2) in order to multiply the effects of their efforts apply such complex tools that considerable qualifications are required before working with them, and the slightest difference in a worker's skill may considerably lower or increase their productivity. Levy thus concludes that the existence of relatively modernized societies is a new phenomenon, especially characteristic of modern times.

In his fine essay "Tradition and Modernity Reconsidered," Reinhard Bendix starts out with a somewhat different set of assumptions.[3] He points to the need for examining the developmental processes, and the processes of modernization and industrialization as well, from the viewpoint of factors of timing and sequence. Because of these factors, he says, these processes are unique in every case; modernization cannot occur twice in the same way. We cannot expect the present processes of modernization to be analogous to the past ones, nor can we expect that the industrialization which usually accompanies modernization will have the same effects in the countries now being modernized as it had in the countries that were already industrialized some time ago.

In Bendix's opinion, a basic element in the definition of modernization is that it pertains to the kind of social changes which have occurred since the eighteenth century—changes which have led to political or economic "breakthroughs" in some pioneering societies and which have subsequently caused changes in follower societies. Thus Bendix tells us that in the process of modernization there are always "advanced model countries" and "follower countries." In his opinion, when we speak of modernization, we usually mean the processes of social change similar to those which originated during the industrial revolution in England (1760-1830), and the political revolution in France (1789-1794). These processes transformed England and France into "model" or "pace setter" countries; they were the most highly developed economically, socially, and politically. Other countries strove to catch up with these two; using every "shortcut" they could think of, they were thus able to achieve the level of the model country in a much shorter time. Because of its industrial achievements, England served as a model country for France. Previously, Holland and Sweden, due to their highly developed cannon-making techniques, had served as models for England. In all these cases, the follower country not only followed the experience of the model country, but also used "shortcuts" to catch up with it. Modernization has always consisted of internal changes in a country's economy and structure, but the internal changes have always been consequences of striving to attain the level of the model country. In all modernization processes, says Bendix, the government plays a particularly important role, since it initiates and stimulates modernization, obviously using different methods in different situations. Moreover, the greater the gap between the model and the follower country, the stronger, the role played by the government in the process. Finally, the wide development of communications media puts a premium on education as a means of modernization, because it is more easily available than the capital required for modern technology.

Other writers view modernization as a process of sustained growth or development after the point of "take-off." At the same time, however, it was pointed out that a mere destruction of traditional cultures and structures does not automatically produce modernity, that new regimes which appear with modern façades sometimes have to be embedded in societies which have retained many traditional qualities. Furthermore, although governments and regimes based upon such structures are unstable and shaky, there cannot be a return to the past.[4] Finally, many writers have recently pointed out that traditions continue to have a strong grip on societies, even after they have crossed the Rubicon to modernity; they especially have the capacity to permeate the new culture and structure, and regenerate even after it seems that they have disappeared forever. In many Asian societies tradition and modernity especially seem to be inseparable. Modernity embraces the traditional order, and the traditional culture permeates the new social and political structures, often exercising a strong impact on the functions of the modern economy.[5] Opinions are divided at this point. Some experts think that even though such societies are strongly rooted in the traditional order, they are nonetheless modern; others take the opposite view, arguing that modernity under such circumstances is only a façade.

While some writers nowadays tend to regard any process of development as modernization, others (as, for instance, J. A. Ponsioen) say that modernization by itself does not mean anything as long as one does not specify exactly what modern standards are.[6] Notwithstanding the fact that his entire book is actually an attempt to explain what these standards are and how to achieve them, Ponsioen shuns the use of the term "modernization" and instead persistently speaks about "development."

David E. Apter's work contains a complex analysis of the multitudinous aspects and problems to both the theory and the practice of modernization.[7] Apter considers the topic on different levels of abstraction. Explorations of exemplary cases are built into the discussion. Thus he combines normative, behavioral, structural, and functional dimensions and allows the reader to look at the same issues simultaneously from diverse angles. Structure is treated dynamically as a process, and process as a permutation of one structure into another. Great importance is attributed to the impact of traditional cultures on the attitude toward modernization, and diverse cases are examined which illustrate the problems. Finally, Apter introduces a typology of systems of political modernization as alternative instruments for inducing and promoting the transformation of modernizing societies. Thus he distinguishes systems of mobilization, reconciliation, theocratic and military oligarchy, and neo-mercantilism. I will return to some of these points in the course of further discussion. At this time it is pertinent to recall Apter's general statement on the nature of modernization. He says:

> Development, modernization, and industrialization, although related phenomena, can be placed in a descending order of generality. Development, the most general, results from the proliferation and integration of functional roles in a community [defined earlier in this study as growing systemness]. *Modernization is a particular case of development.* Modernization implies three conditions—a social system that can constantly innovate without falling apart (and that includes among its essential beliefs the acceptability of change); differentiated, flexible social structures; and a social framework to provide the skills and knowledge necessary for living in a technologically advanced world. Industrialization, a special aspect of modernization, may be defined as the period in a society in which the strategic functional roles are related to manufacturing. It is possible to attempt the modernization of a given country without much industry, but it is not possible to industrialize without modernization.[8]

The following instances of development can be distinguished: (a) Industrial modernization as development; (b) Nonindustrial modernization as development; (c) Premodernizational development. The application of these distinctions would allow us to treat modernization as a special, important instance of the development of societies, an instance where conscientious efforts are made to achieve higher chosen standards.

In this chapter, as in other parts of this book, I have adopted the method of discussing elements from the theories of other writers as opinions on the subject at hand, and as blocks of material with which to structure my own theory. Instead of exposing the "bad guys" against the "good guys," my method is to discuss elements of relevant theories as complements of one another. It is an attempt to account for various factors, aspects, and evaluations, and a means by which to approach the topic from various points and with a wide perspective. The preceding presentation on some views on the essence of the process of modernization should suffice to adumbrate the subject in the spirit outlined above. It should also provide enough material for a further, more detailed analysis of the various aspects of the processes of modernization. By drawing some conclusions from the theories of modernization which have already been introduced and by introducing some new points, we may say that the term "modernization" denotes a process of bridging the gap between the level of development in a society (or in some sphere of its life) and a more advanced and modern form already achieved in the spheres of life in other societies. It is a process which aims at standards in the patterns of behavior, modes of action, ways of thinking which are regarded as more up-to-date, more rational (if fashion is excluded), more profitable and generally more instrumental. It is thus a striving for successes already attained by a reference group or "pace setter."

When we speak of the modernization of new nations (and this is the connotation in which the concept is now most often applied), it is to indicate those developmental processes or measures which are meant to transform these countries into up-to-date nations. Thus, modernization is not a self-sustaining evolutionary process progressing on its own. Rather, it is a process of emulation, of the transplantation of patterns and products from the achievements of other countries to one's own. It is a striving to equalize one's own level of development with the most advanced and modern achievements of others. As Bendix has pointed out, there are always model and follower countries (or model and follower groups) involved in this process.* However, this is not a case of slavish copying, of the blind acceptance of somebody else's achievements, but an effort to achieve the desirable results in a way suited to one's own needs and conditions. What is even more important is that in the course of "following," the follower countries or groups often invent new, more efficient modes of action which allow them to outrun the previous pace setter, as well as to establish new patterns of modernity which are not necessarily in the same sphere as the previous leading country had established. This does not mean, however, that the process of modernization is a sort of international race, or even an organized competition. Sometimes it is a run for life. Other times, it is a mutual challenge. In still other cases, modernization is a striving for a better way to live.

For a comparative analysis one can even design a sort of semimeasurement of the distance between the pace setter and the followers. Thus the gap between the model country (or sector or group) and the follower can be measured on a time scale. The gap is equivalent to the number of years the former took to evolve from the level of development now represented by the latter to its present level. In other words, the gap between the model country X and the follower country Y is twenty years if twenty years ago country X looked more or less the way country Y looks today. This is said, of course, without illusions that this is a truly quantitative

* Some writers who challenge this view argue that terms such as "developed," "leading," "pace setter," "pioneering," and "following" contain strong ideological implications. They argue that modernization is a universal fact. Every society is modernizing, and the universal, worldwide community is continuously advancing and modernizing. In this understanding of the term, however, modernization obtains the same meaning as development in the theories on the general cultural evolution of humanity.

method for the comparative analysis of modernization. It should help only as a contrast.

A necessary prerequisite for all modernization processes is contact and communication among various societies, so that they can constantly compare their respective achievements in different fields. It may generally be said that modernization in Europe—that is, the closing of the gap between one European country and another—has involved appreciable changes in the modes of production and technology, and particularly in the replacement of animate power with inanimate power; not only have these countries experienced rapid scientific development, but what is more important, they have taken over others' scientific achievements in order to produce their own even more advanced achievements. Thus it is justifiable to some extent to view the introduction of technological innovations on the one hand, and the spread of education and the growth of scientific (including the social sciences) on the other hand, as the most salient symptoms of modernization. Again the intensity of modernization may be ranked in correlation to the volume of investments made and the scientific progress achieved. It is worth pointing out that technical innovations and the generation of new scientific knowledge are the very two fields of activity which have the most explicit developmental appearance. Modernization is not, of course, confined to those two kinds of changes, but consists in manifold transformations with a pervasive influence on all spheres of social life and culture. In Europe, it was either changes in the modes of production and technical innovations which spearheaded processes of social and political change, or, conversely, it was social and political reforms and revolutions which paved the way for technical innovations and economic growth. Although it is possible to speak of the modernization of social relations, patterns of behavior, or the style of organization, in modern times in Europe and America, at least, innovations in production have been inseparable attributes of modernization.

Also typical of the European processes of modernization was the comparative insignificance in the gap between the model societies or sectors and the follower societies or sectors when compared to analogous differences now obtaining in the Third World. In the process of modernization which occurred in nineteenth- and twentieth-century Europe, the gap between the model countries and the follower countries ranged from a few years to 40 or 50, or 100 years at the very most, and it was usually bridged in relatively short periods of time. In addition, in many cases the same country was a "follower" of modernization in one sphere and a "pace setter" in another. The gap between the Third World countries and their model countries is much greater. While the gap is bridged in some areas

—for instance, as a result of the spread of education in the new nations after they have acquired independence—it still keeps widening in other respects, due to the now even faster development of the industrialized countries. It is true that in European societies as well modernization did not advance evenly in all spheres of life, that it advanced while clusters of backwardness and underdevelopment still lagged behind; however, the process on the whole was more or less comprehensive. In the Third World countries, and especially in Africa, modernization is not comprehensive. It very strongly affects some spheres of life, some institutions and geographical areas, while other areas undergo modernization very slowly. Thus the internal gap between the pace setters and the followers and potential followers is also widely stretched.

Finally, there is still another, highly important difference: Third World countries usually modernize without industrialization. If they are partially in pace with industrialization, it is a different kind than the one in eighteenth- and nineteenth-century Europe and America. In any case, industrialization is not the main gate for new nations into the modern era. African and Asian nations usually begin the process of modernization with nation-building and the elevation of modern political systems. They aim at a transformation of their social structure, a spread of new norms and values. They disseminate education, while the local industry is developed only very slightly, and grows only later. While industrialization in Europe gave birth to modernization, in Africa and Asia the present modernization processes may—though not in all cases—create favorable conditions for the industrialization that will come.

The Klondike atmosphere which surrounded modernization theories in the fifties and early sixties now seem to have passed. The mood has changed. More and more writers discuss the problems of modernization under the heading of "Is it worth it?" They point out that modernization has neither brought happiness nor reduced tensions, that on the contrary, it intensified them in many instances. Why enter the rat race if the prize is illusory? Is it worth it, they ask, to strive intensively, to struggle for the right to live in the iron cages of bureaucratic orders in polluted, crime-ridden societies? There is something more important for which to struggle: the preservation of traditions and traditional cultures. It is there that one should search for the source of new living, they say. Modernization? If so, then at least not the sort that occurred in Europe, the Soviet Union, and America.

A strange transmogrification in attitudes thus seems to be under way. The radicals preach conservation and conservatism and call for an orientation toward traditions and the past. The conservatives call for an incessant striving toward revolutionary modernization and transformation.

The pace setters and reference groups, though still striving for higher standards of living, become more and more regarded as objects of warning. Thus modernization becomes a process of learning—learning about the vices and virtues in the achievements of others—and a process of paving the roads and bridges into the future of new nations with blocks of concentrated experience from other nations. These are often very winding roads. Although they seem to lead in the same direction as the roads which were already passed by industrial nations, all posters and signs along the way say the old roads lead nowhere. The new ones lead into a new past.

Nullum est jam dictum quod non dictum sit prius—Nothing can be said now that has not been said before, says an old Roman maxim. Thus, although the concept and theory of modernization are relatively new in origin and the writers on the subject do not refer to any predecessors, some resemblances and parallels can nonetheless be traced between modernization theories and other theories from the past. I refer in particular to the so-called diffusionist theories in cultural anthropology. In England the trend was represented by E. Smith and W. J. Perry; in Germany, where it flourished most, its representatives were F. Graebner, L. Frobenius, P. W. Schmidt, and numerous others. In the United States a number of distinguished scholars can be listed as adherents of this school. The diffusionists were not interested in the prospects of development in the future; rather, they were concerned with development in the past. In their interpretation, the whole process of development in traditional societies (and they most often considered traditional societies) was but a process of the migration of cultures, borrowings, superimpositions, transmissions of objects and elements of civilizations which inspired and catalized the generation of new developments in new places. They tended to distinguish a number of centers of origin of civilizations, out of which, in their opinion, the changes spread circularly into new places.

The early functionalists were the major opponents of the theory of cultural diffusion. Their primary argument was that similar objects of culture, similar structures, and similar systems could have been developed in different places independently. Most of the diffusionist argument could in fact no longer be sustained. At the beginning of the twentieth century critics were able to disprove a great many of their beliefs. Yet even if the naïve claims contained in such theories about the spread of worldly culture from just a few leading centers or about the superiority of some people above others can be disregarded, there is still something left to be learned from the diffusionists. Even if the diffusionist theory as a whole was wrong, some observations made by writers of that trend may yet be valuable for studies which construct theories of modernization.

Another theory worth mentioning in connection with this discussion is W. F. Ogburn's theory on cultural lag.[9] Especially useful for comparative analysis of modernization in diverse spheres is his point that changes in the material culture often outdistance the ways of using the products of change. Thus, different elements of the culture—and different systems as well—develop at a different pace, producing periods of maladjustment, or, as Ogburn called it, culture lag.

After this general review of the concept and general understandings of the process of modernization, I now wish to proceed with a discussion of the various aspects of modernization by examining the case of modernization of Sub-Saharan Africa.

2. Three Forms of Modernization in Sub-Saharan Africa

Analyzing the various historical phenomena and modernization processes in Africa, we can in general claim that modernization occurred in one of three ways: (1) As a consequence of the industrialization of a country (industrialization itself is a very important process of modernization, as Apter has already pointed out). Industrialization generates a lag which necessitates a change in the attitudes and behavior producing a new value-orientation. Changes in values and motivations in turn generate further industrialization. (2) Spontaneously, as the consequence of a confrontation between the more developed or somewhat developed societies and cultures and the less developed ones. (3) As a result of a purposeful, planned governmental activity, which aims at uplifting the economy and the culture to the level considered as most modern; this can be done because of the dissemination of education and scientific achievements from the rest of the world, and in general it means patterning one's way of life after that of a country or countries or other reference groups that are considered worthy of being followed. Once started, modernization tends to spread and penetrate ever wider strata of society.

It is pertinent to begin the discussion of modernization in Sub-Saharan Africa with an analysis of that area in the precolonial era. Such an analysis should explore, among other things, the mutual cultural impacts of diverse tribal groups and precolonial states and the exchanges between Africa and other continents at those times. However, since data on that subject are extremely scant, and pure speculations on such a sensitive and complex issue are pointless, we have to begin with the early period of colonialism.

By including Africa in their spheres of influence and commercial activity, the colonial powers infected Africa with the germ of European modernization. At the same time, however, the colonial system and all the implications which resulted from it precluded the possibility of modernizing Africa in a comprehensive and thorough way. In order to rule Africa, the colonialists and the colonial administrations had to change her. It was in their interest, however, to see to it that modernization affected only a small part of the population, and only superficially at that. Colonialism was dependent on modernization, but too much modernization meant the end of colonialism. Diverse policies were adopted by the different colonial authorities in the pursuit of their objectives.* Wage labor, private ownership of land, missionary activities, school education, the employment of Africans in lower level white-collar jobs, commerce organized by Europeans and Asians, attitudes and patterns of behavior characteristic of and displayed by the functionaries of colonial administration and the foreign settlers, the introduction of colonial legislation—all these things gave an initial impetus to modernization, and at the same time they generated protest, and struggle against colonialism.

The process of modernization might be said to culminate in the struggle for national liberation, which the African nations use as a means to broaden and deepen it. The struggle for independence was, on the one hand, one of the new, worldwide, overlapping revolutions; on the other hand, it was an era of transition to a wide new period of modernization organized by the African governments themselves. The spontaneous drive to fight against misery and economic backwardness and for independence was born during colonial rule: it is now being transformed in the independent states into a conscious effort (and in some countries a planned effort) toward growth and development. Three forms or models of modernization since the beginning of colonialism in Sub-Saharan Africa can be characterized as follows:

The industrialization of a country and the construction of new enterprises considerably steps up employment. Apart from causing changes in the modes of production, increasing productivity, and replacing animate power with technical equipment, industrialization also leads to manifold social changes. Employment outside the field of agriculture increases. The family ceases to be the unit of productive organization, and the production process itself comes to be separated from family affairs. As industrialization progresses, the entire social structure undergoes a profound change, social mobility intensifies, new patterns of social strati-

* As we know, the French colonial policy was based on three fundamental goals: assimilation (or the transformation of Africans into "black Frenchmen"); association (or the transformation of the colonial territories into overseas departments of France), and paternalism. The Portuguese colonial policy was similar. So was the British colonial policy, although it was based on a system of indirect rule, aimed at a partial change of the traditional sociopolitical system; it thus contained elements of modernization.

fication come into being, and the urbanization drive gains momentum.

Industrialization creates new material conditions and needs, stimulates the adoption of new attitudes and value orientations, and produces a new social division of labor and exchange of services. Along with the rise in industrialization, a complementary interdependence in societal structures develops; new roles, organizations, and systems of activity become differentiated. Modernization of this type arises out of the necessity to adapt the social organization to the requirements of industry. It might thus be called *industrial modernization.* So far, it has not been a frequent phenomenon in Sub-Saharan Africa. Where it did happen, it mostly sprang up from the development of the mining industries.

Quite different is the type of modernization which emerges from a confrontation between two diametrically different cultures—from the emulation by people of one culture of the patterns of behavior accepted in another, from the spread of information about the way of life in other countries, and, finally, from the dissemination of a system of education which originated in another country and which was designed for the youth raised in another culture. This type of modernization develops as a process of selective transplanting of particular elements from other cultures into Africa and subsequently incorporating them into the traditional, homogeneous cultural setting. This does not lead to the replacement of the old institutions or products by the new ones; occasionally the process enriches the traditional culture with new, heterogeneous elements, but very often it leads to its impoverishment, deformation, and, in some instances, to all kinds of cultural and social abnormalities.

Thus the superimposition of the foreign culture on the traditional culture created a new semidevelopmental, buffer culture, belonging neither to the traditional African society nor to the foreign culture alone. It promoted a duality of norms, patterns of behavior, attitudes, and structural affiliations. It implied that people could behave according to the norms of the old culture or of the new one, depending on the circumstances. A whole world of syncretic phenomena is generated by the buffer culture: new languages, religions, and social and cultural institutions appear within it. Under such conditions, modernization amounts primarily to processes that social anthropologists call "acculturation."[10] I shall here call it *acculturative modernization.* It, too, may lead to profound changes; it may especially cause the breakdown of static traditional societies under the pressure of new social divisions and new cultural elements.

Acculturative modernization was typical of the colonial systems when the traditional African cultures found themselves under particularly strong pressure from the cultures of the colonialists. It is more a seduction than an introduction to modernization, and the basic means of that seduction is money. The African was shown the "supreme" virtues and pleasures of European life—in this case, the pleasures available to the colonial administrator. He was told that such pleasures are for sale should he have money. Of course, not all forms of pleasure were open to him; some were reserved for Europeans only. Still others were available in return for certain services. Pecuniary taxes were imposed on the African population; to pay them and to still have some money to spend on the cheap products of European culture, the African had to modernize. He had to sell his services or his labor, or to raise crops especially wanted by the Europeans. Thus he became involved in the process of modernization and industrialization which was advancing somewhere far away. He was on the fringe of it, and he contributed to it with his blood and sweat. In return he was given some gadgets of white culture. He proudly wore and used them in the hopes that it would increase his status in the tribal society. He did not know that the gadgets and the money that he received were the kiss of death to his tribal identity, and were at the same time a sign of his inferiority, for he had been thus marked by the strangers.

The acculturated African became a superior inferior, a man between cultures. He did not belong, so he had to produce his own buffer culture to isolate himself from both the vituperating adulation of the tribal society and the burning contempt of the detestable foreigners. He had to develop his own identity to differ from both that of the tribal Africans and the Europeans. Thirty years ago, Bronislaw Malinowski, who is sometimes accused of being in the service of British colonialism, characterized the buffer culture as a unique cultural phenomenon, a product that cannot again be subdivided into separate European and African parts. It is a product of the interpenetration of elements of two different races and cultures. He points out that to understand the process we should begin with a hypothesis that one culture absorbs the elements of the other. However, this is not a satisfactory explanation. The process is in fact much more complex.

> What really takes place is an interplay of specific contact forces: race prejudice, political and economic imperialism, the demand for segregation, the safeguarding of a European standard of living, and the African reaction to all this. . . . No sorting of elements is possible; no invoicing back to a previous culture as an element of reality. For we have to deal with a vast phenomenon which in its essence is defined by a set of economic, legal, and social arrangements which have arisen in response to a new need. . . . The fallacy of regarding such a phenomenon as a heap of fragments "borrowed" from Black and White parent cultures is evident.[11]

Malinowski goes on to point out that one can draft a long list of what we have given to Africa. Yet, "it would be easy to see that it is not a matter of 'give' nor yet a matter of generous 'offering' but usually a matter of 'take.' "[12] Land was taken, men were shipped to America and other territories, the soul was taken, and the people changed as a result. When the intelligent Africans discover what is happening, they begin to look upon tribalism, "not as to be despised but as a symbol of their racial heritage, the nationalistic hopes, of a future cultural independence."[13] But it is too late. The tribal past is gone; there is no way to return to it. The only thing which is still possible is a struggle for a new way of life, for independence.

Acculturative modernization is a process of alienation. The African is alienated from his society and transformed into a superior inferior, as previously mentioned. He is told that since he has acquired some European habits he has become superior; at the same time, however, the European colonizer treats him as an inferior. The African who is still part of the traditional society looks upon him as a superior, since he has acquired an education, knows the European way of life, and is usually relatively rich. But he also sees him as an inferior who does not live in the old ways. The process of acculturative modernization is a process of detribalization; with detribalization there is gradual substitution of the old security once provided by the traditional, ascriptive allocation of roles and positions by a new security based on individual achievement within a new social and political organization of the society.

Of course, life in tribal societies was not idyllic. There were constant wars, food scarcities, the terror of elders and of tradition, and witch hunts. Yet to many Africans (and, indeed, to Black Americans today) it appears to have been beautiful. Some would like to restore it, without its ugly aspects, of course. But there is no return to the past, and modern Africans cannot become tribesmen again.

Colin M. Turnbull calls the alienated, acculturated African the lonely African. Both George Padmore and Ndabaningi Sithole describe the process of acculturation (or, as they say, assimilation) in nearly identical terms.[14] Sithole, a clergyman, freedom-fighter, and politician, writes that apart from its negative aspects, colonialism also performed a positive role. He characterizes the acculturated Africans as *assimilados*. Franz Fanon calls them men with a black skin and a white mask and he seeks the disalienation of the black man. Yet could such a disalienation come about simply by taking off the mask? The mask in the meantime has slowly, in a process of osmosis, become the face itself. There are no longer any faces behind the white masks. And although it is painful to live in a white mask, although one may scream from pain wearing it and with hatred against those who originally seduced him to try it, the mask

can no longer be taken off. To remove the mask is to take off the head.*
We are all born in the iron cage of civilization; there is no longer a world
outside it, and even if there were one, we would not be able to live in it.

Bernard B. Dadié, the brilliant writer of the Ivory Coast, has a marvelous story which I wish to retell in abbreviated form here. Once upon
a time the peaceful and prosperous life of the people under the rule of
Queen Poku was interrupted by an enemy attack. The enemy was numerous, and the people had to leave their fields and huts and run away
from the shores of the ocean rich with fish. They ran through a big forest,
and all the animals laughed at them. The enemy continued to persecute
them, so they ran faster and faster. Finally, they reached the shores of a
wide river. The crowd again began to sing the song of exile, but the
river rumbled and its waves rose as high as the peaks of the trees, over
and over again. Was it the same water which had fed them in the past?
Or was it now under the control of a bad spirit? Then the priest came
to the front and announced that the water was angry and would not be
satisfied until they gave her their dearest possession. People started to
throw golden necklaces and bracelets into the river, but the river rumbled just as before. "It does not want your jewelry; it wants him," said the
priest, pointing to the six-month-old prince whom the beautiful queen
was holding. The horrified mother embraced her boy. Then she smiled,
raised her child above her head and threw him into the abyss. The river
calmed down, and huge hippopotamuses formed a bridge across which
the people crossed to escape. The queen came last. She said, "Bauli!," and
this is now the name of the people.

* One could find many illustrations of this situation in modern African writings. Thus,
for instance, Robert Muema Mbato ("Identity," in *Bursara* /Nairobi/ Vol. 2, No. 3,
1969, pp. 31-34) is asking, in search of his identity, Who am I? "I am not a
Mkamba, yet I am Mkamba. I was born of Kamba parents. In my veins there flows
Kamba blood. . . . I know a number of Kamba customs, but what I know is so
little that I am ashamed. . . . Can I claim to be a European? A black European?
Now wait a minute! In my veins, there flows Kamba blood. My skin is black like a
Mkamba's. . . . And when I eat European food my stomach rebels. It wants most of
all the Kamba dish—*isyo*—maize with beans and green vegetables. . . .

I speak the English language. I write in English. I even dress like English people. In my best clothes, I look like an Englishman. I struggle hard to learn the manners of the English people. . . . I fall short of European customs and culture. When
they say 'Don't be silly,' I feel I have been insulted. Yet it's not so. When a daughter
kisses her father, my blood says 'Oh no!' It is odd to me. . . .

When I was a young boy, I was 'Kambanized.' I learned how to make bows and
arrows, the Kamba traditional weapons. . . . I don't know how to dance the traditional Kamba dances. I went to school too early to learn them. At school I learned
English and Scottish dances. Yet I don't know why the English and Scottish dances
are danced. . . .

What then, am I? A conglomeration of indigenous and borrowed ideas and
ideals. As such, I must find my footing in the whole nation, and indeed in the whole
human race. I am not a Mkamba, yet a Mkamba, in whose veins Kamba blood flows."

The acculturated African is the wonderful prince who has to be sacrificed for the sake of his people. The river which the people crossed is of no return. Ahead of them was the new land of independence, a land to be inhabited and built into prosperity.

The third form of modernization which takes place in Sub-Saharan Africa, to which I shall devote most of my attention here, is *induced modernization*. It consists of patterning a country's organizations, institutions, and value orientations after those of industrialized countries. However, while these were a product of industrialization itself in the industrial countries, in the new countries they are introduced irrespective of whether the process of industrialization has achieved any significant proportions, or whether it has even started at all. In a way, this is a process of introducing the consequences of the modernization of industrial countries without the groundwork which paved the way for it. I call it induced modernization because the changes and transformations—particularly in the sphere of social relations—which are involved, and which are usually government-initiated, lead to the acceptance in the new society of the norms, values, and organization of the industrial societies. Thus, this is a process induced by the existence of industrial societies elsewhere in the world.

Induced modernization consists of introducing modern forms of government and administration, education, universities, research institutes, universal suffrage, and communications media into an industrially underdeveloped country, without having previously industrialized the country. Induced modernization arises primarily out of the desire to catch up with the more developed societies, especially in the spheres of political organization and education, and partly because of the desire to have easy accessibility to the products of modern technical progress. The institutions created in the process of this kind of modernization are not only modeled on the most modern achievements in these spheres, but they are themselves meant to induce modernization processes in all other spheres of life—particularly in the sphere of economic growth, which will eventually lead to beginning the industrial era in the country. It is not a mere imitation of foreign patterns, but an effort at the maximal development of a country's own potential, so that it can achieve a high level of development by itself while employing the technology and methods invented by others.

Induced modernization germinated in the colonial past. In the colonial era, induced modernization could be seen in the creation of political parties apart from the colonial rule; the creation of African schools under native initiative apart from those run by missions or the colonial government; the birth of modern literature and the social sciences (especially history). Having once gained independence, the African countries carried out induced modernization in several ways: through social reforms which transformed the traditional society, by expanding the education system, creating a modern system of administration and state authorities, disseminating the achievements of modern scientific knowledge, organizing more productive processes in the rural areas, initiating systems of African entrepreneurs and state enterprises, and reorganizing the social structure with a special emphasis on the incorporation of all tribal groups into the ongoing birth development of the nation. In a sense induced modernization can be identified with nation-building. It is thus aimed at a transformation of the whole population into a new, self-contained entity, while a significant part of the traditional culture (norms, symbols, patterns of behavior, and parts of the social structure) is consciously preserved and even incorporated into the new one. The government and the ruling political party are the chief organizers and implementers of induced modernization.

Sub-Saharan Africa today is witness to all three forms of modernization, and they are taking place simultaneously. Industrial modernization is still of negligible significance in the overall process. Acculturative modernization, whether regarded as desirable or not, is still under way, though now in somewhat weakened form. Induced modernization plays the dominant part.

This division of the forms of modernization is based on logical differentiation. In practice, the elements of all three forms intermingle and sometimes even stem from one another. Thus, although this division cannot be considered as a classification, it might be considered as a base of classification criteria as in the following schematic diagram:

MODERNIZATION	SPONTANEOUS	ORGANIZED BY GOVERNMENT
Based on *industrialization*	Industrial modernization in capitalist societies	Industrial modernization in communist societies
Based on *cultural contact*	Acculturative modernization	Induced modernization

The towns are the centers of modernization processes. Here these processes appear in the most intensive forms, and it is from here that they spread to the rest of the country. In Europe the creation of towns was correlated with the industrialization process. Apart from its other social roles, urbanization was always a factor, as well as a consequence, of industrial modernization. In Africa (and also in Asia) cities and towns are now growing (and they grew in colonial times) irrespective of whether the country is industrialized or not. To be sure, they grow faster where the country is industrialized, but even when the country remains essentially rural, the population in urban areas is on the increase. Urbanization here is a product of extreme poverty in the rural areas. The majority of African urban dwellers are jobless migrants who are not fully urbanized. Those who come to towns, whether they find employment or not, acquire new attitudes, orientation, and needs.[15] Thus, towns and cities are hotbeds of modernization, and the migrants affected by it sow the seeds of modernization even in the communities which are still dominated by the traditional order.*

Each of the three forms of modernization (industrial, acculturative, and induced) develops through a differentiation of new roles, the establishment of specialized institutions, and the generation of specific kinds of interdependencies. These subsequently spread and encompass the body of society which had originally been an agglomeration of tribal units often only accidentally fitted together into a single government as a result of the colonial scramble. At the beginning of modernization, the roles are few, and the interconnections are far-reaching and tenuous; thus the network of interactions is rare. The units stick together as a whole either because they are coerced by the central authority, or because it is dangerous for all of them to fall apart, or out of sheer passivity since there is no one to care and it really does not much matter within whose frontiers they exist. Subsequently, however, stronger ties develop. Roles and organizations become connected, a network of institutions of authority is imposed over the whole territory, and it becomes bound by a set of roads and other channels of communication. The powers of social and political gravitation based on the balance of centrifugal and centripetal forces become more manifest. African societies are still economically underdeveloped, and the network of complementary economic interdependencies still consists of rare meshes and tenuous links, and only partial dependencies on the market since there is still a predominance of greatly self-sufficient agricultural units.

* As Lerner sees it, four phenomena which grow in dimension in the process of modernization are systematically related to one another—namely, urbanization, literacy, media participation, and political participation. Thus, for example, Lerner is of the opinion that a country cannot have modernized to any significant degree until at least 10 per cent of the population has come to adopt the urban style of life. Apter, in *The Politics of Modernization* (pp. 70-71), asserts that in comparative studies on modernization the following criteria should be used for a measurement of the degree of modernization: sets of key roles, growth indexes, career and entrepreneurship roles, technology, and national income.

In industrial modernization, the key roles are those of the entrepreneur, worker, inventor, and innovator. These roles may also appear in induced modernization, though in this case the roles of the politician, intellectual, and bureaucrat seem to be of particular importance. Although this does not necessarily happen in other situations, in these peculiar conditions when development is the target the politicians, bureaucrats, and intellectuals must have an innovative orientation. Acculturative modernization is put into effect primarily by the tradesman, migrant, student, and emancipated member of the tribal society.

In the course of modernization new forms of conflict are generated, and they subdivide the society which was originally divided by the conflicts of the traditional order. Apart from the conflicts which usually appear between those who are already caught by the spirit of innovation and modernization, conflicts also develop between the modernizers who are competing for achievements in their pursuits. Modernization destroys the old equilibrium or semiequilibrium based on tradition.

Acculturative modernization takes place amid castelike differences and wide discrepancies and social distance between the European colonizers and the African population. The colonizers and the local population are not components of one homogeneous social structure; they belong to two different societies and two different cultures. Industrial modernization results in the emergence of complex structures of class division. Induced modernization, as I have said, is realized primarily by political and educational means; thus, while economic growth gains in importance only at a later stage, social differentiation leads chiefly to the creation of elites. However, as suprastructures are created, and particularly as the process of economic growth gains momentum, the elites tend to change into the upper classes of society.

All forms of modernization spring primarily from the acceptance of a common set of values. This is one reason why the notion of modernization may be applied to all of them. Very important among the norms and sets of values common to all forms of modernization is the belief that innovations and changes are always desirable, creative processes. In addition to the norms common to all forms of modernization, there are also norms specific to each one of them. From another point of view, in the structure of roles distinguishable in each form of modernization, we may differentiate the roles of its initiators or organizers, its propagators (acting consciously or unconsciously in that capacity), and its consumers.[16]

Modernization processes develop through a diffusion of innovations which are either products of the given society or are derived from another society. However, they become factors of modernization only when they lead to still other innovations. As Zygmunt Bauman writes,

The truly developmental culture is one of continuous change and innovation and it differs from other cultures insofar as it (a) rewards at least one type of deviation (none of the known cultures rewards all types of deviations; approval of deviation is always selective, always based on a choice of a direction of development from among logically distinguishable possibilities); (b) continuously creates groups of people with deviation-type behavior; and (c) has created a mechanism for the assimilation, institutionalization of the selected deviations, i.e. for a continuous modification of the accepted standards and patterns of behavior not only without destroying the institutions of social control and sanctions, but with their active assistance. . . . Finally the acceptance of certain types of innovations must come to be reflected in the mentality typical of the developmental culture. This can only be achieved if the past is deprived of its authority over the present, and the positive stress is shifted from the old to the new. . . .[17]

We may also add that modernization gains in momentum when the new is subsequently able to find in the old some sources to sanction its endeavors and inspire its action as a continuity. A necessary prerequisite for the process of modernization is the social acceptance of selected deviations, which can thus change into institutionalized innovations. For modernization consists, among other things, in the absorption of innovations and in their transformation into norms.

3. Induced Modernization: Diverse Spheres of Activity

Induced modernization is organized from a center, and it therefore usually begins with political decisions. The leaders of new nations who initiate and organize the process of induced modernization have to face the following questions: (1) Diverse nations have achieved high standards of development by applying different policies in different ways. They have had and now have different economic and political organizations, and they differ in regard to the socioeconomic relations and structures which result from these previously mentioned differences. Taking into account the various criteria—the ideological, moral, economic values, the effective achievement of ends, and so forth—which of these nations should the aspiring country follow? (2) On the basis of an analysis of the experiences of industrialized societies is it possible to produce a new model to fit the needs of the African nations themselves, even though they cannot at once enter into a process of intensive industrialization? (3) What sort of political, social, and economic mechanisms have to be set in motion to achieve the goals and spread of modernization? (4) Is it possible to have modernization in one sphere without having it in other spheres? Especially important is the qusetion of whether a kind of modernization is possible which will not destroy certain values, norms, and relations which were inherited from traditional societies and which are highly cherished by the majority of Africans. How can they achieve a high standard of living for the population, a high national income, and general prosperity, while at the same time retaining some of the most important traditions and some elements of the traditional social order? Which part of the highly praised inheritance from the past should be sacrificed in order to attain modernization, and which should be retained even though it may impede modernization?

Answers to these and many other problems which the African leaders have to face must be included in a political formula, an ideology which contains a set of goals to be attained in the process of induced modernization and to be used as an incentive for organized action and the mobilization of the masses.[18] The very nature of inducement requires the possession of such an ideology. Parallel to the ideology, an institutional embodiment for organized action must be built, and a political system must be developed. Thus the governmental structure has to be organized and supplemented with an adequate administration. Decisions must be made concerning the political system, the party structure, and the degree of mass participation in politics. Finally, decisions concerning social and economic policies have to be made. It is a peculiar feature of the situation of the new nations that the political leadership (and very often the leader of the nation) has to make decisions about the direction and character of economic development.*

The process of political modernization can also be characterized differently. As C. E. Welch, Jr. describes it: "The process of political modernization has three major characteristics: (1) an increased centralization of power in the state, coupled with the weakening of traditional sources of authority; (2) the differentiation and specialization of political institutions; (3) increased popular participation in politics, and greater identification of individuals with the political system as a whole."[19] While the first two processes Welch mentions seem to have taken place in modern African states, the third seems to be dissipating.

After independence, most of the African states followed the advice of the French and British colonial administrations and attempted to establish political orders modeled upon the patterns of French or Britain respectively. It was very soon evident, however, that the parliamentary

* In addition, they have to be concerned with and solve mundane problems every other day, such as: How to remain in power; how to earn more money needed to satisfy their own needs and aspirations; how to maintain the administration and army in order to run the system.

multiparty systems of these countries did not fit the needs of African societies and could work there. Multiparty systems tended to become vehicles of tribal struggle. What the young African states needed most was unity. And the unity and cohesion with which the African leaders had to work was fragile. Thus, to preserve unity and to produce an effective instrument for modernization, practically all the African states turned to single-party rule. There was another aspect to the problem: jobs—and especially political jobs—were scarce. Those who were lucky enough to have a position—especially as a member of the government or a leader of a nation, with all the attached privileges—were anxious to keep it. In short, the single-party systems solidified the structure of political systems in the new African states.[20] They were instrumental in mobilizing the masses and raising the spirit of nationalism ("One party, one state, one nation!") Yet, they did not generate a climate conducive for genuine democracy.[21] Some African leaders say that African nations cannot afford to have democracy at that point of development.

Julius Nyerere, the enlightened president of Tanzania, has come up with some proposals for a new model of democracy based on a single party system and reflecting the spirit of the traditional African culture. According to Nyerere's proposal, elections have to be periodical, and a number of candidates have to compete for offices, even though they are from the same party. The choice should be made on the basis of the personal qualifications of the candidate. These ideas are similar to those of the proponents of socialism with a human face in Eastern Europe. Whether such a system will work well in Africa is difficult to say just now. It seems to be quite suitable for the present conditions. On the other hand, one should remember that candidates, especially in Africa, belong to certain groups, that is, extended families, tribes, and by virtue of such affiliations elections could easily be transformed into a competition among groups. The imperfect democracy which the West European societies now enjoy is a product of a long evolution. African states have been in existence for only ten or fifteen years, and this is much too short a time for a successful attempt to create a working political order which will at the same time reflect the spirit of tradition, unify the nation, plan and direct economic development, engage in the modernization of all spheres of life, and fulfill many other functions. And in addition there is a minimum of skilled personnel and a serious lack of experience.

After an incipient and short period of multiparty democracy, single-party systems were introduced in almost all African countries. Yet the period of single-party rule did not last long in many African countries either. It was succeeded by military upheavals. Altogether more than thirty military coups have taken place in Sub-Saharan Africa up to now.

Although the armies are usually small, they are the only well-organized large force. Military regimes usually dissolve the political parties, but retain the civil service and rule through it. The average man lives in the same way as he did before and the military leaders have to deal with the same problems that their civilian predecessors dealt with. Military rule does not solve the problems of corruption that army officers most often proclaim as their target. Life most often goes on as before. Military rule is certainly not a solution for the multitude of accumulated problems in the African societies. It must be realized, however, that the significance of military rule in Africa is different from that in Latin America, for instance. In Latin America upheavals are connected with social revolutions. Not so in Africa. Some theorists regard military rule as an impediment to modernization. Others who consider the example of the Young Turks and of some Arab cases claim that military forces could become strong and efficient modernizers. Neither the first nor the second belief can as yet be confirmed on the basis of the African experience. In some cases, such as Nigeria and the Congo, the size of the armies has increased under military regimes. Again, however, these countries passed through a period of civil war, and compared to other parts of the world, their armies are still small. For the time being, then, the evaluation of the consequences of military rule in Sub-Saharan Africa has to be postponed.

In the meantime, the political formula, the ideology of Africa political parties and governments, has changed considerably. Anticolonialism and nationalism were the propelling ideological formulas in the struggle for independence. Colonialism was overcome and nationalism retained by a generally anti-imperialist orientation. However, a new trend developed at the same time: the ideology of African socialism spread.[22] Many African governments today profess one or another kind of African socialism. As I have discussed earlier, socialism is in general understood here as a brotherhood and unity. The norm of egalitarianism is only rarely stressed, and even less so are the demands for various freedoms. It is true, however, that the more militant African governments include the postulate of struggle against exploitation into the concept of socialism, thus directing it against both foreign and African capitalists, if not entrepreneurs in general. In such countries a strong emphasis is placed on planning and on mobilizing the masses against imperialism in general, and internally for work in self-help schemes, cooperation, and other projects. This is a socialism promoted by governments not by people and revolutionary oppositions.

Some African leaders prefer the Western societies as their models for their development, while others look to the East European nations and the Soviet Union. In either case, however, although they regard these societies and their political orders as models, they stress that they are actually aiming at building different political orders which better reflect the needs of their own societies.

Several diverse types of political systems can be differentiated in new nations (including the African countries) after taking account of all the above factors—the inclinations of a new nation to associate itself with one or another of the big powers, the prevailing features of the developing political order, the ideologies used for the rationalization of political action and decision-making, the methods and degree to which a government uses coercion and information to maintain authority and stability and to increase efficiency, and still other characteristics. David E. Apter's classification of political systems types is most often used. Apter proposes to distinguish between political systems patterned on the sacred-collectivity model and those patterned on the secular-libertarian model. Especially stressing the structural dynamics, he proposes to distinguish among the mobilization system, modernizing autocracy, neomercantilist system, and reconciliation system.[23]

Political modernization in Sub-Saharan Africa is still basically a process of nation-building and the generation of national identities. It is not at the moment a process of growing mass participation in the decision-making processes of the new states. African countries are ruled by small groups—either party leaderships, elites in government, or army regimes. Apart from this, political modernization is important as a process by which to induce modernization in other spheres of life, especially in the transformation of rural life. This is still an incipient process, but this is where wide modernization has to actually begin if it is to become dominant in the society.

It is very difficult to assess the progress in economic development and modernization of the independent states. Books on the economic development of Africa are primarily concerned with problems that have to be solved and not with the assessment of results. Reliable data on economic development are not readily available. Once data are obtained, it is even more difficult to compare them and to draw any relevant conclusions from them. The table which follows may to some extent help in the assessment. The problems are complex and numerous indeed, and since I cannot devote enough time to present their complexity, it would be better to direct the reader to an excellent book on the subject and to limit myself to a few very general comments.[24]

In general it can be said that African countries have not yet entered the take-off stage. Industries are few, and basically of two kinds, mining and the production of basic commodities for local consumption. In most African countries the stress is on agricultural development and on build-

Gross National Product in 1965 Prices[25]

A. Total GNP
(Million Dollars)

Country	Annual Growth Rate[a] (Percent)	1960	1961	1962	1963	1964	1965	1966[E]	Exchange Rate Per US Dollar
Ethiopia	3.5[b]	n.a.	1,020	1,050	1,090	1,131	1,171	1,212	2.500 Ethiopian dollars
Ghana	2.6	1,919	1,980	2,087	2,142	2,203	2,210	2,237	0.714 cedis
Kenya	5.4	786	787	859	908	966	985	1,080	7.143 shillings
Morocco	2.3	2,228	2,152	2,395	2,543	2,572	2,606	2,555	5.060 dirhams
Nigeria[c]	5.0	3,809	3,927	4,146	4,310	4,548	4,852	5,115	0.357 pounds
Rhodesia, Southern	0.5	910	934	933	940	967	1,022	940	0.357 pounds
Sierra Leone	n.a.	n.a.	n.a.	n.a.	319	340	353	n.a.	0.714 leones
South Africa Rep.[d]	6.4	8,006	8,195	8,805	9,666	10,390	10,940	11,610	0.714 rands
Sudan[e]	3.6	1,175	1,181	1,330	1,339	1,359	1,387	1,453	0.348 pounds
Tanganyika	4.2	617	594	637	657	709	730	789	7.143 shillings
Tunisia	4.1	734	784	797	817	882	933	935	0.525 dinars
Uganda	3.6	554	545	545	604	633	667	686	7.143 shillings
Zambia	6.5	594	605	590	609	671	842	867	0.357 pounds

For explanations of a, b, c, d, e, E, n.a., see *Note* on table on the next page.

B. Per Capita GNP[25]
(Dollars)

Country	Annual Growth Rate[a] (Percent)	1960	1961	1962	1963	1964	1965	1966[E]	Exchange Rate Per US Dollar
Ethiopia	2.0[b]	n.a.	48	49	50	51	52	53	2.500 Ethiopian dollars
Ghana	-0.1	283	284	292	292	292	286	282	0.714 cedis
Kenya	2.4	97	94	100	103	106	105	112	7.143 shillings
Morocco	-0.5	192	179	194	201	198	196	186	5.060 dirhams
Nigeria[c]	2.8	99	100	103	105	109	114	117	0.357 pounds
Rhodesia, Southern	-2.6	250	248	340	234	234	240	214	0.357 pounds
Sierra Leone	n.a.	n.a.	n.a.	n.a.	139	146	149	n.a.	0.714 leones
South Africa, Rep.[d]	3.9	445	445	468	502	526	541	561	0.714 rands
Sudan[e]	0.8	101	99	108	106	104	104	106	0.348 pounds
Tanganyika	2.1	67	63	66	67	71	72	76	7.143 shillings
Tunisia	2.8	177	186	187	190	202	211	209	0.525 dinars
Uganda	1.2	83	80	78	84	86	83	89	7.143 shillings
Zambia	3.4	185	183	174	174	186	227	226	0.357 pounds

Note: Data shown for those countries where GNP estimates are available on trend basis. Such estimates are necessarily crude and are unadjusted for inequalities in purchasing power among countries. Excluding South Africa, countries listed represent 59% of the estimated GNP of less developed Africa in 1965. Including South Africa, countries listed represented 70% of the estimated GNP of all Africa in 1965 (LDC's listed 43%, South Africa 27%).

E—Estimate.   n.a.—Not available.

a—Average annual rate 1960 to 1966.   b—For 1961 to 1966.

c—Fiscal years beginning April 1.   d—Includes Botswana, Lesotho, South-West Africa and Swaziland.   e—Fiscal years ending June 30.

Source: AID estimates based on country publications.

Agricultural Production
(Index: 1957-59 = 100)

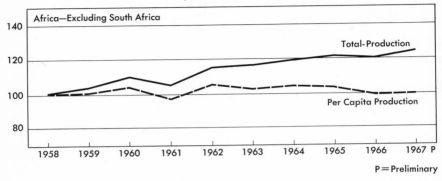

Production of Selected Commodities Total-Production
(Index: 1958 = 100)

ing the infrastructure to some extent. Although the agricultural output has increased substantially in most cases, it cannot be assessed adequately, partially due to the fact that it is difficult to account for the rise in producer's consumption, and partially because even though African countries now produce more, prices on their main agricultural commodities are often lower than they were in the past. Thus, even though they produce more, they do not receive more money in return for their exports. The number of wage and salary earners has increased, yet this is not a good indicator of economic changes since these are often employees of the administration, police, or army. The rate of unemployment is high. In conclusion, African countries have increased their production (especially in agriculture); the number of wage and salary earners is now greater than before their independence; and more people are involved in market relations, but it is still difficult to speak about significant economic change and development.* Yet even these developments have resulted in important social changes and have especially led to a more intensive generation of two separate classes—the African entrepreneurs and the African peasantry.

It is in the development of education that African governments have achieved the greatest success, and education is truly the spearhead for any other modernization there. According to UN data, prior to independence in all the territories of so-called French West Africa only about 5 per cent of school-age children were attending classes.** In French Equatorial Africa the figure was only 2.5 per cent, and in Portuguese territories, even less than 1 per cent. Under British rule the percentages were somewhat higher.

The data on education in Africa (excluding South Africa) tell us that in 1968 there were 19,227,000 pupils in primary schools and 1,615,000 pupils in secondary schools; together they comprised 8 per cent of the African population (compare this with U.S. figures, where 25 per cent of the population are regarded as pupils). In addition 221,000 Africans are listed as being in vocational schools. Most of the major African countries now have their own universities; Nigeria has a number of them. Literacy in general went up from roughly 5 per cent prior to independence to 20 per cent at the end of the 1960's.[27]

A. Peshkin and R. Cohen assert that

> Economic development is, perhaps, the predominant goal of social change in the developing nations; in fact, at times it appears that other types of change are advocated solely for their contribution to economic change rather than as valid ends in themselves. In many instances, changes in economic values provide the impetus to value change in other categories. National governments develop, transportation and communication systems evolve, and modified social structures appear in response to needs and goals in the national economy.[28]

Although this concept also applies to Africa, it is the party-state and the education system that have to be regarded as the principal institutional instruments of modernization in present-day Sub-Saharan Africa. Economics, though very important and undoubtedly a goal both in governmental and individual endeavors, seems to still be lagging far behind these two as the third principal institutional instrument.

---

* A. M. Kamarck, *The Economics of African Development*, (p. 27), asserts: "Africa is a poor continent. The total gross national product (GNP) of Africa, excluding the Mediterranean countries, is estimated at about $30 billion equivalent (at current exchange rates) for 1966. This is nominally less than 5 percent of the American GNP in money terms." He also evaluates the average African per-capita GNP (excluding South Africa) as to be somewhat around $100 equivalent.
** It is acknowledged that "school-age children" is a very ambiguous term. These data, however, were the only ones that I was able to obtain.

Whether controlled by civilian or military forces, the party and the state over all Sub-Saharan Africa as a rule constitute two sides of the same institutional structure. In countries where a militant populist ideology is professed, the party is usually said to be supreme; in the less militantly oriented countries, on the contrary, the government and state administration are dominant.

African political parties differ from political parties in any other part of the world. As a rule, they are composed of a hierarchical skeleton of party leadership, around which a great part of the population is amassed, in a loose membership to participate in the sporadic activities initiated by the party. It is neither a cadre party as in Eastern Europe and the Soviet Union, nor an interest group or ideological faction as in Western Europe, nor a caucus or elected assembly as in the United States. Its basic functions can be outlined as follows: The party provides a frame for national formation and social and political integration, although in some cases it may be dominated by one or several of the more influential tribes in the country. It is an instrument for the generation of a supratribal society which will eventually encompass all the people and, in doing this, will generate political power. The party and state are organizers of the process of modernization, either by means of a mobilization of the masses, or by a stimulation of private initiative and entrepreneurship, or as a collective entrepreneur itself. African governments and the ruling political parties respectively do not just rule, govern, and maintain law, order, and stability. They are expected to be developers as well. They provide the society with mobilizing symbols, an adequate ideology, and even a national identity.[29] Thus the party-states in Africa are simultaneously nation-builders, organizers of the political systems, and generators of the political culture. They are creators and participants at the same time. In addition, the party is a springboard for the birth and elevation of the political elite of the new African states; by virtue of this it is a ladder of social mobility for individuals, and a generator of a supratribal structure of social stratification. Because of lack of means for industrialization and intensive economic development it is much easier to mobilize the masses against than for, than in attainment of definite economic achievements.

Profuse benefits are connected with political office-holding in Africa. The holder of a political office not only has a high status and a salary which allows him to maintain a high standard of living, but he also benefits from many privileges. Sometimes people view his office as the succession to a chief's position. Though he may be hated, he is respected at the same time, either as an officeholder, an influential personality, or a smart man who knows how to make money. Traditionally, holders of political offices also help their relatives to obtain political positions, obtain an education, and engage in entrepreneurial activities.

Education is the other major instrument of modernization—so it too is a generator of the supratribal nation now in transmutation into stratified societies. Education, just like political offices, provides prestige, yields good jobs, and with them privileges and money. However, the present situation in Africa is changing rapidly: until recently, educated people, even with primary or secondary education, were in great demand, but the demand is now lessening. Political and administrative vacancies are few, and they cannot be increased much more. Industries which could have absorbed school and university graduates are growing slowly, and the output of educated people in many countries is already exceeding the capacity to absorb them. In some African countries like Ghana, Nigeria, Dahomey, Kenya, and Senegal, there is already a substantial number of educated unemployed. Indeed, they are strongly achievement-oriented and prone to form the ranks of political opposition. Education generates a new world outlook, new needs and desires for general modernization, and for personal success within the new framework. In conditions when these needs cannot be satisfied, a tense crisis of expectation (as experts phrase it) is engendered.

In addition to the earlier groups of politicians, the military, the educated classes and traditional chiefs, who were all born elites, a new elite of an African business class is now emerging in countries where economic development has made some progress. The business elite is most often composed of people who were themselves members of either the political or the educated elite or were relatives of such people. In some cases the new African businessmen come from families of former chiefs and other branches of aristocracy.[30] These are people who were able to make money by means other than engaging in business. Now they use it in entrepreneurial activities.

4. The Stratified Supratribal National Society— The Product of Modernization

The new African national societies which have emerged during the current process of induced modernization are supratribal and stratified and show a tendency to become even more stratified. In a sense they are superimposed on the traditional tribal structure, out of which they draw their membership. It is possible to distinguish different degrees of belonging in the new society. Thus, it can be said that detribalized urban dwellers, sometimes of the second, third or even earlier generation, and often offspring of parents of different tribal origins, belong more (socially and economically, not legally) to the supratribal society than do people with a dual attachment to the supratribal society and to a far-away tribal entity, or people who still think of themselves as primarily, if not exclusively, members of a tribal entity. Stratification also naturally results from the existence of a political order. The political elite, subdivided according to the various positions in the diverse levels of the authority hierarchy, occupies the apex of this order.

a. The Elite

African elites may be regarded, at least to a certain degree, as the vanguards of ruling class, if not as the ruling class itself. At the same time, since by belonging to them one obtains many privileges (including a high standard of living and the best education for one's children), the elites can be regarded as the fountainheads from which a more coherent ruling upper class emerges. This brings us to the problem of class structure, which must be considered as a product of modernization and still another form of stratification which encompasses the modern, emerging, supratribal society.

The process of the generation and articulation of separate social classes is, in fact, very evidently in progress in many societies of Sub-Saharan Africa.[31] To be sure, the class structure of such societies springs from different origins and inducements and does not constitute a single, homogeneous structure which relates one class to another. In the past (as well as to some extent in our own times) class-producing developments were, for the most part, an outcome of foreign activities in Africa —they resulted from the introduction of plantations for export needs, the spread of private land ownership, the employment of hired (wage) labor, or the inducement for entrepreneurial activities. Each of the existing social classes emerged in a separate course of development and not as an element of a coherent structure. Only now are such classes starting to relate to one another.

b. The Working Class

The working class emerged first. It arose from the introduction of hired and wage labor, when plantations and mines belonging to Europeans started to appear under colonialism. The working class in Africa differs in many respects from the working classes in other parts of the world. Both in the past and in the present it has been a very peculiar working class, insofar as it consists mainly of poorly paid migrants who belong to it only temporarily. Furthermore, these migrants were and are more often unemployed than employed; an insignificant number of them is employed as real workers, whereas the majority work as servants, cooks, gardeners, guards, and so forth; only very few persons in that class possess any vocational training. They adhere to norms and values which are as a rule not homogeneous and certainly do not form class principles. Psychologically they were and still are under a strong spell of the rules and tenets of kinship and tribal solidarity. To the present day the working class has permanently experienced a kind of rotation of the majority of its members. For this reason it can be truthfully said that there is a large working class in Sub-Saharan Africa, a class which enormously exceeds the number of employed workers. But, at the same time, it is a working class to a great extent without workers. The majority of those who claim to belong to the working class as a rule live only temporarily in the urban setting or other locations where they can find work. They earn a substantial part of their livelihood from sources other than employment as workers. At the same time they belong to tribal communities, and by virtue of this membership, they retain their rights to the land, of which they make use, if need be.

Of course, the working class in Africa should not be described as a static entity. It is a class in the making, both with respect to its numerical growth and the qualitative changes taking place within it. The part which is composed of full-time, permanent workers is increasing. It is a class which already possesses an eventful economic and political history of class struggle from the times of the colonial system. Yet that had been a struggle against foreigners and was conducted under the banner of opposition to imperialism and colonialism. Now, for the first time, the African working class has begun to confront African employers, both the private ones and the state. As I have already stated, the progress of industrialization in Africa is still very low. In any African country the number of job seekers is usually several times greater than the number of jobs available. Social security for workers and lower-ranking employees is practically nonexistent. Wages are very low, though they are now much better than they were in colonial times. Unions exist, but since independence their activities have been limited. They are especially restricted in organizing militant actions, and in raising strong demands on behalf of workers against the employer state. They are told that the situation is now different from what it was under colonialism, since they are working for themselves because the state is now theirs.

While the standard of living and the earnings of workers in Africa are still very low, the workers, even when they are temporarily unemployed, enjoy a highly privileged position when compared to the population in rural areas. Their wages, especially if they earn them regularly, seem nearly to be a fortune in the eyes of the poor tribesmen in the remote rural areas, to the peasants who produce for the market, or to the migrant laborers. Thus, Fanon and other writers assert that the proletariat in new nations—and especially in Africa—unlike the proletariat in capitalist societies, is a privileged class, and especially privileged are the qualified workers. Thus, also, G. Balandier points out that the working class in Africa is not and cannot be a revolutionary class.[32] He is right. The workers in Africa are engaged in a tense competition for jobs. They have not developed a strong class consciousness or class ideology. They have retained the recourse of returning and retreating to the rural areas, where in most cases they still have rights to the land (unlike the workers in the early stages of European industrialization, who could not return to the villages). The tribal hinterland provides security for them. Because they are privileged and because they have recourse to the land, they do not feel desperate. Thus the working class in Africa is, and will probably for a long time remain, a "class in itself" rather than a "class for itself."

c. The Class of Entrepreneurs

In contrast to Asian and Arab countries there was practically no local bourgeoisie in Sub-Saharan Africa prior to or during the time of colonialism. Of course, indigenous trade was widespread both prior and during colonialism. Yet the traditional traders, such as the Hausa in West Africa, could hardly be regarded as a bourgeoisie. Even independence did not make them bourgeois. The colonial authorities and the European or Asian enterprises active in colonial Africa tried to prevent all attempts by the Africans to start and expand entrepreneurial activities. In some countries where race discrimination had legal sanctions, there were laws in force to prohibit the Africans from formally entering upon any such scheme. In places where legal barriers were not erected, the African entrepreneur who embarked upon that new and unfamiliar undertaking was faced with competition from long-established European and Asian firms who possessed the proper experience, credit, and the support of the colonial authorities. It was very difficult for an African entrepreneur to obtain bank credit. Banks refused to grant financial assistance on the ground that Africans did not own private land or other real estate to serve as a security for credit.[33] They were particularly reluctant to extend credit to African trade or industrial undertakings. African entrepreneurs, as suggested above, lacked experience. It was no wonder, therefore, that the prospects and possibilities of developing African business initiative were slight. In spite of, or perhaps regardless of, these obstacles West Africa saw a considerable expansion of African business initiative, especially native street peddling and itinerant trade. Some of the traders—including the famous market women of Ghana and Nigeria—were able to amass relatively sizable amounts of capital considering their modest scope of activity, and they could even employ, on various terms, quite a few sellers.

When independence came, many of the barriers erected to prevent African entrepreneurship were removed, but this alone could not and did not produce conditions for the immediate rise of a big business class. Besides, some of the leaders of the newly independent African states were against such developments and tried to impede or stop them. African entrepreneurship has focused on trade (mainly retail) and has started small production enterprises or transportation businesses. For the most part Africans still do not possess sufficient capital for investment in complex industries, mining, or other enterprises which require a long-term amortization.

The new upstart class of entrepreneurs has to surpass a mountain of obstacles and difficulties. The African entrepreneur does not have sufficient capital, and he usually has to draw it from other than strictly business sources, such as plantations, loans from friends and relatives, or by exploiting the support from friends or relatives in government offices. The African businessman still has difficulties in obtaining credit from banks. His experience in running a business is usually scant. Some manage well in spite of this; the majority have difficulties. The competition from foreigners is still strong, and "they have to succeed in an economy which is inter-related from the peasant farmer to Covent Garden, from textile mills in India through the wholesaler in Mombassa to the tailor in a country market, in an economy where they bank money in the branches of European companies, and compete with products manufactured a hundred or thousand miles away. But they are socially isolated from the wider economy by a profound mutual ignorance."[34]

The African entrepreneur is under the pressure of two patterns of behavior which reduce his capacity to accumulate capital and restrain the momentum of enterprise. On the one hand, he is trying to imitate the way of life—or rather the way of spending money—peculiar to the European entrepreneur in Africa. His expenses often exceed what he can afford, considering the amount of capital at his disposal; they even exceed what a European businessman with the same income would spend. At the same time, the African is urged by tribal standards of conduct to assist and support numerous relations and members of his native community, plus various kinds of organizations. Finally, he has to overcome or bypass the aversion of his own government, which is often either formally against a development of private African initiative in business, or when officially promoting the cause of the Africanization of the business in Africa, is still trying to take all the bread and leave the entrepreneur only with the crusts. The government imposes exceedingly heavy taxes which beginners find it difficult to meet. The African entrepreneur has to act under very unstable, constantly changing political conditions which are not conducive to far-flung planning and investments in the anticipation of a steady (though relatively small) accelerating profit.

Thus the African entrepreneur finds himself, either in competition with much stronger competitors—the European and Asian businessmen—or he has to fight the reticence of his own government. When it is possible, he has to make hay while the sun shines; if he has connections with important officials, he must use them and engage, if necessary, in fradulent deals. In any case, he does not carry on his business under stable, "normal" conditions. The reasons for buttressing expanding African business are multitudinous. The stimulation and expansion of African entrepreneurship is important as a factor of the general economic and social development of the new nations in Africa. African business could generate the links and interdependencies necessary for an economic unification of the countries. Profits from business conducted by Africans in an African country can be retained there for reinvestment and capital formation. This would generally increase the wealth of the African countries. African governments are even less equipped than governments in the Soviet Union and Eastern Europe to handle retail trade and a wide network of small shops, restaurants, coffee shops, and other similar enterprises. Thus they either fail if they try to do it themselves (as in Guinea), or, as in Tanzania, Africans are dissuaded from engaging in entrepreneurial activities in order to prevent them from becoming a class of indigenous exploiters. At the same time the government allows Asians to do these jobs and then condemns them for amassing riches. African entrepreneurs could create outlets for farming and other local production initiatives, thus promoting economic growth in general and on a wide scale. They could free African countries from immigrant communities and overseas initiative, or at least make them less dependent on them. On the other hand, however, the creation of a wide, fairly established African structure of entrepreneurship leads at the same time to the growth of capitalism, and with it to explicit class differentiation, and maybe even to class conflict, all of which are against the ideology of brotherhood and socialism that many African leaders promote.

d. The Peasantry[35]

The most important social consequence of the process of modernization (especially of economic modernization) in Sub-Saharan Africa today is, in my opinion, the birth of an African peasantry. The discussion on this subject must begin with the assertion that peasants exist in Africa, and that the peasantry is growing there right now. While the term *paysan africain* is used in the French literature on Africa as referring to a self-evident phenomenon, and while one can frequently read about peasants in the English literature published in Africa, the American and English sources published elsewhere have strangely enough, carefully avoided the term peasant in regard to Africa. Authors write about agriculturalists, cultivators, or tribesmen working in the fields, the Africans on their land, or sometimes about farmers, but they treat the concept of African peasantry as taboo. Some writers, however, have written that it is improper to speak about peasants in Africa since the "common folk" in the complex African societal structure can hardly be regarded as a peasantry or compared to the peasants in Latin America, Europe, or Asia. In my opinion, the Africans certainly are peculiar peasants, since they live under peculiar conditions; yet they share most of the basic traits of peasants in other parts of the world.

What is a peasant? Some writers who use the term "peasantry" characterize entire societies; others regard the peasants only as a part, or stratum, or segment of a society. In a book he published recently, E. R. Wolf points out that it is correct to define the peasantry primarily in terms of its subordinate relationships to a group of controlling outsiders.[36] This is, in fact, a pattern commonly adopted. Thus, Redfield distinguishes the peasant society as intermediate between the two extremes on a folk-urban continuum embracing all societies from the simplest to the most complex. Kroeber, the classical writer to whom many social anthropologists discussing this subject refer most often, stressed that "Peasants are definitely rural—yet live in relation to market towns: they form a class segment of a larger population which usually contains urban centers, sometimes metropolitan capitals. They constitute part-societies with part-cultures."[37] Marx sometimes viewed the peasants as a class related to another class, that of the landlords. He also spoke of peasants as aggregates of agricultural producers who live under similar conditions, but who, because of the mode of production in which they are engaged, are isolated one from another. From this point of view, they are a sort of semiclass, an agglutination of "localized microcosms," without a distinctive revolutionary class consciousness.[38] Indeed, the topic "peasantry" can be discussed from many angles, and the topic "African peasantry" seems to be an even more complex topic.

From an economic point of view, the peasantry can be placed somewhere in the middle of a continuum with an abstract notion of subsistence economy at one pole and an abstract notion of a pure business farm economy at the other. The strict delineation of the peasantry in this continuum is difficult to point out, yet it could be said in general that the peasantry is distinct from both the subsistence and the business farm economy. It developed out of the first. It is based on small-scale technological simple agricultural production, mostly on a family-group basis designed primarily for the family's own consumption but also producing a substantial output either for the landlord or directly for the market. Under conducive conditions (and especially in modern times) it tends to transform itself into the business farm economy. The subsistence economy (keeping in mind the fact that pure subsistence economies are ideal types or logical concepts) tends to produce everything it needs and nearly exclusively for its own consumption. It is isolated and not linked with the market. The business market economy, on the other hand, is usually a highly specialized economy which tends to produce primarily agricultural products for the market. It is often based on outside inputs, such as capital investments or hired wage labor. While the increase of the output of the business farm economy depends on the availability of capital, labor and especially on the increase of market demands, the increase of the output of the peasant economy depends first of all on the increase of its internal needs, most often in connection with the increase of the number of dependents in the household.[39]

Prior to the advent of the Europeans and the involvement of African cultivators in production for the world market, most of African agricultural production was for direct consumption. Today, African producers are in varying stages of transformation from producing for direct consumption to producing for the market. This process of transition is a continuous one, but it is possible, as some writers have pointed out, to identify four major stages in the move up, or in other words, four major forms of involvement in the marketing economy.[40]

(1) Most production is for direct consumption; occasional exchanges of agricultural products take place. (2) Most inputs are devoted to production for self-consumption; there is constant marginal production for the market. (3) The greater proportion of input and output is for the market, but there is still production for direct consumption. (4) All inputs are for specialized production for the market, other than minor and insignificant inputs for home consumption.

Few producers in Sub-Saharan Africa, excluding the European and Asian planters, are either below the first stage or at the top of the ladder. This is why African agricultural producers seem to belong (from an economic point of view) to the peasantry. The move up from subsistence economy or nearly exclusively subsistence economy to economies basically oriented toward the market is so wide in its scope and so significant in its magnitude that it alone could be regarded as the most important modernization in contemporary Africa. This is a process which pertains to about 85 per cent of the population. The fate of modernization in Sub-

Saharan Africa, if one can use such an expression, depends, in fact, on the extent to which this population will (from an economic point of view) be involved in the process of becoming a peasantry, in producing for the market, and becoming in itself a market for industrial development—in short, the degree to which it will become intermeshed with a national economy which generates from the urban centers and with the worldwide economy as a whole. This depends on various factors—on the extent to which the African rural population will be willing to engage in such an endeavor, the degree to which it will find markets for its products (and thus the degree to which the world market will be able to absorb its production), the degree to which African governments and African entrepreneurs will be able to channel the agricultural production of their countries into international markets, and whether they will be able to obtain for it sufficiently good returns so as to enable modernization to go on.

The peasantry can be regarded as a social class different from other classes and composing a social structure together with them. It has often been assumed that peasant classes in this sense were part of the European and Asian feudal or medieval social orders. In fact, however, the peasantry in such societies formed estates rather than classes. They came to be viewed as classes only from a retrospective point of analysis, in which the past was viewed through the prism of the capitalist present in an attempt to discover the same elements in any social structure.

In the feudal structure the peasants were part of either the lordly or the prebendal domains (they had to work on the landlords' farms or pay tributes in kind or money to either the landlords or the officials appointed by the state or king). Peasants were producers, but not owners, or at least not full owners, of the land. In Europe in the eighteenth and nineteenth centuries, and in Asia more recently, the former peasants were freed from their legal dependence on the landlords; they obtained the rights of citizens, among them the right to own land. New social classes emerged in the social structure in which the peasants too were incorporated. To be a peasant began to mean being a person who, with his family, earns a living by tilling the land he owns, and producing goods partially for the market. Hence, the class of peasants becomes the class of small landholders. Its relation to other classes, especially to the landlords, loses its importance. As a class, the peasantry becomes internally stratified. In many East European countries and in the Soviet Union where, under communist rule, private ownership of land was abolished, the notion of the peasant class has taken on still another meaning. It denotes people who do not own land but who are members of agricultural cooperatives and earn their living by working in them.

The landlord-peasant relationship did not exist in most societies of

Sub-Saharan Africa. Some sort of a prebendal system emerged only in the recent past in the interlacustrine and Hausa kingdoms. Private ownership of land was also nonexistent in African societies. Land was usually regarded as the property of the gods or ancestors and was held in trust on behalf of the people by the chiefs, who were responsible for its distribution.

The private ownership of land began to appear in Africa only during the colonial era. In some parts of the continent it sprang up from the expropriation of Africans and the seizure of their lands by the European settlers. Also, some European companies were endowed with large landholdings for mining, timber, or plantations (especially under the rule of the French and Portuguese). All the consequences of colonial land usage will not be discussed here, but it is worth pointing out that this produced a situation of sharp class conflict and tension between the European landlords and the African land laborers.

Another form of private land ownership was established by the British in Buganda. The treaty of the British protectorate in Uganda concluded in 1900 introduced the so-called *mailo* system of land ownership. The arable land of Buganda was to become the private property of the king (Kabaka) of Buganda and a thousand of his most important chiefs. Thus Buganda became the first African country with an African class of large landowners. Later some land was redistributed or sold; today within the territory of Buganda there are about 50,000 landholders and landowners. In many West African countries, such as Nigeria, Senegal, the Cameroons, and the Ivory Coast, the increase in plantations for cocoa, coffee, bananas, and other products has been followed by a marked expansion of private land ownership.[41] Land is owned, held, and used in these countries today on the basis of a variety of titles of land use and principles which function side by side with the traditional land tenure system—that is, family ownership, group ownership, individual ownership. In East Africa, especially in Kenya, Uganda, and Zambia (which was at that time Northern Rhodesia), the privatization of land ownership on a wide scale was introduced in the late fifties and early sixties, under a system of land reform organized and initiated by the colonial administration. The vast majority of the African population (especially in other parts of the continent), though increasingly market-oriented, still does not own land.

Land ownership in itself is neither enough of a basis by which to differentiate the European peasantry as a class nor to analyze it comprehensively. It is even less sufficient a criterion by which to distinguish the African peasantry as a class. To use it to single out the class of peasants in Africa means practically to once again single out a privileged minority (as was done when the working class was defined and discussed above).

There is, however, another way of viewing the problem which seems to be more adequate to the African reality. This is to stretch the limits of the concept of class and to use occupation and inhabitance as the criteria by which to delineate the peasantry. This, on the one hand, takes us back to the economic interpretation of the peasantry. On the other hand, it implies a contrast between rural and urban dwellers. The latter is the main topic and the distinction especially emphasized by Redfield and his followers.

Redfield regards the peasantry as a historical formation which resulted from the impingement of town and city on the tribal culture. There were no peasants before the first cities, he stresses. As cities and towns grow, their influence on the surrounding rural area becomes more acute. Taxes are imposed on the rural cultivator. The local authority is subordinated to the urban center. Resident strangers appear in the village community. Village people have to go to town either for work or for the exchange of goods. Family cohesion and village solidarity dwindle. Sacred sanctions lose their importance. Hence, peasants are people in transition. Inwardly they are oriented to the local community, but outwardly they relate to the town. All traits of the peasantry are derived from these characteristics. The argument follows that even though it is constantly affected by the city life, and even though it is persistently opposed to it, the peasant society produces a folk culture of its own, which is neither traditional nor urban. And, in contrast to the urban technical culture, folk culture is regarded as the distinguishing mark of a peasantry. Hence some of Redfield's followers conclude that the peasantry does not exist where there is no urban or other elite culture distinct from a folk culture.

Undoubtedly the urban-rural dichotomy is an important analytical instrument which allows us to depict some of the characteristics of peasant societies. Yet it seems that it should not be regarded as the only, or even the most decisive, criterion for discussing the subject. Cities exercise a stimulating and decisive influence on the formation and growth of peasant economies and social structures, but that influence may differ considerably under different circumstances. The urban-rural relations of town and village (if we agree that these relations inevitably characterize peasant societies) can be, and indeed sometimes are, very distant, far-stretched, and intermediate. In Africa the rural population is connected not only with the towns and cities in Africa, but also, through various media, with the faraway cities and cultures of Europe, America, and Asia—by means of the international market for which it produces at least part of its agricultural crops, the colonial administration (in the past), the system of education, and numerous other ways. Modern means of transportation and communication shorten these distances considerably.

How relevant is the dimension of urban-rural relations to the analysis of the African peasantry past and present?

Precolonial African societies have mostly been described as homogeneous, tribal, and composed of corporate, unilineal descent groups; hence, with no social stratification attributed to them. As a matter of fact, however, some of these societies were quite stratified—the Hausa, the Dahomey tribes, and some interlacustrine kingdoms, to mention only a few examples. I do not believe that the leisure classes (as Herskovits calls them) —the town-dwellers, the artisans, and the traders of the old African cities —did not have cultures quite distinct from the cultures of the people living in the countryside, especially in West Africa. The point is that the subject has not been investigated thoroughly enough, and the early European explorers tended to describe the culture of the courts and commoners as identical to that of the tribe. Strangers often tend to attribute what they are able to observe to nations and cultures as a whole, rather than to the specific segments with which they have come in contact.

Today, even from the point of view of the contrast between the urban and rural cultures, there is an increasing body of evidence on the emergence and growth of a distinctive African peasantry. As was noted earlier, cities, towns, and urban centers in general are growing rapidly in modern Africa. Within their precincts a new urban culture is growing as well. It partially stems from, or overlaps with, what I earlier described as the buffer culture, but it also has other new traits. To anyone who has lived in those cities, it is absolutely evident, but I cannot, because of the lack of space, elaborate on its characteristics. The new urban culture, as in other parts of the world, increasingly impinges upon the African hinterland. The use of modern mass media communications, the spread of school education, and still other channels also allow the spread of elements of the cultures which come from the distant cities of Europe and America. Subsequently, these new elements induce the generation of a new rural culture in the Africa of today.

The course of induced modernization begins in the sphere of politics and spreads into urban life to generate subsequent changes in the structure and culture of the rural population. Yet the success of the process of modernization depends on how much the rural population becomes affected by the striving for modernity and how much feedback is produced from the rural areas to the urban centers. It is also worth pointing out that there is now enough material to begin a study of the African folk culture by differentiating the peasantry on the basis of economic and social traits, and to then distinguish the culture of the people living in rural areas as that of the African peasants.

Generally speaking, peasants live in small, relatively isolated rural communities. To a great degree peasant families retain the quality of corporate units, in which family and productive roles coincide. Their productive activities are conducted in the first place for the fulfillment of the family's own consumption needs, and only in the second place for the market. Each member of the society is subject to the strong controls of the local community. These traits produce not only a specific peasant culture but a specific life attitude as well. Of course, each peasant society has its own problems and hence has specific attitudes toward them. However, from a macrosociological perspective it is possible to discern some general patterns of peasant life attitudes which are common to all peasant societies. Thus peasants usually have a semiworshipping attitude toward the land; they have a strong attachment to the locality, an orientation to self-sufficiency, a distrust of strangers, a strong respect for traditions, and so on. Peasant societies can also be characterized from the standpoint of such attitudes.

It is fascinating to examine modern rural life in Africa in the hopes of answering the question of whether the same patterns of behavior are present in African villages as in other parts of the world. Suffice it to say that in that respect African rural life has also increasingly become peasant, more than it ever was in the past. Due to divergent present conditions, a different past, differing forms of land ownership, different types of cultivation, we must add that there is currently not a single one but a number of peasantries in Sub-Saharan Africa. And this generation of peasantries, though not a transformation of Africa into smaller Americas, Russias, or Europes, is an important, if not the most important, step forward in the process of modernization on that continent. It is a modernization of and from the grass roots, and it is necessarily a widespread modernization which is only a beginning.

5. Induced Modernization: Change Within Continuity

The peculiarity of induced modernization in general and in Africa in particular consists, among other things, in the fact that it is not a homogeneous process which can at once encompass the whole society and all the spheres of activity to an equal degree. Although the lifting up process is generally oriented toward the most modern patterns of achievement, in some spheres it proceeds quickly, while in others it goes at a very slow pace, and in still others it does not begin at all because of a strong resistance to change, the absence of conditions for it, or the lack of suitable means to promote it (as is the case, for instance, with industrialization). Thus it is a gradual, uneven process; it sparks up in different fields simultaneously, yet at the same time very incongruently. It often produces some modernization in the existing institutions, patterns of behavior, life expectations and activities, though it rarely immediately achieves the higher levels of modernity which are the model. In short, until now it has rarely produced equalization with the pacesetters. Africa must at the same time deal with high unemployment, due both to its economic under-development and lack of industries and to the problems stemming from automation and modern technology. The problem of illiteracy and a lack of skilled personnel is coupled with the problem of a surplus of school and university graduates. While people still cannot read, they are often well informed about events in other parts of the world through radio and, in some African countries, television.

At the levels of government, the universities, health, education, bank-ing, and mass media, modernization in Africa means the introduction of the necessary means, techniques, organization, and the most modern thinking in the world. Yet the number of people who have access to these innovations is still very small. Although some achievements have been introduced into the cities, city life, with the negative consequences of modern town living, can on the whole be compared to city life in Eu-rope on the verge of industrialization. In rural areas the transformation of semisubsistence economies into market economies is progressing, yet still could hardly be regarded as advanced enough.

Modernization as development means a differentiation of new roles, specializations, organizations, and the generation of specialized agencies and systems. Because of the unevenness and heterogeneity of the process of development, these roles, agencies, and organizations are incongruent. They may be functionally complementary, but this is a complementarity based not so much on the mutual exchange of services as on the supple-mentation of activities. The man who sits in the market and who for a shilling or so types dictated letters to the friends, family, or offices of street customers, the street tailor, or even the herbalist or traditional healer who applies pills and drugs given to him by a physician are simul-taneously agents of modernity and servants of the traditional society. They complement the bureaucratic organization of the state, the market econ-omy, and the modern health service, respectively. Modernization of the center and modernization organized by it stirs up responses along nu-merous autonomous chains of change. Bridges and links among the sepa-rately progressing chains of modernization are generated in the second order. The same applies to the social structure. Social classes are not re-lated one to another as in Europe, and each class appears rather in-dependent at first in response to external inducements. Subsequently, however, these classes are linked together in a more unified structural interdependence to produce a cohesive society.

Modernization and development are synonymous with drastic changes, but these are also changes within a continuity. In addition to other interpretations of the concepts of modernization and development, it can also be said that development consists in cumulative changes which produce new traits, but which are at the same time parts of an ongoing continuity. Continuity in Africa means a continuity of the traditional societies. Modernity looks promising to Africans, whether they are intellectuals, politicians, or peasants, but it is still not very accessible to the majority. The past, the traditional society, as it begins to fall apart, also begins increasingly to look valuable. To many it was advantageous, if not from the point of view of the standards of living and the possibilities for individual achievement, at least because it could offer higher moral standards, more care for the individual, and a stronger sense of belonging. The fascination with modernity, and especially with its technology, cannot suppress the nostalgia for the declining traditional order in which each man had his place ascribed by tradition and could count on the help and concern of the other members of the community. Thus traditions are worshiped, and all kinds of attempts are made to preserve them and to build modernity on the foundations of tradition.

There is nothing unusual in the desire to preserve something that is uniquely African, the African culture. Any kind of modernization is an attempt to improve the individual, group, or national standard of living, degree of security, or position in the internal societal or the international coexistential interdependence. The people of Sub-Saharan Africa have a great respect and desire for modern technology. They look to it as a means by which to raise their standards of living to the level of modernity. Yet, although all people are for it, the number of Africans (educated or not) who are frightened by the eventual consequences of industrialization and the introduction of modern technology is increasing. The more the Africans learn about Europe, America, or the Soviet Union, the less they would like their societies to become like the societies of the whites. Thus they look to traditions as a barrier against the evils of modernity. They look to traditions as a means of containing and absorbing modernity. Of course, there are diverse traditions in Africa and not all could or have to be preserved; on the whole, however, the course is toward a modernity which is an extension of the traditional—development as change within continuity. Although I have examined this process in regard to Africa, it seems to be a spreading attitude in other nations, even in the already industrialized and developed nations of today.

Development and modernization in Sub-Saharan Africa proceed through a superimposition of new political orders, social structures, and cultures and institutions over the earlier existing ones. The new orders encompass the old ones, and in the process they are also permeated by the traditional culture. Economic development is still slow in Africa. It advances as islands of modernity are formed which create some economic activities for the market. Although economic modernity is slow and although it looks insignificant on a scale of increasing GNP, it has exercised a tremendous impact on the traditional society, its social structure and culture. Meanwhile, although the traditional culture and structure have been shattered from both the inside and the outside by the innovations and introduction of modernity, they still continue to exist, and they often dominate the scene. The disruption of traditions alone does not create a new order. Behind the façade of modernity ancient Africa continues to live as it always has.

Apart from physical migration, there is also the phenomenon of pendular "spiritual" migration. It has become very common in modern Africa. All Africans take part in it. It is a migration from the traditional to the modern, and from the modern to the traditional, and it goes back and forth. The politician or intellectual or bureaucrat who is emancipated from the traditional society, the migrating laborer, the new entrepreneur —all these and any African living in the sphere of modernity are involved in numerous role performances. And a great number of these roles are still in the traditional society in the home of one's origin. They actually live in two worlds, but the two worlds eventually fuse in a process of mutual permeation.

Modernization is a mode of introducing development from above. However, it is only the inducement that comes from above. Modernization is successful only if it sparks a reciprocal trend at the grass roots, an orientation toward change, variant innovations in pursuit of higher standards of living. Development, especially economic development, has to result from modernization, and it begins when the majority of the people in a country have a chance to participate in it. It means (as I have emphasized many times) specialization and an accelerating differentiation of roles (especially the new roles of innovators), as well as a differentiation of specialized agencies and organizations in a simultaneous expansion of interdependencies and a growing network of exchanges which transform the agglomeration of people into a cohesive social, economic, and political entity. Government plays an important role in inducing modernization. Success depends on engaging the whole population. In Africa, it can now proceed only through the generation of a peasantry which constitutes the foundation of a new supratribal society, and an incipient market for an incipient industry—the new nation in the full sense of the word. The growth of the peasantry is the most conspicuous result of modernization and development.

Not all of what pertains to Africa could be applied to modernizing nations in other areas. Yet Africa provides an example of a most interesting instance of modernization because the distances that have to be passed are far stretched, because it is an attempt at combining tradition with modernity, because the scope of changes that have to be introduced are wider, more drastic, and revolutionary than in any other part of the world. Africa is therefore the greatest laboratory of development and modernization that has ever existed. Modernization is an attempt to attain the level of development of others in a much shorter time and in a more effective way. But it does take time.

To summarize this chapter I would like to say a few words generally about the Third World and its problems. It must be reiterated that the Third World nations must simultaneously face and solve problems accumulated through the ages, those which originated in the precolonial era, the residual problems of colonialism and the new problems which have appeared since independence. I think that the most urgent need is for jobs, which are needed in order to create a market for the nations' industries, to raise the standard of living of the population. Modern complex industries, however, become highly automated and do not absorb much unskilled labor. There are also no markets for their products in the poor nations. Increased agricultural production may improve the diet of the people but it cannot solve quickly and effectively enough the problem of raising incomes and creating more jobs. The European and American markets are, as we said above, glutted with agricultural products of the Third World nations. If the production of these goods were to be increased, prices for them on the international market would go down. The gain would not be so great as to be worth the effort. Some say the solution lies in small industries, yet their introduction is a slow process. People in the Third World cannot wait any longer; they need an urgent solution which is unfortunately not available.

The big industrialized powers, the U.S.S.R. and the U.S.A., seem to become increasingly less prone to render any sort of effective assistance to the Third World nations. Every five or ten years the standard military equipment of the armies of the United States and the Soviet Union becomes remodernized. Some armaments are stored in large quantities and are never in use. Both sides, but especially the Soviet Union, are quite happy to sell or give away this equipment as assistance, for they would otherwise have to demolish it. The Third World nations find other assistance increasingly difficult to obtain. As was mentioned, many intellectuals and some politicians of the Third World nations are against industrialization. They view it as europeanization, as the dissemination of European culture which would destroy their native value systems which are very precious to them. Of course, industrialization has been painful to the European peasant as well, and has eradicated their folk-culture, local identity, and parochial attachment. This, however, is not very often remembered.

Thus it is said in general that the problems of the Third World are difficult to solve, and that the gap between the already developed and underdeveloped nations is steadily widening instead of being bypassed. Representatives of the Third World nations lament this situation during each of the sessions of the United Nations. Some intellectuals write books on this subject, appealing to the consciousness and ethical values of the rich nation. On the whole, however, as with other contemporary problems, people have become used to it, and while regarding it as a terrible situation, feel that they cannot master it or change it.

Kenneth E. Boulding, who is regarded as an authority on that subject, recently analyzed trends of the widening gap between rich and poor nations, attributing its causes to the exploitation of the Third World by European nations, especially in the past, and predicts that in the future the gap will become even wider. He tells us that the causes of the increasing gap are changing somewhat at present. "We may look forward therefore, to a world in which the Temperate Zone countries form a belt of increasing homogeneity and affluence, all really very much like each other in spite of their diverse political philosophies. [He includes here both capitalist and communist countries—S. C.] whereas the tropical belt falls further and further behind the Temperate Zone, and may even collapse into famine, internal war, and massive disorganization."[42]

Is the gap really widening, and should we accept this prediction as the only future prospect? It must be first pointed out that we must actually consider not one particular gap, but a number of gaps in the Gross National Product, in the degree of industrialization, in the overpopulation, in the number of educated people with modern know-how per head of population in the country, in the position held by a country in international relations, and so forth.

I do think that each of these gaps, while interrelated and intertwined with others, must be a subject for a separate analysis. Here I can only point out that it is true that the gap in the Gross National Product is widening. Yet some of the tropical countries have great mineral resources and already have high returns from these. The question is that of the utilization of these returns. It is worthwhile to remember that at one time Spain and Portugal had more wealth and controlled wider areas of the world than other countries, and yet they have never become highly industrialized and prosperous. The diagram below seems to illustrate well

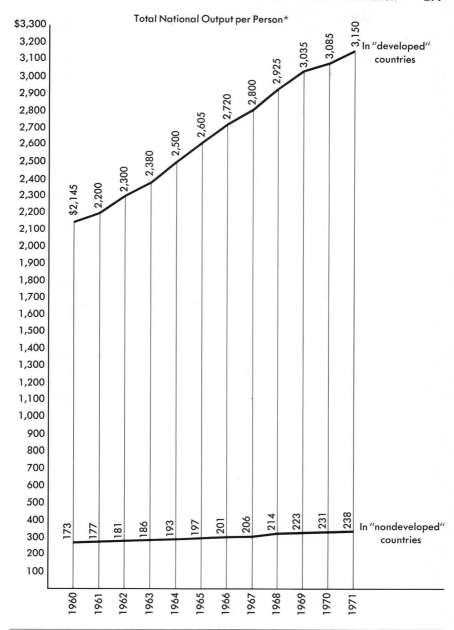

Total National Output per Person*

$3,300
3,200
3,100
3,000
2,900
2,800
2,700
2,600
2,500
2,400
2,300
2,200
2,100
2,000
1,900
1,800
1,700
1,600
1,500
1,400
1,300
1,200
1,100
1,000
900
800
700
600
500
400
300
200
100

$2,145
2,200
2,300
2,380
2,500
2,605
2,720
2,800
2,925
3,035
3,085
3,150

In "developed" countries

173
177
181
186
193
197
201
206
214
223
231
238

In "nondeveloped" countries

1960
1961
1962
1963
1964
1965
1966
1967
1968
1969
1970
1971

*Basic data: U.S. Agency for International Development.
Output is in 1970 dollars to eliminate effect of inflation.

the situation of the widening gap between rich and poor nations, taking the GNP as an indicator.

While the total national output per person in 1971 in the United States was $4,833, in Sweden $4,042, in Canada $3,900, in West Germany $3,092, in the U.S.S.R. $2,240, in Ethiopia it was only $70, in India $97, in Indonesia $100, in Pakistan $133, in Uganda $131. The gap between various levels of industrialization of the rich and poor nations is growing and no one seems to have a solution for this. To be sure, a number of previously underdeveloped countries have been rapidly making a considerable advancement in the introduction of modern industries, for instance, India, Taiwan, Brazil, and Mexico. This does not however, change the total grim picture. The gap in industrialization will probably grow wider in the near future. One may hope only that for some reason in a more distant future it will become convenient to set up highly automated factories right in the middle of the Sahara or Mongolia, rather than in central California or close to Odessa in the U.S.S.R. Even if the less developed nations will permit such investments this will not solve the problem of badly needed jobs in the Third World nations. Automated industry does not need many laborers. It may, however provide some additional income for the poor nations. Will this money be utilized in industrialization and generally in the development of poor nations? The current experience of the major oil-exporting countries, enjoying in some instances a GNP growth rate close to 9 per cent provides evidence to the contrary. Money earned in these countries is quite often located by rulers of such countries in European banks which utilize it for new investments in already industrialized nations.

The problem of overpopulation is probably the most difficult problem to solve, and here the gap is still growing. Demographers now expect that by year 2040 nations currently considered as underdeveloped with a population of 2.6 billion will have a population of 13.9 billion while the developed nations which now have a population of about 1.1 billion will reach 1.8 billion.

Some of the other gaps, at least, are slowly being bridged to some extent. The number of educated people in the Third World nations is growing and illiteracy is declining. Until recently the future Indian and African intellectuals, those who were educated in developed nations as scientists, surgeons, agriculturalists, and so forth, were looking for jobs in the U.S.A., Canada, and other wealthy nations. Today when the industrialized countries are beginning to have a substantial unemployment rate among their own highly educated specialists, the drain of specialists from Third World nations will probably begin to decline. We should then expect that local specialists knowing both the conditions of their own countries as well as the achievements of the European and American sciences would more easily find solutions to problems of their own countries than Europeans, especially when the local specialists will have to compete for jobs in their own countries on the basis of the criteria of excellence and innovative know-how. The needs and ability to cope with problems of a literate population will also change in comparison with that which existed in the past when most of the Asians, Africans, and Latin Americans were illiterate. If we take another of the mentioned gaps, the position of the Third World nations in international relations tremendously improved, and will probably continue to do so in the future.

The gap still does exist, and everything possible must be done to bridge it. However, I do think that the Third World nations, despite their all too frequent political turmoils and the fact that they have not developed as fast as expected after independence, are slowly but steadily beginning to find their own solutions, even though it will take a long time before the gaps will be bridged altogether.

A few more facts must be taken into consideration. The Third World nations do have some commodities to offer which might become very dear in the future, such as resources of minerals which have very often not yet been explored. In spite of the overpopulation they still have unpolluted water and air, which—who knows—may also become a rare resource in the future. In addition, since our planet is shrinking because of overpopulation and the spreading of faster means of communication, I would guess that we are approaching that time when we will no longer be able to afford having any underdeveloped areas on our planet. The space and the markets of consumers will both be needed for the increasing output of productivity.

The final point is that, as has been believed, in their search for solutions, the Third World nations will have to decide whether they want their development to be based on the principles of complementary interdependence adopted from the West, or semiorganismic interdependence adopted from the Soviet Union. In the first stages these nations attempt to closely follow one or another pattern. In learning of the faults and vices of both these systems, they began to experiment on their own in trying to combine the experience of both the West and communist countries. Who knows, perhaps a better social and political system combining the elements of complementary and semiorganismic interdependencies to solve the problems of the interdependence of coexistence simultaneously will be found in the Third World.

At the beginning of the seventeenth century in England, France, or Germany, the idea that America would become the leading industrial and political nation of the world would have been the subject of much ridicule. Who would have believed, at the beginning of the twentieth century, and even after the Bolshevik revolution, that in only fifty years the Soviet Union was to become one of the mightiest powers in the world? While casting many gloomy predictions about the growing gap between the developed and underdeveloped nations, Kenneth E. Boulding also writes: "Perhaps one can visualize a world, 100 years or more from now, in which the tropical countries, having passed through a period of agony, have learned to control their population, to educate their children, and to come into the modern world. Looking even further ahead, one can perhaps visualize a time in which the main centers of human life and activity will be in the Tropics."[43] Whether this vision is correct or not I do not know, but certainly the leaders and intellectuals of the Third World do not want this to be the case in a hundred years; they want to achieve this much sooner. To anyone who has lived in the Third World, this may at present appear impossible, yet who knows what the future will bring?

Conclusion: Variables
of the Sixth Approach

The process of societal development in different parts of the world under different political systems has been analyzed here from the perspective of diverse approaches and theories. On each occasion I attempted to derive from such comparisons some new perspectives for viewing the topic. These are neither advices nor prescriptions on how to organize or improve societal or political development; nor are they theories claiming to contain the entire or the only correct explanation and solution of the problems. This has been a search for new analytical tools enabling us to develop comparative studies of development of industrialized and non-industrialized societies, of societies under Western and Communist types of political order. I think that the comparisons of different approaches presented here, and the new proposals derived from them allow us now to pinpoint a number of variables, which in combination could constitute a frame for a multidimensional analysis of societal development from a new perspective. These variables have been mentioned; however, I now wish to outline them again with some elaboration in a concise form.

1. Conflict Within Consensus

Because of the recurrent generation of scarcity of goods and wealth on diverse levels of needs determined by culture; because political power and any form of prestige cannot be distributed equally and inevitably becomes a subject of competition; because of inevitable differentiation of interests and differentiation of opinions about the ways of implementation of these interests, about individual and societal goals and about modes of concerted action in their attainment, conflict inevitably appears in all and any societal structure. It may be destructive in some instances but it is constructive and productive in others if regulated, exploited, and directed accordingly by the parties involved. It often divides, but it also often unites and unifies in action against those others, whether they personally have chosen so or not. Although the mere fact of belonging to groups and societies creates conflict, the need to coexist in the same societal order in spite of conflict, and the need to cooperate regardless of hostilities generates consensus and an order of authority and power for concerted action, regulation, and resolution of conflicts. Thus conflict and consensus are inevitably interconnected and tend to generate each other.

Conflict within consensus is also the source of those activities objectively producing diverse forms of development. People engaged in conflict and competition, whether economic, political, cultural, group, or personal, are striving to improve their chances and positions in confrontations with the other parties by innovations of all kinds, technological, organizational, political, social. The scope of innovation introduced in any society in the course of resolution of conflict depends on the availability of means and experience, the already attained level of development, the accumulated resources of knowledge, the conditions for introduction of innovations produced by authorities, and numerous other factors. In societies with a strong traditional orientation innovations are barely rewarded and sometimes even punished. Thus the society is not developmentally oriented. Conflicts are resolved in accordance with rules of tradition, thereby the pace of development is slow. Developmental-oriented societies are as a rule highly competitive. Competition is here most often the way of life, and numerous conflicts transformed into competitions become simultaneously a part of the consensus structure. Though conflict and competition are the source of developmental activities, it is only so if they are conducted at least partially by means of invention and innovation. In a sense, conflict is a clash of potentialities and the release of these potentialities produces development.

Development of societies is a process of growing systemness. People all live in systems. And the more a society is economically developed and industrialized, the more it consists of numerous overlapping and intermeshed systems. Systemic relations proliferate and become attenuated and more systemic in the course of the specialization of individuals, the differentiation of roles, institutions, and organizations, and the separation of systems of special areas of organizational activities. Systemic relations are generated in the course of societal, economic, political, and other interactions; men produce them in the course of confrontation with other men, in pursuit of greater efficiency, greater productive outputs, and better conditions of life. They are simultaneously interactions of consensus and conflict, in some cases with the prevalence of consensus, and in others of conflict. In both cases they relate to and generate systemic interdependencies. Societal systems differ from organismic and mechanical systems in that they are constituted of autonomous units and thinking individuals generating systemic interconnections and the energy flowing through them both in the pursuit of their individual or group goals as well as in the service of maintenance of the system in which they are engaged. Only a system theory which includes conflict can explain in a satisfactory manner the accelerating, spreading, and engulfing process of general development comprising numerous specific developments, in other terms, the process of growing societal systemness. Yet system theories in sociology and political science have until now rarely included conflict as a part of their premises. To combine the system approach with conflict theory would be a formidable task.

2. Differentiation Within Growing Interdependence

I view societal development as a process of growing systemness. As we have seen, it seems to be not an entirely new idea, as it is contained in numerous classical writings especially in sociology, in works of Marx, Toennies, Durkheim, Weber, and lately of Smelser. In other words, the process of societal development can be characterized as a process of ongoing accelerating differentiation within growing greater interdependence, as a continuity irreversibly directed toward greater complexity. At the same time it is uneven in the sense that it does not encompass to the same degree and at the same time either all societies, or in each concrete society all elements of a societal or political or economic structure; it proceeds at an uneven pace. In some instances it becomes stagnant, in others interrupted. Yet, in any case, it cannot be reversed. In such an understanding, development does not imply a movement toward an equifinality or the implementation of a predestination. Neither does it imply inevitability as a linkage of the chain of events. To be sure, there is an inevitable linkage with the past, the conglomeration of activities and factors which existed earlier generated those existing now. Yet at any point in the present, in this one-way street from the past to the future, men have numerous options (if one excludes exceptional situations when they are prevented from making decisions by themselves). Apart from some predictable elements, each choice contains numerous unpredictable elements. The further stretched are our plans and the greater the number of factors in them, the more they change from plans into desires. Of course we can anticipate, and with the progress of science and knowledge we can anticipate more and more accurately. Yet any predictions have to contain at least one element which is impossible to predict—men, their inventions, their changing beliefs, and modes of action. All that can be said with certainty is that if development continues it will produce a greater complexity of societal relations, more differentiation within a growing interdependence, and more systemness. It is also evident that continuous differentiation within growing interdependencies leads to situations in which units are too differentiated, too specialized, and cannot relate by themselves on their own initiative but must be related by specialized institutions erected solely for the purpose or acquiring this function.

I have especially emphasized that the development of societies—of social, political, and economic structures—advances and is manifest in the generation of specialized roles, agencies, structures, and systems which because of their specialization and complementarity are interdependent, or have to be made so by special agencies. It is a process of separation and proliferation of systems, of specialized activities and systemic interconnections within these systems, their expansion over other systems and areas, and their mutual interpenetration and permeation.

Systemic interdependencies are channels for the exchange of goods, services, ideas, cultural patterns, and cooperation. They are also channels of bargaining and thus of competition and conflict (at least when societal systems are considered). This is especially evident in the sphere of economics where growth is as a rule a concomitant process of the expansion of market relations, growing productivity, and increasing general and per capita national incomes.

I distinguished three types of interdependencies increasing and densifying in the course of societal development: the interdependence of the coexistence of actors not engaged in cooperation but merely existing in proximity; the complementary interdependence of autonomous units or constituents engaged in a process of exchange on their own account and calculation; the semiorganismic interdependence of allocation of positions, functions and rewards from a center, in total subordination to it and without freedom of autonomous action for the units. These three types of interdependencies are present in any society, yet societies differ according to the prevalence and domination of one of them. The three interdependencies develop simultaneously though not congruently in the course of growing specialization and differentiation of roles, agencies, and so forth, in short in the course of what may be termed societal development. This, however, is not an inevitable evolution. It is simply a process which has taken place in the past and which is observable in many societies in the present.

The interdependence of coexistence seems to be absent in conditions where proximity of coexistence does not become a factor impinging on the autonomy of individuals, groups, and units of societal structures. It has not been a major societal problem until recently. With the increase of population, the reduction of the space available for inhabitation per capita, the narrowing of the distance of intercommunication as a result of the development of transportation and communication, the interdependence of coexistence is transformed into a factor of impingement painfully affecting the autonomy of individuals and groups in the society.

The semiorganismic interdependence generated by the state, bureaucracies, and organizational structures increases as a means of regulating the impingement of the interdependence of coexistence. However, it too limits individual autonomy. The growth of both the complementary and semiorganismic interdependencies result in a greater output of goods and services, yet it also turns into a process of increasing limitation of freedoms, standardization of life, uniformity, and depersonalization. This is especially true for the semiorganismic interdependence. In societies where it constitutes the principal frame of societal structure, men and any other units of society are regarded as corpuscles and organs whose sole purpose of existence is as a part of the system. Hence rights and freedoms of individuals against the state in such orders or regimes are reduced to a minimum.

Both constantly growing and densifying interdependencies of coexistence and of the semiorganismic type are nowadays impinging more and more, and so are painfully felt by the average man in many aspects of his life. His freedoms are increasingly shrinking because of the activities of other competitors, the control and regulation by the various administrations and government, and the declining possibility of influencing the decisions upon which he is dependent. While future developments may bring even higher standards of living, elimination of underdevelopment in many areas of the world, elimination of the poverty still existing in industrial societies, and perhaps resolve many of the other problems plaguing men and modern societies, they may and probably will produce many new even more complex problems which can hardly be anticipated at present.

Nevertheless, future societies need not inevitably and necessarily become super-rational and totalitarian as some writers predict.* This may happen if men passively or under the spell of some persuasion allow themselves to become totally subordinated to the functions and needs of

---

* The fact that rational may have different meanings, and that something may be rational from one point of view but not rational from another, especially if one takes into account that even the rationality of applying right means to selected goals is only relatively right, is usually not taken into account in such predictions.

systems created in the pursuit of greater gain, greater output of productivity, and better efficiency.

There is still another possibility that man, freed from many time-consuming activities of today, endowed with greater education, knowledge, and understanding of the factors constituting the systems on which they are dependent, having at their disposal more free time, relieved from the painful need to worry about means of subsistence, and so forth, will be able to devote his life to creative activities; creative not necessarily in the sense of producing great works for eternity, but creative because he will produce them in his individual way, for his own satisfaction and enjoyment. People, however, will probably not even be happy then. Perhaps they will have more problems than we have today. Yet their problems, and predictions about their problems, are outside the scope of this discussion.

The distinction introduced here between the three types of societal interdependencies do not exhaust the topic fully. From another point of view, or for other analytical purposes, diverse types of interdependencies characterizing such interactions as cooperation and subordination in horizontal and vertical orders can be distinguished as more important. This is the subject of organizational theory. For the sake of brevity I have not engaged in the discussion of these interdependencies. The interdependencies which I have discussed—coexistence, complementarity and semiorganismic—are as a rule asymmetrical, more beneficial in certain or in all respects for some partners of the interdependencies than for others. The asymmetry of interdependence reflects the inequality within and between societies.

3. Development As Generated by Insecurity Within Security

Men rarely, if ever, engage in developmental activities for the sake of generating growing systemness of differentiation within a growing interdependence. Developmental activities are pursued for the sake of their fruits. If people engage in such activities, it is in pursuit of personal benefits of wealth, prestige or political power, or in an attempt to change the world in accordance with their own beliefs which in turn are expected to produce benefits for the individual in question, a group or society as a whole, if not all mankind. In some cases men seek direct and immediate profits, in others—in a distant future. Men are concerned not only with the present and the past but even more with the future which they would like to make more predictable and more secure. Development is a springboard into a more secure future. Striving for security is probably one, if not *the*, most important motivation for developmental activities. In his quest for individual, group, and general societal security in his attainment of greater physical, economic, political, spiritual, psychological, and other securities, man establishes institutions, enters interaction, and maintains systemic interdependencies with other people, accepts consensuses, engages in conflict and competition, and invents new modes and means of action. Apart from their own value wealth, power and prestige are valued as securities. Man, groups, and societies are in constant, incessant, and obstinate striving for greater security. Depending on the prevailing structure of beliefs and the value-orientation in a society, this striving for security finds diverse vehicles of expression. It is carried by variant motivations of action, especially of action with anticipation of gain. In Anglo-Saxon culture it takes shape primarily in individual achievement motivations. On the other hand, German and Japanese cultures traditionally have sought security in the implementation of duties and callings imposed by the society, although they too are increasingly carrying out their search through individual achievement motivation. In the Soviet Union and other communist societies, the Party and government promote policies and ideologies of total subordination of individual achievements to the tasks and targets of collective achievement.

Apart from diverse societal and technological arrangements generating protection and providing security for individuals and for groups the most natural, important, and reliable source of security is man's sense of belonging to a society, family, kinship group, tribe, class, estate, caste, guild, or professional group. The greater his involvement and feeling of belonging, the stronger is his sense of the security provided by his community. In modern times citizenship is the most universal institution of security. It provides protection against the encroachment of foreign powers upon the society and its members, it guarantees each individual rights and freedoms and the protection by authorities against encroachment of fellow citizens. Rich contemporary societies even include social securities among the securities of citizenship. They provide essential means for living to those members of the society who are unable to obtain them themselves due to unemployment or other reasons. General objective security is conducive to far-flung entrepreneurial activities in expectation of profits and benefits to come. It induces members of the society to undertake risks, to engage in activities which will bear fruits in the distant future. It provides subjective and practical material protection for investments, property, and individual achievements. It is an important factor in the calculation of fulfillment of expectations. It reduces the uncertainty of the future. It can be provided only by the state and the political organization of the society.

General development of the society and especially economic devel-

opment depends greatly on the amount of security provided by the political system for innovators, inventors, deviant personalities coming forward with new ideas, and achievers. Thus conditions generated by the
political set-up determine greatly the pace, direction, and scope of economic and social development, as well as that of the whole society. In
accordance with this belief I related the theory of development primarily
and especially to the structure and function of political systems. Provided
that other means such as skills and material resources are available, the
course of developments in society is determined greatly, if not primarily,
by political conditions, by the state of security in society generated by the
political system.

Another factor which I considered important for development was
stimulating subjective insecurity within a general objective societal security. When society provides a high degree of general security for all its
members but individual security, especially in the economic sphere, depends on individual undertakings within the general frame, then members
of the society will be most prone to engage in intensive innovations and
inventions which will accelerate the process of development. Individual
insecurity within security is common in political systems simultaneously
maintaining a stable order as the basis of common security and a structure
allowing wide and varied competition rewarded profusely by high grati-
fication for achievements. These are political systems with a strong inclination toward egalitarian principles and highly balanced institutionalization of conflict and competition within consensus.

Taking into account the importance of the above factors, I propose
to regard insecurity within security as another variable of the general
theory of societal development. Yet, apart from motivations stemming
from and directed consciously or unconsciously at the attainment of security, other motivations too may be important in the generation of developmental action. Man may explore, invent, innovate, and consequently
produce development to fulfill his urge of curiosity, his love for risk-
taking, or his urge to prove his worth to others. And still other explanations are possible.

Development from above, modernization organized by governments
and specialized agencies in a concerted action toward the attainment of
standards achieved elsewhere has to include manipulation of men and
their induction by adequate motivations toward the attainment of goals
and rewards propounded by the modernizers. Success in such activities
depends highly on the selection of proper motivations and incentives
which will generate profuse responses in the desired activities. In practice this means avoiding the imposition of values incongruent with the

traditional culture; it means utilizing elements of the culture of the people who are mobilized as motivation vehicles to induce action.

4. Change Within Continuity

The role of culture in development is important for another reason. Development is patently a process of cumulative changes advancing in a continuity, and this characteristic especially describes the cultural aspect of the societal process. I discussed it here in terms of the example of Sub-Saharan Africa, yet it is a valid variable for any characteristic of the developmental processes. Developments produced by men can never be cultural-free. Man is part of the culture in which he was born, has lived, and has become socialized, and he is its carrier and disseminator as well as the producer of additions to it. The culture of one society cannot be substituted for another—it can only be changed; in this process some of its elements are exposed more than others, and it is these which are utilized in new action. Culture is not static. Inherently or under exogenous inducement it continuously changes, yet at the same time it remains the most constant element of societal structure and often serves as a decisive factor in the maintenance, under apparently different systems, of a continuity of norms, habits, and structures generated in the past.

We are living in a time of accelerating changes. Everything seems to be mobile, transient, temporary, in the process of becoming more modern. People tend to value innovations more than they have ever done in the past. They now attach less importance to objects and things which were very dear in the past, as they are easily replaceable today. In this constant restless race for innovations, novelties, new experience, and new patterns of life, we still remain rooted in the past. True, many people view the past and history as irrelevant for activities of today. Others, however, still attach great importance to it or are proud of their national heritage and origin. Concurrently with introducing new styles of life, many people emphasize that they are the bearers of traditions, of all that comes from the past, or at least of some traditions that are dear to them.

There are problems about which humanity ponders throughout all its existence. Modern existentialists, Marxists, revolutionary anarchists, New Left radicals, and phenomenologists asking new questions, viewing new problems of modernity or the future still pose the same questions which were posed by Aristotle, Plato, Socrates, Hobbes, Rousseau, Marx, and Hegel. Plays written by Aristophanes, Molière and Shakespeare, as well as books written by classical writers perplex intelligent contemporary youth who have a concern for humanity as they did in the past. True, the youth views these works as a prism through which to see the problems of today, yet they value them highly even while enjoying contemporary writers. Young people today have a taste for an entirely different music and art than that of ten, twenty, or fifty years ago. But when they have a real feeling for music, they listen to Beethoven, Bach, Tchaikovsky, Mozart, Handel, and other great nineteenth- and twentieth-century composers with the same admiration and profound enjoyment as did their elders. One may attend any exhibition of great artists of the past to see with what great delight and interest young people assess their mastery and yet expressed youths' feeling and visions and even objects of interest. The Soviet Union, which was probably the first country to proclaim the slogan that the culture of the ancient regime of the decadent classes of exploiters is obsolete, now spends millions preserving its palaces, art, and cultivating its folk heritage.

The pace of change is constantly accelerating. Every day brings innovations, new styles, views, and ideas. However, modernity is rooted in the past, and in any of its forms it is a continuation of it, sometimes even a complete return to old traditions and styles. In the throw-away culture of modern times, we do not throw away the treasures of men's creativity and greatness of the past.

5. The Political Aspects of Economic Development and the Economic Aspects of Political Development

From the perspective of the analysis presented in this book, economic and political developments can be regarded as part-developments, as aspects or constituents of the general process of societal development. From another point of view, they can also be regarded as goals of developmental action, although not in the sense of an equifinality or a target set up by anonymous forces which put in motion the societal process. If they are goals, they are set forth by groups, governments, or individuals in pursuit of desired results in economic productivity or political integration. They are goals organized for purposeful action when people viewing other societies or their own past decide that they want them as goals. They result from innovative changes, from increased productivity in economics, from increased macrostructural integration in the sphere of politics, and above all from increased differentiation and interdependence in societies.

From the standpoint of the propositions presented in this book, economic development can be characterized as a growing specialization and differentiation in the sphere of economics which transcends proliferations and densification of market relations engulfing the society. It intermeshes with other similar developments and on the whole engenders through overlapping interdependencies and increased efficiency, greater economic outputs, and subsequently a growth in both the general national and per capita incomes. I believe that the scope of expansion of market relations matters much in this process, since it generates important social consequences transforming the whole structure of the society. Cases are known of countries which amass wealth as a result of conquest or exchange for valuable minerals or fuels (oil) on the international market yet do not engage in economic development. In the sixteenth and seventeenth centuries Spain and Portugal controlled most of the colonial territories and had the greatest influx of gold and other valuable resources, yet they never became as industrialized as Britain. Most economists believe that the growth of GNP can be regarded as the best indicator of economic growth and development. Since it results, in most cases, from the growth of economic systemness, it has to be accepted as the most comprehensive definition of economic development.

Economic development can be regarded as a self-expanding and inexhaustible goal. Though targets can be set and reached in its implementation there is no end to the extent to which economic development can be expanded, intensified, and accelerated. In any society the objectives of economic development are regarded as most desirable, yet its character, organization, targets, and to a degree, even its consequences differ according to the level of economic development already attained and the structure of organization of the societal and political order. Though common features of economic development and economic growth in general can be discerned, in diverse conditions determined by the character of political organization and the already attained level of economic development they can mean different things. Three branches of the theory of economic development dealing with different problems and defining its aspects differently exist in economics, applying to the capitalist, communist, and newly established societies.

In the discussion of political development I proposed to distinguish (a) development of political entities—the nations; (b) development of political systems; (c) development of political culture; (d) the process of etatization of modern societies. These developments do not seem to be congruent. Neither is economic development and political development or, as a matter of fact, development of any of the other spheres of societal activities congruent one with another. Yet these developments are interdependent to a degree and tend to stimulate processes of change and growth in other spheres of activities. I characterized development of political systems as a collateral and reciprocal process. On one end, it advances through differentiation of autonomous political interest groups encompassed by a framework of unified interests, in an overlapping structure of networks of differing political and ideological proclivities. Social allegiances are frequently related to the diversity of economic interest in society. On this end it also develops as expanding egalitarianism and increasing competitiveness for desired positions in society. Thus it consists of an increasing generation of mutually balanced overlapping structures of conflict contained and pervaded by structures of consensus.

On the other end, it advances through differentiation and integration generated by the authority in reciprocity with grass-roots developments, in institutionalization of specialized governmental agencies, in increased capacity of the government order evident in performances responsive to the other directional trend. One-sided developments within political systems, especially of expanding institutionalization of the authoritarian structure are "pathological" and anomic. Though it could result in a greater permeation of the societal structure by governmental agencies, though it might produce greater subordination to the center and more order, it also eradicates grass-roots upward initiative and paralyzes the interplay between political agencies and other units and constituents of the socioeconomic and political structure. The political system in such a situation becomes turgid and redundant. It is always constituted of men and organizations. Organizational structures stiffening and congealing men as motionless corpuscles in the name of organizational rationality usually become inefficient and obsolete. Their imposed capacity to generate energy declines in proportion to the congealing effect of the imposed societal order. Societal and political systems need moral and intellectual energy to run effectively, and such energy can be harnessed only by and from free and free-thinking men.

The opposite one-sided antiorganizational development is devastating as well. It leads to dissipation of the system, and modern men cannot live as a mass without unifying systems. Since economic and other developments depend highly on conditions generated by political systems, one-sided developments within political systems affect them disastrously too.

We live in surroundings produced as a result of development. Most of the things that we enjoy in life are either products or refinements of processes of various developments, and especially of industrialization. Yet development begins to result more and more in things and products that we do not enjoy at all. It impinges upon our human identity. As a result of the growth and development of the semiorganism, men are wedged into the cages of systemic interdependencies and subordination. As a result of economic development, interactions are transformed into market commodities exchanges. Superfluous social development leads to depersonalization, sterile exchangeability of partners and parties, and loneliness; it generates all present-day urban problems. Industrial development produces affluence but also pollution. Development is one of the great forces that man originally unleashed, but of which he still fears to lose control. It alienates men, and it alienates itself. Yet mankind needs still more development to solve its problems, and the new nations need it even more than those already developed. And when these problems are solved, more development will be needed to solve the new problems engendered in the meantime. From man's benefactor, development can change into his enemy. There is no alternative to development, however, though all its consequences cannot be anticipated. The only choice is between mindful and mindless development.

It is common now to speak about various limits of growth of mankind. Perhaps the critics of such theories are right. Perhaps the described limits of growth are not as narrow as in the adumbration by MIT experts, who recently published their report for the Club of Rome. We are certainly capable of finding new sources of energy. Human creativity cannot be accounted for in such anticipation. Irregardless of whether the MIT experts' conclusions are or are not accepted, it is evident that the future should bring more choices, along with more regulations, restrictions, and systemic dependencies.

Whether we are or are not approaching the so-called limits of growth, it is doubtful, at least for the present, that it will be possible to impose any limits or restriction on the growth of the Soviet Union, the New Nations, and on various spheres of activities in Western societies. It is also doubtful that a flexible equilibrium, as suggested by these analysts, will provide any solution. An equilibrium means the maintenance of the status quo, and who, especially among the poorer people and nations, will be happy perpetuating the status quo? Redistribution of wealth? How could it be redistributed satisfactorily?

In this book I have attempted to explore the various aspects of societal development and its consequences. Perhaps, as in the African story introducing this book, in pursuit of societal development, regardless of whether it is a conscious effort or a consequence of various processes, we are chasing our own tail. It might be different, however. Perhaps becoming more self-conscious and aware of the various aspects of societal development, we will be able to find better ways to solve the predicaments which we are now facing. Perhaps the understanding of societal development will help us to overcome the current or any other limits of growth. Global solutions or perspectivistic approaches to the future, and whether or not they accept the idea of limits of growth, future macrosocietal changes within or beyond any limits of growth will inevitably have to involve more, newer societal developments.

Notes

Preface

1. See Thomas S. Kuhn, *The Structure of Scientific Revolutions* (2 ed. Chicago: University of Chicago Press, 1970), p. 4.
2. Walter Buckley, *Sociology and Modern Systems Theory* (Englewood Cliffs, N.J.: Prentice-Hall, 1967), p. 60.

Introduction

1. See A. Angyal, *Foundations for a Science of Personality* (Cambridge, Mass.: Harvard University Press, 1941), Chapter 8.

i The First Approach: Evolutionary Theories

1. Dale B. Harris (ed.), *The Concept of Development: An Issue in the Study of Human Behavior* (Minneapolis: University of Minnesota Press, 1967), p. 189.
2. Ibid. pp. 211-12.
3. Ibid. p. 129.
4. Sir Isaiah Berlin, *Historical Inevitability* (London: Oxford University Press, 1954), p. 31.
5. Harris (ed.), *Concept of Development,* p. 3.
6. J. A. Ponsioen, *National Development: A Sociological Contribution* (The Hague: Mouton, 1968), p. 13.
7. See Robert A. Nisbet, *Social Change and History: Aspects of Western Theory of Development* (New York: Oxford University Press, 1969).
8. Karl Marx, "Retrospective Preface to a Contribution to the Critique of Political Economy," *Selected Works,* edited by V. Adoratsky (New York: International Publishers, n.d.), Vol. I, p. 356.
9. Auguste Comte, *A General View of Positivism* (New York: Dutton, 1898), p. 221.
10. Ibid. p. 222.
11. Herbert Spencer, *The Principles of Sociology* (New York: D. Appleton, 1901), Vol. I, pp. 498ff.
12. Ibid. pp. 505ff.

13. John C. Burnham, *Lester Frank Ward in American Thought* (Washington: Washington Public Affairs Press, 1956), p. 1.
14. See Samuel Chugerman, *Lester F. Ward, The American Aristotle: A Summary and Interpretation of His Sociology* (New York: Octagon Books, 1965).
15. Israel Gerver, "Introduction," *Lester Frank Ward: Selection from His Work, with an Introduction* (New York: Crowell, 1963), p. 5.
16. Richard Hofstadter, *Social Darwinism in American Thought* (New York: George Braziller, 1969), p. 71.
17. See Lester F. Ward, *Dynamic Sociology Based Upon Social Science As Based Upon Statical Sociology and the Less Complex Sciences* (New York: D. Appleton, 1911).
18. See Lester F. Ward, *Pure Sociology* (New York, London: Macmillan, 1903).
19. Ibid. p. 465.
20. Ibid. p. 553.
21. Marshall D. Sahlins (ed.), *Evolution and Culture*. Foreword by Leslie A. White (Ann Arbor: University of Michigan Press, 1960).
22. Ibid. p. vii.
23. Leslie A. White, *The Science of Culture: A Study of Man and Civilization* (New York: Farrar, Straus & Giroux, 1969).
24. Ibid. p. 366.
25. See ibid. p. 367.
26. See ibid. p. 368.
27. Ibid. p. 374.
28. Ibid. p. 385.
29. Ibid. p. 369.
30. See Karl Popper, *The Poverty of Historicism* (Boston: Beacon Press, 1957).
31. Berlin, *Historical Inevitability*, p. 10.
32. Ibid. p. 15.
33. Morris Ginsberg, *Evolution and Progress* (London: William Heinemann, 1961), p. 252.
34. Ibid. p. 237.
35. See Karl Mannheim, *Ideology and Utopia: An Introduction to the Sociology of Knowledge*. Translated from the German by Louis Wirth and Edward Shils. (New York: Harcourt, Brace & World, 1970); and Kuhn, *The Structure of Scientific Revolutions*.

ii   The Second Approach Development: The Growing Societal Systemness

1. Nisbet, *Social Change and History*, p. 240.
2. Wilbert E. Moore, *Social Change* (Englewood Cliffs, N.J.: Prentice-Hall, Inc., 1963).
3. Charles H. Cooley, *Social Organization* (Glencoe, Ill.: The Free Press, 1956), p. 23.
4. Ferdinand Toennies, *Community and Society (Gemeinschaft and Gesellschaft)*. Translated and introduced by Charles P. Loomis (East Lansing, Mich.: Michigan State University Press, 1957), p. 35.
5. Ibid. p. 76.
6. Ibid. pp. 76-77.
7. Emile Durkheim, *The Division of Labor in Society*. Translated by George Simpson (Glencoe, Ill.: The Free Press, 1949), p. 37.

8. See Max Weber, *The Theory of Social and Economic Organization.* Translated by A. M. Henderson and Talcott Parsons. Edited with an Introduction by Talcott Parsons (New York: The Free Press, 1966), p. 136.

9. See Ely Chinoy, *Sociological Perspective* (Garden City, N.Y.: Doubleday, 1964), pp. 81-86.

10. Francis S. Sutton, "Representation and the Nature of Political Systems," *Comparative Studies in Society and History* (Ann Arbor, Mich.), Vol. II, No. 1, October 1959.

11. Talcott Parsons, *The Social System* (Glencoe, Ill.: The Free Press, 1951), pp. 101ff.

12. Talcott Parsons and Edward Shils (ed.), *Toward a General Theory of Action* (New York and Evanston, Ill.: Harper & Row, 1951), pp. 76 ff.

13. See Bert F. Hoselitz, *Sociological Aspects of Economic Growth* (Glencoe, Ill.: The Free Press, 1960).

14. Neil J. Smelser, *Essays in Sociological Explanation* (Englewood Cliffs, N.J.: Prentice Hall, 1968).

15. Here he is quoting M. Nash, "Some Notes on Village Industrialization in South and East Asia," *Economic Development and Cultural Change,* Vol. III, No. 3 (1954), p. 271.

16. Smelser, *Essays in Sociological Explanation,* p. 126.

17. Ibid. p. 129.

18. Ibid. p. 138.

19. See especially Ludwig von Bertalanffy, *General System Theory: Foundations, Development, Applications* (New York: Braziller, 1968).

20. See Peter M. Blau, *Exchange and Power in Social Life* (New York: Wiley, 1967), pp. 89-90.

21. Robert Michels, *Political Parties: A Sociological Study of the Oligarchical Tendencies of Modern Democracy.* Translated by Eden and Cedar Paul. Introduction by Seymour Martin Lipset (New York: The Free Press, 1962).

22. See Lucy Mair, *Primitive Government* (Harmonsdsworth, Middlesex: Penguin Books, 1962).

23. See also M. Gluckman, *Custom and Conflict in Africa* (Oxford: Basil Blackwell, 1963).

24. See Melville J. Herskovits, *Dahomey: An Ancient West African Kingdom* (Evanston, Ill.: Northwestern University Press, 1938), Vol. I.

25. See also David E. Apter, *The Political Kingdom in Uganda* (Princeton, N.J.: Princeton University Press, 1961), Chapter IV.

26. Mair, *Primitive Government,* pp. 107-8.

27. S. N. Eisenstadt, *The Political Systems of Empires* (Glencoe, Ill.: Free Press, 1963), p. 5.

28. See Sutton, "Representation. . . ."

29. See Robert Redfield, *Peasant Society and Culture* (Chicago: University of Chicago Press, 1963).

30. See Max Weber, "Politiks als Beruf" in *Gesammelte Politische Schriften.* Edited by Johannes Winckelmann (Tübingen: J. C. B. Mohr [Paul Siebeck], 1971); Marc L. B. Bloch, *Feudal Society.* Translated from the French by L. A. Hanyan (London: Routledge & Kegan Paul, 1965), 2 Vol. Rushton Coulborn, *The Origin of Civilized Societies* (Princeton, N.J.: Princeton University Press, 1959).

31. Eisenstadt, *The Political Systems* . . .

32. Ibid. p. 16.
33. Ibid. p. 24.
34. Lorenz von Stein, *Der Socialismus und Kommunismus des heutigen Frankreichs* (Leipzig: O. Wigand, 1848) Abt. III. "Die Bewegung der Gesellschaft," and Abt. IV. "Der Gegenzatz in der heutigen europeischen Gesellschaft."
35. See Witold Kula, *Teoria ekonomiczna ustroju feudalnego* (Warsaw: Panstwowe Wydawnictwo Naukowe, 1962).
36. Benjamin Nelson, *The Idea of Usury: From Tribal Brotherhood to Universal Otherhood* (Chicago: University of Chicago Press, 1969).
37. Barrington Moore, Jr., *Social Origins of Dictatorship and Democracy* (Boston: Beacon Press, 1966), p. 5.
38. Ibid. p. 13.
39. Ibid. p. 11.
40. Ibid. pp. 461-62.
41. Marion J. Levy, Jr., *Modernization and the Structure of Societies* (Princeton, N.J.: Princeton University Press, 1966), Vol. I, pp. 35 ff.
42. Buckley, *Sociology and Modern Systems Theory.*
43. Von Bertalanffy, *General Systems Theory,* p. 55.
44. A. Angyal, "A Logic of Systems," in F. E. Emery (ed.), *Systems Thinking* (Harmondsworth, Middlesex: Penguin Books, 1969), p. 21.
45. R. L. Ackoff, "Systems, Organizations and Interdisciplinary Research," in F. E. Emery, ibid. p. 332.
46. Buckley, *Sociology and Modern Systems Theory,* p. 41.
47. Warren F. Ilchman and Norman T. Uphoff, *The Political Economy of Change* (Berkeley and Los Angeles: University of California Press, 1969); and Talcott Parsons and Neil J. Smelser, *Economy and Society* (London: Routledge & Kegan Paul, 1957).
48. See Wlodzimierz Brus, *Ogolne problemy funkcjonowania gospodarki socjalistycznej* (Warsaw: Panstwowe Wydawnictwo Naukowe, 1961), pp. 116-17. Also Gregory Grossman, "The Solidary Society: A Philosophical Issue in Communist Economic Reforms," in Grossman (ed.), *Essays in Socialism and Planning in Honor of Carl Landauer* (Englewood Cliffs, N.J., 1970).
49. See Ralf Dahrendorf, *Essays in the Theory of Society* (Stanford, Calif.: Stanford University Press, 1968), especially pp. 25-38.

iii   Comparison of Some Cases of Growing Systemness in Diverse Societies

1. C. Kerr, J. T. Dunlop, F. H. Harbison, and C. A. Myers, *Industrialism and Industrial Man* (New York: Oxford University Press, 1960).
2. Ibid. p. 49.
3. See especially Barrington Moore, Jr., *Terror and Progress—USSR* (New York: Harper & Row, 1954). Also his *The Social Origin of Dictatorship and Democracy.*
4. Wright Mills, *The Power Elite* (New York: Oxford University Press, 1956).
5. Vladimir I. Lenin, "The Fifth Congress of the R.S.D.L.P." in *Collected Works* (Moscow: Foreign Languages Publishing House, 1962), Vol. 12, p. 464.
6. Lenin, "Tenth All-Russia Conference of the R.C.P.(B)," *Collected Works* (Moscow: Foreign Languages Publishing House, 1969), Vol. 32, p. 408.
7. J. Stalin, "The Tasks of Business Executives," in *Problems of Leninism* (Moscow: Foreign Languages Publishing House, 1947), p. 356.

8. Apter, "Notes for a Theory of Non Democratic Representation," in *Some Conceptual Approaches to the Study of Modernization* (Englewood Cliffs, N.J.: Prentice-Hall, 1968), p. 305.
9. See Andrew Shonfield, *Modern Capitalism. The Changing Balance of Public and Private Power* (London: Oxford University Press, 1965); John K. Galbraith, *The New Industrial State* (London: Hamish Hamilton, 1967); Peter d'Alroy Jones, *The Consumer Society: A History of American Capitalism* (London: Pelican Books, 1965).
10. Joseph A. Schumpeter, *Capitalism, Socialism and Democracy* (London: Unwin University Books, 1966), pp. 73-74.
11. See Thorstein Veblen, *The Theory of Leisure Class: An Economic Study of Institutions*. With a Foreword by Stuart Chase (New York: Modern Library, 1934); David Riesman, *Thorstein Veblen: A Critical Interpretation* (New York: Scribner's, 1960), Chapter III.
12. Paul A. Baran and Paul M. Sweezy, *Monopoly Capital: An Essay on the American Economic and Social Order* (New York: Monthly Review Press, 1966), p. 80.
13. Ibid. p. 109.
14. See Alex Inkeles, "Social Stratification and Mobility in the Soviet Union: 1940-1950," *American Sociological Review*, Vol. 15, No. 4, 1950; Alex Inkeles and Raymond Bauer, *The Soviet Citizen: Daily Life in a Totalitarian Society* (New York: Atheneum, 1968); Milovan Djilas, *The New Class: An Analysis of the Communist System* (New York: Praeger, 1957); H. Gordon Skilling and Franklyn Griffiths (eds.), *Interest Groups in Soviet Politics* (Princeton, N.J.: Princeton University Press, 1971); Robert A. Feldmesser, "Stratification and Communism" in Allen Kassof, *Prospects for Soviet Society* (New York: Praeger, 1968).
15. J. W. Hall, "Changing Conception of the Modernization of Japan," in Marius B. Jensen, *Changing Japanese Attitudes Toward Modernization* (Princeton, N.J.: Princeton University Press, 1965), p. 36.
16. Moore, *Social Origins . . .* , p. 246.
17. Ibid. p. 273.
18. R. P. Dore, "The Legacy of Tokugawa Education," in *Changing Japanese Attitudes . . .* , p. 101.
19. See Chapter VI, pp. 263 ff.
20. See Chodak, "Social Classes in Sub-Saharan Africa," *Africana Bulletin* (Warsaw, 1966), No. 4.
21. On setbacks in organized development in Africa see René Dumont, *False Start in Africa*. Translated by Phyllis Nauts Ott (New York: Praeger, 1969); Stanislav Andreski, *The African Predicament: A Study in Pathology of Modernization* (New York: Atherton, 1968).
22. See Alfred G. Meyer, "Theories of Convergence," in Chalmers Johnson (ed.), *Change in Communist Systems* (Stanford, Calif.: Stanford University Press); Peter Wiles, "Will Capitalism and Communism Spontaneously Converge?" *Encounter*. Vol. XX, June 1963, pp. 84-90.
23. A. I. Berg, B. V. Birukov, I. B. Novik, A. T. Spirkin, "Kibernetika—Metodologicheskie Problemy," *Vestnik Akademii Nauk SSSR* (hereafter referred to as VAN), No. 9, 1971.
24. See Albert Parry, *The New Class Divided—Russian Technology, Science Versus Communism* (New York: Macmillan, 1966); Gregory Grossman, "The Economist as a Catalyst of Change in the USSR and Eastern Europe," *Paper for the AAS-*

WSA in Denver, Colorado. March, 1971; A. Brzeski, "Poland as a Catalyst of Change in the Communist Economic System," *The Polish Review,* Vol. XVI. No. 2, Spring 1971.

25. See N. P. Fedorenko. *O Razrabotke sistemy optimalnogo funkcyonirovanya ekonomiki* (Moscow, 1968); N. P. Fedorenko, "K voprosu o postroenii sistemy optimalnogo perspektivnogo planirovanya narodnogo khoziaystva." *VAN,* No. 5, 1971; N. P. Fedorenko, "Ekonomisty—matematiki—narodnomu khoziaystvu," *VAN,* No. 1, 1971; John P. Hardt et al., *Mathematics and Computers in Soviet Economic Planning* (New Haven, Conn.: Yale University Press, 1967); Michael Ellman, *Soviet Planning Today: Proposals for an Optimally Functioning Economic System* (Cambridge: Cambridge University Press, 1971).

26. See M. V. Keldysh, "Vstupitelnoye slovo Presidenta Akademii Nauk SSSR," *VAN,* No. 5, 1971.

27. N. P. Fedorenko, "O sostoyanii i perspektivakh sozdanya aftomatizirovanykh sistem upravlenya promyslennymi predpriyatiyami," *Ekonomika i matematischeskiye metody* (Moscow, 1972), Vol. 3, No. 2, 1972.

28. N. Y. Petryakov, "Voprosy teorii optimalnogo upravleniya ekonomikoy," *Izvestiya Akademii Nauk SSSR, Serya ekonomicheskaya,* No. 2, 1972.

29. A. Kucev, M. Goryakov, *Matematika i upravleniye proizvodstvom* (Moscow: Moskovski Rabotchyi, 1969).

30. See *Problemy funkcyonirovanya bolshikh ekonomicheskikh sistem* (Papers of the Conference in Moskow. 4-7 October, 1967) (Moscow, 1969); B. M. Smekhov, *Perspektivnoye narodno-khoziaystviennoye planirovanye* (Moscow, 1968).

31. Petryakov, "Voprosy teorii . . . ," p. 86.

32. Ibid.; See also I. G. Shilin, "Problemy planirovanya i stimulirovanya tekhnicheskogo progressa," *Vestnik Moskovskogo Universiteta,* No. 6, 1971.

33. Shilin, "Problemy planirovanya . . . ," p. 73.

34. See P. G. Oldak, A. P. Dubnov, B. D. Grober, "Programmnyi podkhod k planirovaniyu ekonomicheskogo razvitya," *Izvestya Sibirskogo Otdelenya Akademii Nauk SSSR. Serya Obshchestvennykh Nauk* (Novosybirsk, 1971), No. 6.

35. A. G. Granberg, "O primenenii optimizacyonnykh modeley v prognosirovanyi razvitya i razmeschennya proizvoditelnykh sil," *Izvestiya Akademii Nauk SSSR, Serya ekonomicheskaya,* No. 2, 1971.

36. See papers in *Ekonomika i matematicheskie metody* (Moscow: Gos. Izdat 1970, 1971).

37. A. Y. Boyarskyi, "Eshcho ob optimalnom planirovanii," *Izvestiya Akademii Nauk SSSR, Serya ekonomicheskaya,* No. 2, 1971.

38. Ibid. p. 100.

39. A. A. Modin, "Aftomatizirovannye sistemy upravlenya i problemy ikh razrabotki," *Vestnik Akademii Nauk SSSR,* No. 3, 1972. p. 20.

40. Hannah Arendt, *Totalitarianism* (New York: Harcourt, Brace & World, 1968); Merle Fainsod, *How Russia Is Ruled* (Cambridge, Mass.: Harvard University Press, 1963); C. J. Friedrich and Z. Brzezinski, *Totalitarian Dictatorship and Autocracy* (New York: Praeger, 1965).

41. Inkeles and Bauer, *The Soviet Citizen;* Moore, *Terror and Progress: USSR;* F. C. Barghoorn, *Politics in the USSR* (Cambridge, Mass.: Harvard University Press, 1950); Zbigniew Brzezinski and Samuel P. Huntington, *Political Power: USA/USSR* (New York: Viking, 1967).

42. Allen Kassof, "The Administered Society: Totalitarianism Without Terror," *World Politics,* XVI, No. 4, July 1964; Alfred G. Meyer, *The Soviet Political System: An*

Interpretation (New York: Random House, 1965); Kassof (ed.), *Prospects for Soviet Society*.

43. Thomas R. Malthus, *An Essay on the Principle of Population or a View of Its Past and Present Effects on Human Happiness* (New York: Augustus M. Kelley, 1971), p. 6.

44. *Hegel's Philosophy of Right*. Translated with notes by M. Knox (Oxford, The Clarendon Press, 1965), p. 156.

45. See Ernst B. Haas, *Beyond the Nation State: Functionalism and International Organization* (Stanford, Calif.: Stanford University Press, 1964).

46. See Matus Gustavo Lagos, *International Stratification and Underdeveloped Countries* (Chapel Hill: The University of North Carolina Press, 1963).

47. Karl W. Deutsch, *The Analysis of International Relations* (Englewood Cliffs, N.J.: Prentice-Hall, 1968), pp. 174-79.

48. Haas, *Beyond the Nation State*, pp. 53-54.

49. Ibid. pp. 484-97.

50. Ibid. p. 82.

51. Ibid. pp. 48 and 487; see also Ernst B. Haas, "Collective Security and the Future International System," *Monograph Series in World Affairs*, Vol. V, Monograph No. 1, 1967-68, pp. 22-25.

52. Ibid. pp. 26-27.

53. Deutsch, *The Analysis* . . . , p. 8.

54. Karl W. Deutsch, *Political Community at the International Level* (Garden City, N.Y.: Doubleday, 1964), p. 29.

55. Deutsch, *The Analysis* . . . , p. 174.

56. See Morton A. Kaplan, *System and Process in International Politics* (New York: Wiley, 1957). For a general discussion of system theories in international relations see Jerome Stephens, "An Appraisal of Some System Approaches in the Study of International Systems," *International Studies Quarterly*, Vol. XVI, No. 3, September 1972.

57. Out of the six mentioned, these two are discussed in a reformulated version in Morton A. Kaplan, "The Systems Approach to International Politics," in Morton A. Kaplan (ed.), *New Approaches to International Relations* (New York: St. Martin's Press, 1965).

58. See Haas, *Beyond the Nation State*, pp. 464-75; K. R. Minogue, *Nationalism* (London: B. T. Batsford, Ltd., 1967); Karl W. Deutsch and William J. Foltz, *Nation Building* (New York: Atherton Press, 1963).

59. Jacques Ellul, *The Technological Society*. Translated from the French by John Wilkinson with an Introduction by Robert K. Merton (New York: Knopf and Random House, 1964), p. 284.

60. Ibid. p. 287.

61. Ibid. pp. 432-33.

62. Ibid. p. 430.

63. Brzezinski and Huntington, *Political Power*.

64. Ibid. p. 436.

65. Ibid. p. 426.

66. Ibid. p. 413.

67. See W. G. Afanasiev, *Nauchnyi Kommunism* (Scientific Communism) (Moscow: Gosizdat, 1966). There are also a number of articles by various authors without names of the editors: *Nekotorye Problemy Teorii i Praktiki Stroitelstva Kommunisma* (Some Problems of Theory and Practice in Building Communism)

(Moscow, 1961); *Dialektika Stroitelstva Kommunisma* (The Dialectic of Building Communism) (Moscow, 1968), etc.

68. See Harry G. Shaffer and Jan S. Prybyla, *From Underdevelopment to Affluence: Western Soviet and Chinese Views* (New York: Appleton-Century-Crofts, 1968).

69. See Andrei D. Sakharov, *Progress, Coexistence and Intellectual Freedom*. Translated by the New York *Times*. With Introduction, Afterword, and Notes by Harrison E. Salisbury (New York: Norton, 1968).

70. Ibid. pp. 27-28.

71. Andrei Amalrik, *Will the Soviet Union Survive Until 1984?* Preface by Henry Kamm, Commentary by Sidney Monas (New York: Harper & Row, 1970), p. 22.

72. Ibid. p. 29.

73. Clark Kerr, *Marshall, Marx and Modern Times: The Multidemensional Society* (Cambridge: Cambridge University Press, 1969).

74. Ibid. p. 124.

75. Ernst B. Haas, *Tangle of Hopes: American Commitments and World Order* (Englewood Cliffs, N.J.: Prentice-Hall, 1969), p. 220.

76. Ibid. p. 58.

77. Robert K. Merton, *Social Theory and Social Structure* (New York: The Free Press, 1967), pp. 60ff.

78. Von Stein, *Der Sozialismus* . . . , Abteilung IV.

79. Chodak, *Systemy partyjne Europy Zachodniej: pochodzenie ewolucja, funkcje spleczne. Studia Socjologiczno-polityczne*, Vol. 9 (Warsaw, 1961).

80. William G. Sumner, *Folkways: A Study of the Sociological Importance of Usages, Manners, Customs, Mores and Morals* (Boston: Ginn, 1906).

81. J. O. Hertzler, *Social Institutions* (Lincoln, Neb.: University of Nebraska Press, 1946), pp. 89-90.

iv   The Third Approach: Development and Innovation in Search for Security

1. See Tom Burns and S. B. Saul (eds.), Introduction to Michael Argyle, Reinhard Bendix, M. W. Flinn, Everett E. Hagen, *Social Theory and Economic Change* (London: Tavistock, 1967), p. 2.

2. Max Weber, *The Protestant Ethic and the Spirit of Capitalism*. Translated by Talcott Parsons with a Foreword by R. H. Tawney (New York: Scribner's, 1958), p. 76.

3. Ibid. p. 17.

4. Ibid. pp. 58-59.

5. Ibid. p. 117.

6. Max Weber, *Werk und Person: Dokumente*. Ausgewählt und kommentiert von Eduard Baumgarten (Tübingen: J. C. B. Mohr /Paul Siebeck/, 1964), p. 183.

7. See S. N. Eisenstadt, "The Protestant Ethic: Thesis in an Analytical and Comparative Framework"; and E. Fischoff, "The Protestant Ethic and the Spirit of Capitalism: The History of a Controversy," in S. N. Eisenstadt (ed.), *Protestant Ethic and Modernization: A Comparative View* (New York: Basic Books, 1968). See also Robert W. Green (ed.), *Protestantism and Capitalism: The Weber Thesis and Its Critics* (Boston: D. C. Heath, 1959). This small book contains extracts from earlier criticism of Weber: E. Troelsch, W. Sombart, R. H. Tawney, W. S. Hudson, and others.

8. H. M. Robertson, *Aspects of the Rise of Economic Individualism: A Criticism of Max Weber and His School* (London: Cambridge University Press, 1933).

9. Ibid. p. xiv.
10. Ibid. p. 30.
11. Kurt Samuelsson, *Religion and Economic Action,* translated from the Swedish by E. Geoffrey French, edited and with an introduction by D. C. Coleman (New York: Basic Books, 1961).
12. Ibid. p. 50.
13. Ibid. pp. 151-52.
14. See H. Lüthy, "Variationen über ein Thema von Max Weber: Die Protestantische Ethik und der Geist des Kapitalismus," in *In Gegenwart der Geschichte. Historische Essays* (Berlin: Kiepenheuer und Witsch, 1967).
15. Ibid. pp. 84-85.
16. H. R. Trevor-Roper, *The Crisis of the Seventeenth Century: Religion, the Reformation and Social Change* (New York: Harper & Row, 1968).
17. Julien Freund, *The Sociology of Max Weber* (New York: Random House, 1968).
18. Raymond Aron, *Main Currents in Sociological Thought.* Translated by Richard Howard and Helen Weaver (London: Weidenfeld and Nicolson, 1967), Vol. II. See especially pp. 205-19.
19. Reinhard Bendix. *Max Weber: An Intellectual Portrait* (Garden City, N.Y.: Doubleday, Anchor Books, 1962), p. 57.
20. Benjamin Nelson, "In Defense of Max Weber," *Encounter,* No. 131, August 1964; Review of K. Samuelsson's *Religion and Economic Action,* in *American Sociological Review,* Vol. XXVII, 1962; *The Idea of Usury,* pp. 236-46, "Conscience and the Making of Early Modern Cultures: The Protestant Ethic Beyond Max Weber," *Social Research,* Vol. XXXVI, No. 1, 1969.
21. Benjamin Nelson, "Scholastic Rationales of 'Conscience,' Early Modern Crisis of Credibility, and the Scientific-Technocultural Revolutions of the 17th and 20th Centuries," *Journal for Scientific Study of Religion,* Vol. VII, No. 2, 1968, p. 162.
22. Ibid. pp. 162-63.
23. Ibid. p. 168.
24. Robert N. Bellah, *Tokugawa Religion: The Values of Pre-Industrial Japan* (New York: Free Press, 1957). See also Robert N. Bellah (ed.), *Religion and Progress in Modern Asia* (New York: Free Press, 1965).
25. Clifford Geertz, *Peddlers and Princes: Social Change and Economic Modernization in Two Indonesian Towns* (Chicago: University of Chicago Press, 1963), p. 49.
26. See Everett E. Hagen, *On the Theory of Social Change: How Economic Growth Begins* (Homewood, Ill.: Dorsey Press, 1962), p. 93.
27. Ibid. p. 97.
28. Ibid. p. 186.
29. Ibid. p. 242.
30. Ibid. p. 261.
31. L. Kasdan, "Family Structure, Migration and the Entrepreneur," in *Comparative Study of Society and History,* Vol. VII, No. 4, 1967.
32. Ibid. p. 346.
33. See Benjamin Higgins, *Economic Development: Principles, Problems and Policies* (New York: Norton, 1968), pp. 249-57.
34. In the discussion of David C. McClelland's theory of achievement motivation I will rely basically on two of his books: *The Achieving Society* (Princeton, N.J.: Van Nostrand, 1961) and the book by David C. McClelland, David G. Winter with Sara K. Winter and others, *Motivating Economic Achievement* (New York:

Free Press, 1969). See also John W. Atkinson and Norman T. Feather (eds.), *A Theory of Achievement Motivation* (New York: Wiley, 1966); H. Heckhausen, *The Anatomy of Achievement Motivation,* translated by Kay F. Butler, Robert C. Birney, and David C. McClelland (New York: Academic Press, 1967).

35. McClelland, *Achieving Society,* p. 38.
36. M. R. Winterbottom, "The Relation of Need for Achievement to Learning Experiences in Independence and Mastery," in J. W. Atkinson (ed.), *Motives in Fantasy, Action and Society* (Princeton, N.J.: Van Nostrand, 1958). Quoted in McClelland, *Achieving Society.*
37. Ibid. pp. 45 and 65.
38. Ibid. p. 36.
39. Ibid. p. 205.
40. Ibid. p. 168.
41. J. N. Morgan, "The Achievement Motive and Economic Behavior," in J. W. Atkinson and N. T. Feather (eds.), *Motives in Fantasy . . . ,* p. 207.
42. Max Weber, *The Protestant Ethic . . . ,* p. 76.
43. McClelland, *Achieving Society,* pp. 236-37.
44. McClelland and others, *Motivating Economic Achievement,* pp. 21-23.
45. McClelland, *Achieving Society,* pp. 210-25; H. Heckhausen, *Anatomy of Achievement Motivation,* pp. 58-61; G. H. Litwin, "Achievement Motivation, Expectancy of Success, and Risk-Taking Behavior" in Atkinson and Feather (eds.), *Motives in Fantasy . . . ,* pp. 103-15.
46. McClelland, *Achieving Society,* pp. 225-28; see various studies in Bernhard C. Rosen, Harry J. Crockett, Jr., and Clyde Z. Nunn (eds.), *Achievement in American Society,* with Foreword by James S. Coleman (Cambridge, Mass.: Schenkman, 1969).
47. McClelland, *Achieving Society,* pp. 229-30.
48. Ibid. p. 231.
49. Robert A. Le Vine, *Dreams and Deeds: Achievement Motivation in Nigeria,* with assistance of Eugene Strangman and Leonard Unterberger (Chicago: University of Chicago Press, 1966).
50. M. Brewster Smith, "The Achieving Society, by David C. McClelland" in *History and Theory,* Vol. III, No. 3, 1964, p. 380.
51. Warren E. Ilchman and Norman T. Uphoff, *The Political Economy of Change* (Berkeley and Los Angeles: University of California Press, 1969), pp. 262-67. See also B. Higgins, pp. 241-49.
52. D. C. McClelland et al., *Motivating.*
53. See George A. De Vos, "Achievement and Innovation in Culture and Personality," in Edward Norbeck, Douglas Price-Williams, William M. McCord (eds.), *The Study of Personality: An Interdisciplinary Appraisal* (New York: Holt, Reinhart & Winston, 1968).
54. Ibid. p. 361.
55. See B. C. Rosen et. al., *Achievement in American Society.*
56. B. Bettelheim, *Obsolete Youth* (San Francisco: San Francisco Press, 1970), p. 13.
57. See George A. De Vos, "The Relation of Guilt Towards Parents to Achievement and Arranged Marriage Among the Japanese," in Neil J. Smelser and William T. Smelser (eds.), *Personality and Social Systems,* 2nd Edition (New York: Wiley, 1964), pp. 150-67.
58. *Fundamentals of Marxism-Leninism: Manual* (Moscow: Foreign Languages Publishing House, 1961), pp. 175, 755.

59. Vladimir I. Lenin, "The Tasks of the Youth Leagues," *Selected Works* (Moscow: Progress Publishers, 1967), Vol. III, p. 468.
60. Ibid. pp. 169-70.
61. See, for example, Alfred G. Meyer,￼*The Soviet Political System*, pp. 82-83, 338-56; Karel and Irene M. Hulicka, *Soviet Institutions: The Individual and Society.* Boston: Christopher Publishing House, 1967, pp. 28-33, 532-37; Alex Inkeles, *Public Opinion in Soviet Russia: A Study in Mass Persuasion* (Cambridge, Mass.: Harvard University Press, 1950).
62. I. V. Stalin, "New Conditions—New Tasks in Economic Construction," in *Problems of Leninism* (Moscow: Foreign Languages Publishing House, 1947), p. 359. See also Alex Inkeles and Raymond Bauer, *The Soviet Citizen: Daily Life in a Totalitarian Society.* With the assistance of David Gleicher and Irving Rosow (New York: Atheneum, 1968), pp. 255-58.
63. McClelland, *Achieving Society,* p. 168.
64. See H. G. Barnett, *Innovation: The Basis of Cultural Change.* (New York: McGraw-Hill, 1953). On diverse motivation in entrepreneurial activities see F. Redlich, *Der Unternehmer* (Göttingen: Vanderhoech and Ruprecht, 1964), pp. 201-21, 355-59.
65. Max Weber, *The Protestant Ethic,* pp. 53-54.
66. Ibid. p. 80.
67. Immanuel Kant, *Critique of Practical Reason and Other Writings In Moral Philosophy,* translated and edited with an introduction by Lewis White Beck (Chicago: University of Chicago Press, 1949), p. 193.
68. Kuno Francke, *The German Spirit* (New York: Henry Holt, 1916), pp. 49, 64-65.
69. See Thorstein Veblen, *The Higher Learning in America: A Memorandum on the Conduct of Universities by Business Men.* Reprints of Economic Classics (New York: Augustus M. Kelley, 1965), pp. 195-206.
70. Joseph A. Schumpeter, *Capitalism, Socialism and Democracy* (London: Unwin University Books, 1966), pp. 127, 124.
71. Ralph Linton, *The Cultural Background of Personality* (London: Routledge & Kegan Paul, 1964), p. 6.
72. See Sydney Hook, "A Philosopher's View," in E. J. Faulkner (ed.), *Man's Quest for Security: A Symposium* (Lincoln: University of Nebraska Press, 1966), p. 5.
73. Harold D. Lasswell and Abraham Kaplan, *Power and Society* (New Haven: Yale University Press, 1968), p. 61.
74. See A. L. Knutson, "Personal Security as Related to Station in Life," in *Psychological Monographs,* Vol. LXVI, No. 336, 1952.
75. Hook, "A Philosopher's View," p. 17.
76. Thomas S. Power, "A Military Scientist's View," in Faulkner, *Man's Quest . . . ,* p. 184.
77. See Karen Horney, *Our Inner Conflict: A Constructive Theory of Neurosis* (New York: Norton, 1957); N. S. Sullivan, *The Interpersonal Theory of Psychiatry* (New York: Norton, 1953). In a special category not related to psychoanalysis one should include the theory of W. E. Blatz, *Human Security* (Toronto: University of Toronto Press, 1966). Some of the ideas of the writer correspond to those of Erich Fromm, who also has to be regarded as a follower of the cultural school of psychoanalysis.
78. Erich Fromm, *The Sane Society* (New York: Rinehart, 1955), p. 196.
79. On security in traditional societies see Abram Kardiner, *The Individual and His Society: The Psychodynamics of Primitive Social Organization.* With a foreword

and two ethnological reports by Ralph Linton. (New York: Columbia University Press, 1965) espe. Chapter IV, "Security System and Basic Personality Structure."

80. See Immanuel Wallerstein (ed.), *Social Change: The Colonial Situation* (New York: Wiley, 1966), Part VI. B. G. M. Sundklar, *Bantu Prophets in South Africa*, 2nd ed. (London: Oxford University Press, 1961).
81. Arthur H. Cole, *Business Enterprise in Its Social Setting* (Cambridge, Mass.: Harvard University Press, 1959), p. 108.
82. B. Nelson, "Communities, Societies. Civilizations. Postmillennial Views on the Masks and Faces of Change," in Manfred Stanley (ed.), *Social Development: Critical Perspectives*. (New York: Basic Books, 1972), p. 105.
83. Eric J. Hobsbawn, *The Age of Revolution: Europe 1789-1848* (London: Weidenfeld & Nicolson, 1962), p. 28.
84. See Reinhard Bendix, *Nation Building and Citizenship: Studies of Our Changing Social Order* (Garden City, N.Y.: Doubleday, 1969), pp. 89-90.
85. Ibid. pp. 90-91.
86. See Sebastian De Grazia, *The Political Community: A Study of Anomie* (Chicago: University of Chicago Press, 1948).
87. See Everet M. Rogers, *Diffusion of Innovations* (New York: Free Press of Glencoe, 1962), p. 194.
88. On marginal men, see E. V. Stonequist, *The Marginal Man: A Study in Personality and Cultural Conflict* (New York: Russell & Russell, 1961).
89. On activities of members of other Protestant churches in the field of industries and entrepreneurial endeavours, contribution in the development of science and spread of innovation see, Arthur Raistrick, *Quakers in Science and Industry: Being an Account of the Quaker Contributions to Science and Industry During the 17th and 18th Centuries* (New York: Kelley, 1968); Thomas S. Ashton, *Economic History of England: The Eighteenth Century* (London: Methuen, 1955); Wellman J. Warner, *The Wesleyan Movement in the Industrial Revolution* (London: Longmans, Green, 1930): On a case study of a marginal group in another continent and culture see Dharam P. Ghai, *Portrait of a Minority: Asians in East Africa* (Nairobi, Oxford University Press, 1965).
90. Warner, *The Wesleyan Movement* . . . , p. 47. See also De Grazia, *Political Community,* pp. 62-63.
91. Jean Paul Sartre, *Anti-Semite and Jew,* translated from the French by George J. Becker (New York: Schocken Book, 1948), pp. 83, 97, 98.
92. Ibid. pp. 144-45.
93. Berthold F. Hoselitz, "Introduction to the American Edition" of Werner Sombart, *The Jews and Modern Capitalism,* translated by M. Epstein (Glencoe, Ill.: The Free Press, 1951), p. 12.
94. See Bettelheim, *Obsolete Youth.*
95. See S. De Grazia, *Political Community,* pp. 178-83.
96. Charles Hampden-Turner, *Radical Man: The Process of Psycho-Social Development* (Cambridge, Mass.: Schenkman, 1970), pp. 48-50. See also Theodore Roszak, *The Making of Counter Culture* (Garden City, N.Y.: Doubleday, 1969).
97. See Herbert Marcuse, *One-Dimensional Man: Studies in Ideology of Advanced Industrial Society* (Boston: Beacon Press, 1964), p. 171.

v   The Fourth Approach: Economic and Political Development

1. See, for example, B. Higgins, *Economic Development: Principles, Problems and Policies.*

2. Henry J. Bruton, *Principles of Development Economics* (Englewood Cliffs, N.J.: Prentice-Hall, 1967), p. 1.
3. Gerald M. Meier and Robert E. Baldwin, *Economic Development: Theory, History, Policy* (New York: Wiley, 1957), p. 2. For a similar standpoint, see Harvey Leibenstein, *Economic Backwardness and Economic Growth: Studies in Theory of Economic Development* (New York: Wiley, 1957); Irma Adelman, *Theories of Economic Growth and Development* (Stanford, Calif.: Stanford University Press, 1961); W. Arthur Lewis, *The Theory of Economic Growth* (New York and Evanston: Harper & Row, 1965).
4. Meier and Baldwin, *Economic Development*, pp. 2-3.
5. S. Herbert Frankel, *The Economic Impact on Underdeveloped Societies: Essays in International Investment and Social Change* (Oxford: Blackwell, 1953), pp. 29-55; Simon Smith Kuznets, "Problems in Comparisons of Economic Trends" in Kuznets, Wilbert E. Moore, Joseph J. Spengler (eds.), *Economic Growth: Brazil, India, Japan* (Durham, N.C.: Duke University Press, 1955); McClelland, *Achieving Society*, pp. 80-82.
6. See Witold Kula, *Problemy i metody historii gospodarczej* (Warsaw: Panstwowy Instytut Wydawniczy, 1963), especially pp. 331-35.
7. Leibenstein, *Economic Backwardness and Economic Growth*, p. 8.
8. See Higgins, *Economic Development*, pp. 106-7.
9. See A. W. Sametz, "Production of Goods and Services: The Measurement of Economic Growth" in Eleanor B. Sheldon and Wilbert E. Moore (eds.), *Indicators of Social Change: Concepts and Measurements* (New York: Russell Sage, 1968). It is applied to the analysis of United States; Kenneth K. Kurihara, *National Income and Economic Growth* (London: Allen and Unwin, 1961). Iakov A. Kronrod, *Obshchestvennyi produkt i ego struktura pri socyalizme* (Moscow: Gosudarstvennoe Izdatelstvo Politicheskoi Literatury, 1958); Adam Przeworski, "Niektore problemy metodologiczne socjologii rozwoju gospodarczego," *Studia Socjologiczne*, No. 3 (14), (Warsaw, 1967).
10. McClelland, *Achieving Society*, pp. 85-97.
11. Meier and Baldwin, *Economic Development*, p. 8.
12. See Adam Smith, *An Inquiry into the Nature and Causes of the Wealth of Nations* (London: Methuen, 1961).
13. Bert F. Hoselitz, "Theories of Stages of Economic Growth" in Hoselitz (ed.), *Theories of Economic Growth* (Glencoe, Ill.: Free Press, 1960), pp. 193-95.
14. Neil J. Smelser, *The Sociology of Economic Life* (Englewood Cliffs, N.J.: Prentice-Hall, 1963), Chapter II; Leibenstein, *Economic Backwardness and Economic Growth*, Chapter 12.
15. See Hoselitz, "Theories of Stages. . . ."
16. See Walt W. Rostow, *The Stages of Economic Growth: A Non-Communist Manifesto* (London: Cambridge University Press, 1960). For criticism of Rostow, see S. S. Kuznets, *Economic Growth and Structures: Selected Essays*. On a different proposal on stages of development of societies taking into consideration especially agriculture, see Guy Hunter, *Modernizing Peasant Societies: A Comparative Study in Asia and Africa.* (London: Oxford University Press, 1969), pp. 24-29.
17. See J. Buttrick, "Toward a Theory of Economic Growth: The Neoclassical Contribution" in Hoselitz (ed.), *Theories of Economic Growth*, p. 158.
18. Joseph A. Schumpeter, *The Theory of Economic Development: An Inquiry into Profits, Capital, Credit, Interest and the Business Cycle.* Translated from German by Redvers Opie (Cambridge, Mass., Harvard University Press, 1961), p. 16.

19. Here I am following the lead of I. Adelman, *Theories of Economic Growth and Development*, pp. 94-99.
20. H. J. Bruton, "Contemporary Theorizing on Economic Growth" in Hoselitz (ed.), *Theories of Economic Growth*, p. 239.
21. Ibid. p. 295.
22. Ibid. pp. 297-98.
23. Meier and Baldwin, *Economic Development*, p. 110.
24. Ibid. p. 124.
25. *Fundamentals of Marxism-Leninism*, p. 704.
26. Oscar Lange, *The Political Economy of Socialism: Two Lectures* (The Hague. Institute of Social Studies, No. 16, 1958, p. 7). See also "Ekonomia polityczna socjalizmu" in Lange (ed.), *Zagadnienia ekonomii politycznej socjalizmu* (Warsaw: Panstwowe Wydawnictwo Naukowe, 1960).
27. Lange, *The Political Economy of Socialism*, p. 8.
28. Ibid. pp. 10-11.
29. Ibid. p. 15.
30. Ragnar Nurske, *Problems of Capital Formation in Underdeveloped Countries* (New York: Oxford University Press, 1957). See Chapter 1.
31. On criticism of the concept of vicious circles, see Gunnar Myrdal, *Economic Theory and Underdeveloped Regions* (London: Methuen, 1957), Chapter 2; Meier and Baldwin, *Economic Development*, pp. 319-24.
32. Leibenstein, *Economic Backwardness and Economic Growth*, p. 187.
33. See, for instance, Ignacy Sachs (ed.), *Obstacles to Growth: Demographic, Economic and Social* (Warsaw: Polish Scientific Publishers, 1967); Peter T. Bauer and Basil S. Yamey, *The Economics of Underdeveloped Countries* (Chicago: University of Chicago Press, 1963).
34. On political systems, see David Easton, "An Approach to the Analysis of Political Systems," *World Politics*, Vol. IX, April 1957; David Easton, *Systems Analysis of Political Life* (New York: Wiley, 1965); David Easton (ed.), *Varieties of Political Theory* (Englewood Cliffs, N.J.: Prentice-Hall, 1966); Gabriel A. Almond and C. Bingham Powell, *Comparative Politics: A Developmental Approach* (Boston: Little Brown, 1966); Deutsch, *The Nerves of Government*; Herbert V. Wiseman, *Political Systems: Some Sociological Approaches* (London: Routledge & Kegan Paul, 1966).
35. Lucian W. Pye, *Aspects of Political Development* (Boston: Little, Brown, 1966), p. 63.
36. Ibid. p. 67.
37. Ibid. p. 45.
38. See Samuel P. Huntington, "Political Development and Political Decay," *World Politics*, Vol. XVII, No. 3 (1965).
39. Gabriel A. Almond, *Political Development: Essays in Heuristic Theory* (Boston: Little, Brown, 1970).
40. Ernest Renan, "The Meaning of Nationality," in Hans Kohn, *Nationalism: Its Meaning and History* (Princeton, N.J.: Van Nostrand, 1955), p. 136.
41. See "The Nature of Nations," in *Nationalism: A Report by a Study Group of Members of the Royal Institute of International Affairs*. Frank Cass and Comp. Ltd. 1963), pp. 249-63.
42. Walter Sultzbach, *National Consciousness* (New York: American Council on Public Affairs, 1949).

43. K. R. Minogue, *Nationalism* (London: B. T. Batsford, 1967).
44. See Leonard Binder, "National Integration and Political Development," *The American Political Science Review*, Vol. LVIII, No. 3 (September 1964); Karl W. Deutsch, "The Growth of Nations: Some Recurrent Patterns of Political and Social Integration," *World Politics*, Vol. V (January 1953).
45. See Sutton, "Representation and the Nature of Political Systems," F. G. Riggs, "Agraria and Industria: Toward a Typology of Comparative Administration" in W. J. Siffin (ed.), *Toward a Comparative Study of Public Administration* (Bloomington, Ind.: Indiana University Press, 1957), pp. 27-38.
46. Seymour M. Lipset, *Political Man: The Social Basis of Politics* (Garden City, N.Y.: Doubleday, 1960); Edward Shils, *Political Development in the New States* (s-Gravenhage: Mouton, 1962); Gabriel A. Almond and James S. Coleman, *The Politics of the Developing Areas* (Princeton, N.J.: Princeton University Press, 1960).
47. Joseph La Palombara and Myron Weiner (ed.), *Political Parties and Political Development* (Princeton, N.J.: Princeton University Press, 1965); Chodak, *Systemy partyjne Europy zachodniej* . . . , David E. Apter, "Notes for a Theory of Non-Democratic Representation" in *Some Conceptual Approaches to the Study of Modernization* (Englewood Cliffs, N.J.: Prentice-Hall, 1968).
48. Almond, "A Comparative Study of Interest Groups and the Political Process" in Almond, *Political Development* . . . , Otto Stammer, "Interessenverbände und Parteien" in *Kölner Zeitschrift für Soziologie und Socialpsychologie*, No. 4, 1957.
49. Joseph La Palombara (ed.), *Bureaucracy and Political Development* (Princeton, N.J.: Princeton University Press, 1963); Samuel P. Huntington, *Political Order in Changing Societies* (New Haven, Conn.: Yale University Press, 1968); Almond, "Political Development: Analytical and Normative Perspectives" in Almond, *Political Development.* . . .
50. A. F. K. Organski, *The Stages of Political Development* (New York: Knopf, 1965).
51. Huntington, "Political Development. . . ."
52. Chodak, "Societal Functions of Single-Party Systems in Sub-Saharan Africa" in Erik Allardt and Yrjö Littunen (eds.), *Cleavages: Ideologies and Party Systems* (Helsinki: The Academic Bookstore, 1964).
53. See Almond, "Political Development: Analytical and Normative Perspectives," in *Political Development*, pp. 291ff.
54. Ibid. pp. 210-11.
55. See S. E. Finer, "Almond's Concept of 'The Political System'; A Textual Critique," in *Government and Opposition*, Vol. V, No. 1 1969-1970.
56. See Deutsch, *The Nerves of Government*, pp. 250-54.
57. See J. Roland Pennock and John W. Chapman, *Privacy* (New York: Atherton, 1971); J. Rosenberg, *The Death of Privacy* (New York: Random House, 1969); Alan F. Westin, *Privacy and Freedom* (New York: Atheneum, 1967); Malcolm Warner and Michael Stone, *The Data Bank Society: Organizations, Computers and Social Freedom* (London: Allen & Unwin, 1970).
58. A. R. Radcliffe Brown, "Preface" to M. Fortes and E. E. Evans-Pritchard, *African Political Systems* (London: Oxford University Press, 1961).
59. Gabriel A. Almond and Sidney Verba, *The Civic Culture: Political Attitudes and Democracy in Five Nations* (Boston and Toronto: Little, Brown, 1965).
60. Ibid. p. 19.

61. Ibid. p. 30.
62. J. P. Nettl, *Political Mobilization: A Sociological Analysis of Methods and Concepts* (London: Faber & Faber, 1967).
63. Ibid. p. 68.
64. Ibid. pp. 72-78.
65. Ibid. pp. 79, 89.
66. See George P. Murdock, "The Cross-Cultural Survey," *American Sociological Review,* Vol. V, No. 3, 1940, pp. 364-69.
67. Apter, *The Politics of Modernization* (Chicago: University of Chicago Press, 1965), pp. 83-95.
68. See Zygmunt Bauman, *Kultura i społeczenstwo: Preliminaria* (Warsaw: Państwowe Wydawnictwo Naukowe, 1966).
69. See Kenneth E. Boulding, *Beyond Economics: Essays on Society, Religion, and Ethics* (Ann Arbor: University of Michigan Press, 1968), pp. 98-111.
70. Arne Naess, *Democracy, Idealogy and Objectivity* (Oslo: Oslo University Press and Oxford: Basil Blackwell, 1956).
71. Karl Marx, "On the Jewish Question" in Lloyd D. Easton and Kurt H. Guddat (ed.), *Writings of the Young Marx on Philosophy and Society* (Garden City, N.Y.: Doubleday, 1967), p. 241.
72. See J. Stalin, "On the Draft Constitution of the U.S.S.R." *Problems of Leninism,* pp. 540 ff.
73. George Lichtheim, *A Short History of Socialism* (New York: Praeger, 1970).
74. *Colloque sur les politiques de développement et les diverses voies africaines vers le socialisme* (Paris, 1963), p. 12.
75. Léopold Sédar Senghor, *On African Socialism.* Translated and with an introduction by Mercer Cook (New York: Praeger, 1964), p. 108.

vi   The Fifth Approach: Modernization

1. See John Brode, *The Process of Modernization: An Annotated Bibliography on the Sociocultural Aspects of Development,* foreword by Inkeles (Cambridge, Mass.: Harvard University Press, 1970); Allan A. Spitz, *Developmental Change: An Annotated Bibliography* (Lexington: University of Kentucky Press, 1969).
2. Marion J. Levy, Jr. *Modernization and the Structure of Societies* (Princeton: N.J.: Princeton University Press, 1966), Vol. I, p. 35.
3. Reinhard Bendix, "Tradition and Modernity Reconsidered," *Comparative Studies in Society and History,* Vol. IX, No. 3, April 1967.
4. See S. N. Eisenstadt, *Tradition. Change and Modernity: Some Reflections on Theories of Modernization.* Paper for the VII World Congress of IPSA, September 18-23, 1967. Also see his *Modernization: Protest and Change* (Englewood Cliffs, N.J.: Prentice-Hall, 1966).
5. See Lloyd I. Rudolph, Susanne H. Rudolph, *The Modernity of Tradition. Political Development in India* (Chicago: The University of Chicago Press, 1967); Donald N. Levine, "The Flexibility of Traditional Culture," *The Journal of Social Issues,* Vol. XXIV, No. 4, October 1968; see also articles in this issue.
6. See Ponsioen, *National Development,* p. 13.
7. See Apter, *The Politics of Modernization.*
8. Ibid. p. 67 (our emphasis). Also p. 42.
9. See William F. Ogburn, *Social Change: With Respect to Culture and Original*

Nature. New edition with Supplementing Chapter (New York: Viking, 1950), pp. 200-213.

10. On theory of acculturation in cultural anthropology see Bronisław Malinowski, *A Scientific Theory of Culture and Other Essays.* With a Preface by Huntington Cairns (Chapel Hill: The University of North Carolina Press, 1944); Bronisław Malinowski, *The Dynamic of Culture Change: An Inquiry into Race Relations in Africa,* Edited by Phylis M. Kaberry (New Haven, Conn.: Yale University Press, 1955). Herskovits, *Man and His Works: The Science of Cultural Anthropology* (New York: Alfred K. Knopf, 1958). William R. Bascom and Melville J. Herskovits (eds.), *Continuity and Change in African Cultures* (Chicago: University of Chicago Press, 1959).

11. Malinowski, *The Dynamic of Culture Change,* pp. 23-26.

12. Ibid. p. 57.

13. Ibid. p. 60.

14. Collin M. Turnbull, *The Lonely African* (New York: Simon & Schuster, 1962); George Padmore, *Pan-Africanism or Communism? The Coming Struggle for Africa* (London: D. Dobson, 1956), pp. 209-10; Nbadinge Sithole, *African Nationalism* (Capetown, London: Oxford University Press, 1959).

15. Daniel Lerner, *The Passing of Traditional Society: Modernizing of the Middle East,* With the collaboration of Lucille W. Pevsner and introduction by David Riesman (Glencoe, Ill.: Free Press, 1958), pp. 56-62.

16. Apter, *The Politics of Modernization,* pp. 49, 60, 169-72; see also L. W. Pye, "Administrators, Agitators, Brokers," *Public Opinion Quarterly,* No. 22 (1958).

17. Zygmunt Bauman, "Bieguny analizy kulturowej," *Studia socjologiczne* No. 3 (19), 1964, p. 65.

18. See Dunduza K. Chisiza, *Africa: What Lies Ahead* (New Delhi: Indian Council for Africa, 1961).

19. Claude E. Welch, Jr. (ed.) "The Comparative Study of Political Modernization," *Political Modernization* (Belmont, Calif.: Wadsworth, 1967), p. 7. See also Myron Weiner (ed.), *Modernization. The Dynamics of Growth* (New York: Basic Books, 1966).

20. See Aristide R. Zolberg, *Creating Political Order: The Party States of West Africa* (Chicago: Rand McNally, 1966).

21. See M. F. Lofchie, "Representative Government, Bureaucracy, and Political Development: The African Case," *The Journal of Developing Areas,* Vol. 2, No. 1 (October 1967).

22. See William H. Friedland and Carl G. Rosberg (eds.), *African Socialism* (Stanford: Stanford University Press, 1964). *Africa Report* (African-American Institute), Vol. 8, No. 5, May 1963. Julius K. Nyerere, *Freedom and Unity: A Selection from Writings and Speeches 1952-1965* (Dar es Salaam: Oxford University Press, 1966); Nyerere, *Freedom and Socialism: A Selection from Writings and Speeches 1965-1967* (Dar es Salaam, Oxford University Press, 1968); Leopold Sédar Senghor, *On African Socialism,* Kwame Nkrumah, *Class Struggle in Africa* (New York: International Publishers, 1970); Jitendra Mohan, "Nkrumah and Nkrumahism," *The Socialist Register 1967: A Survey of Movements and Ideas,* edited by Ralph Miliband & John Suville (London: Merlin Press).

23. Apter, *The Politics of Modernization,* pp. 22-45.

24. Andrew M. Kamarck, *The Economics of African Development* (New York: Praeger, 1967).

25. Reproduced from *Overseas Business Reports* (Washington, D.C.: U.S. Department of Commerce, April 1968), p. 11.
26. Ibid., p. 14.
27. All data here are according to *Overseas Business* . . . , pp. 6-9. For data on education in Africa, see also *International Yearbook of Education* (UNESCO, 1969), Vol. XXXI.
28. A. Peshkin and R. Cohen, "The Values of Modernization," *The Journal of Developing Areas,* Vol. II, No. 1, October 1967.
29. James S. Coleman and Carl J. Rosberg (eds.), *Political Parties and National Integration in Africa* (Berkeley, Los Angeles: University of California Press, 1964).
30. See Kofi A. Busia, *The Position of the Chief in the Modern Political System of Ashanti* (London, New York: Oxford University Press, 1963); Ramkrishna Mukherjee, *The Problem of Uganda: A Study in Acculturation* (Berlin: Berlin Akademie Verlag, 1956); L. A. Fallers (ed.), *The King's Men: Leadership and Status in Buganda on the Eve of Independence.* With a Foreword by A. I. Richards (London, New York, Nairobi, 1964), especially Chapter 3, "The Modernization of Social Stratification"; Y. Wane, "Organisation 'traditionnelle' et modernisation sociale au Senegal," *Cahiers internationaux de sociologie,* No. 1, 1971; Benjamin Memberger, "Classless Society and One-Party State Ideology in Africa," *African Studies Review,* Vol. XIV, No. 2, 1971; J. A. Hebga, "Evolution des armées africaines," *Cahiers Congolais,* No. 1 (Mars/avril), 1970; Dudley Jackson, "Economic Development and Income Distribution in Eastern Africa," *The Journal of Modern African Studies,* Vol. 9, No. 4, 1971. P. Anyang-Nyongo, "The Civil Servant in Uganda," *East African Journal* (Nairobi), Vol. 8, No. 4, 1971; John Michael, *African Armies and Civil Order* (New York: Praeger, 1969).
31. See Georges Balandier, "Problématiques des classes sociales en Afrique Noire," and Paul Mercier, "Les classes sociales et les changements politiques récents en Afrique noire," both in *Cahiers internationaux de sociologie,* Vol. XXXVIII, 1965; K. C. Doktor and H. Gallis, "Size and Characteristic of Wage Employment in Africa: Some Statistical Estimates," *International Labour Review,* Vol. LXXXXIII, No. 2, February 1966; Raymond Barbe, "Les classes sociales en Afrique Noire," *Economie et politique,* March 1964; Peter C. W. Gutkind, *The Passing of Tribal Man in Africa* (Leiden: Brill, 1970); Arthur Tuden and Leonard Plotnicov, *Social Stratification in Africa* (New York: The Free Press, 1970); Martin L. Kilson Jr., "Nationalism and Social Classes in British West Africa," *The Journal of Politics.* Vol. XX, 1958; Richard Sandbrook, "Patrons, Clients and Factions: New Dimensions of Conflict Analysis in Africa," *Canadian Journal of Political Science,* Vol. V, No. 1, March 1972; Immanuel Wallerstein, "Class, Tribe and Party in West African Politics," *Transaction of the Fifth World Congress of Sociology,* September 1962 (International Sociological Association, 1964), Vol. III; Irving L. Markovitz, "Traditional Social Structure, The Islamic Brotherhoods, and Political Development in Senegal," *The Journal of Modern African Studies,* Vol VIII, No. 1, 1970.
32. G. Balandier, "Problématique . . ."
33. B. Galletti, K. D. S. Baldwin, and I. O. Dina, *Nigerian Cocoa Farmers: An Economic Survey of Yoruba Farming Families* (London: Oxford University Press, 1956).
34. Peter Marris, "The Social Barriers of African Entrepreneurship," *The Journal of Development Studies,* Vol. V, No. 1, October 1968.
35. This topic is more elaborated in Chodak, "The Birth of an African Peasantry,"

Canadian Journal of African Studies, Vol. V, No. 3, 1971; and Chodak, "Brother-hood or Otherhood? Some Aspects of Modernization in Rural Africa," *Sociologia Ruralis,* Vol. XII, No. 3/4, 1972.

36. See Eric R. Wolf, *Peasants* (Englewood Cliffs, N.J.: Prentice-Hall, 1966), p. 13.
37. A. L. Kroeber, *Anthropology: Race, Language, Culture, Psychology.* New edition, revised (New York: Harcourt, Brace, 1948), p. 284.
38. See David Mitrany, *Marx Against the Peasant: A Study in Social Dogmatism* (New York: Collier Books, 1961), pp. 36-40 and 57.
39. On this topic, see M. Nash, *Primitive Peasant Economic Systems* (San Francisco: Chandler, 1966); Daniel Thorner, Basil Kerblay, and R. E. F. Smith (eds.), *Chayanov Aleksandr Vasil'evich: Theory of Peasant Economy* (New York: R. D. Irvin, 1966); Gerge Dalton (ed.), *Tribal and Peasant Economies: Readings in Economic Anthropology* (Garden City, N.Y.: Natural History Press, 1967).
40. Compare: Montague Yudelman, *African on The Land: Economic Problems of African Agricultural Development in Southern, Central, and East Africa with Special Reference to Southern Rhodesia* (Cambridge, Mass.: Harvard University Press, 1964), p. 172.
41. See Daniel Biebuyck (ed.), *African Agrarian Systems: Studies Presented and Discussed.* Foreword by Daryll Forde. Published for the International Institute (London: Oxford University Press, 1963); Edwin Ardener, Shirley Ardener and W. A. Warmington, *Plantation and Village in the Cameroons* (Nairobi, London: Oxford University Press, 1967); S. M. Makings, *Agricultural Problems of Developing Countries in Africa* (Nairobi: Oxford University Press, 1967); Colin Leys, "Politics in Kenya; the Development of Peasant Society," *British Journal of Political Science,* Vol. I, Part 3, July 1971; Guy Hunter, *Modernizing Peasant Societies: A Comparative Study in Asia and Africa* (London, New York: Oxford University Press, 1969); Polly Hill, *Studies in Rural Capitalism in West Africa* (London: Cambridge University Press, 1970); B. B. Quaraishy, "Land Tenure and Economic Development in Ghana," *Présence Africaine,* No. 1, 1971.
42. Kenneth E. Boulding, "The Gaps between Developed and Developing Nations" in C. S. Wallia (ed.), *Toward Century 21: Technology, Society, and Human Values* (New York: Basic Books, 1970), p. 129.
43. Ibid. p. 131.

Selected Bibliography

Abegglen, James C. *The Japanese Factory: Aspects of its Social Organization*. New York: The Free Press, 1958.

Adelman, Irma. *Theories of Economic Growth and Development*. Stanford, Calif.: Stanford University Press, 1961.

Ake, C. *The Theory of Political Integration*. Homewood, Ill.: The Dorsey Press, 1967.

Allardt, Erik and Yrjö Littunen (eds.). *Cleavages: Ideologies and Party Systems*. Helsinki: The Academic Bookstore, 1964.

Almond, Gabriel A., and G. Bingham Powell. *Comparative Politics: A Development Approach*. Boston: Little, Brown and Company, 1966.

————. *Political Development: Essays in Heuristic Theory*. Boston: Little, Brown and Company, 1970.

———— and Sidney Verba. *The Civic Culture: Political Attitudes and Democracy in Five Nations*. Boston: Little, Brown and Company, 1965.

———— and James S. Coleman. *The Politics of Developing Areas*. Princeton, N.J.: Princeton University Press, 1960.

Amalrik, Andrei. *Will the Soviet Union Survive Until 1984?* New York and Evanston: Harper & Row, 1970.

Amstrong, John. *The Soviet Bureaucratic Elite*. New York: Frederick A. Praeger, 1955.

Andreski, Stanislav. *The African Predicament: A Study in Pathology of Modernization*. New York: Atherton Press, 1968.

————. *Military Organization and Society*. Berkeley and Los Angeles, Calif.: University of California Press, 1968.

Apter, David E. *The Political Kingdom in Uganda*. Princeton: Princeton University Press, 1961.

————. *The Politics of Modernization*. Chicago: University of Chicago Press, 1965.

————. *Some Conceptual Approaches to the Study of Modernization*. Englewood Cliffs, N.J.: Prentice-Hall, 1968.

Ardener, Edwin, Shirley Ardener, and W. A. Warmington. *Plantation and Village in Cameroon*. London: Published for Institute of Social and Economic Research by Oxford University Press, 1960.

338   Selected Bibliography

Arendt, Hannah. *Totalitarianism.* New York: Harcourt, Brace & World, 1956.
Aron, Raymond. *Main Currents in Sociological Thought.* Two volumes. London: Weidenfeld and Nicolson, 1967.
Ashby, W. Ross. *An Introduction to Cybernetics.* New York: John Wiley & Sons, 1956.
Asher, Robert E., et. al. *Development of the Emerging Countries: An Agenda for Research.* Washington: The Brookings Institution, 1962.
Ashton, Thomas S. *Economic History of England: The 18th Century.* London: Methuen, 1955.
Atkinson, John W. and Feather, Norman T. (eds.). *A Theory of Achievement Motivation.* New York: John Wiley & Sons, 1966.
Balandier, Georges. "Problématique des classes sociales en Afrique Noire" in *Cahiers Internationaux de Sociologie,* Vol. XXXVIII, 1965.
Banfield, Edward C. *The Moral Basis of a Backward Society.* New York, London: Collier-Macmillan Limited, 1958.
Baran, Paul A., and Sweezy, Paul M. *Monopoly Capital: An Essay on the American Economic and Social Order.* New York: Monthly Review Press, 1966.
Barbe, Raymond. "Les classes sociales en Afrique Noire" in *Économie et Politique,* No. 3, March 1964.
Barghoorn, F. C. *Politics in USSR.* Cambridge, Mass.: Harvard University Press, 1950.
Barnett, H. G. *Innovation: The Basis of Cultural Change.* New York: McGraw-Hill, 1953.
Bascom, William R., and Herskovits, Melville J. (eds.). *Continuity and Change in African Culture.* Chicago: University of Chicago Press, 1959.
Bauer, Peter T., and Yamey, Basil S. *The Economics of Underdeveloped Countries.* Chicago: Chicago University Press, 1963.
Bauman, Zygmunt. *Kultura i społeczenstwo.* Warsaw: PIW, 1966.
Baumgarten, Eduard. *Max Weber. Werk und Person. Dokumente. Ausgewählt und Kommentiert.* Tübingen: I. C. B. Mohr [Paul Siebeck], 1964.
Bay, Christian. *The Structure of Freedom.* Stanford, Calif.: Stanford University Press, 1970.
Bellah, Robert N. *Religion and Progress in Modern Asia.* New York: The Free Press, 1965.
———. *Tokugawa Religion: The Values of Pre-Industrial Japan.* New York: The Free Press, 1957.
Bendix, Reinhard. *Max Weber: An Intellectual Portrait.* Garden City, N.Y.: Doubleday, Anchor Books, 1962.
———. *Nation Building and Citizenship: Studies of Our Changing Social Order.* Garden City, New York: Doubleday, 1969.
———. "Tradition and Modernity Reconsidered" in *Comparative Studies in Society and History,* Vol. IX, No. 3, 1967.
Berlin, Isaiah Sir. *Historical Inevitability.* London: Oxford University Press, 1954.
Bertalanffy, Ludwig von. *General System Theory: Foundations, Development, Applications.* New York: George Braziller, 1968.
———. *Robots, Man and Minds: Psychology in the Modern World.* New York: George Braziller, 1967.
Bettelheim, Bruno. *Obsolete Youth.* San Francisco: San Francisco Press, 1970.
Biebuyck, Daniel (ed.). *African Agrarian Systems: Studies Presented and Discussed.* Foreword by Daryll Forde. London: Oxford University Press, 1963.
Blatz, W. E. *Human Security.* Toronto: University of Toronto Press, 1966.

Blau, Peter M. *Exchange and Power in Social Life.* New York: John Wiley & Sons, 1967.

Bluhm, William T. *Theories of the Political System.* Englewood Cliffs, N.J.: Prentice-Hall, 1965.

Boulding, Kenneth E. *The Meaning of the Twentieth Century: The Great Transition.* New York: Harper & Row, 1964.

Brenner, Y. S. *Theories of Economic Development and Growth.* New York: Frederick A. Praeger, 1966.

Brentano, Lujo. *Der Unternehmer.* Berlin: Leonhard Simion, 1907.

Brode, John. *The Process of Modernization: An Annotated Bibliography on the Sociocultural Aspects of Development.* Foreword by Alex Inkeles. Cambridge, Mass.: Harvard University Press, 1970.

Bruton, Henry J. *Principles of Development Economics.* Englewood Cliffs, N.J.: Prentice-Hall, 1967.

Brzezinski, Zbigniew and Samuel P. Huntington. *Political Power: USA/USSR.* New York: The Viking Press, 1967.

Buckley, Walter. *Sociology and Modern Systems Theory.* Englewood Cliffs, N.J.: Prentice-Hall, 1967.

Burnham, John C. *Lester Frank Ward in American Thought.* Washington: Washington Public Affairs Press, 1956.

Burns, Tom and Saul S. B. (eds.). *Social Theory and Economic Change.* London, New York: Tavistock Publications, 1967.

Busia, Kofi A. *The Position of the Chief in the Modern Political System of Ashanti.* London, New York: Oxford University Press, 1951.

Chapman, Janet C. *Real Wages in Soviet Russia Since 1928.* Cambridge, Mass.: Harvard University Press, 1963.

Chinoy, Ely. *Sociological Perspective: Basic Concepts and Their Application.* Garden City, N.Y.: Doubleday, 1954.

Chisiza, Dunduza K. *Africa: What Lies Ahead.* New Delhi: Indian Council for Africa, 1961.

Chodak, Szymon. "Social Class in Sub-Saharan Africa," *Africana Bulletin.* Warsaw, No 4, 1966.

—— and Jerzy Kleer. *Socjalizm a modernizacja w czarnej Afryce.* Warsaw: KiW, 1967.

——. "Some Aspects of Modernization of Sub-Saharan Africa," *Africana Bulletin.* Warsaw, No 7, 1967.

——. *Systemy partyjne Europy Zachodniej: pochodzenie, ewolucja, funkcje społeczne, Studia Socjologiczno-polityczne,* No 9. Warsaw: Panstwowy Instytut Wydawniczy, 1961.

Chugerman, Samuel. *Lester F. Ward, The American Aristotle: A Summary and Interpretation of His Sociology.* New York: Octogon Books, 1965.

Cofer, Charles N. and M. H. Appley. *Motivation: Theory and Research.* New York: John Wiley and Sons, 1964.

Cole, Arthur H. *Business Enterprise in its Social Setting.* Cambridge, Mass.: Harvard University Press, 1959.

Coleman, James S. and Carl G. Rosberg (eds.). *Political Parties and National Integration in Africa.* Berkeley and Los Angeles: University of California Press, 1964.

Comte, Auguste. *A General View of Positivism.* New York: E. P. Dutton, 1898.

Cooley, Charles H. *Social Organization*. Glencoe Ill.: The Free Press, 1962.

Coulborn, Rushton. *The Origin of Civilized Societies*. Princeton: Princeton University Press, 1959.

Dahrendorf, Ralph. *Class and Class Conflict in Industrial Society*. Stanford, Calif.: Stanford University Press, 1959.

————. *Essays in the Theory of Society*. Stanford, Calif.: Stanford University Press, 1968.

Deutsch, Karl W. *The Analysis of International Relations*. Englewood Cliffs, N.J.: Prentice-Hall, 1968.

————. *Nationalism and Its Alternatives*. New York: Alfred A. Knopf, 1969.

———— and William J. Foltz (eds.). *Nation Building*. New York: Atherton Press, 1963.

————. *Political Community at the International Level*. Garden City, N.Y.: Doubleday, 1964.

————. "The Growth of Nations: Some Recurrent Patterns of Political and Social Integration," *World Politics*, Vol. V, January 1953.

————. *The Nerves of Government: Models of Political Communication and Control*. New York: The Free Press, 1966.

Djilas, Milovan. *The New Class: An Analysis of the Communist System*. New York: Frederick A. Praeger, 1957.

Dobriner, William M. *Social Structures and Systems*. Pacific Palisades, Calif.: Goodyear Publishing Company, 1969.

Doktor, D. C. and H. Gallis. "Size and Characteristics of Wage Employment in Africa; Some Statistical Estimates," *International Labour Review*, Vol. 93, No. 2, February 1966.

Dumont, René. *False Start in Africa*. Translated by Phyllis Nauts Ott, Introduction by Thomas Balogh. New York: Frederick A. Praeger, 1966.

Durkheim, Emile. *The Division of Labor in Society*. Translated from the French by George Simpson. Glencoe, Ill.: The Free Press, 1933.

Easton, David. *Systems Analysis of Political Life*. New York: John Wiley and Sons, 1965.

————. *The Political System: An Inquiry into the State of Political Science*. New York: Alfred A. Knopf, 1960.

———— (ed.). *Varieties of Political Theory*. Englewood Cliffs, N.J.: Prentice-Hall, 1966.

Easton, Lloyd D. and Kurt H. Guddat (eds.). *Writings of the Young Marx on Philosophy and Society*. Garden City, N.Y.: Doubleday, 1967.

Eisenstadt, S. N. *Modernization: Protest and Change*. Englewood Cliffs, N.J.: Prentice-Hall, 1966.

————. *The Political Systems of Empires*. London: Collier, Macmillan, Ltd., The Free Press of Glencoe, 1963.

———— (ed.). *The Protestant Ethic and Modernization: A Comparative View*. New York: Basic Books, 1968.

Ellul, Jaques. *The Technological Society*. Translated from the French by John Wilkinson with an Introduction by Robert M. Merton. New York: Alfred A. Knopf, 1964.

Emery, F. E. (ed.). *Systems Thinking*. Harmondsworth, Middlesex: Penguin Books, Ltd., 1969.

Evans-Pritchard, Edward Evan. *The Nuer: A Description of the Modes of the Livelihood and Political Institutions of a Nilotic People*. Oxford: Clarendon Press, 1940.

Fainsod, Merle. *How Russia is Ruled*. Cambridge, Mass.: Harvard University Press, 1953.

Fallers, Lloyd A. (ed.). *The King's Men*. London, New York: Oxford University Press, 1964.

Fanon, Frantz. *Black Skin, White Masks*. New York: Grove Press, 1967.

———. *The Wretched of the Earth*. New York: Grove Press, 1968.

Faulkner, E. J. (ed.). *Man's Quest for Security: A Symposium*. Lincoln, Nebr.: University of Nebraska Press, 1966.

Foerster, Hans von and G. W. Zopf, Jr. (eds.). *Symposium on Principles of Self-Organization*. Oxford, New York: Pergamon, 1962.

Fortes, Meyer and Edward E. Evans-Pritchard (eds.). *African Political Systems*. London: Oxford University Press, 1940.

Francke, Kuno. *The German Spirit*. New York: Henry Holt, 1916.

Frankel, Sally H. *The Economic Impact on Underdeveloped Societies: Essays in International Investment and Social Change*. Oxford: Blackwell, 1953.

Friedland, William H., and Rosberg, Carl G. *African Socialism*. Stanford, Calif.: Stanford University Press, 1964.

Friedrich Carl J. and Z. K. Brzezinski. *Totalitarian Dictatorship and Autocracy*. New York: Frederick A. Praeger, 1961.

Freund, Julien. *The Sociology of Max Weber*, New York: Random House, 1968.

Fromm, Erich. *The Sane Society*. New York: Reinhart, 1955.

Fundamentals of Marxism, Leninism. Manual. Moscow: Foreign Languages Publishing House, 1961.

Galbraith, John Kenneth. *The New Industrial State*. London: Hamish Hamilton, 1967.

Galletti, R., K. D. S. Baldwin, and I. O. Dina, *Nigerian Cocoa Farmers: An Economic Survey of Yoruba Cocoa Farming Families*. London: Oxford University Press, 1956.

Geertz, Clifford (ed.). *Old Societies and New States*. Glencoe, Ill.: The Free Press, 1963.

———. *Peddlers and Princes. Social Change and Economic Modernization in Two Indonesian Towns*. Chicago: University of Chicago Press, 1963.

Gershenkron, Alexander. *Continuity in History and other Essays*. Cambridge, Mass.: Belknap Press of Harvard University, 1968.

———. *Economic Backwardness in Historical Perspective: A Book of Essays*. Cambridge, Mass.: Belknap Press of Harvard University, 1962.

Gerver, I. *Lester Frank Ward: Selection from His Work with an Introduction*. New York: Thomas Y. Crowell, 1963.

Ghai, Dharam P. *Portrait of a Minority: Asians in East Africa*. London: Oxford University Press, 1965.

Ginsberg, Morris. *Evolution and Progress*. London: Heinemann, 1961.

Gluckman, Max. *Custom and Conflict in Africa*. Oxford: Basil Blackwell, 1963.

Goldman, Marshall I. *The Soviet Economy: Myth and Reality*. Englewood Cliffs, N.J.: Prentice-Hall, 1968.

Gouldner, Alvin W. *The Coming Crisis of Western Sociology*, New York: Basic Books, 1970.

Grant, Arthur J. *The Hugenots*. London: Thornton Butterworth, Ltd., 1934.

De Grazia, Sebastian, *The Political Community: A Study of Anomie*. Chicago: University of Chicago Press, 1948.

Grossman, Gregory (ed.). *Essays in Socialism and Planning in Honor of Carl Landauer*. Englewood Cliffs, N.J.: Prentice-Hall, 1970.

Haarelmo, Trygve. *A Study in Theory of Economic Evolution*. Amsterdam: North Holland Publishing Company, 1954.

Haas, Ernst B. *Beyond the Nation State: Functionalism and International Organization*. Stanford, Calif.: Stanford University Press, 1964.

———. *Tangle of Hopes: American Commitments and World Order*. Englewood Cliffs, N.J.: Prentice-Hall, 1969.

Hagen, Everett E. *On the Theory of Social Change*. Homewood, Ill.: The Dorsey Press, 1962.

Hampden-Turner, Charles. *Radical Man: The Process of Psycho-Social Development*. Cambridge, Mass.: Shenkman Publishing Company, 1970.

Harris, Dale B. (ed.). *The Concept of Development*. Minneapolis, Minn.: University of Minnesota Press, 1957.

Harvey, O. J. (ed.). *Motivation and Social Interaction: Cognitive Determinants*. New York: Ronald Press, 1963.

Heckhausen, H. *The Anatomy of Achievement Motivation*. Translated by Kay F. Butler, Robert C. Birney, and David C. McClelland. New York: Academic Press, 1967.

Heilbroner, Robert L. *The Making of Economic Society*. Englewood Cliffs, N.J.: Prentice-Hall, 1970.

Hellpach, Willy. *Der Deutsche Charakter*. Bonn: Athenäum Verlag, 1954.

Herskovits, Melville J. *Man and His Works: The Science of Cultural Anthropology*. New York: Alfred A. Knopf, 1948.

Hertzler, J. O. *Social Institutions*. Lincoln, Neb.: University of Nebraska Press, 1946.

Higgins, Benjamin. *Economic Development: Principles, Problems and Policies*. New York: Norton, 1968.

Hobsbawm, Eric J. *The Age of Revolution: Europe 1789-1848*. London: Weidenfeld and Nicolson, 1962.

Hodgkin, Thomas. *African Political Parties*. Harmondsworth: Penguin Books, 1961.

Hoffman, S. "International Systems and International Law," *World Politics*, Vol. XIV, No I, 1961.

Hofmann, Walter. *Stellung und Bedeutung der Unternehmerpörseinlichkeit in der modernen Wirtschaftsorganisation*. Leipzig: G. A. Gloeckner, 1933.

Hofstadter, Richard. *Social Darwinism in American Thought*. Boston: Beacon Press, 1959.

Horney, Karen. *Our Inner Conflict: A Constructive Theory of Neurosis*. New York: W. W. Norton and Company, 1957.

Hoselitz, Berthold F. *Sociological Aspects of Economic Growth*. Glencoe, Ill.: The Free Press, 1960.

——— et al. *Theories of Economic Growth*. Glencoe, Ill., The Free Press, 1960.

Hulicka, Karel and Irene M. Hulicka. *Soviet Institutions: The Individual and Society*. Boston: The Christopher Publishing House, 1967.

Humprey, Marshall T. *Class, Citizenship and Social Development*. Garden City, N.Y.: Doubleday, 1964.

Hunter, Guy. *Modernizing Peasant Societies*. New York: Oxford University Press, 1969.

Huntington, Samuel P. *Political Order in Changing Societies*. New Haven: Yale University Press, 1968.

Ilchman, Warren F., and Uphoff, Norman T. *The Political Economy of Change*. Berkeley and Los Angeles: University of California Press, 1969.

Inkeles, Alex. *Public Opinion in Soviet Russia. A Study in Man's Persecution.* Cambridge: Harvard University Press, 1950.
———. "Social Stratification and Mobility in the Soviet Union," *American Sociological Review,* Vol. 15, No. 4, 1950.
———, and Raymond Bauer. *The Soviet Citizen: Daily Life in a Totalitarian Society.* New York: Atheneum, 1968.
Jansen, Marius B. (ed.). *Changing Japanese Attitudes Toward Modernization.* Princeton: Princeton University Press, 1965.
Johnson, Chalmers (ed.). *Change in Communist Systems.* Stanford, Calif.: Stanford University Press, 1970.
Jones, Peter d'Alroy. *The Consumer Society: A History of American Capitalism.* Harmondsworth: Penguin Books, Ltd., 1965.
Kahn, Herman, B. Bruce Briggs. *Things to Come. Thinking about the 70's and 80's.* New York: Macmillan, 1972.
Kamarck, Andrew M. *The Economics of African Development.* New York: Frederick A. Praeger, 1967.
Kaplan, Morton A. *New Approaches to International Relations.* New York: St. Martin's Press, 1968.
———. *System and Process in International Politics.* New York: John Wiley and Sons, 1957.
Kardiner, Abram. *The Individual and His Society: The Psychodynamics of Primitive Social Organization.* New York: Columbia University Press, 1965.
Kasdan, L. "Family Structure, Migration and the Entrepreneur," *Comparative Study of Society and History,* Vol. VII, No 4, 1967.
Kassof, Allen (ed.). *Prospects for Soviet Society.* New York: Frederick A. Praeger, 1968.
———. "The Administered Society: Totalitarianism Without Terror," *World Politics,* Vol. XVI, No 4, July 1964.
Kedourie, Elle. *Nationalism.* London: Hutchinson, 1960.
Kerr, Clark, John T. Dunlop, Frederick Harbison, H. Harbison, and Charles A. Myers. *Industrialism and Industrial Man: The Problems of Labor and Management in Economic Growth.* Cambridge, Mass.: Harvard University Press, 1960.
———. *Marshall, Marx and Modern Times: The Multi-dimensional Society.* London: Cambridge University Press, 1969.
Kohn, Hans. *Nationalism: Its Meaning and History.* New York: Van Nostrand, 1955.
Kolkowicz, Roman. *The Soviet Military and the Communist Party.* Princeton: Princeton University Press, 1967.
Kroeber, Alfred L. *Configurations of Culture Growth.* Berkeley and Los Angeles: University of California Press, 1944.
Kronrod, Iakov A. *Obshchestviennyi produkt i ego struktura pri socjalizmye.* Moscow: Gosudarstvyennoe Izdatelstvo Politicheskoy Literatury, 1958.
———. *Zakon Stoimosti i ego ispolzovanye v narodnom khoziaystvye SSSR.* Moscow: Gosudarstvyennoye Izdatelstvo Politicheskoy Literatury, 1959.
Kuhn, Thomas S. *The Structure of Scientific Revolutions.* Chicago: University of Chicago Press, 1970.
Kula, Witold. *Problemy i metody historii gospodarczej.* Warsaw: Panstwowy Instytut Wydawniczy, 1963.
———. *Teoria ekonomiczna ustroju feudalnego.* Warsaw: Panstwowy Instytut Wydawniczy, 1962.

Kuper, Leo and M. G. Smith (eds.). *Pluralism in Africa.* Berkeley and Los Angeles: University of California Press, 1969.

Kurihara, Kenneth K. *National Income and Economic Growth.* London: George Allen and Unwin, Ltd., 1961.

Kuznets, Simon Smith. *Economic Change: Selected Essays in Business Cycles. National Income and Economic Growth.* New York: W. W. Norton, 1953.

————, Wilbert E. Moore, Joseph J. Spengler (eds.). *Economic Growth. Brazil, India, Japan.* Durham, N.C.: Duke University Press, 1955.

————. *Toward a Theory of Economic Growth with Reflection on the Economic Growth of Modern Nation.* New York: W. W. Norton, 1968.

Lagos, Matus Gustavo. *International Stratification and Underdeveloped Countries.* Chapel Hill: The University of North Carolina Press, 1963.

Lamont, Corliss. *Freedom of Choice Affirmed.* Boston: Beacon Press, 1963.

Landau, Martin. "On the Use of Metaphor in Political Analysis," *Social Research,* Vol. XXVIII, No 3, Autumn 1961.

————. "Redundancy, Rationality, and the Problem of Duplication and Overlap," *Public Administration Review,* Vol. XXIX, No 4, 1969.

Lange, Oskar. *The Political Economy of Socialism: Two Lectures.* The Hague: Institute of Social Studies. Publications on Social Change, No 16, 1958.

————. *Wholes and Parts: A General Theory of System Behavior.* Oxford, New York: Pergamon Press, 1965.

LaPalombara, Joseph. *Bureaucracy and Political Development.* Princeton: Princeton University Press, 1963.

Lasswell, Harold D. *Politics: Who Gets What, When, How.* New York: Meridian Books, 1958.

———— and Abraham Kaplan. *Power and Society: A Framework for Inquiry.* New Haven: Yale University Press, 1950.

Leibenstein, Harvey. *Economic Backwardness and Economic Growth: Studies in Theory of Economic Development.* New York: John Wiley and Sons, 1957.

Lenski, Gerhard. *Power and Privilege.* New York: McGraw-Hill, 1966.

Lerner, Daniel (ed.). *Parts and Wholes.* New York: The Free Press, 1963.

————. *The Passing of Traditional Society,* with the collaboration of Lucille W. Pevsner and introduction by David Riesman. Glencoe, Ill.: The Free Press, 1958.

Le Vine, Robert A. *Dreams and Deeds: Achievement Motivation in Nigeria,* with assistance of Eugene Strangman and Leonard Unterberger. Chicago: University of Chicago Press, 1966.

Levy, Marion J., Jr. *Modernization and the Structure of Societies.* Vols. I and II. Princeton: Princeton University Press, 1966.

Lewis, W. Arthur. *The Theory of Economic Growth.* New York and Evanston: Harper & Row, 1965.

Lichtheim, George. *A Short History of Socialism.* New York: Frederick A. Praeger, 1970.

Link, Henry C. *The Way to Security.* Garden City, N.Y.: Doubleday, 1970.

Linton, Ralph. *The Cultural Background of Personality.* London: Routledge and Kegan Paul, Ltd., 1964.

Lipset, Seymour Martin. *Political Man: The Social Bases of Politics.* Garden City, N.Y.: Doubleday, 1960.

———— (ed.). *Politics and the Social Sciences.* New York: Oxford University Press, 1969.

Lockwood, David. "Some Remarks on 'The Social System,'" *British Journal of Sociology*, No. 7, 1956.

Lockwood, William W. (ed.). *The State of Economic Enterprise in Japan: Essays in the Political Economy of Growth*. Princeton: Princeton University Press, 1965.

Loewenstein, Karl. *Political Power and Governmental Process*. Chicago: University of Chicago Press, 1957.

Lofchie, Michael F. "Representative Government, Bureaucracy, and Political Development: The African Case." *The Journal of Developing Areas*, Vol. II, No. 1, October 1967.

Lowie, Robert. *The German People: A Social Portrait in 1914*. New York: Farrar and Reinhart, 1945.

Lüthy, Herbert. *In Gegenwart der Geshichte: Historische Essays*. Berlin: Kiepenheuer und Witsch, 1967.

Mac Iver, Robert M. *The Web of Government*. New York: The Free Press, 1965.

Madsen, K. B. *Theories of Motivation: A Comparative Study of Modern Theories of Motivation*. Kent, Ohio: Kent State University Press, 1968.

Mair, Lucy. *Primitive Government*. Harmondsworth, Middlesex: Penguin Books, 1962.

Makarenko, Anton C. *Vospitaniye v Sovyetskoi Shkhole*. Moscow: Prosveshchenye, 1966.

Makings, S. M. *Agricultural Problems of Developing Countries in Africa*. Nairobi, Oxford University Press, 1967.

Malinowski, Bronislaw. *A Scientific Theory of Culture and Other Essays*. With a Preface by Huntington Cairns. Chapel Hill: University of North Carolina Press, 1944.

———. *The Dynamic of Culture Change: An Inquiry into Race Relations in Africa*. Edited by Phylis M. Kaberry. New Haven: Yale University Press, 1945.

Mannheim, Karl. *Freedom, Power and Democratic Planning*. Edited by Hans Gerth and Ernest K. Bramstedt. London: Routledge & Kegan Paul, Ltd., 1968.

———. *Ideology and Utopia: An Introduction to the Sociology of Knowledge*. Translated from the German by Louis Wirth and Edward Shils. New York: Harcourt, Brace & World, 1970.

Marcuse, Herbert. *One-Dimensional Man: Studies in the Ideology of Advanced Industrial Society*. Boston: Beacon Press, 1964.

Marris, Peter and Anthony Somerset. *African Businessmen: A Story of Entrepreneurship and Development in Kenya*. London: Routledge & Kegan Paul, 1971.

———. "The Social Barriers of African Entrepreneurship," *The Journal of Development Studies*. Vol. I, No. 1, 1968.

Martini, Winfried. *Das Ende Aller Sicherheit*. Stuttgart: Deutsche Verlage Anstalt, 1954.

Meier, Gerald M. and Robert E. Baldwin. *Economic Development: Theory. History. Policy*. New York: John Wiley & Sons, 1957.

Mercier, P. "Les classes sociales et les changements politiques récents en Afrique Noire," *Cahiers Internationaux de Sociologie*, Vol. XXXVIII, 1965.

Merton, Robert K. *Social Theory and Social Structure*. New York: The Free Press, 1957.

Meyer, Alfred G. *The Soviet Political System: An Interpretation*. New York: Random House, 1965.

Michels, Robert. *Political Parties: A Sociological Study of the Oligarchical Tendencies of Modern Democracy.* Translated by Eden and Cedar Paul. Introduction by Seymour Martin Lipset. New York: The Free Press, 1958.

Mills, Charles Wright. *The Power Elite.* New York: Oxford University Press, 1956.

————. *The Sociological Imagination.* New York: Oxford University Press, 1959.

Minogue, K. R. *Nationalism.* London: B. T. Batsford, Ltd., 1967.

Mitrany, David. *Marx Against the Peasant: A Study in Social Dogmatism.* New York: Collier Books, 1961.

Mitzman, Arthur. *The Iron Cage: An Historical Interpretation of Max Weber.* New York: Alfred A. Knopf, 1970.

Moore, Barrington, Jr. *Terror and Progress—USSR: Some Sources of Change and Stability in the Soviet Dictatorship.* New York: Harper & Row, 1954.

————. *The Social Origins of Dictatorship and Democracy: Lord and Peasant in the Making of the Modern World.* Boston: Beacon Press, 1967.

Moore, Wilbert E. *Order and Change: Essays in Comparative Sociology.* New York: John Wiley & Sons, 1967.

————. *Social Change.* Englewood Cliffs, N.J.: Prentice-Hall, 1963.

Mukherjee, Ramkrishna. *The Problem of Uganda: A Study in Acculturation.* Berlin: Berlin Akademie Verlag, 1956.

Myrdal, Gunnar. *Economic Theory and Underdeveloped Regions.* London: Methuen, 1957.

McClelland, David C. *Studies in Motivation.* New York: Appleton-Century-Crofts, 1955.

McClelland, David C., John W. Atkinson, Russell A. Clark, Edgar L. Lowell, *The Achievement Motive.* Appleton-Century-Crofts, 1953.

————. *The Achieving Society.* Princeton, N.J. Van Nostrand, 1961.

————, David G. Winter, with Sara K. Winter and others. *Motivating Economic Achievement.* New York: The Free Press, 1969.

Naess, Arne. *Democracy, Ideology and Objectivity.* Oslo: Oslo University Press, 1956.

Nash, Manning. *Primitive and Peasant Economic Systems.* San Francisco: Chandler Publishing Company, 1966.

Nationalism: A Report by a Study Group of Members of the Royal Institute of International Affairs. London: Frank Cass and Company, Ltd., 1963.

Nelson, Benjamin. "Conscience and the Making of Early Modern Cultures: The Protestant Ethic Beyond Max Weber," *Social Research,* Vol. XXXVI, No. 1, 1969.

————. "Scholastic Rationales of 'Conscience,' Early Modern Crisis of Credibility and the Scientific-Technocultural Revolutions of the 17th and 20th Centuries," *Journal for Scientific Study of Religion,* Vol. VII, No. 2, 1968.

————. *The Idea of Usury: From Tribal Brotherhood to Universal Otherhood.* Chicago: University of Chicago Press, 1969.

Nettl, J. P. *Political Modernization: A Sociological Analysis of Methods and Concepts.* London: Faber and Faber, Ltd., 1967.

Nisbet, Robert A. *Social Change and History: Aspects of the Western Theory of Development.* New York: Oxford University Press, 1969.

————. *The Sociological Tradition.* New York: Basic Books, 1966.

Norbeck, Edward, Douglass Price-Williams, W. M. McCord (eds.). *The Study of Personality.* New York: Holt, Rinehart and Winston, 1968.

Nove, Alec. *The Soviet Economy: An Introduction.* London: George Allen and Unwin, Ltd., 1968.

Nurske, Ragnar, *Problems of Capital Formation in Underdeveloped Countries.* New York: Oxford University Press, 1957.

Nyerere, Julius, *Freedom and Socialism: A Selection from Writings and Speeches 1965-1967.* Dar es Salaam: Oxford University Press, 1968.
——. *Freedom and Unity: A Selection from Writings and Speeches 1952-65.* Dar es Salaam: Oxford University Press, 1966.
Ogburn, William F. *Social Change with Respect to Culture and Original Nature.* New York: The Viking Press, 1950.
Organski, A. F. K. *The Stages of Political Development.* New York: Alfred A. Knopf, 1965.
Ortega y Gasset, José. *Man and People.* Authorized translation from Spanish by Willard R. Trask. New York: W. W. Norton, 1957.
Padmore, George. *Pan-Africanism or Communism? The Coming Struggle for Africa.* London: D. Dobson, 1956.
Pannier, J. *L'expansion française outre-mer et les protestants français.* Paris: Société des missions évangeliques, 1931.
Parry, Albert. *The New Class Divided: Science and Technology versus Communism.* New York: Macmillan, 1966.
Parsons, Talcott and Neil J. Smelser. *Economy and Society.* London: Routledge & Kegan Paul, Ltd., 1957.
——. *Essays in Sociological Theory.* Glencoe, Ill.: The Free Press, 1954.
——. *The Structure of Social Action.* Glencoe, Ill.: The Free Press, 1949.
—— and Edward Shils (eds.). *Toward a General Theory of Action.* New York: Harper & Row, 1951.
Peshkin, A. and Ronald Cohen. "The Values of Modernization," *The Journal of Developing Areas,* Vol. II, No 1, October 1967.
Ponsioen, J. A. *National Development: A Sociological Contribution.* The Hague, Mouton, 1968.
——. *The Analysis of Social Change Reconsidered: A Sociological Study.* 'S-Gravenhage, Mouton, 1962.
Popper, Karl Raimond. *The Poverty of Historicism.* London: Routledge & Kegan Paul, Ltd., 1957.
Pritchard, Harold A. *Moral Obligations.* Oxford: Clarendon Press, 1949.
Przeworski, Adam. "Niektóre problemy metodologiczne socjologii rozwoju gospodarczego," *Studia socjologiczne,* Warsaw, No. 3 (14), 1967.
Pye, Lucian W. "Administrators, Agitators, Brokers," *Public Opinion Quarterly,* No. 22, 1958.
——. *Aspects of Political Development.* Boston: Little, Brown and Company, 1966.
Raistrick, Arthur. *Quakers in Science and Industry.* New York: Philosophical Library, 1950.
Redfield, Robert. *Peasant Society and Culture.* Chicago: University of Chicago Press, 1965.
Redlich, Fritz. *Der Unternehmer.* Göttingen: Vanderhoech and Ruprecht, 1964.
Reuck, Anthony de and Julie Knight (eds.). *Conflict in Society.* London: J. and A. Churchill, Ltd., 1966.
Riesman, David. *Thorstein Veblen: A Critical Interpretation.* New York: Charles Scribner's & Sons, 1953.
Robertson, H. M. *Aspects of the Rise of Economic Individualism: A Criticism of Max Weber and His School.* London: Cambridge University Press, 1933.
Rogers, Everet M. *Diffusion of Innovations.* New York: The Free Press, 1962.
Rose, Arnold M. (ed.). *Human Behavior and Social Process: An Interactionist Approach.* Boston: Houghton Mifflin Company, 1962.

Rosen, Bernard C., and Harry Crokket, Jr., and Clyde Z. Nunn (eds.). *Achievement in American Society*. Cambridge, Mass.: Schenkman Publishing Company, 1969.

Rostow, Walt W. *The Process of Economic Growth*. New York: W. W. Norton, 1952.

———. *The Stages of Economic Growth: A Non-Communist Manifesto*. London: Cambridge University Press, 1960.

Roszak, Theodore. *The Making of Counter Culture*. Garden City, N.Y.: Doubleday, 1969.

Rudolph, Lloyd I. and Susanne H. Rudolph. *The Modernity of Tradition: Political Development in India*. Chicago: University of Chicago Press, 1967.

Sachs, Ignacy (ed.). *Obstacles to Growth: Demographic, Economic and Social*. Warsaw: Polish Scientific Publishers, 1967.

Sahlins, Marshall D. (ed.). *Evolution and Culture*. Foreword by Leslie A. White. Ann Arbor: University of Michigan Press, 1960.

Sakharov, Andrei D. *Progress, Coexistence, and Intellectual Freedom*. Translated by the *New York Times*. With Introduction, Afterword, and Notes by Harrison E. Salisbury. New York: W. W. Norton, 1968.

Samuelsson, Kurt. *Religion and Economic Action*. Scandinavian University Book, 1961.

Sartre, Jean-Paul. *Anti-Semite and Jew*. Translated by George J. Becker. New York: Schocken Books, 1948.

Schmidt-Freytag, C. G. (ed.). *Die Autorität und die Deutschen*. Munich: Deutsche Verlagsbuch Handlung, 1966.

Schultze, Charles L. *National Income Analysis*. Englewood Cliffs, N.J.: Prentice-Hall, 1967.

Schumpeter, Joseph A. *Capitalism, Socialism and Democracy*. London: Unwin University Books, 1966.

———. *The Theory of Economic Development: An Inquiry into Profits, Capital, Credit, Interest and the Business Cycle*. Translated from the German by Redvers Opie. Cambridge, Mass.: Harvard University Press, 1934.

Senghor, Léopold Sédar. *On African Socialism*. Translated and with an Introduction by Mercer Cook. New York: Frederick A. Praeger, 1964.

Shaffer, Harry G. and Jan S. Przybyla, *From Underdevelopment to Affluence: Western, Soviet and Chinese Views*. New York: Appleton-Century-Crofts, 1968.

Sheldon, Eleonor B. and Wilbert E. Moore. *Indicators of Social Change: Concepts and Measurements*. New York: Russel Sage Foundation, 1968.

Shils, Edward. *Political Development in the New States*. 'S-Gravenhage: Mouton & Co., 1962.

Shonfield, Andrew. *Modern Capitalism: The Changing Balance of Public and Private Power*. London: Oxford University Press, 1965.

Siffin, William J. (ed.). *Toward a Comparative Study of Public Administration*. Bloomington, Ind.: Indiana University Press, 1959.

Simmel, Georg. *Conflict: The Web of Group Affiliations*. Translated by Kurt H. Wolff and Reinhard Bendix. New York: The Free Press, 1966.

Sithole, Ndabaningi. *African Nationalism*. London: Oxford University Press, 1959.

Skilling, H. Gordon and Franklyn Griffits (eds.). *Interest Groups in Soviet Politics*. Princeton: Princeton University Press, 1971.

Skinner, B. F. *Beyond Freedom and Dignity*. New York: Alfred A. Knopf, 1971.

Small, Albion W. *General Sociology*. Chicago: University of Chicago Press, 1905.

Smelser, Neil J. *Essays in Sociological Explanation*. Englewood Cliffs, N.J.: Prentice-Hall, 1968.

————. and William T. Smelser. *Personality and Social System*. New York: John Wiley and Sons, 1970.

————. *The Sociology of Economic Life*. Englewood Cliffs, N.J.: Prentice-Hall, 1963.

Smith, Adam. *An Inquiry into the Nature and Cause of the Wealth of Nations*. London: Methuen, 1961.

Smythe, Hugh H. and Nabel M. Smythe, *The New Nigerian Elite*. Stanford, Calif.: Stanford University Press, 1960.

Sombart, Werner. *Luxury and Capitalism*. Introduction by Philip Siegelman. Translated by W. R. Dittman. Ann Arbor: University of Michigan Press, 1967.

————. *The Jews and Modern Capitalism*. Translated by M. Epstein and with an Introduction to the American edition by Bert F. Hoselitz. Glencoe, Ill.: The Free Press, 1951.

Spencer, Herbert. *The Principles of Sociology*. Three Volumes. New York: D. Appleton, 1901.

Stein, Lorenz von. *Der Socialismus und Kommunismus des heutigen. Frankreichs*. Leipzig: O. Wigand, 1848.

Stanley, Manfred (ed.). *Social Development: Critical Perspectives*. New York: Basic Books, 1972.

Stonequist, E. V. *The Marginal Man: A Study in Personality and Culture Conflict*. New York: Russell & Russell, 1961.

Strumilin, S. "Zakon stoimosti i planirovaniye," *Voprosy Ekonomiki*, Moscow: No 7, 1959.

Sumner, William G. *Folkways: A Study of the Sociological Importance of Usages, Manners, Customs, Mores and Morals*. Boston: Ginn and Company, 1906.

Sutton, Francis X. "Representation and the Nature of Political Systems," *Comparative Studies in Society and History*. Vol. II, No. 1, 1959.

Tawney, Richard H. *Religion and the Rise of Capitalism*. Gloucester, Mass.: P. Smith, 1954.

Thorner, Daniel, Basile Kerblay, and R. E. F. Smith (eds.). *Chayanov Aleksandr Vasil'evich's Theory of Peasant Economy: Published for the American Economic Association*. Homewood, Ill.: R. D. Irvin, 1966.

Tocqueville, Alexis de. *The Old Regime and the Revolution*. New York: Harper and Brothers, 1956.

Toennies, Ferdinand. *Community and Society (Gemeinschaft and Gesellschaft)*. Translated and introduced by Charles P. Loomis. East Lansing, Mich.: Michigan State University Press, 1957.

Turnbull, Colin M. *The Lonely African*. New York: Simon & Schuster, 1962.

Tymowski, A. "Dochody a sposob wydatkowania," *Studia Socjologiczne*. Warsaw, No. 3, 1962.

Veblen, Thorstein. *The Higher Learning in America: A Memorandum on the Conduct of Universities by Business Men*. New York: Augustus M. Kelley, 1965.

————. *The Instinct of Workmanship and the State of Industrial Art*. New York: B. W. Huebsch, 1918.

————. *The Theory of the Leisure Class: An Economic Study of Institutions*. New York: The Modern Library, 1934.

Wallerstein, Immanuel M. (ed.). *Social Change: The Colonial Situation*. New York: John Wiley & Sons, 1966.

Wallia, C. S. (ed.). *Toward Century 21. Technology, Society and Human Values*. New York: Basic Books, 1970.

Ward, Lester F. *Pure Sociology*. New York: Macmillan, 1903.

Warner, Wellman J. *The Wesleyan Movement in the Industrial Revolution*. London: Longsman, Green and Company, 1930.

Watts, Alan W. *The Wisdom of Insecurity*. New York: Vintage Books, 1951.

Weber, Max. *The Protestant Ethic and the Spirit of Capitalism*. Translated by Talcott Parsons, with a Foreword by R. H. Tawney. New York: Charles Scribner's Sons, 1969.

————. *The Theory of Social and Economic Organization*. Translated by A. M. Henderson and Talcott Parsons. Edited with an Introduction by Talcott Parsons. New York: The Free Press, 1966.

Weiner, Myron. "Political Integration and Political Development," *The Annals*, Vol. 358.

Weiner, Myron (ed.). *Modernization: The Dynamics of Growth*. New York: Basic Books, 1966.

Welch, Claude E., Jr. *Political Modernization: A Reader in Comparative Political Change*. Belmont, Calif.: Wadsworth Publishing Company, 1967.

White, Leslie A. *The Evolution of Culture: The Development of Civilization to the Fall of Rome*. New York: McGraw-Hill, 1959.

————. *The Science of Culture: A Study of Man and Civilization*. New York: Farrar, Straus and Giroux, 1969.

Wiles, Peter. "Will Capitalism and Communism Spontaneously Converge?" *Encounter*, No. 6, June 1963.

Wiseman, Herbert V. *Political Systems: Some Sociological Approaches*. London: Routledge and Kegan Paul, Ltd., 1966.

Wolf, Eric R. *Peasants*. Englewood Cliffs, N.J.: Prentice-Hall, 1966.

Worsley, Peter. *The Third World*. London: Weidenfeld and Nicolson, 1964.

Yudelman, Montague. *Africans on the Land*. Cambridge, Mass.: Harvard University Press, 1964.

Zolberg, Aristide R. *Creating Political Order: The Party-States of West Africa*. Chicago: Rand McNally and Company, 1966.

Index

DATE DUE

NO 23 '83	NOV 8 '83		
GAYLORD			PRINTED IN U.S.A